Key to map symbols

ELEVATION

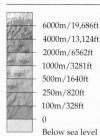

6000m/19,686ft
4000m/13,124ft
2000m/6562ft
1000m/3281ft
500m/1640ft
250m/820ft
100m/328ft
0
Below sea level

▲ Mountain

• Depression

BORDERS

▬ ▬ ▬ Full international

– – – Disputed *de facto*

• • • • • Territorial claim

×–×–×–× Cease-fire line

··········· Undefined

———— State/Province

NAVIGATOR

DRAINAGE FEATURES

——— River

——— Seasonal river

⊥⊥⊥⊥⊥⊥⊥ Canal

◯ Lake

⬭ Seasonal lake

SETTLEMENTS

● Capital city

◎ Major town

○ Minor town

• Major port

COMMUNICATIONS

nd
amazing .... from
around the world

The navigator device can be used to quickly move around the atlas. Using this example, the next map to the north of page 128 can be found on page 120.

4
Atlas contents

Atlas contents

North & West Asia 94-95

South & East Asia 106-107

Australia & Oceania 124-125

Country factfiles 138-359

See overleaf for contents

Factfile contents

8
The Political World

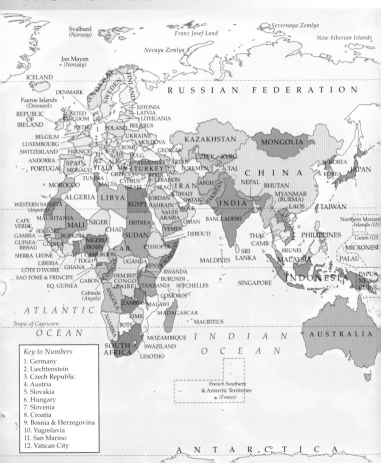

Svalbard *(Norway)*
Franz Josef Land
Severnaya Zemlya
New Siberian Islands
Jan Mayen *(Norway)*
Novaya Zemlya
ICELAND
DENMARK
Faeroe Islands *(Denmark)*
REPUBLIC OF IRELAND
UNITED KINGDOM
NETH.
BELGIUM
LUXEMBOURG
SWITZERLAND
ANDORRA
PORTUGAL
SPAIN
MONACO
MOROCCO
TUNISIA
MALTA
ALGERIA
LIBYA
WESTERN SAHARA *(disputed)*
MAURITANIA
CAPE VERDE
MALI
NIGER
SENEGAL
GAMBIA
GUINEA-BISSAU
BURKINA
GUINEA
SIERRA LEONE
LIBERIA
CÔTE D'IVOIRE
GHANA
TOGO
BENIN
NIGERIA
SAO TOME & PRINCIPE
EQ. GUINEA
CAMEROON
GABON
CONGO
Cabinda *(Angola)*
C.A.R.
CHAD
SUDAN
ERITREA
DJIBOUTI
ETHIOPIA
UGANDA
KENYA
RWANDA
BURUNDI
DEM. REP. CONGO *(ZAIRE)*
TANZANIA
ANGOLA
ZAMBIA
MALAWI
MOZAMBIQUE
ZIMB.
BOTS.
NAMIBIA
SOUTH AFRICA
SWAZILAND
LESOTHO
MADAGASCAR
COMOROS
SEYCHELLES
MAURITIUS

NORWAY
SWEDEN
FINLAND
RUSSIAN FEDERATION
ESTONIA
LATVIA
LITHUANIA
BELARUS
POLAND
UKRAINE
MOLDOVA
ROM.
BULG.
GEORGIA
ARMENIA
AZERB.
AZ.
TURKEY
GREECE
CYPRUS
SYRIA
LEBANON
ISRAEL
JORDAN
IRAQ
IRAN
KUWAIT
BAHRAIN
QATAR
SAUDI ARABIA
EGYPT
YEMEN
OMAN
SOMALIA
KAZAKHSTAN
UZBEK.
TURKMEN.
KYRG.
TAJ.
AFGH.
PAKISTAN
NEPAL
BHUTAN
INDIA
BANGLADESH
MYANMAR *(BURMA)*
LAOS
THAI.
CAMB.
SRI LANKA
MALDIVES
MONGOLIA
CHINA
N. KOREA
S. KOREA
JAPAN
TAIWAN
Northern Mariana Islands *(US)*
Guam *(US)*
PHILIPPINES
MICRONESIA
PALAU
BRUNEI
MALAYSIA
SINGAPORE
INDONESIA
PAPUA NEW GUINEA
AUSTRALIA

ATLANTIC OCEAN
Tropic of Capricorn
INDIAN OCEAN
French Southern & Antarctic Territories *(France)*

ANTARCTICA

Key to Numbers
1. Germany
2. Liechtenstein
3. Czech Republic
4. Austria
5. Slovakia
6. Hungary
7. Slovenia
8. Croatia
9. Bosnia & Herzegovina
10. Yugoslavia
11. San Marino
12. Vatican City

The Political World

ARCTIC OCEAN

Greenland
(Denmark)

Arctic Circle

Alaska
(US)

C A N A D A

Aleutian Islands (US)

ATLANTIC OCEAN

PACIFIC OCEAN

Midway Islands
(US)

UNITED STATES
OF AMERICA

Bermuda (UK)

MEXICO

Hawaii
(US)

Puerto Rico (US)
ST KITTS & NEVIS
ANTIGUA & BARBUDA
DOMINICA
ST LUCIA
BARBADOS
ST VINCENT &
THE GRENADINES
GRENADA
TRINIDAD & TOBAGO

DOM. REP.

Tropic of Cancer

BAHAMAS

BELIZE CUBA

HAITI

JAMAICA

MARSHALL
ISLANDS

WALLIS & FUTUNA (France)

Palmyra Atoll (US)

GUATEMALA
EL SALVADOR
HONDURAS
NICARAGUA

COSTA RICA

PANAMA VENEZUELA

COLOMBIA

French Guiana (France)

NAURU

TUVALU

KIRIBATI

Tokelau
(NZ)

Galapagos Islands
(Ecuador)

GUYANA

SURINAME

Equator

SOLOMON
ISLANDS

Cook
Islands
(NZ)

ECUADOR

B R A Z I L

VANUATU

Niue (NZ)

French
Polynesia
(France)

Pitcairn
Islands
(UK)

PERU

FIJI

TONGA

American
Samoa (US)

BOLIVIA

CHILE PARAGUAY

Tropic of Capricorn

New
Caledonia
(France)

SAMOA

PACIFIC OCEAN

ARGENTINA

URUGUAY

NEW
ZEALAND

CONTINENTAL COLORS

North & Central
America

South America

Africa

Europe

NW/SE Asia

Australasia
& Oceania

Falkland Islands (UK)

South Georgia &
South Sandwich Islands
(UK)

CHILE

ANTARCTICA

Antarctic Circle

The Physical World

ARCTIC

Spitsbergen
Franz Josef Land
Severnaya Zemlya
New Siberian Islands
Greenland Sea
Novaya Zemlya
Laptev Sea
Barents Sea
Kara Sea
Arctic Circle
Denmark Strait
Norwegian Sea
Iceland
Scandinavia
Yenisey
Lena
Khrebet Cherskogo
Siberia
Ural Mountains
Ob
North European Plain
British Isles
North Sea
Sea of Okhotsk
Volga
Lake Baikal
EUROPE
Alps
Danube
Lake Balkhash
Altai Mountains
Amur
Sakhalin
Bay of Biscay
Caucasus
Black Sea
Aral Sea
Tien Shan
Gobi
Manchurian Plain
Hokkaido
Azores
Iberian Peninsula
Caspian Sea
Hindu Kush
Yellow River
Sea of Japan
Madeira
Atlas Mts
Mediterranean Sea
Anatolia
Iranian Plateau
Plateau of Tibet
Honshu
Canary Islands
Syrian Desert
Zagros Mts
Himalayas
Yangtze
East China Sea
Kyushu
Tropic of Cancer
Sahara
Thar Desert
Mount Everest 8848m
Taiwan
AFRICA
Nile
Arabian Peninsula
Deccan
South China Sea
Philippine Sea
Sahel
Arabian Sea
Bay of Bengal
Philippine Islands
Cape Verde Islands
Lake Chad
Niger
Ethiopian Highlands
Horn of Africa
Sri Lanka
Mekong
Malay Peninsula
Borneo
Celebes
East Indies
New Guinea
Equator
Gulf of Guinea
Congo Basin
Lake Victoria
Kilimanjaro 5895m
Somali Basin
Seychelles
Sumatra
Java Sea
ATLANTIC
Congo
Timor Sea
Angola Basin
INDIAN
Java
Namib Desert
Zambezi
Mauritius
Réunion
Great Sandy Desert
OCEAN
Kalahari Desert
Madagascar
Mozambique Channel
OCEAN
AUSTRALIA
Tropic of Capricorn
Cape Basin
Nullarbor Plain
Darling
Cape of Good Hope
Ninetyeast Ridge
Mid-Atlantic Ridge
Southwest Indian Ridge
Tasmania
Southeast Indian Ridge
Kerguelen
South Indian Basin
Antarctic Circle

ANTARCTICA

OCEAN

East Siberian Sea

Chukchi Sea

Bering Strait

Kamchatka

Bering Sea

Aleutian Islands

Northwest Pacific Basin

Mid-Pacific Mountains

Micronesia

Polynesia

Hawaiian Islands

PACIFIC OCEAN

Solomon Islands

Coral Sea

Fiji

New Caledonia

Tasman Sea

South Island

North Island

New Zealand

Southwest Pacific Basin

East Pacific Rise

Easter Island

Beaufort Sea

Brooks Range

Mackenzie

Mount McKinley (Denali) 6194m

Coast Mountains

Gulf of Alaska

Vancouver Island

Coast Ranges

Great Bear Lake

Great Slave Lake

Rocky Mountains

Great Plains

NORTH AMERICA

Great Lakes

Mississippi

Appalachian Mts

Gulf of Mexico

West Indies

Caribbean Sea

Galapagos Islands

Queen Elizabeth Islands

Ellesmere Island

Baffin Island

Baffin Bay

Hudson Bay

Greenland

Labrador Sea

Grand Banks of Newfoundland

North American Basin

Mid-Atlantic Ridge

ATLANTIC OCEAN

Arctic Circle

Tropic of Cancer

Equator

Amazon

Amazon Basin

SOUTH AMERICA

Andes

Peru Basin

Brazil Basin

Cerro Aconcagua 6959m

Gran Chaco

Pampas

Patagonia

Argentine Basin

Tropic of Capricorn

Falkland Islands

South Georgia

Tierra del Fuego

Cape Horn

Drake Passage

South Sandwich Islands

Antarctic Peninsula

Antarctic Circle

Time zones

Time zones

The
World's
Regions

North & Central America

EUROPE

ICELAND

Franz Josef Land
(to Russia)

Svalbard
(to Norway)

Jan Mayen
(to Norway)

Greenland
(Denmark)

Arctic Circle

Labrador
Sea

Labrador

North
Pole

Baffin
Bay

Baffin Island

Hudson
Bay

ARCTIC

OCEAN

Queen Elizabeth
Islands

Reindeer Lake

Lake Winnipeg

Great Bear
Lake

Great Slave Lake

Lake Athabasca

C A N A D A

Beaufort
Sea

Arctic Circle

ASIA

Mackenzie

Gr

R o c k y   M o

Bering Strait

ALASKA

Yukon

Bering Sea

Gulf of
Alaska

Snake

Aleutian Islands

PACIFIC

OCEAN

St Pierre &
Miquelon
(France)

ATLANTIC
OCEAN

S a r g a s s o S e a

Bermuda
(UK)

Virgin Islands (UK)
British Virgin
Islands (UK)
Anguilla (UK)
ST KITTS &
NEVIS
ANTIGUA &
BARBUDA
Guadeloupe
(to France)
ST LUCIA
BARBADOS

Turks & Caicos
Islands (UK)

DOMINICAN
REPUBLIC
Puerto
Rico (US)
Montserrat (UK)
DOMINICA
Martinique (France)
ST VINCENT & THE GRENADINES
GRENADA
Netherlands
Antilles
(Neth.)

TRINIDAD
& TOBAGO

Equator

SOUTH
AMERICA

BAHAMAS

C U B A
HAITI
JAMAICA

Cayman
Islands (UK)

BELIZE
HONDURAS
GUATEMALA
EL SALVADOR
NICARAGUA
COSTA RICA
PANAMA

Aruba (Neth.)

A n d e s

UNITED STATES
OF AMERICA

Great
Lakes
Lake
Superior
Lake Huron
Lake Ontario
Lake Erie
Lake
Michigan

Appalachian Mountains

Ohio
Missouri
Mississippi
Arkansas

P l a i n s

Rio Grande

Gulf of Mexico

M E X I C O

Sierra Madre Occidental

Colorado

PACIFIC
OCEAN

Galapagos Islands
(Ecuador)

Clipperton Island
(French Polynesia)

Equator

Tropic of Cancer

1000
1000

0 km
0 miles

ATLANTIC
OCEAN

Western Canada & Alaska

◆ In 1867 William Henry Seward negotiated the purchase of Alaska from Russia for the price of $7,200,000, which amounted to around two cents per acre (0.4 hectares).

◆ The Aleutian Islands span some 1200 miles (1800 km) and by crossing the 180° line of longitude, form both the most easterly and westerly extents of the USA.

◆ On July 9, 1958 a massive landslide dropped 40 million cubic yards (30.6 million cu m) of rock into Lituya Bay creating a wave 1720 ft (524 m) high.

RUSSIAN FEDERATION

Wrangel I.

ARCTIC OCEA

Attu I.

Bering Sea

Rat Is.

Aleutian Islands

Umnak I.
Dutch Harbor
Unalaska I.

St. Lawrence I.

Nunivak I.

Kodiak I. Kodiak

Bering Strait

Arctic Circle

Yukon

Brooks Range

Prudhoe Bay

ALASKA
(part of USA)

Mt McKinley
6194m

Alaska Range

Anchorage

Valdez
Cordova

Fairbanks

YUKON TERRITORY

WHITEHORSE

Gulf of Alaska

JUNEAU

Rocky

PACIFIC OCEAN

Ketchikan

Prince Rupert
Queen Charlotte Is.
Queen Charlotte Sound

Port Hardy
Vancouver I.

BI
CO

0 km   400
0 miles   400

VICTORIA

160°   140°   120°   100°   80°   60°   80°   40°

Greenland
(Danish external territory)

Ellesmere I.

Axel Heiberg I.

◇ Despite an area of 769,900 sq miles (1,994,000 sq km) the northerly province of Nunavut has only 13 miles (21 km) of highway.

Queen Elizabeth Is.

Bathurst I.

Devon I.

Baffin Bay

Melville I.

Resolute   Lancaster Sound

Somerset I.

Davis Strait

Viscount Melville Sound

Banks I.   Prince of Wales I.

Baffin I.

eaufort Sea

Amundsen Gulf

Victoria I.

King William I.

uvik

Kugluktuk

Arctic Circle

IQALUIT

N U N A V U T

Hudson Strait

ent Bear L.

60°

NORTHWEST

Southampton I.

Mackenzie

ERRITORIES   YELLOWKNIFE

Great Slave L.

Dubawnt

Rankin Inlet

Hudson Bay

QUEBEC

Hay River   Fort Smith

ISH   ALBERTA

Fort St. John

Churchill

L. Athabasca

Fort McMurray   **MANITOBA**

C A N A D A

Grande Prairie   **SASKATCHEWAN**

Flin Flon   Thompson

O N T A R I O

EDMONTON

Leduc

Saskatchewan

Prince Albert

Saskatoon

L. Winnipeg

◇ Some 7% of Canada's 3.5 million sq miles (9.2 million sq km) land area is devoted to grain production yielding around 26 million tons (tonnes) of wheat every year.

Red Deer

Yorkton

ce   ge

Calgary   REGINA   Brandon   WINNIPEG

mloops

ancouver   Kelowna   Lethbridge   Estevan

U S A

100°   80°

Eastern Canada

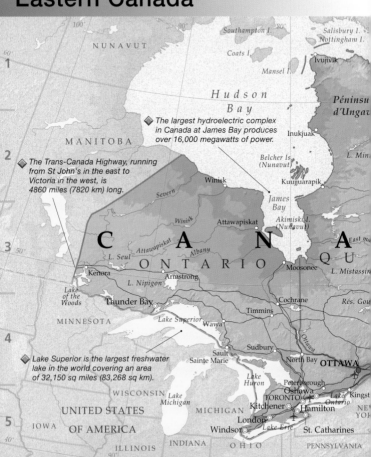

The largest hydroelectric complex in Canada at James Bay produces over 16,000 megawatts of power.

The Trans-Canada Highway, running from St John's in the east to Victoria in the west, is 4860 miles (7820 km) long.

Lake Superior is the largest freshwater lake in the world covering an area of 32,150 sq miles (83,268 sq km).

NUNAVUT

MANITOBA

Hudson Bay

Péninsu d'Unga

Southampton I.

Coats I.

Mansel I.

Salisbury I.
Nottingham I.

Ivujivik

Inukjuak

L. Min

Belcher Is
(Nunavut)

Kuujjuarapik

James Bay

Winisk

Akimiski I.
(Nunavut)

C A N A D A

Q U

Severn

*Wini*sk

Attawapiskat

East

L. Mistassin

O N T A R I O

Attawapiskat

Albany

Moosonee

L. Seul

Kenora

L. Nipigon

Armstrong

Res. Gou

Lake
of the
Woods

Thunder Bay

Cochrane

MINNESOTA

Lake Superior

Wawa

Timmins

Sault
Sainte Marie

Sudbury

North Bay

OTTAWA

UNITED STATES

OF AMERICA

WISCONSIN *Lake Michigan*

MICHIGAN

*Lake
Huron*

Peterborough

Oshawa

TORONTO

Kitchener

Hamilton

London

Windsor

Kingst

Lake Ontario

NE

St. Catharines

Lake Erie

IOWA

ILLINOIS

INDIANA

OHIO

PENNSYLVANIA

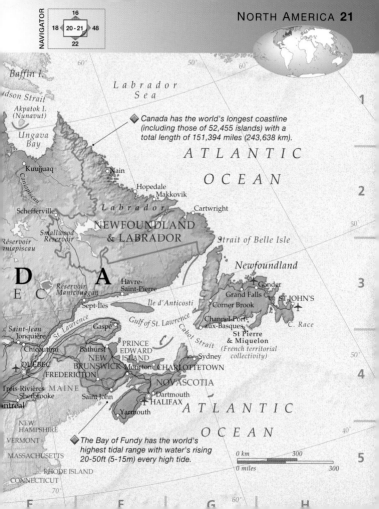

Baffin I.

dson Strait

Akpatok I.
(Nunavut)

*Ungava
Bay*

*Labrador
Sea*

60°   50°   60°

◆ Canada has the world's longest coastline
(including those of 52,455 islands) with a
total length of 151,394 miles (243,638 km).

A T L A N T I C

O C E A N

Kuujjuaq

Nain

Hopedale
Makkovik

Labrador

Scefferville

*Smallwood
Reservoir*

Cartwright

Strait of Belle Isle

NEWFOUNDLAND
& LABRADOR

Newfoundland

*Réservoir
niapiscau*

50°

Caniapiscau

D   **A**

E
C

*Réservoir
Manicouagan*

Havre-
Saint-Pierre

Ile d'Anticosti

Gander

Grand Falls

Corner Brook   ST JOHN'S

Sept-Îles

St. Lawrence

Gulf of St. Lawrence

C. Race

Gaspé

Cebot Strait

Channel-Port
aux-Basques

**St Pierre
& Miquelon**
*(French territorial
collectivity)*

Saint-Jean
Jonquière

Chicoutimi

Bathurst

PRINCE
EDWARD
ISLAND

50°

QUÉBEC

NEW
BRUNSWICK

Moncton

Sydney

Trois-Rivières MAINE

FREDERICTON

CHARLOTTETOWN

NOVASCOTIA

Sherbrooke

ntreal

Saint John

Dartmouth
HALIFAX

NEW
HAMPSHIRE

Yarmouth

A T L A N T I C

VERMONT

O C E A N

40°

MASSACHUSETTS

◆ The Bay of Fundy has the world's
highest tidal range with water's rising
20-50ft (5-15m) every high tide.

0 km   300

RHODE ISLAND

0 miles   300

CONNECTICUT

70°   60°

F   **G**   **H**

USA: The Northeast

95°   90°   85°   80°

MINNESOTA

1   Lake Superior

Superior   ONTARI   C A

Ironwood

Marquette
Sault Ste Marie

Iron Mountain

Ladysmith   Cheboygan

45°   W I S C O N S I N   Lake Huron

2   M I C H I G A N

Eau Claire   Traverse City

Green Bay   Lake Michigan   Bay City

La Crosse   Oshkosh   Saginaw   Flint

I O W A   MADISON   Grand Rapids

Milwaukee   LANSING   Detroit

Mississippi   Rockford   Waukegan   Ann Arbor   Lake Erie   Er

◆ The Chicago River
originally flowed into
Lake Michigan, but was
reversed in 1900 by
the completion of
a canal.

Chicago   Toledo   Clevelan

Aurora   South   Youngstown

Rock Island   Joliet   Gary   Bend   Akron

Galesburg   Fort Wayne   Mansfield   Canton

3   Peoria   Wheeling

I L L I N O I S   I N D I A N A   O H I O

40°   Champaign   Muncie   COLUMBUS

4   SPRINGFIELD   INDIANAPOLIS

Decatur   Dayton

Effingham   Terre Haute   Cincinnati

Missouri   Bloomington   Huntington

East St Louis   Louisville   CHARLESTON

Mt. Vernon   Evansville   FRANKFORT   Lexington   WEST

M I S S O U R I   Carbondale   Owensboro   Richmond   VIRGIN

5   K E N T U C K Y   London

Paducah   Bowling Green

Hopkinsville

ARKANSAS   90°

A   B   C   D

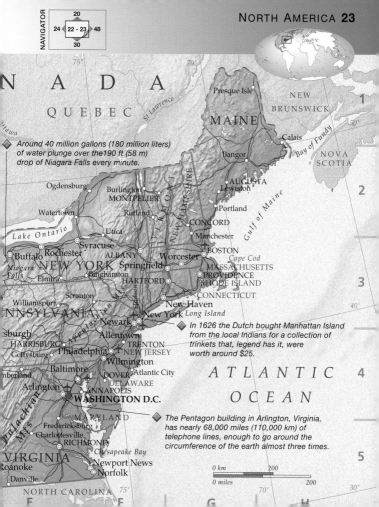

NAVIGATOR
20
24 22 - 23 48
30

C A N A D A

QUEBEC

MAINE

NEW BRUNSWICK

Presque Isle

St Lawrence

Ottawa

◆ Around 40 million gallons (180 million liters) of water plunge over the 190 ft (58 m) drop of Niagara Falls every minute.

Calais

Bay of Fundy

NOVA SCOTIA

Bangor

Ogdensburg

Burlington
MONTPELIER

AUGUSTA
Lewiston

NEW HAMPSHIRE

VERMONT

Portland

Watertown

Rutland

Gulf of Maine

Lake Ontario

Utica

CONCORD

Manchester

Buffalo Rochester Syracuse

ALBANY

Worcester

BOSTON

Cape Cod

Niagara
Falls Elmira

NEW YORK

Springfield

MASSACHUSETTS

Binghamton

HARTFORD

PROVIDENCE
RHODE ISLAND

Scranton

CONNECTICUT

Hudson

New Haven

Williamsport

PENNSYLVANIA

Newark

New York Long Island

◆ In 1626 the Dutch bought Manhattan Island from the local Indians for a collection of trinkets that, legend has it, were worth around $25.

Allentown

Pittsburgh

HARRISBURG

TRENTON
NEW JERSEY

Gettysburg

Philadelphia

Wilmington

Baltimore

Atlantic City

Cumberland

DOVER
DELAWARE

A T L A N T I C

Arlington

ANNAPOLIS

O C E A N

WASHINGTON D.C.

MARYLAND

Fredericksburg

Charlottesville

RICHMOND

Chesapeake Bay

◆ The Pentagon building in Arlington, Virginia, has nearly 68,000 miles (110,000 km) of telephone lines, enough to go around the circumference of the earth almost three times.

VIRGINIA

Roanoke

Newport News

Norfolk

Danville

NORTH CAROLINA

Appalachian Mts

0 km   200

0 miles   200

USA: Central States

At 20,016 ft (6104 m), or almost 4 miles (6 km) in length, the Fort Peck Dam is the largest earth-filled hydraulic dam in the US.

The Great Salt Lake is a remnant of the prehistoric Lake Bonneville, which once covered almost 20,000 square miles (51,800 sq km) of western Utah.

The world's largest organism is a 200 acre (81 hectares) grove of aspen trees in Utah. Derived from a single tree it has hundreds of suckers growing from its root system.

100°   95°   90°   50°   85°

C A N A D A

MANITOBA   *Lake of the Woods*   O N T A R I O   1

Lake Superior

M I N N E S O T A

Grand Forks   Virginia

AKOTA   Moorhead   Duluth   45°   2

SMARCK   Fargo   Brainerd

◇ Access to the St Lawrence Seaway via the Great Lakes makes Duluth the most westerly Atlantic port in the US, some 1100 miles (1770 km) from the Atlantic ocean.

St Cloud   **W I S C O N S I N**   M I C H I G A N

AKOTA   Minneapolis   SAINT   *Lake Michigan*

PIERRE   Watertown   PAUL

Mitchell   Rochester

Sioux Falls   Mason City   OHIO   3

Missouri

Dubuque

Sioux City   **I O W A**   Cedar Rapids   40°

ASKA   Columbus   DES MOINES   Davenport   I N D I A N A

North   Omaha   Council Bluffs   I L L I N O I S   Ohio

Platte   LINCOLN   Burlington

Hastings   ◇ Between 1950 and 1994 Kansas suffered over 2000 tornadoes, claiming around 200 lives and causing in excess of $1.2 billion damage.

Kirksville

St Joseph   Mississippi

akley   Hays   Kansas City   Independence

TOPEKA   Kansas City   Saint   4

ANSAS   JEFFERSON CITY   Louis   Ohio   K E N T U C K Y

Dodge   Wichita   **M I S S O U R I**   Missouri

City   Pratt   Springfield   85°

Ozark Plateau   T E N N E S S E E   5

Arkansas

0 km   200

O K L A H O M A   **A R K A N S A S**   0 miles   200

100°   95°   90°   90°

E   F   G   H

Hells Canyon is the deepest in the US, with cliffs up to 7900 ft (2408 m) high.

At Black Rock Desert on October 15, 1997, ThrustSSC, driven by Andy Green, became the first land vehicle to break the sound barrier by achieving a speed of 763 mph (1228 km/h).

Death Valley is not only the lowest point in North America at 282 ft (86 m) below sea level, it is also the hottest, with a maximum air temperature of 134°F (57°C) recorded in 1913.

The Golden Gate Bridge, completed in 1937, has 80,000 miles (129,000 km) of wire in its two main cables, weighing a total of 22,200 tons (tonnes).

U T A H

N E V A D A

A R I Z O N A

C A L I F O R N I A

M E X I C O

Sierra Nevada

Coast Ranges

San Joaquin Valley

Mojave Desert

Death Valley

Lake Mead

Salton Sea

Santa Rosa I.
Santa Cruz I.
Santa Catalina I.
San Nicolas I.
San Clemente I.

Channel Islands

P A C I F I C

O C E A N

Susanville
Tulelake
Pyramid Lake
Reno
Sparks
Chico
Yuba City
Ukiah
SACRAMENTO
Santa Rosa
Berkeley
Oakland
San Francisco
San Jose
Santa Cruz
Monterey
Salinas
Santa Barbara
Oxnard
Ely
Fallon
Hawthorne
CARSON CITY
Lake Tahoe
Stockton
Modesto
Merced
Fresno
Visalia
Bishop
Tonopah
Las Vegas
Bakersfield
Mojave
Lancaster
Barstow
Pasadena
Los Angeles
Long Beach
Huntington Beach
San Bernardino
Riverside
Santa Ana
Oceanside
San Diego
Chula Vista
Palm Springs

Mt. Whitney
4418m

80m

Colorado

Colorado

Joaquin

0 km   200
0 miles 200

USA: The Southwest

◆ The Colorado River has cut down some 6242 ft (2000 m) into the Colorado Plateau to form the Grand Canyon, exposing rock strata over 2 billion years old.

◆ Meteor Crater was formed when a meteor about 150 ft (46 m) across struck the desert at about 40,000 mph (64,372 km/h) with a force equivalent to 20 million tons (tonnes) of TNT.

◆ The first atomic bomb was tested at Trinity Site near Alamogordo on July 16, 1945 yielding an explosive force equivalent to 20,000 tons (tonnes) of TNT from around 2.2 lbs (1 kg) of plutonium-239.

NEVADA UTAH COLORADO
L. Powell
Farmington
Grand Canyon
L. Mead Painted Desert
Colorado Plateau
Los Alamos SANTA FE
Gallup Rio Grande
Flagstaff Albuquerque
Pecos
Prescott
CALIFORNIA ARIZONA NEW
Glendale Scottsdale MEXICO
PHOENIX Mesa
Sonoran Roswell
Yuma Alamogordo
Desert Artesia
Casa Grande Las Cruces Carlsbad
Tucson
El Paso
Douglas
Rio Grande

Baja California Golfo de California MEX

PACIFIC
OCEAN

0 km   200
0 miles   200

K A N S A S

100°

95°

1

Ponca City

Enid

Tulsa

Arkansas

Broken Arrow

35°

O K L A H O M A

ARKANSAS

Borger

OKLAHOMA CITY

Pampa

Shawnee

Amarillo

Norman

nadian

Red River

Lawton

2

vis

Vernon

Red River

wnfield

Lubbock

Wichita Falls

Paris

◇ On January 10, 1901
the Lucas Gusher blew
oil 100 ft (30 m) into the
air, flowing at 100,000
barrels a day until it was
eventually capped nine
days later.

Denton

Hobbs

Fort Worth

Arlington

Longview

Big Spring

Abilene

Dallas

Tyler

Sweetwater

Brazos

Jacksonville

Odessa

Midland

Waco

Toledo Bend Res.

3

Pecos

San Angelo

Colorado

Neches

T E X A S

LOUISIANA

Bryan

30°

Edwards

L. Travis

Beaumont

Plateau

AUSTIN

Houston

Port Arthur

San Antonio

Pasadena

Del Rio

Victoria

Texas City

Galveston

San Antonio

Freeport

Eagle Pass

4

C O

Corpus Christi

Gulf

Laredo

Kingsville

o f

Padre Island

M e x i c o

Rio Grande

Brownsville

5

100°

95°

25°

USA: The Southeast

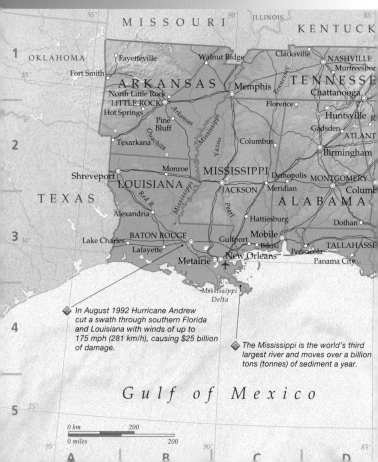

In August 1992 Hurricane Andrew cut a swath through southern Florida and Louisiana with winds of up to 175 mph (281 km/h), causing $25 billion of damage.

The Mississippi is the world's third largest river and moves over a billion tons (tonnes) of sediment a year.

MISSOURI
ILLINOIS
KENTUCKY
OKLAHOMA
Fayetteville
Walnut Ridge
Clarksville
NASHVILLE
Murfreesbor
Fort Smith
ARKANSAS
Memphis
TENNESSE
Chattanooga
North Little Rock
Florence
Huntsville
LITTLE ROCK
Gadsden
Hot Springs
Pine Bluff
ATLANT
Texarkana
Columbus
Birmingham
Monroe
MISSISSIPPI
Demopolis
MONTGOMERY
Shreveport
JACKSON
Meridian
Columb
LOUISIANA
Red R.
ALABAMA
TEXAS
Alexandria
Hattiesburg
Dothan
Lake Charles
BATON ROUGE
Mobile
TALLAHASSE
Lafayette
Gulfport
Biloxi
Pensacola
Metairie
New Orleans
Panama City

Mississippi Delta

Gulf of Mexico

0 km 200
0 miles 200

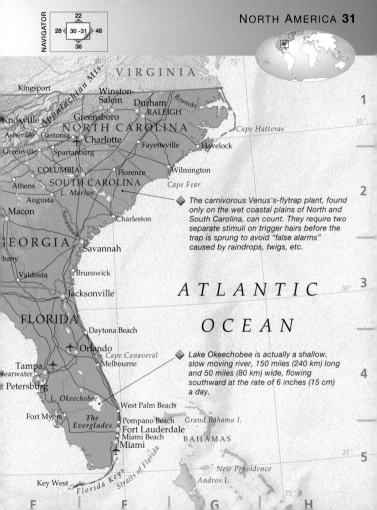

VIRGINIA

Kingsport

Winston-Salem
Durham
RALEIGH
Roanoke

Knoxville
Appalachian Mts.
NORTH CAROLINA
Cape Hatteras

Asheville
Gastonia
Greensboro
Charlotte

Greenville
Spartanburg
Fayetteville
Havelock

COLUMBIA
SOUTH CAROLINA
Florence
Wilmington

Athens
Cape Fear

Augusta
L. Marion

◆ The carnivorous Venus's-flytrap plant, found only on the wet coastal plains of North and South Carolina, can count. They require two separate stimuli on trigger hairs before the trap is sprung to avoid "false alarms" caused by raindrops, twigs, etc.

Macon

Charleston

GEORGIA

Savannah

Savannah

bany

Brunswick

ATLANTIC

Valdosta

Jacksonville

OCEAN

FLORIDA

Daytona Beach

◆ Lake Okeechobee is actually a shallow, slow moving river, 150 miles (240 km) long and 50 miles (80 km) wide, flowing southward at the rate of 6 inches (15 cm) a day.

Orlando
Cape Canaveral

Tampa
Melbourne

learwater

t Petersburg

L. Okeechobee
West Palm Beach

Fort Myers
The Everglades
Pompano Beach
Fort Lauderdale
Grand Bahama I.

Miami Beach
Miami
BAHAMAS

New Providence

Key West
Florida Keys
Straits of Florida
Andros I.

Mexico

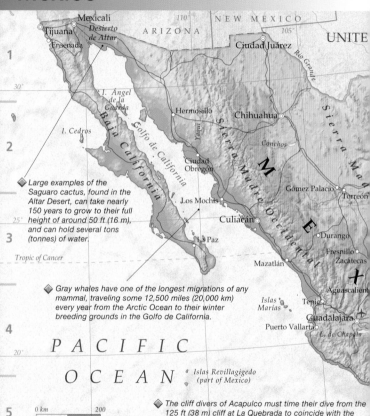

◆ Large examples of the Saguaro cactus, found in the Altar Desert, can take nearly 150 years to grow to their full height of around 50 ft (16 m), and can hold several tons (tonnes) of water.

◆ Gray whales have one of the longest migrations of any mammal, traveling some 12,500 miles (20,000 km) every year from the Arctic Ocean to their winter breeding grounds in the Golfo de California.

◆ The cliff divers of Acapulco must time their dive from the 125 ft (38 m) cliff at La Quebrada to coincide with the incoming swells to avoid being dashed on the rocks in the shallow inlet.

PACIFIC OCEAN

Islas Revillagigedo
(part of Mexico)

0 km   200
0 miles   200

STATES OF AMERICA | LOUISIANA

T E X A S

1

Río Grande

Nuevo Laredo

25°

nclova
Reynosa

G u l f

2

o f

Monterrey
Matamoros
Tropic of Cancer

altillo

M e x i c o

85°

Ciudad Victoria

3

Cancún

Mérida

20°

San Luis
Potosí
Tampico

Isla
Cozumel

Río Verde
Ciudad Valles

Dolores Hidalgo

Campeche

Yucatan
Peninsula

eón
apuato

Querétaro

Poza Rica

Bahía de Campeche

4

Tulancingo
Pachuca

Xalapa

MEXICO
CITY
Veracruz

Morelia

Coatzacoalcos
Villahermosa

Cuernavaca
Puebla
Minatitlán

BELIZE

ruapan
Tehuacán

Balsas

O

Sierra Madre del Sur

Oaxaca
Tuxtla

15°

Acapulco

HONDURAS

Golfo de
Tehuantepec
Tapachula

GUATEMALA

EL SALVADOR

100°
15°
95°
90°

E | E | F | G | H

In spring 2001, the Rio Grande stopped flowing into the Gulf of Mexico for the first time in recorded history, allowing illegal immigrants to simply walk into the US.

It is thought that "The Ballgame," a ritual sport played by Maya and Aztec civilizations, and a forerunner of soccer, often ended with the losing team being sacrificed.

Central America

MEXICO

Belize City

BELMOPAN

Flores

San Ignacio

BELIZE

Islas de la Bahía

GUATEMALA

Gulf of Honduras

Puerto Cortés

Trujillo

Huehuetenango

Cobán

Puerto Barrios

San Pedro Sula

La Ceiba

Lago de Izabal

Zacapa

HONDURAS

Patuca

Quezaltenango

GUATEMALA CITY

Santa Rosa de Copán

Comayagua

Juticalpa

Escuintla

La Esperanza

TEGUCIGALPA

SAN SALVADOR

Santa Ana

EL SALVADOR

San Miguel

Choluteca

Somoto

Jinotega

NICARAGUA

Estelí

Matagalpa

Gulf of Fonseca

Chinandega

Corinto

León

Juigalpa

MANAGUA

PACIFIC

Granada

Lago de Nicaragua

OCEAN

Rivas

◈ Unique freshwater species of shark and swordfish have evolved in the long period since Lake Nicaragua was cut off from the Pacific Ocean by a belt of volcanic cones.

Península de Nicoya

Liberia

Puntarenas

Alajue

SAN JOSÉ

◈ The strongest living creature is the Rhinoceros Beetle found in the jungles of Costa Rica, which can support up to 850 times it's own body weight, equivalent to a human carrying about 70 tons (tonnes).

0 km   200

0 miles   200

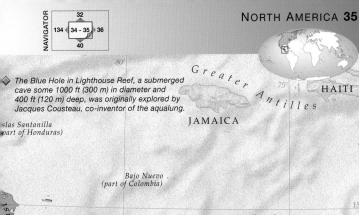

◆ The Blue Hole in Lighthouse Reef, a submerged cave some 1000 ft (300 m) in diameter and 400 ft (120 m) deep, was originally explored by Jacques Cousteau, co-inventor of the aqualung.

Greater Antilles

HAITI

*slas Santanilla
(part of Honduras)*

JAMAICA

*Bajo Nuevo
(part of Colombia)*

C a r i b b e a n

Cayos Miskitos

S e a

*I. de Providencia
(part of Colombia)*

*I. de San Andrés
(part of Colombia)*

Islas del Maíz

uefields

◆ Gatun Locks on the Panama Canal are 110 ft (33 m) wide and 1000 ft (303 m) long, took four years to build and required 2 million cubic yards (1.5 million cu m) of concrete.

OSTA
RICA

Limón

Colón

*Gulf
of
Darien*

PANAMA

PANAMA CITY

Penonomé

*Panama
Canal*

*Isla del
Rey*

David

*Golfo
de
Chiriquí*

Santiago

Chitré
Las Tablas

*Golfo
de
Panamá*

COLOMBIA

The Caribbean

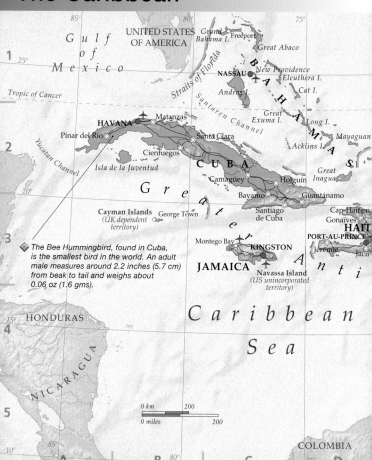

The Bee Hummingbird, found in Cuba, is the smallest bird in the world. An adult male measures around 2.2 inches (5.7 cm) from beak to tail and weighs about 0.06 oz (1.6 gms).

Gulf of Mexico

UNITED STATES OF AMERICA

Straits of Florida

Tropic of Cancer

Yucatan Channel

HAVANA

Matanzas

Pinar del Rio

Santa Clara

Cienfuegos

Isla de la Juventud

CUBA

Camagüey

Holguín

Bayamo

Guantánamo

Santiago de Cuba

Cayman Islands
(UK dependent territory)

George Town

Montego Bay

KINGSTON

JAMAICA

Navassa Island
(US unincorporated territory)

Grand Bahama I.

Freeport

Great Abaco

New Providence

NASSAU

Eleuthera I.

Andros I.

Cat I.

Great Exuma I.

Long I.

Santaren Channel

B A H A M A S

Mayaguan

Acklins I.

Great Inagua

Cap-Haïtien

Gonaïves

HAÏTI

PORT-AU-PRINCE

Jérémie

Jacn

G r e a t e r   A n t i l l e s

C a r i b b e a n

S e a

HONDURAS

N I C A R A G U A

0 km   200

0 miles   200

COLOMBIA

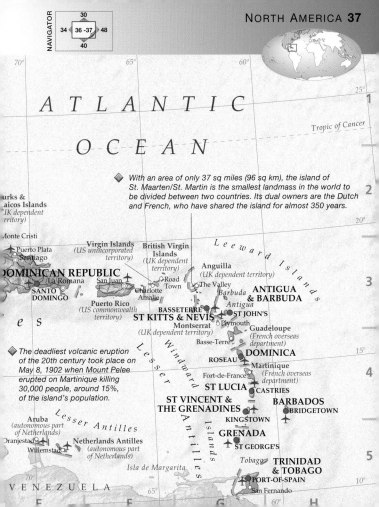

1

25°

Tropic of Cancer

ATLANTIC

OCEAN

◇ With an area of only 37 sq miles (96 sq km), the island of St. Maarten/St. Martin is the smallest landmass in the world to be divided between two countries. Its dual owners are the Dutch and French, who have shared the island for almost 350 years.

2

20°

urks & aicos Islands *(UK dependent territory)*

Monte Cristi

Puerto Plata

Santiago

DOMINICAN REPUBLIC

La Romana

SANTO DOMINGO

es

s

Virgin Islands *(US unincorporated territory)*

San Juan

Charlotte Amalie

Puerto Rico *(US commonwealth territory)*

British Virgin Islands *(UK dependent territory)*

Road Town

The Valley

L e e w a r d   I s l a n d s

Anguilla *(UK dependent territory)*

Barbuda

ANTIGUA & BARBUDA

BASSETERRE

ST KITTS & NEVIS

Antigua

ST JOHN'S

Montserrat *(UK dependent territory)*

Plymouth

Basse-Terre

Guadeloupe *(French overseas department)*

3

15°

◇ The deadliest volcanic eruption of the 20th century took place on May 8, 1902 when Mount Pelée erupted on Martinique killing 30,000 people, around 15%, of the island's population.

L e s s e r

W i n d w a r d

ROSEAU

DOMINICA

Martinique *(French overseas department)*

Fort-de-France

ST LUCIA

CASTRIES

4

ST VINCENT & THE GRENADINES

KINGSTOWN

I s l a n d s

A n t i l l e s

BARBADOS

BRIDGETOWN

Aruba *(autonomous part of Netherlands)*

Oranjestad

Lesser Antilles

Netherlands Antilles *(autonomous part of Netherlands)*

Willemstad

GRENADA

ST GEORGE'S

Tobago

TRINIDAD & TOBAGO

5

10°

Isla de Margarita

VENEZUELA

PORT-OF-SPAIN

San Fernando

70°   65°   60°

South America

ATLANTIC OCEAN

Equator

Caribbean Sea

Greater Antilles

Lesser Antilles

Puerto Rico

Hispaniola

Jamaica

Trinidad

COLOMBIA

VENEZUELA

GUYANA

SURINAME

French Guiana (France)

(claimed by Venezuela)

(claimed by Suriname)

Guiana Highlands

Orinoco

Meta

Magdalena

Cauca

Rio Negro

Canal

Represa Balbina

Içá

Japurá

Putumayo

Napo

Marañón

Ucayali

Juruá

Purus

Amazon

Tapajós

Xingu

Tocantins

Madeira

Araguaia

Beni

Madre de Dios

Serra do Roncador

Serra do Cachimbo

Serra Formosa

Amazon Basin

BRAZIL

BOLIVIA

PERU

ECUADOR

Andes

Chimborazo

Altiplano

Lake Titicaca

Planalto de Mato Grosso

Chapada dos Parecis

Pantanal

Brazilian Highlands

Planalto Borborema

São Francisco

Represa de Sobradinho

Turtuc Humac Mountains

Equator

rapids

Tropic of Capricorn

ATLANTIC

OCEAN

URUGUAY

Lagoa dos Patos

Mirim Lagoon

Serra do Mar

Serra Geral

Uruguay

Ibicuí

Río de la Plata

PARAGUAY

ARAGUAY

Paraná

Paraná

Mesopotamia

Pilcomayo

Gran Chaco

Bahía Blanca

Colorado

Bahía Blanca

Río Negro

Golfo San Matías

Península Valdés

Gulf of San Jorge

Chubut

Deseado

Chico

Bahía Grande

Patagonia

ARGENTINA

CHILE

Cerro Ojos del Salado 6893m

Atacama

Cerro Aconcagua 6960m

Isla San Ambrosio (Chile)

Isla San Félix (Chile)

Islas Juan Fernández (Chile)

Isla de Chiloé

PACIFIC

OCEAN

Tropic of Capricorn

Strait of Magellan

Tierra del Fuego

Cape Horn

Drake Passage

West Falkland

East Falkland

Falkland Islands
(UK)

Scotia Sea

South Shetland Islands

ANTARCTICA

South Georgia
(UK)

South Sandwich
Islands
(UK)

South Orkney Islands

0 km   1000

0 miles   1000

Northern South America

Caribbean Sea

Gulf of Venezuela

Ríohacha
Santa Marta
Maicao
Coro
CARACA
Barranquilla
Maracaibo
Cartagena
Valledupar
Cabimas
Maracay
Ciudád Ojeda
Barquisimeto
Valencia
Lago de
Maracaibo
Acarigua
Sincelejo
Mérida
Valera
Guanare
San Juan
Montería
de los Morros
Cúcuta
Barinas
San Cristóbal
San Fernando
Bucaramanga
Arauca
Bello
Barrancabermeja
VEN
Medellín
Itagüí
Quibdó
Puerto Carreño
Tunja
Manizales
Yopal
Pereira
Meta
Armenia
BOGOTÁ
Buenaventura
Ibagué
Guaviare
Cali
Villavicencio
COLOMBIA
Popayán
Neiva
San José
del Guaviare
Pasto
Mocoa
Florencia
Mitú
Esmeraldas
Tulcán
Ibarra
QUITO
Aguarico
Manta
Santo Domingo
de los Colorados
Portoviejo
Ambato
Caquetá
Guayaquil
Riobamba
Milagro
ECUADOR
Putumayo
Golfo de
Guayaquil
Cuenca
Machala
Loja

PANAMA

PACIFIC OCEAN

Cauca
Magdalena

Apure
Guanare
Arauca
Orinoco

80°
70°
Less
10°
0° Equator
5°
75°
80

PERU

◇ Nestling between snow capped
peaks, at 9350 ft (2850 m)
Quito is the second highest
capital in the world.

◇ The first coffee
seedlings were
brought to
Colombia in
1804 by Jesuit
Missionaries;
today Columbia
produces over
a million tons
(tonnes) of
coffee beans
every year.

Antilles
GRENADA
ATLANTIC
OCEAN

Isla de Margarita
Carúpano
TRINIDAD
& TOBAGO
Cumaná
Barcelona
Maturín
Tucupita
El Tigre
The Serpent's Mouth
n o s
Orinoco
Ciudad Bolívar
Ciudad Guayana

◇ The Guyana shield is one of the
Earth's oldest surfaces, formed
around 4 billion years ago.

(claimed by Venezuela)

*Embalse
de Guri*
Cuyuni

ZUELA

*Salto
Ángel*

Caroní

G u i a n a

Paragua

H i g h l a n d s

Orinoco

◇ Angel Falls
(Salto Ángel)
plunge 3121 ft
(951 m) to form
the world's
highest waterfall.

Bartica
Rockstone
Linden

GEORGETOWN
New Amsterdam

GUYANA

Essequibo

Acarai Mts.

*(claimed by
Suriname)*

Nieuw
Amsterdam
St-Laurent-
du-Maroni
PARAMARIBO
Sinnamary
Kourou

*W.J. van
Blommesteinmeer*

SURINAME

Courantyne

**French
Guiana**
*(French overseas
department)*

Maroni

CAYENNE

(claimed by Suriname)

◇ The European Space Agency launch
facility at Kourou takes advantage
of the Earth's spin near the
Equator to gain 10 percent
more payload than an equivalent
launch at Cape Canaveral in the US.

Equator

A m a z o n

B   R   A   Z   I   L

B a s i n

Amazon

◇ 2.47 acres (one hectare) of Amazon rain forest
can contain more than 750 types of trees and
1500 plant species, amounting to around
900 tons (tonnes) of living plant material.

0 km   200

0 miles   200

Peru, Bolivia & North Brazil

COLOMBIA

VENEZUELA

GUYANA

Boa Vista

Guian

Represa Balbina

Rio Negro

Manaus

Equator

ECUADOR

Napo

Putumayo

Amazon

Iquitos

Amazon

Marañón

Moyobamba

Tarapoto

Amazon Basin

Juruá

B   **R**   **A**

Piura

Chiclayo

Purus

Saña

Pucallpa

Porto Velho

Madeira

Trujillo

Chimbote

Huaraz

Huanuco

Rio Branco

Madre de Dios

Riberalta

Huacho

La Oroya

Puerto Maldonado

Beni

Guaporé

Callao

LIMA

Huancayo

P

E

R

U

Trinidad

PACIFIC OCEAN

Ayacucho

Pisco

Ica

Cusco

BOLIVIA

Nazca

Puno

LA PAZ

Cochabamba

Montero

◆ Lake Titicaca is the largest lake in South
America at 3220 sq miles (8340 sq km)
and with an altitude of 12,500 ft (3810 m)
it is also the world's highest navigable lake.

Arequipa

Lake Titicaca

Santa Cruz

Tacna

Oruro

Puerto Suáre

Lago Roopó

SUCRE

Potosi

CHILE

Uyuni

Tupiza

PARAGUA

Tarija

BOLIVIA'S TWO CAPITALS

La Paz - legislative and
administrative capital

Sucre - legal capital

ARGENTINA

50°

French Guiana
(French overseas department)

RINAME

Highlands

Macapá

Ilha Caviana de Fora

40°

◇ The Amazon River is 4195 miles (6751 km) long with a peak flow of 7 million cubic feet (198,229 cu m) of water entering the Atlantic Ocean every second.

ATLANTIC

Equator

1

Ilha de Marajó

Belém

OCEAN

Amazon

Santarém

São Luís

Paranaíba

Represa de Tucuruí

Fortaleza *de Noronha*
San Fernando
(part of Brazil)

2

Xingu

Imperatriz

Teresina

Mossoró

Z

I

L

Carolina

L

Juàzeiro do Norte

Campina
Grande

Natal
João
Pessoa

Araguaia

Tocantins

Represa de Sobradinho

São Francisco

Juàzeiro

Recife

Maceió

les Pires

3

10°

Aracaju

Mato Grosso

Taguatinga

Feira de Santana

Salvador

Cuiabá

Brazilian

Itabuna

Anápolis

BRASÍLIA

Highlands

Vitória da Conquista

4

Goiânia

Montes Claros

Governador Valadares

Campo Grande

Uberaba

Uberlândia

Divinópolis

Belo Horizonte

Vitória

Ribeirão Preto

Paraná

Marília

Nova
Iguaçu

Campos

5

20°

Londrina

Campinas

Juiz de Fora

Sorocaba

Taubaté

Rio de Janeiro

Tropic of Capricorn

São Paulo

40°

30°

Paraguay, Uruguay & South Brazil

◆ Formed by river deposits washed
down from the Andes and Brazilian
Shield, the Gran Chaco is virtually
free of stones. It is composed of
sand and silt sediments that are
up to 10,000 ft (3050 m) thick.

◆ The Itaipú hydroelectric scheme is
able to produce more power than
10 average nuclear reactors; it supplies
26% of the electrical power consumption
of Brazil and 78% for Paraguay.

BOLIVIA

BRA

São José do Rio Preto

Campo Grande

Presidente
Prudente

Marili

Baur

General Eugenio A. Garay

Fuerte Olimpo

Dourados

Ourinhos

Mariscal
Estigarribia

Londrina

PARAGUAY

Concepción

Maringá

Tropic of Capricorn

Pozo Colorado

Ponta Grossa

Coronel
Oviedo

Ciudad
del Este

Guarapuava

Curitiba

ASUNCIÓN

Villarrica

Iguaçu

Lambaré

Caazapá

Jøinville

San Juan
Bautista

Blumenau

Pilar

Encarnación

Pelotas

Florianópolis

Lajes

Erechim

Passo Fundo

Carazinho

Caxias do Sul

São Borja

Uruguaiana

Santa Maria

Canoas

Artigas

Rivera

Bagé

Porto Alegre

ARGENTINA

Salto

Lagoa dos Patos

Tacuarembó

Pelotas

Paysandú

Melo

Rio Grande

Fray Bentos

URUGUAY

Mirim Lagoon

Mercedes

Trinidad

Durazno

Chuy

Las Piedras

MONTEVIDEO

San Carlos

Río de la Plata

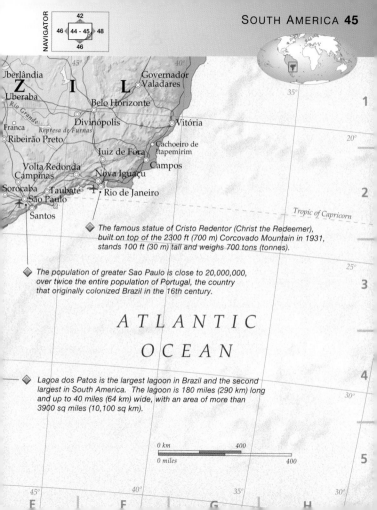

Iberlândia
Z I L
Uberaba
Rio Grande
Governador Valadares
Belo Horizonte
Franca
Divinópolis
Represa de Furnas
Vitória
Ribeirão Preto
Juiz de Fora
Cachoeiro de Itapemirim
Volta Redonda
Campos
Campinas
Nova Iguaçu
Sorocaba
Taubaté
Rio de Janeiro
São Paulo
Santos

Tropic of Capricorn

◆ The famous statue of Cristo Redentor (Christ the Redeemer), built on top of the 2300 ft (700 m) Corcovado Mountain in 1931, stands 100 ft (30 m) tall and weighs 700 tons (tonnes).

◆ The population of greater Sao Paulo is close to 20,000,000, over twice the entire population of Portugal, the country that originally colonized Brazil in the 16th century.

A T L A N T I C

O C E A N

◆ Lagoa dos Patos is the largest lagoon in Brazil and the second largest in South America. The lagoon is 180 miles (290 km) long and up to 40 miles (64 km) wide, with an area of more than 3900 sq miles (10,100 sq km).

0 km 400
0 miles 400

Southern South America

BRAZIL

BRAZIL

PERU

BOLIVIA

PARAGUAY

URUGUAY

ARGENTINA

CHILE

The world's tallest, active volcano is the Guallatiri volcano in northern Chile. It stands 19,918 ft (6071 m) tall, and last erupted in 1987.

The driest place on earth is the Atacama Desert in Chile with an average rainfall of 0.004 inches (0.1 mm) per year. Until recently some places had received no rain for over 400 years.

Tropic of Capricorn

Tropic of Capricorn

Tropic of Capricorn

PACIFIC

OCEAN

Posadas
Formosa
Corrientes
Concordia
BUENOS AIRES
La Plata
Gualeguaychú
Resistencia
Vera
Santa Fe
Paraná
Rosario
Junín
Córdoba
Río Cuarto
Villa Mercedes
San Salvador de Jujuy
Salta
San Miguel de Tucumán
Santiago del Estero
La Rioja
San Juan
Mendoza
Godoy Cruz
Rancagua
SANTIAGO
Chuquicamata
Calama
Copiapó
Chañaral
Vallenar
La Serena
Coquimbo
Illapel
La Ligua
Viña del Mar
Valparaíso
San Antonio
Pichilemu
Talca
Linares
Curicó
Arica
Iquique
Tocopilla
Antofagasta

Desierto de Atacama

Gran Chaco

Pampas

Pilcomayo

Bermejo

Paraná

Paraguay

Uruguay

Salado

Laguna Mar Chiquita

Cerro Aconcagua 6959 m

Islas Juan Fernández (to Chile)

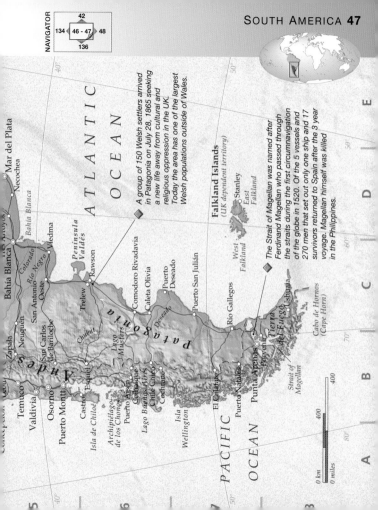

A T L A N T I C

O C E A N

Mar del Plata

Necochea

Los Arroyos

Bahía Blanca

Bahía Blanca

Colorado

Río Negro

San Antonio
Oeste

Viedma

*Península
Valdés*

Kawson

Trelew

Comodoro Rivadavia

Caleta Olivia

Puerto
Deseado

Puerto San Julián

A group of 150 Welsh settlers arrived
in Patagonia on July 28, 1865 seeking
a new life away from cultural and
religious oppression in the UK.
Today the area has one of the largest
Welsh populations outside of Wales.

Falkland Islands
(UK dependent territory)

Stanley

East
Falkland

West
Falkland

The Strait of Magellan was named after
Ferdinand Magellan who passed through
the straits during the first circumnavigation
of the globe in 1520. Of the 5 vessels and
270 men that set out only one ship and 17
survivors returned to Spain after the 3 year
voyage. Magellan himself was killed
in the Philippines.

Temuco

Zapala

Neuquén

Valdivia

San Carlos
de Bariloche

Osorno

Puerto Montt

Castro

Esquel

Chubut

Río Gallegos

Isla de Chiloé

*Archipiélago
de los Chonos*

Puerto Aisén

Coihaique

*Lago
Musters*

Deseado

Coyhaique

Chile Chico

Cochrane

Lago Buenos Aires

*Lago
General
Carrera*

*Isla
Wellington*

El Calafate

Puerto Natales

Punta Arenas

Porvenir

*Tierra
del Fuego*

Ushuaia

*Cabo de Hornos
(Cape Horn)*

*Strait of
Magellan*

P a t a g o n i a

A n d e s

P A C I F I C

O C E A N

0 km   400

0 miles   400

The Atlantic Ocean

A R C T I C   O C E A N

Svalbard
(Norway)

Barents
Sea

Arctic Circle

Scandinavia

Black Sea

Red Sea

EUROPE

Danube

Baltic Sea

Alps

Port Said

Nile

Tropic of Cancer

Greenland
Sea

Jan Mayen
(Norway)

Faeroe Is.
(Denmark)

Rotterdam

North
Sea

British
Isles

Mediterranean Sea

Atlas Mts.

S a h a r a

AFRICA

USSR

Denmark Strait

Iceland

Gibraltar

Azores
(Portugal)

Madeira
(Portugal)

Canary Is.
(Spain)

Canary Basin

Lake

Greenland
(Denmark)

♦ The North Atlantic Deep Water
Current is an oceanic "river"
that carries around twenty
times more water than all the
rivers of the world put together.

Newfoundland
Basin

CAPE VERDE

Cape V.

Mid-Atlantic Ridge

Ellesmere I.

Baffin
Bay

Baffin I.

Davis Strait

Labrador
Sea

Grand Banks

St. Lawrence

♦ The Gulf Stream travels across
the Atlantic Ocean at up to
110 miles (170 km) a day.

New York

Bermuda (UK)

Sargasso Sea

West Indies

Caribbean
Sea

Arctic Circle

Hudson
Bay

Great Lakes

N O R T H

A M E R I C A

Gulf of
Mexico

Mississippi

Tropic of Cancer

A   B   C   D   E

Equator

Tropic of Capricorn

Lake Victoria

Congo

Lake Nyasa

Gulf of Guinea

● **Cape Town**

Cape of Good Hope

Angola Basin

Cape Basin

ATLANTIC OCEAN

St Helena (UK)

Ascension I. (St Helena)

Walvis Ridge

Tristan da Cunha (St Helena)

Gough I. (Tristan da Cunha)

Bouvet I. (Norway)

Atlantic-Indian Ridge

Atlantic-Indian Basin

ANTARCTICA

Antarctic Circle

Brazil Basin

Fernando de Noronha (Brazil)

Ilha da Trindade (Brazil)

Mid-Atlantic Ridge

◆ Every cubic mile of seawater holds over 150 million tons (tonnes) of minerals.

Rio Grande Rise

Argentine Basin

SOUTH AMERICA

Amazon

● **Rio de Janeiro**

● **Buenos Aires**

Paraná

Andes

PACIFIC OCEAN

Tropic of Capricorn

Falkland Is. (UK)

South Georgia (UK)

Scotia Sea

South Orkney Is.

South Sandwich Is. (UK)

Cape Horn

South Shetland Is.

Weddell Sea

Bellingshausen Sea

Equator

0 km   2000
0 miles   2000

Africa

Caspiann Sea

The Gulf

Tropic of Cancer

Arabian Peninsula

A S I A

Caucasus

Black Sea

E U R O P E

Syrian Desert

Crete

Mediterranean Sea

Red Sea

Gulf of Aden

SOMALIA

ERITREA

DJIBOUTI

Ethiopian Highlands

ETHIOPIA

Lake Turkana

UGANDA

Blue Nile

White Nile

Nile

EGYPT

SUDAN

Sudd

Ubangi

CENTRAL AFRICAN REPUBLIC

Congo

LIBYA

Libyan Desert

Tibesti

CHAD

Ahaggar

S a h a r a

NIGER

Sicily

Melilla (Spain)

Atlas Mountains

TUNISIA

ALGERIA

MOROCCO

Ceuta (Spain)

Iberian Peninsula

Madeira (Portugal)

Islas Canarias (Spain)

ATLANTIC OCEAN

WESTERN SAHARA (disputed)

Tropic of Cancer

MAURITANIA

MALI

Senegal

SENEGAL

GAMBIA

GUINEA-BISSAU

GUINEA

SIERRA LEONE

LIBERIA

Niger

S a h e l

BURKINA

CÔTE D'IVOIRE (IVORY COAST)

GHANA

TOGO

BENIN

NIGERIA

Niger

CAMEROON

EQUATORIAL GUINEA

Gulf of Guinea

COMOROS

Mayotte (France)

MADAGASCAR

Tropic of Capricorn

BURUNDI

DEM. REP. CONGO (ZAIRE)

TANZANIA

Lake Nyasa

Lake Tanganyika

MALAWI

Mozambique Channel

INDIAN OCEAN

ANGOLA

ZAMBIA

Zambezi

MOZAMBIQUE

ZIMBABWE

Cabinda (Angola)

NAMIBIA

BOTSWANA

Kalahari Desert

SWAZILAND

LESOTHO

SOUTH AFRICA

Orange River

Namib Desert

Cape of Good Hope

ATLANTIC OCEAN

Ascension I. (St Helena)

St Helena (UK)

Tropic of Capricorn

Tristan da Cunha (St Helena)

Gough Island (Tristan da Cunha)

0 km   1000
0 miles   1000

Northwest Africa

SPAIN

ATLANTIC
OCEAN

1

◆ On March 27, 1977, two Boeing 747s
carrying 583 passengers and crew collided
on the runway at Los Rodeos Airport in
the world's worst ever air disaster.

Madeira
(Portugal)

ALGIERS
Mostaganem
Tanger   Ceuta (Spain)   Oran
Tetouan   Melilla   Sidi Bel
(Spain)   Abbes
Kénitra   Fès   Tlemcen
RABAT   Oujda
Casablanca
Khouribga   Figuig   Ghardaïa
Safi   Beni
Essaouira   Mellal   Er Rachidia   Béchar
Marrakech   **MOROCCO**
Agadir

Islas Canarias
(Spain)

La Palma
Tenerife   Lanzarote
Gran   Fuerte-
Canaria   ventura
LAÂYOUNE   Tan-Tan

3

ALGER

Smara   Tindouf   I-n-Sale

**WESTERN
SAHARA**
*(disputed territory under
Moroccan occupation)*   Reggane

Tropic of Cancer   Ad Dakhla

◆ The region of Tidikelt
in Algeria once went
for ten years without
a drop of rain.

4

◆ The Sahara desert covers an area of
around 3,565,600 sq miles (9,234,904 sq km),
an area roughly the size of Europe.

Lagouira

MAURITANIA

5

0 km   400
0 miles   400

MALI

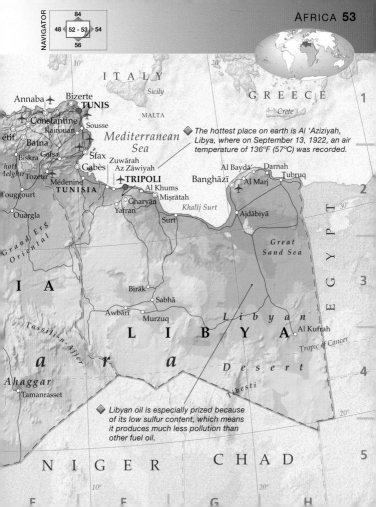

10°

I T A L Y

Sicily

20°

G R E E C E

1

Annaba ✈ Bizerte
TUNIS
Constantine
étif Sousse
Batna Kairouan
Biskra Gafsa
hott Tozeur
lelghir Sfax
Touggourt Médénine Gabès
Ouargla **TUNISIA**

Crete

MALTA

*Mediterranean
Sea*

Zuwārah
Az Zāwiyah
✈ **TRIPOLI**
Al Khums
Gharyān Mişrātah
Yafran
Surt

◈ The hottest place on earth is Al 'Aziziyah,
Libya, where on September 13, 1922, an air
temperature of 136°F (57°C) was recorded.

Al Baydā Darnah
Banghāzī Tubruq
◈ Al Marj
Ajdābiyā

Khalīj Surt

30°

2

E G Y P T

Grand Erg
Oriental

I A

Tassili-n-Ajjer

a

r a

Birāk
Awbārī
Sabhā
Murzuq

L I B Y A

Libyan

Al Kufrah

*Great
Sand Sea*

3

Tropic of Cancer

20°

Ahaggar
Tamanrasset

D e s e r t

Tibesti

◈ Libyan oil is especially prized because
of its low sulfur content, which means
it produces much less pollution than
other fuel oil.

4

N I G E R

10°

C H A D

20°

5

F

E

F

G

H

When first opened in 1869, the Suez Canal consisted of a channel, 26 ft (8 m) deep and 200 to 300 ft (60 to 90 m) wide at the surface. Construction involved the excavation and dredging of 97 million cubic yards (74 million cubic metres) of material.

For thousands of years the Nile has supported cultivation in the Aswan region, despite it being one of the driest places on Earth, with an average of only 0.02 inches (0.5 mm) of rain per year.

E D C B A

IRAN

IRAQ   *The Gulf*   Tropic of Cancer

SYRIA   40°   SAUDI   20°

JORDAN   ARABIA   YEMEN   Gulf of Aden

LEBANON   Boossaso

ISRAEL   Red Sea   DJIBOUTI
CYPRUS   Port Said   DJIBOUTI
Ismā'iliya   ERITREA   Aseb
Suez Canal   Massawa
Suez   Sinai   ASMARA   Mek'ele
Mediterranean   Hurghada   (administered by   Himora   Desē
Sea   Sudan)   Keren   Gonder
Alexandria   Qena   Port Sudan   Bahir
Nile Delta   Luxor   Kassala   Gedaref   Blue Nile
CAIRO   Sohag   Isna   Aswan   Atbara
El Gîza   Asyût   Idfu   Abu   Wad Medani
Beni Suef   Lake Nasser   Omdurman   El Obeid
El Mînya   (administered by Egypt)   KHARTOUM
Monkhafad   El Khârga   Dongola   Dilling
el Qatt âra   Wadi Halfa
-133m   E G Y P T   S U D A N

LIBYA   Nubian
Libyan   *Desert*
Desert   Darfur   El Fasher
Tropic of Cancer   El Geneina   Nyala
CHAD

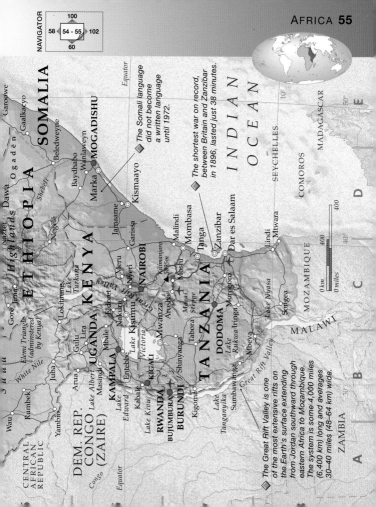

West Africa

Tropic of Cancer

WESTERN
SAHARA
*(disputed territory
under Moroccan occupation)*

Bîr
Mogrein

'Erg Iguîdi
Kâghet   El Hank

S

Fdérik   Zouérat

Ouarâne

◆ *Despite a population of 2,500,000 there are
fewer than 6000 telephones in Mauritania,
roughly one for every 416 people.*

Nouâdhibou

Akchâr

Choûm

Atâr

El Mreyyé

**CAPE
VERDE**

Ilhas de Barlavento

Santo
Antão
São
Vicente São
Nicolau
Santiago
Fogo   **PRAIA**
Ilhas de Sotavento

Sal
Boa Vista
Maio

NOUAKCHOTT

Akjoujt

Rkiz   Aleg

Kiffa

M A U R I T A N I A

Aoukâr

S

Saint Louis

SENEGAL

DAKAR

Mbaké
Diourbel
Kaolack

Kaédi

Nioro

Kayes

Ségou

BAMAK

S

BANJUL
GAMBIA

Bignona

BISSAU

**GUINEA-
BISSAU**

Gaoual

Boké

Labé

Kindia

GUINEA

Niger

Siguiri

Kankan

Bougouni

Dio

Odienne

**CÔTE
D'IVOIR
IVORY CO**

**A T L A N T I C

O C E A N**

◆ *Gambia is only around 20 miles (32 km)
wide and 300 miles (483 km) long;
its unusual shape and size are down
to territorial compromises arising from
19th-century Anglo-French rivalry
in western Africa.*

CONAKRY

FREETOWN

**SIERRA
LEONE**

Bo

◆ *Monrovia, named after the fifth US President
James Monroe, was founded in 1830 by the
American Colonization Society as a settlement
for freed American slaves.*

Tubmanburg

MONROVIA

LIBERIA

YAMOUSSOUKRO

Buchanan

Zwedru

◆ *A Ruppell's Griffen Vulture collided with a
commercial airliner at 37,000 ft (11,277 m) above
Cote d'Ivoire to earn the posthumous distinction
of the highest flying bird ever recorded.*

Harper

Ab

Ga

Senegal

Gambia

Bafing

Niger

A L G E R I A

L I B Y A

◆ In the late 1960s and early 1970s a series of
catastrophic droughts caused the Sahara Desert
to advance southward up to 60 miles (100 km) into
the Sahel region. The loss of human life by starvation
and disease was estimated in 1973 to be 100,000.

Tropic of Cancer

udenni

h   *a*   *r*   *a*

Tibesti

Tessalit

Assamakka

Ténéré
du
Tafassâsset

Adrar des
Ifôghas

Massif
de l'Aïr

Ténéré

Azaouâd

M A L I

N I G E R

Grand Erg de Bilma

C H A D

Tombouctou
Lac
Niangay

Gao
Ansongo

Agadez

Hombori

Tahoua

h   *e*   *l*

Zinder

Nguigmi

Lake Chad

BURKINA

NIAMEY

Maradi

Gouré

OUAGADOUGOU

Sokoto

Katsina

Maiduguri

Edda-
Ngourma

Gusau

Kano

Zaria

Kandi

Kainji
Reservoir

N I G E R I A

Kaduna

Kumo

BENIN

Natitingou

Jos
Plateau

Parakou

Tamale

Niger

ABUJA

Sekode

Ilorin

Oyo

GHANA

Lake
Volta

Abomey

Ede

Ogbomosho

Benin
City

Enugu

C.A.R.

Ibadan

Lagos

Onitsha

Aba

Calabar

LOMÉ   PORTO-
NOVO

Sapele

ACCRA

Bight of Benin

Port Harcourt

Gulf of Guinea

Mouths
of the Niger

CAMEROON

EQUATORIAL
GUINEA

ake Volta is one of the largest man-made
akes in the world covering 3283 sq miles
8502 sq km), or 3.6% of Ghana's area

Central Africa

The eye of an ostrich is bigger than it's brain. They are the largest bird on earth. An adult male can stand 8 ft (2.5 m) tall, weigh up to 300 lbs (135 kg), and run at around 30 mph (48 km/h).

Pygmies that inhabit the Congo Basin grow to be only 3 or 4 feet (0.9 to 1.2 m) tall at adulthood. The name, "Pygmy," is derived from the Greek word, pyme, which means "a cubit in height."

The vast sand flats surrounding Lake Chad were once covered by water. Changing climatic patterns caused the lake to shrink and desert now covers much of its previous area.

EGYPT

LIBYA

SUDAN

NIGER

ALGERIA

NIGERIA

CENTRAL AFRICAN REPUBLIC

CHAD

Sahara

Tibesti

Ennedi

Tropic of Cancer

Faya

Biltine

Abéché

Mongo

Am Timan

Ati

Mao

NDJAMENA

Bongor

Sarh

Goré

Lai

Bol

Chari

Koussèri

Bria

Ndélé

Massif des Bongo

Bossangoa

Moundou

Lake Chad

Maroua

Guider

Garoua

Ngaoundéré

Banyo

Bamenda

Tropic of Cancer

L. Albert
Bunia
Isiro
Uele
Butembo
Equator
UGANDA
L. Edward
Goma
L. Kivu
RWANDA
Bukavu
BURUNDI
TANZANIA
Kindu
Monts Mitumba
Kalemie
L. Tanganyika
Likasi
Manono
Kolwezi
Lubumbashi
Z A M B I A

Gemena
Ubangi
Bumba
Congo
Kisangani
Congo Basin
Mbandaka
DEM. REP.
CONGO
(ZAIRE)
Lodja
Kasongo
Kabinda
Mbuji-Mayi
L. Mweru
Kamina
Kananga
Mwene-
Ditu
Dilolo
A N G O L A

Ouésso
Impfondo
Owando
CONGO
Bandundu
Ilebo
Tshikapa
Kasai

YAOUNDÉ
CAMEROON
Ebolowa
Oyem
Bata
EQUATORIAL
GUINEA
LIBREVILLE
Djambala
Mossendjo
Kwilu
Kikwit
KINSHASA
BRAZZAVILLE
Dolisie
Matadi
Kwango

SÃO TOMÉ
& PRÍNCIPE
Príncipe
SÃO TOMÉ
São Tomé
Equator
G A B O N
Lambaréné
Massoukou
Pointe-Noire
Boma
Cabinda
(Angola)
Port-Gentil

A T L A N T I C
O C E A N

The only major river that
flows both north and south
of the equator is the Congo.
It crosses the equator twice.

0 km   400
0 miles   400

5

6

7

8

A   B   C   D   E

DEM. REP.
CONGO
(ZAIRE)

Congo

Tangan

Cabinda
(Angola)
Cabinda

Uíge

Ambriz

N'Dalatando

Lucapa

Saurimo

LUANDA

Malanje

Ndola
Mufulira

Sumbe

ANGOLA

Kuito

Zambezi

Chingola

Kitwe
Luanshya

Lobito
Benguela

Huambo

Menongue

Cuanza

Zambezi

ZAMBIA

Lubango

Namibe

N'Giva

Cuango

Okavango

LUSAKA

Choma

Livingstone

La
Kar

Chitung

*ATLANTIC
OCEAN*

Tombua

Cunene

Rundu

*Victoria
Falls*

ZIMI

◆ The Okavango River pours
some 14.4 billion cubic yards
(11 billion cu m) of water into
the Okavango Delta each year.
It drains away through a maze of
lagoons, channels, and islands
covering around 5800 sq miles
(15,000 sq km) before eventually
disappearing into the sands of the
Kalahari Desert to the south.

*Etosha
Pan*

Tsumeb

Okavango Delta

Maun

Bulawayo

Grootfontein

Francistown

NAMIBIA

Ghanzi

Namib Desert

BOTSWANA

Swakopmund

WINDHOEK

Kalahari

Mahalapye

Limpo

Walvis Bay

Rehoboth

GABORONE

Tropic of Capricorn

◆ The Kalahari Desert is the largest
continuous sand surface in the world.
Iron oxide gives a distinctive red
color to the sand, which is over
200 ft (60 m) deep in places.

Desert

Lobatse

Mmabatho

PRETO

Keetmanshoop

Soweto

Johannesburg

Lüderitz

Karasburg

Orange R.

Kimberley

Vaal

Kro

MAS

BLOEMFONTEIN

LESOTHO

SOUTH AFRICA'S THREE CAPITALS
Pretoria – administrative capital
Cape Town – legislative capital
Bloemfontein – financial capital

**SOUTH
AFRICA**

Middelburg

Beaufort West

Drakens

Bellville

East
Lon

CAPE TOWN

Cape of Good Hope

George

Port
Elizabeth

0 km   400
0 miles   400

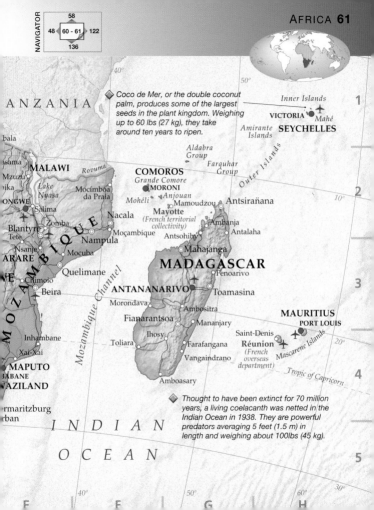

1

◆ Coco de Mer, or the double coconut palm, produces some of the largest seeds in the plant kingdom. Weighing up to 60 lbs (27 kg), they take around ten years to ripen.

Inner Islands

VICTORIA
Mahé
SEYCHELLES

Amirante Islands

ANZANIA

bala

Aldabra Group

Farquhar Group

Outer Islands

asama

MALAWI

Rovuma

COMOROS
Grande Comore
◉MORONI
Anjouan
Mohéli

2

10°

Mzuzu

Lake
Nyasa

ONGWE

pika

Moçimboa
da Prata

Mamoudzou

Antsirañana

Salima

Mayotte
(French territorial collectivity)

Blantyre

Zomba
Tete

Nacala

Moçambique

Antsohihy

Ambanja

Antalaha

Nsanje

Nampula

Mahajanga

ARARE

Mocuba

MADAGASCAR

VE

Chimoio

Quelimane

Fenoarivo

3

Beira

ANTANANARIVO

Toamasina

Morondava

Ambositra

MAURITIUS
PORT LOUIS

Fianarantsoa

Mananjary

Inhambane

Ihosy

Saint-Denis

Xai-Xai

Toliara

Farafangana

Réunion
(French overseas department)

Mascarene Islands

20°

MAPUTO

Vangaindrano

BABANE

Tropic of Capricorn

AZILAND

Amboasary

4

rmaritzburg
rban

◆ Thought to have been extinct for 70 million years, a living coelacanth was netted in the Indian Ocean in 1938. They are powerful predators averaging 5 feet (1.5 m) in length and weighing about 100lbs (45 kg).

I N D I A N

O C E A N

5

40°

50°

60°

30°

F

F

G

G

H

MOZAMBIQUE

Mozambique Channel

Europe

40°   60°   *Limit of winter pack ice*   *Lo*

ICELAND

*Norwegian
Sea*

40°

Faeroe Islands
(Denmark)

Shetland Islands

*Outer
Hebrides*   *Orkney
Islands*

*British
Isles*   **North
Sea**

Ireland

**REPUBLIC
OF
IRELAND**   Isle of Man
(to UK)   *N o r*

DENMARK

*Celtic
Sea*   *Britain*

**UNITED
KINGDOM**

NETHERLANDS

English Channel   **No r**

BELGIUM   **GERMANY**

Channel Is
(UK)   *Seine*   **LUX.**   **CZE
REPU**

40°

*A T L A N T I C
O C E A N*

Loire   *Rhine*

FRANCE   **LIECH**

Bay of Biscay   *Massif
Central*   **SWITZ.**   **AUST**

Alps   **SLOVE**

▲ Mont Blanc
4807m   *Po*

Garonne   *Pyrenees*   **MONACO**

PORTUGAL   *Duero*   *Ebro*   **ANDORRA**   **SAN
MARINO**   **CRO**

Iberian   **BO:
& H**

Tagus   **SPAIN**   *Corsica*

**VATICAN
CITY**   **ITA**

*Madeira
(to Portugal)*   *Peninsula*

Guadalquivir   *Balearic Islands*   *Sardinia*   *Tyrrhenian
Sea*

Strait of Gibraltar

Gibraltar
(UK)   *M e d i t e r r a n e*

20°   *Sicily*

*Canary Islands
(to Spain)*   *A t l a s   M o u n t a i n s*

AFRICA   **MALTA**

1

2

3

4

5

0 km   800

0 miles   800

20° 40° 60° 80°

Barents Sea

North Cape   Ostrov Kolguyev

Arctic Circle

1

Kola
Peninsula

White
Sea

Northern Dvina

Ural Mountains

Ob'

Irtysh

80°

FINLAND

f Bothnia

Lake Onega

Lake
Ladoga

R U S S I A N

2

Åland

ESTONIA

LATVIA

THUANIA

ropean Plain

Central
Russian
Upland

F E D E R A T I O N

Volga Uplands

Volga

Ural

Aral Sea

Syr Darya

80°

3

BELARUS

AND

Pripet
Marshes

Bug

Dnieper Lowlands

Don

Dnieper

Ural

Amu Dary

UKRAINE

Dniester

arpathian Mountains

AKIA

MOLDOVA

Caspian Sea

60°

GARY

Sea
of
Azov

Crimea

C a u c a s u s

El'brus
5642m

4

ROMANIA

VIA

Danube

BULGARIA

lkan Mountains

Black Sea

MACED-
NIA

TURKEY

A S I A

Aegean
Sea

REECE

Anatolia

Zagros Mountains

60°

5

eloponnese

ê

Crete

Cyprus

Euphrates

Tigris

40°

E   F   F   G   H

The North Atlantic

◆ At 840,000 sq miles (2,175,600 sq km), Greenland is the largest island in the world. However, 650,000 sq miles (1,638, 400 sq km) of this is a massive ice sheet so heavy that the central land area has sunk to form to a basin more than 1000 ft (300 m) below sea level.

◆ The Jakobshavn Glacier, often moving 100 feet (30 m) a day, is among the world's fastest glaciers, and calves around 1350 icebergs every year.

Arctic Circle

NUNAVUT

Hudson Bay

CANADA

QUEBEC

Péninsule d'Ungava

Hudson Strait

Baffin Island

Frobisher Bay

Ungava Bay

NEWFOUNDLAND

Labrador Sea

Devon Island

Ellesmere Island

Nares Strait

Qaanaaq

Innaanganeq

Savissivik

Qimusseriarsuaq

Knud Rasmussen Land

Baffin Bay

Kullorsuaq

Limit of summer pack ice

Davis Strait

Qeqertarsuaq

Qeqertarsuaq

Qasigiannguit

Sisimiut

Kong Frederik IX Land

Greenland
(Danish external territory)

Kong Christian IX Land

Maniitsoq

NUUK

Gunnbj
Fjeld
3700?

Paamiut

Ivittuut

Ammassalik

Kong Frederik VI Kyst

Denmar

Qaqortoq

Nanortalik

Nunap Isua
(Kap Farvel)

Limit of winter pack ice

ATLANTIC OCEAN

0 km   800

0 miles   800

Fe

ARCTIC OCEAN

Lincoln Sea

Kap Morris Jesup

Wandel Sea

Nord

Kong Frederik VIII Land

Christian X Land

Daneborg

Kong Oscar Fjord

Ittoqqortoormiit

Ittivvaq

Kangikajik

Strait

Limit of winter pack ice

Greenland Sea

ICELAND

Siglufjördhur

yri

Húsavík

Seydhisfjördhur

REYKJAVÍK

foss

rtsey

Zemlya Frantsa-Iosifa

Novaya Zemlya

Kvitøya

Nordaustlandet

Svalbard
(Norwegian dependency)

Kong Karls Land

Spitsbergen

Barentsøya

Longyearbyen

Storfjorden

Edgeøya

Barentsberg

Barents Sea

Bjørnøya
(Norway)

Nordkapp
(North Cape)

Jan Mayen
(Norway)

Norwegian Sea

RUSSIA

FINLAND

NORWAY

SWEDEN

Arctic Circle

Gulf of Bothnia

Faeroe Islands
(Denmark)

Tórshavn

Shetland Islands

◆ With temperatures ranging from 59° F (15° C) in the summer to -40° F (-40° C) in the winter, vegetation on Svalbard consists mostly of lichens and mosses; the only trees are the tiny polar willow and the dwarf birch.

◆ Greenland's deeply indented coastline is 24,430 miles (39,330 km) long, a distance roughly equivalent to the Earth's circumference at the Equator.

◆ The people of Iceland consume more Coca-Cola per capita than any other nation.

Scandinavia & Finland

ARCTIC OCEAN

RUSSIAN FEDERATION

Barents Sea

◆ The North Cape Current warms the northern coasts of Norway, Finland, and Russia's Kola Peninsula with water temperatures of 39–54° F (4–12° C), allowing this area of the Barents Sea to remain free of pack ice throughout the winter.

Vardø

Kirkenes

Nordkapp (North Cape)

Hammerfest

FINLAND

Sodankylä

Inari

Ounasjoki

Kemijärvi

Rovaniemi

Kemijoki

Kuusamo

Kajaani

Oulujärvi

Oulu

Oulujoki

Kemi

Tornio

Piteå

Skellefteå

Kokkola

Luleå

Gällivare

Kiruna

Muonionjoki

Torniojoki

Nordkapp

Tromsø

◆ The sun is continuously visible from late May to late July in Tromsø because of its position well north of the Arctic Circle.

Harstad

Narvik

Vesterålen

Lofoten

Bodø

Mo i Rana

Ångermanälven

S C A N D I N A V I A

Norwegian Sea

◆ Scandinavia is still recovering from the last ice age, when the land was depressed 2000 ft (600 m) by the weight of the ice. Today the earth's crust is "rebounding" at the rate of 0.3 inches (9 mm) a year in the Gulf of Bothnia.

Arctic Circle

Steinkjer

Trondheimsfjorden

0 km   200

0 miles   200

VARKAUS

Savonlinna
Imatra
Lappeenranta
Kouvola
Kotka

Jyväskylä

Tampere
Hämeenlinna
Riihimäki
Vantaa **HELSINKI**
Espoo

Pori
Rauma
Turku
Åland
Mariehamn

Gulf of Finland

ESTONIA

LATVIA

LITHUANIA

BELARUS

KALININGRAD
(part of Russian
Federation)

POLAND

GERMANY

Sundsvall

*Gulf
of
Bothnia*

Gävle

Falun
Borlänge
Uppsala
Västerås **STOCKHOLM**
Örebro
Nyköping
Norrköping
Linköping

Karlstad
Skövde
Vättern
Jönköping

Vänern

Borås

Göteborg

Visby
Gotland

Öland
Kalmar
Karlskrona
Kristianstad

*Baltic
Sea*

Bornholm
Rønne

Trollhättan
Frederikshavn
Halmstad
Helsingborg
Malmö
Sjælland

Hjørring
Ålborg
Randers
DENMARK
Silkeborg
Århus
Vejle **COPENHAGEN**
Herning
Esbjerg
Odense
Åbenrå
Nyköbing

Jylland

Bergen
Haugesund
Stavanger
Kristiansand

Skagerrak
Seresdal

Arendal
Porsgrunn
Drammen
OSLO
Moss
Fredrikstad
Halden

Hønefoss
Gjøvik
Hamar
Lillehammer

Hønnansverk

The sauna is a Finnish institution with some 2 million sauna facilities to serve a population of just 5 million.

The 10-mile (16-km) bridge and tunnel link across the Øresund sound is one of the largest infrastructure projects in European history. It connects the Danish capital Copenhagen to the Swedish port of Malmö.

The Low Countries

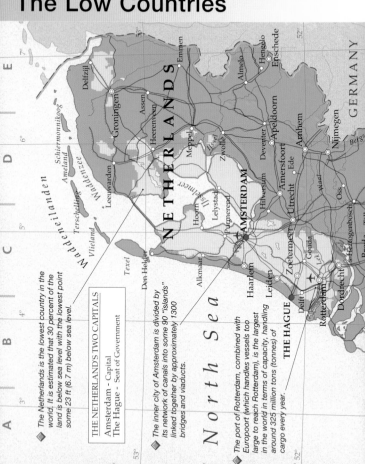

THE NETHERLANDS'S TWO CAPITALS

Amsterdam - Capital
The Hague - Seat of Government

◆ The Netherlands is the lowest country in the world. It is estimated that 30 percent of the land is below sea level with the lowest point some 23 ft (6.7 m) below sea level.

◆ The inner city of Amsterdam is divided by its network of canals into some 90 "islands" linked together by approximately 1300 bridges and viaducts.

◆ The port of Rotterdam, combined with Europoort (which handles vessels too large to reach Rotterdam), is the largest in the world in terms of capacity, handling around 325 million tons (tonnes) of cargo every year.

GERMANY

Belgium and the Netherlands have an underground boundary that differs from the surface boundary shown on maps. In 1950, the two countries agreed to move the underground boundary so as not to divide coal mines between the two countries.

LUXEMBOURG

Moselle

Diekirch

LUXEMBOURG

Arlon

Esch-sur-Alzette

Venlo

Heerlen

Maastricht

Verviers

Liège

Seraing

Ourthe

Meuse

Namur

Ardennes

Eifre

Bastogne

Our

Genk

Hasselt

Tienen

Charleroi

Dinant

Sambre

Turnhout

Antwerpen

Leuven

Mechelen

Aalst

BRUSSELS

La Louvière

Mons

B E L G I U M

Tournai

Zeebrugge

Oostende

Brugge

F l a n d e r s

Schelde

Sint-Niklaas

Gent

Roeselare

Kortrijk

Mouscron

Ieper

Ieper

F R A N C E

On August 23, 1914 three weeks after Britain entered World War I, the 70,000 strong British Expeditionary Force encountered the advancing German army for the first time at the battle of Mons.

Echternach is the home of the only religious dancing procession remaining in the Western world. Every year since the 15th century thousands of pilgrims have marched down the streets of the town performing a ritual dance involving specific movements, music, and prayers.

0 km 50

0 miles 50

A B C D E

The British Isles

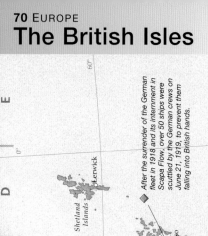

After the surrender of the German fleet in 1918 and its internment in Scapa Flow, over 50 ships were scuttled by the German crews on June 21, 1919, to prevent them falling into British hands.

With a depth of 788 ft (240 m) and a length of about 23 miles (36 km), Loch Ness contains the largest volume of fresh water in Great Britain.

Midges have the fastest wing-beat of any insect, and are able to flap their wings at around 63,000 beats per minute.

The Giant's Causeway comprises approximately 37,000 dark basalt polygonal columns packed together; they were formed by volcanic activity some 55 million years ago.

North Sea

ATLANTIC

OCEAN

Faeroe Islands

Newcastle upon Tyne

Lerwick

Shetland Islands

Orkney Islands

Kirkwall

Thurso

Aberdeen

Dundee

Perth

Elgin

Inverness

Firth of Forth

EDINBURGH

Moray Firth

Ullapool

SCOTLAND

Grampian Mts.

Ben Nevis

Loch Ness

Stirling

Firth of Forth

Southern Uplands

The Minch

Fort William

Isle of Skye

The Little Minch

Isle of Mull

Oban

Loch Lomond

Greenock

Glasgow

UNITED KINGDOM

Iona

Isle of Arran

Ayr

Islay

Isle of Lewis

Stornoway

Outer Hebrides

North Uist

South Uist

Barra

Map labels

Kingston upon Hull
Norwich
Ipswich
Southend-on-Sea
Dover
Channel Tunnel

York
Leeds
Grimsby
Lincoln
Peterborough
Cambridge
Colchester
LONDON
Canterbury
Brighton

Bradford
Manchester
Sheffield
The Wash
The Fens

Blackpool
Preston
Bolton
Liverpool
Chester
Stoke-on-Trent
Derby
Nottingham
ENGLAND
Leicester
Coventry
Stratford-upon-Avon
Oxford
Reading
Southampton
Portsmouth
Isle of Wight

Lancaster

Douglas
(UK crown dependency)

Birmingham
Worcester
Gloucester
Swindon
Thames
Bath
Salisbury

Bangor
WALES
Snowdonia
Shrewsbury
Severn
Newport
Bristol

Anglesey
Holyhead

Cardigan Bay
Aberystwyth

CARDIFF
Swansea
Brecon Beacons
Exmoor
Taunton

Fishguard
Milford Haven
Barnstaple
Exeter
Dartmoor
Bournemouth

English Channel

Channel Islands
(UK crown dependency)
Guernsey
St. Peter Port
St. Helier
Jersey

FRANCE

Newry
Dundalk
Irish Sea

Sligo
Athlone
Lough Ree
DUBLIN

Galway
Ennis
Limerick
Lough Derg
Killarney
Tralee
Bantry Bay
Cork
Blackwater

IRELAND

Wicklow Mts.
Wexford
Waterford
Barrow

Lough Corrib

Shannon

Land's End
Penzance
Plymouth

Isles of Scilly

ATLANTIC OCEAN

50°
0°
5°
10°

Annotations

Seven percent of Ireland's barley crop goes into the production of Guinness stout.

The River Severn has the second highest tidal range in the world, as much as 50 ft (15 m), often giving rise to a tidal bore. In September 1996 one such wave carried a surfer for 5.7 miles (9 km).

0 km   100
0 miles   100

A   B   C   D   E
5   6   7   8

France, Andorra & Monaco

GERMANY

NETHERLANDS

North Sea

BELGIUM

LUXEMBOURG

UNITED

KINGDOM

English Channel

Strasbourg

Colmar

Mulhouse

Vosges

Belfort

Thionville

Metz

Épinal

Vesoul

Besançon

Nancy

Moselle

Meuse

Dijon

Bourgogne

Saône

Laon

Reims

Châlons-
en-Champagne

Bar-
le-Duc

Marne

Troyes

Auxerre

Dunkerque

Calais

Lille

Arras

Douai

Amiens

Beauvais

Somme

PARIS

Bourges

Channel
Tunnel

Boulogne-
sur-Mer

Rouen

Dieppe

Seine

Versailles

Mantes-la-Jolie

Chartres

Orléans

Blois

Cherbourg

Le Havre

Caen

Normandie

Alençon

Le Mans

Tours

Loire

Poitiers

St-Lô

St-Malo

Rennes

Laval

Angers

F

R

A

N

C

E

Channel Islands
(UK crown dependency)

Guernsey

Jersey

Île d'Ouessant

Brest

Quimper

Bretagne

St-Brieuc

Lorient

Belle
Île

Nantes

St-Nazaire

la Roche-
sur-Yon

Work began on the 31-mile (50-km) Channel Tunnel in 1987. Earth was removed at the rate of 2400 tons (tonnes) a day until completion, seven years later. Around 10.5 million cu yards (8 million cu m) had been excavated.

Champagne bottles are placed neck down into a freezing brine bath (bac à glace), freezing only the bottle's neck to form a plug that keeps the wine – and the bubbles – in the bottle while sediments are removed.

On July 1, 1916, the British suffered 58,000 casualties on the opening day of the Somme Offensive. Five months later, after advancing only a few miles, there had been 420,000 British, 200,000 French, and 500,000 German casualties.

Ligurian Sea

MONACO
MONACO
Nice
Côte d'Azur

Corse
(Corsica)
Ajaccio

Sardinia

Mediterranean Sea

ITALY

Mont
Blanc
Annecy
Chambéry
Grenoble
A l p s
Villeurbanne
Lyon
St-Étienne
Chamonix
Valence

Provence
Avignon
Aix-en-Provence
Arles
Marseille
Toulon
Îles d'Hyères

Golfe du Lion

◆ The word denim comes from "de Nîmes,"
this being the town where the fabric was
originally produced.

◆ One of history's great leaders,
Napoleon Bonaparte was born
on August 15, 1769, at Ajaccio
in Corsica.

Mâcon
Roanne
Vichy
Clermont-Ferrand
Massif
Aurillac
Central
Mende
Cévennes
Le Puy
St-Chamond

Limoges
Périgueux
Rodez
Albi
Montauban
Tarn
Cahors
Montpellier
Béziers
Narbonne
Perpignan
Nîmes

Lot
Dordogne

Angoulême
Agen
Toulouse
Carcassonne
Auch
Garonne
Tarbes
Pau

P y r é n é e s

ANDORRA
ANDORRA
LA VELLA

Bordeaux
Mont-de-Marsan
Bayonne

Bay of Biscay

SPAIN

Balearic Islands

◆ The Tour de France
bicycle race is typically held over
some 20 day-long stages covering
around 2200 miles (3600 km) for
the coveted yellow jersey.

◆ The lowest point in Andorra is Riu Runer
at 2756 ft (840m) above sea level.

0 km   100
0 miles   100

Spain & Portugal

ATLANTIC

OCEAN

0 km 100
0 miles 100

1

2

40°

3

4

5

35°

Ferrol
A Coruña
Avilés Gijon
Oviedo
Galicia
Santiago
Lugo
Cordillera Cantábrica
León
Pontevedra
Vigo
Ourense
Miño
Emb. de
Ricobayo
Palencia
Valladolid
Viana do Castelo
Braga
Chaves
Bragança
Zamora
Duero
Póvoa de Varzim
Guimarães
Matosinhos
Porto
Vila Real
Vila Nova de Gaia
Douro
S
P
Aveiro
Viseu
Salamanca
Áv
Coimbra
Covilhã
Sistema Central
Figueira da Foz
PORTUGAL
Castelo Branco
Tagus
Plasencia
Tagus
Caldas da Rainha
Cáceres
Guadiana
Sintra
Santarém
Portalegre
Mérida
Cascais
LISBON
Badajoz
Setúbal
Alcácer do Sal
Beja
Sierra Morena
Córdoba
Sines
Guadiana
Sevilla
Guadalquivir
Algarve
Andalucía
Lagos
Huelva
Anteque
Cabo de São Vicente
Faro
Olhão
Málaga
El Puerto de Santa María
Cádiz
Marbel
Algeciras
Gibraltar
(UK)
Ceuta (Sp.)
MOROCCO

◆ Port has been produced in the Duoro Valley under strict regulation since the 1750s. Brandy is added to the grape juice to fortify and strengthen the wine.

◆ Portugal is one of the world's largest producers of cork and has regulations protecting cork trees dating back to 1320.

◆ Gibraltar was seized by a combined Anglo-Dutch fleet under Admiral Rooke in 1704. British sovereignty was then formalized in 1713 by the Treaty of Utrecht, and Gibraltar eventually became a British colony in 1830.

A
B
C
D

Bay of Biscay

FRANCE

Santander

Bilbao   Donostia-San Sebastián

Miranda
de Ebro   Vitoria-
Gasteiz   Pamplona

Burgos   Logroño

Soria   Huesca

Lleida
Zaragoza   Terrassa

Reus   Sabadell

Tarragona

Tortosa

Golfe du
Lion

ANDORRA

Girona   Figueres

Cataluña   Costa Brava

Mataró

Barcelona

L'Hospitalet de Llobregat

◇ Work continues on the Sagrada Família,
Gaudí's unfinished cathedral. Begun in
1882 the masterpiece is still
without a roof.

AIN

egovia

MADRID

Getafe

oledo   Cuenca

Teruel

Castelló
de la Plana

Albacete   Valencia

Gandía

Ciudad Real

Elda   Benidorm

Cieza   Alicante

Linares   Murcia   Elche

Lorca   Costa Blanca

aén

granada

ierra Nevada

Motril   Almería

osta del Sol

Menorca

Palma

Mallorca

Islas Baleares
(Balearic Islands)

Eivissa

Formentera

◇ Seat of many great civilizations
throughout history, the name
Mediterranean translates as
"sea between the lands."

Cartagena

Mediterranean Sea

ALGERIA

E   F   G   H

Germany & The Alpine States

The Kiel Canal is one of the busiest in the world, with around 45,000 ships a year passing between the Baltic and the North Sea

Early in the morning of Sunday, August 13, 1961, work began on the Berlin Wall, which would eventually run for 66 miles (107 km) between east and west Berlin, cutting through 192 streets.

The German Bundestag, or Parliament, based in Berlin, has 672 members and is the world's largest elected legislative body.

HUNGARY

CZECH REPUBLIC

At 528 ft (161 m) the spire of Ulm Cathedral is the tallest in the world.

Bohemian Forest

VIENNA

Hollabrunn

Krems an der Donau

Eisenstadt

Wiener Neustadt

Kapfenberg

Leibnitz

Klagenfurt

Villach

Maribor

Celje

Sava

LJUBLJANA

SLOVENIA

Gulf of Venice

CROATIA

Koper

Drava

Mur

Graz

Judenburg

AUSTRIA

Linz

Wels

Steyr

Enns

Salzburg

Hallein

Hohe Tauern

Inn

Bad Ischl

Berchtesgaden

Born in Salzburg on January 27, 1756, Wolfgang Amadeus Mozart was already writing music by the age of five, and at eleven he produced his first opera.

Regensburg

Landshut

Ingolstadt

Augsburg

München

Innsbruck

Bavarian Alps

LIECHTENSTEIN

NADUZ

Bregenz

Lake Constance

Alps

ITALY

Frankfurt am Main

Offenbach

Darmstadt Würzburg

Mainz

Wiesbaden

Main

Erlangen

Nürnberg

Frankischer Jura

Mannheim

Heidelberg

Heilbronn

Neckar

Stuttgart

Reutlingen

Pforzheim

Karlsruhe

Rhine

Ulm

Schwäbische

Donau

Schaffhausen

Schwarzwald

Freiburg im Breisgau

Zürich

Zugersee

Chur

Zug

Luzern

Lake Maggiore

Lugano

Bellinzona

Lake Lugano

St Gothard tunnel is 10.14 miles (16.32 km) long, making it the second longest road tunnel in the world.

SWITZERLAND

BERN

Thuner See

Berner Alpen

Brig

Basel

Delémont

Neuchâtel

Lake Neuchâtel

Yverdon

Lausanne

Genève

Lake Geneva

Montreux

Rhine

Mosel

Saarbrücken

Kaiserslautern

LUX

FRANCE

The glass roof over the Olympic stadium in München (Munich) measures 914,940 sq ft (85,000 sq m) making it the biggest structure of its kind in the world.

0 km   100
0 miles   100

CZECH REPUBLIC

SLOVAKIA

HUNGARY

SLOVENIA

CROATIA

BOSNIA & HERZEGOVINA

AUSTRIA

GERMANY

FRANCE

SWITZERLAND

LIECHTENSTEIN

Adriatic Sea

Ligurian Sea

◆ *In April 1998 a violin made by Italian master Stradivari at Cremona in around 1680 sold at Christie's in London for £947,500.*

◆ *San Marino formed in AD 301 is the oldest, and, at 24 sq mi (61 sq km), one of the smallest, republics in the world.*

ALPS

Dolomitiche Alpi

Udine

Trieste

Gulf of Venice

Venezia

Mestre

Treviso

Piave

Bolzano

Trento

Lago di Garda

Vicenza

Padova

Adige

Po Delta

Ravenna

Rimini

SAN MARINO

Ancona

Ascoli Piceno

Pescara

L'Aquila

ROME

VATICAN CITY

Viterbo

Terni

Foligno

Perugia

Lago Trasimeno

Arezzo

Firenze

Prato

Siena

Toscana

Grosseto

Arcipelago Toscano

Isola d'Elba

Corsica (part of France)

Livorno

Pisa

Viareggio

La Spezia

Golfo di Genova

Genova

Savona

San Remo

Aosta

Torino

Novara

Alessandria

Milano

Monza

Bergamo

Brescia

Cremona

Piacenza

Parma

Reggio nell'Emilia

Modena

Bologna

Ferrara

Mantova

Verona

Po

Lago di Como

Lago Maggiore

Verona

Forlì

Tevere

ITALY

APENNINES

Gulf of Otranto

Brindisi
Lecce
Gallipoli
Bari
Altamura
Taranto
Golfo di Taranto
Potenza
Benevento
Salerno
Napoli
Torre del Greco
Golfo di Gaeta
Isola di Capri
Golfo di Salerno

Crotone
Catanzaro
Ionian Sea

Calabria

Cosenza

Isola Stromboli
Isola Eolie
Isole Eolie
Isola Lipari
Isola Salina
Isola Vulcano

Reggio di Calabria
Stretto di Messina

Mt Etna began some 300,000 years ago as a submarine volcano and has since grown to a cone with a base 30 miles (48 km) wide and 10,958 ft (3340 m) high.

Messina

Isola d'Ustica

Palermo
Cefalù
Sicilia
(Sicily)
Catania
Siracusa
Ragusa

VALLETTA
MALTA

Mediterranean Sea

Caltanissetta
Agrigento

Gozo

The George cross that appears on the Maltese flag was awarded to the islanders by King George VI of Britain for their heroism during World War II.

Malta Channel

Trapani
Marsala
Isole Egadi

Isola di Pantelleria

Isole Pelagie

The medical school at Salerno is the oldest in Europe, established during the 11th and 12th centuries.

Tyrrhenian Sea

Strait of Sicily

Mediterranean Sea

Sardegna
(Sardinia)

Nuoro
Oristano

Cagliari

Alghero
Oristano
Iglesias

TUNISIA

0 km   100
0 miles   100

Central Europe

BELARUS

LATVIA

LITHUANIA

◆ Warsaw was home to the world's first public library, opened in 1747.

KALININGRAD
(part of Russian Federation)

Baltic Sea

◆ Hitler's demand in 1939 that Gdansk be returned to German control precipitated the invasion of Poland which ultimately led to World War II.

Courland Lagoon

Gulf of Danzig

SWEDEN

Bornholm
(part of Denmark)

Pomeranian Bay

Zalew Szczeciński

DENMARK

GERMANY

◆ In November 1989 the so-called "Velvet Revolution" saw Czechoslovakia split into the Czech Republic and Slovakia.

Białystok

Bug

Lublin

Ostrowiec Świętokrzyski

Narew

Olsztyn

M a z u r y

Ostrołęka

WARSAW

Wisła

Radom

Kielce

Elbląg

Płock

Toruń

Włocławek

Łódź

Warta

Gdynia

Gdańsk

Grudziądz

Bydgoszcz

P O L A N D

Słupsk

Czluchów

Piła

Noteć

Poznań

Kalisz

Wrocław

Oder Oder

Legnica

Koszalin

Warta

Szczecin

Gorzów Wielkopolski

Zielona Góra

Oder

Wisła

Odra

km 0   100
miles 0   100

UKRAINE

Dnestr

Laborec

Carpathian Mts.

Rzeszów
Tarnów
Kraków
Bielsko-Biała
Śląski
Rybnik

Prešov
Poprad
Košice
Rožňava
Ózd
Lučenec
Banská Bystrica

SLOVAKIA

Žilina
Martin
Trenčín
Nitra
Váh
Trnava
Piešťany

BRATISLAVA

ROMANIA

Nyíregyháza
Debrecen
Miskolc
Szolnok
Kecskemét
Szeged
Békéscsaba

Great Hungarian Plain

Tisza
Mureş

BUDAPEST

Danube

H·U·N·G·A·R·Y

Győr
Tatabánya
Székesfehérvár
Veszprém
Baja
Szekszárd
Kaposvár
Pécs
Balaton
Dráva

Sopron
Szombathely
Zalaegerszeg
Nagykanizsa

AUSTRIA

SLOVENIA
ITALY

CROATIA

YUGOSLAVIA

BOSNIA - HERZEGOVINA

Adriatic Sea

Ostrava
Olomouc
Přerov
Prostějov
Brno
Jihlava

CZECH REPUBLIC

Tábor
Pardubice
Elbe
PRAGUE
Kladno
Plzeň
Strakonice
České Budějovice

◆ Built in 1357, Charles Bridge was the only crossing point of the Vltava in Prague until the 19th century.

◆ With a surface area of around 231 sq mi (598 sq km) Lake Balaton has an average depth of only 11 ft (3.25 m).

◆ The Great Hungarian Plain (Alföld) stretches south from Budapest to the borders of Croatia and Serbia and east to Ukraine and Romania. It covers an area of 20,000 sq miles (51,800 sq km) and is almost completely flat.

A B C D E

Southeast Europe

◆ At 11:15 am, on June 28, 1914, Archduke Francis Ferdinand and his wife were shot dead by Gavrilo Princip in Sarajevo. This single act precipitated World War I, which eventually lead to the death of almost 9 million troops.

◆ The Danube forms all or part of the border between nine different European nations. Germany, Austria, Slovakia, Hungary, Croatia, Yugoslavia, Romania, Bulgaria, and the Ukraine.

◆ Born in Zagreb in 1892, Marshall Tito was the president of Yugoslavia from 1953 until his death in 1980.

SLOVAKIA

AUSTRIA HUNGARY

ROMANIA

BUL

SLOVENIA

CROATIA

ZAGREB

Samobor
Karlovac
Ogulin
Rijeka
Pula
Cres
Krk
Pag
Gospić
Zadar
Dugi Otok
Šibenik
Split
Brač
Makarska
Knin
Bihać

Koprivnica
Varaždin
Čakovec
Bjelovar
Virovitica
Sisak
Una
Sava
Kupa
Lika
Sava

Osijek
Đakovo
Slavonski
Brod
Nova
Gradiška
Banja Luka
Prijedor
Ključ
Drava

Sombor
Subotica
Bačka
Vukovar
Vinkovci
Bosanski Šamac
Modriča
Doboj
Rep. Srpska
Zenica
Tuzla
Zvornik
Srebrenica
Jajce

BOSNIA &
HERZEGOVINA
SARAJEVO
Foča
Konjic
Fed. Bosna
I Hercegovina
Mostar
Livno
Dinaric Alps
Dinara

Vojvodina
Novi Sad
Zrenjanin
Vršac
Pančevo
Smederevo
BELGRADE

Serbia

YUGOSLAVIA

Kragujevac
Čačak
Kraljevo
Topola
Loznica
Šabac
Morava
Aleksinac
Niš
Kruševac
Zaječar
Kopaonik

Danube

Danube

RIA

A U S T R I A

KOSOVO

Kumanovo Kočani
Uroševac Skopje Štip Strumica
Prizren Tetovo Veles Vardar Gevgelija
MACEDONIA
Gostivar Prilep Kavadarci
North Albanian Alps Kičevo Bitola
Shkodër Black Drin Ohrid Lake Ohrid
Podgorica Lake Scutari Lake Prespa
Lezhë TIRANA Elbasan Korçë
Durrës Lumi i Devollit
ALBANIA
Lushnjë Berat Tepelenë
Kuçovë Lumi i Vjosës
Fier Vlorë Gjirokastër
Strait of Otranto Sarandë
Konispol

I T A L Y

Palagruža

A d r i a t i c   S e a

G R E E C E

40°

20°

I o n i a n

S e a

Macedonian opium, derived from poppy juice,
contains around fourteen morphine units and
is recognized as the best quality opium
in the world.

European eels migrate thousands of miles from their
birthplace in the Sargasso Sea to live most of their
10-year lives in Lake Ohrid, before returning to the
Atlantic to spawn and die.

Under an extreme communist regime between
1944 and 1991, Albania was for many years the
only officially atheist state in the world.

10°

40°

0 km   100
0 miles   100

A   B   C   D   E

The Mediterranean

ATLANTIC

OCEAN

UNITED
KINGDOM *Thame*

NETHERLANDS
BELGIUM

GERMAN

LUX.

English Channel

Seine

E

FRANCE

Loire

SWITZ.

LIECH

L. *Geneva*

Danube

A

P

Bay
of
Biscay

Dordogne

Massif
Central

Rhône

Genoa

S

Garonne

MONACO

Livorno

Pyrenees

ANDORRA

Golfe
du
Lion

Marseille

Apenn

Po

MAI

VATICA
CIT

Corsica

PORTUGAL

SPAIN

Barcelona

Balearic Is.

Sardinia

M

e

d

Tagus

Iberian
Peninsula

Valencia

Guadalquivir

Algiers

t

i

Gibraltar
(UK)

Gibraltar

Oran

Tell Atlas

Tunis

Strait of Gibraltar

TUNIS

MOROCCO

ALGERIA

Sfax

Tri

*Madeira
(Portugal)*

Atlas Mountains

Chott el Jerid

*Grand Erg
Occidental*

Grand Erg
Oriental

Tyrrh
Se

*Canary Is.
(Spain)*

A

F

R

Saha

0 km   400

0 miles   400

NAVIGATOR
62
48 | 84 - 85 | 94
50

POLAND

UKRAINE

20°

30°

50°

CZECH REP.

1

E U R O P E

Dnieper

Don

STRIA

SLOVAKIA

30°

HUNGARY

Carpathians

MOLDOVA

RUSSIAN

VENIA

Hungarian
Plain

Sea
of Azov

FEDERATION

CROATIA

ROMANIA

Crimea

2

BOS. &
HERZ.

Danube

Caucasus Mts.

YUGO.

Dinaric Alps

BULGARIA

Black Sea

Danube
Delta

tic Sea

ALBANIA

Balkan Mts.

Bosporus

GEORGIA

Pindus Mts.

MACEDONIA

Rhodope Mts.

TALY

40°

Naples

Aegean
Sea

T U R K E Y

Lesbos

Anatolia

GREECE

Lake
Van

Ionian
Sea

Piraeus

Izmir

Sicily

Peloponnese

Taurus Mts.

Euphrates

MALTA

Kós

Tigris

Rhodes

Cyprus

SYRIA

terranean

Crete

Sea

LEBANON

Anti-Lebanon

I R A Q

4

Haifa

Syrian Desert

Gulf of Sirte

ISRAEL

A S I A

Nile
Delta

Port Said

JORDAN

30°

Suez Canal

L I B Y A

SAUDI
ARABIA

C A

E G Y P T

Arabian

5

a

Libyan
Desert

Nile

Peninsula

20°

30°

40°

Red Sea

E

F

G

H

Bulgaria & Greece

Sofia's skyline is dominated by the gold domes of the Alexander Nevski Memorial Church, which took craftsmen and artists some thirty years to build between 1882 and 1912.

Built between 447 and 438 BCE, the Parthenon survived almost unscathed for over 2000 years until, in 1687, a gunpowder magazine beneath the building exploded causing considerable damage.

Labels on map

YUGOSLAVIA

ROMANIA

BULGARIA

MACEDONIA

ALBANIA

GREECE

TURKEY

Black Sea

Marmara
Denizi

Dobrich
Varna
Razgrad
Shumen
Burgas
Ruse
Lovech
Pleven
Vratsa
Gabrovo
Sliven
Yambol
Stara Zagora
Kazanlŭk
Plovdiv
Khaskovo
Komotini
Orestiáda
Alexandroúpoli
Samothráki
Xánthi
Kavála
Dráma
Serres
Thásos
Thracian Sea
SOFIA
Pernik
Pazardzhik
Velingrad
Petrich
Blagoevgrad
Vardar
Kilkís
Thessaloníki
Kalamariá
Kateríni
Kozáni
Véroia
Flórina
Lake Prespä
Lake Ohrid
Kérkyra
Ioánnina
Préveza
Tríkala
Kardítsa
Lárisa
Vólos
Akrotírio
Límnos
Límnos
Akrotírio
Palioúri
Akrotírio
Drépano
Vóreioi
Sporádes

Danube
Olt
Yantra
Iskŭr
Yantra
Maritsa
Struma

Balkan Mountains

Rhodope Mountains

Thermaïkós
Kólpos

Pín dos

Vidin

Danube

TURKEY

Chíos ○Chíos

Sámos

Ikaría

Dodekánisos
(Dodecanese)

Kos

Ródos

Ródos
(Rhodes)

Kárpathos

Aegean Sea

Ándros

Tínos

Míkonos

Náxos

Amorgós

Astypálaia

Kéa

Kykládes
(Cyclades)

Páros

Íos

Thíra

Kritikó Pélagos
(Sea of Crete)

ATHENS

Mílos

Mirtóo Pélagos

Kríti
(Crete)

Korinthakós Kólpos

Peiraiás

Irákleio

Kýthira

Chaniá

Patra

Kórinthos

Tripoli

Kefallinía

Peloponnísos

Spárti

Mediterranean Sea

Kalamáta

ioi Nísoi
nian Islands)

Zákynthos

Ionian
Sea

LIBYA

◆ The Minoans developed the first Hellenic civilisation 4000 years ago, based at the luxurious palace of Knossos. Unfortunately in 1400 BCE this civilization came to an abrupt end, destroyed by a tidal wave.

◆ Only about 100 of the 2000 or so Greek Islands are permanently inhabited.

◆ The first Olympic athletics festival was held at Olympia in around 776 BCE.

◆ The Corinth Canal was completed in 1893 after 11 years of work. The canal is 4 miles (6.3 km) long, 80 ft (25 m) wide and 26 ft (8 m) deep. The central section runs along a 260 ft (79 m) deep cutting through solid rock.

0 km   100
0 miles   100

The Baltic States & Belarus

◆ Rich oil shale deposits in northern Estonia are quarried, crushed, and heated to produce almost 32,000 barrels of oil a day.

◆ Low salinity and the shallow coastal waters cause pack ice to accumulate at the head of the Gulf of Bothnia and of Finland during most winters; occasionally the ice becomes banked up in pressure ridges that are almost 50 ft (15 m) high.

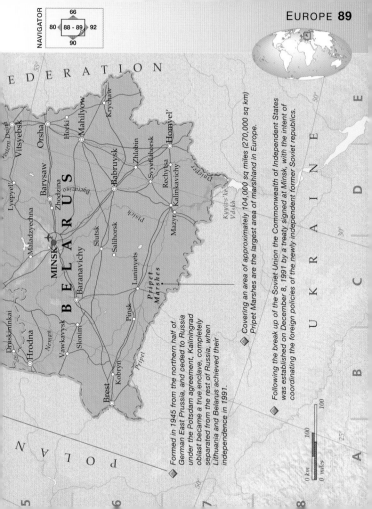

F E D E R A T I O N

Vitsyebsk

Orsha

Mahilyow

Hlorki

Krychaw

Homyel'

Zhlobin

Babruysk

Svyetlahorsk

Rechytsa

Kalinkavichy

Mazyr

Luninyets

Pinsk

Slutsk

Salihorsk

Baranavichy

Slonim

Kobryn

Brest

Vawkavysk

Hrodna

Druskininkai

Maladzyechna

Lyepyel'

Barysaw

Zhodzina

Byerezina

MINSK

B E L A R U S

Pripet Marshes

Pripet

Neman

Ptsich

Dnieper

Kyut's'ke Vdskh.

U K R A I N E

P O L A N D

Western Dvina

Formed in 1945 from the northern half of
German East Prussia, and ceded to Russia
under the Potsdam agreement, Kaliningrad
oblast became a true enclave, completely
separated from the rest of Russia, when
Lithuania and Belarus achieved their
independence in 1991.

Covering an area of approximately 104,000 sq miles (270,000 sq km)
Pripet Marshes are the largest area of marshland in Europe.

Following the break up of the Soviet Union the Commonwealth of Independent States
was established on December 8, 1991 by a treaty signed at Minsk, with the intent of
coordinating the foreign policies of the newly independent former Soviet republics.

0 km   100

0 miles   100

55°

50°

50°

30°

25°

A   B   C   D   E

5   6   7   8

Ukraine, Moldova & Romania

POLAND

BELARUS

◊ On April 25, 1986, engineers accidentally initiated an uncontrolled chain reaction in the number 4 reactor of the Chornobyl' nuclear power plant. The resulting explosion released 8 tons (tonnes) of radioactive material in the world's worst ever nuclear accident.

Pripet
Marshes

Kovel'

Korosten

Luts'k

Rivne

Zhytomyr

L'viv

SLOVAKIA

Ternopil'

U K ~

Ivano-
Frankivs'k

Khmel'-
nyts'kyy

Vinny

◊ Vlad Dracula or Vlad the Impaler was the real life prince upon whom Bram Stoker based his famous Count Dracula. Dracula was born in Transylvania in 1431 in the town of Sighisoara.

Uzhhorod

Kam"yanets'-
Podil's'kyy

Dniester

Chernivtsi

Satu Mare

Ribniṭa
Bălṭi

Suceava

Botoṣani

MOLDOVA

HUNGARY

Baia Mare

Transylvania

Oradea

Dej

Dubăsari

Iaṣi

CHIṢI

Cluj-Napoca

Piatra-Neamt

Tiraspol

Arad

Târgu Mureṣ

Bacău

Tighina

Alba Iulia

Sighisoara

Siret

Basarabeasca

Timiṣoara

Deva

R O M A N I A

Reni

Reṣiṭa

Carpaṭii Meridionali

Sibiu

Focṣani

Tulcea

Râmnicu Vâlcea

Braṣov

Galaṭi

Târgoviṣte

Buzău

Brăila

Drobeta-Turnu Severin

Piteṣti

Ploieṣti

Craiova

BUCHAREST

Constan

YUGOSLAVIA

Eforie Sud

Danube

Corabia

Olt

Giurgui

Mangalia

0 km   100

0 miles   100

BULGARIA

30°   35°   40°

RUSSIAN

FEDERATION

◆ *A monument in central Kiev stands as testament to the 7–12 million Ukrainian peasants who died during the Great Famine of 1932–33.*

Shostka

Chernihiv

Chornobyl'

Kyyivs'ke Vdskh.

Sumy

KIEV

Kaniws'ke Vdskh.

Lubny   Kharkiv   50°

ila Tserkva

A I N E

Donets

Cherkasy   Poltava   Syeverodonets'k

Kremenchuts'ke Vdskh.   Kremenchuk   Slov''yans'k   Luhans'k

Oleksandriya   Pavlohrad   Horlivka   Kostyantynivka

Kirovohrad   Dnipropetrovs'k   Makiyivka   Yenakiyeve

Pivdennyy Buh   Kryvyy Rih   Nikopol'   Donets'k   Krasnyy Luch

Zaporizhzhya

Mykolayiv   *Kakhovs'ka Vdskh.*   Mariupol'

Melitopol'   Berdyans'k

Kherson   Kakhovka

Dnieper   ◆ *In 1872 an ironworks was founded at Donets'k by British industrialist John Hughes (from whom the town's pre-Revolutionary name Yuzovka was derived) to produce rails for the growing Russian transportation network.*

Odesa

Sea of Azov

Karkinits'ka Zatoka

Kryms'kyy Pivostriv

Kerch

RUSSIAN

Yevpatoriya   **FEDERATION**   45°

Simferopol'

Black Sea

Sevastopol'   Yalta

Odesa was one of the major flashpoints in the Russian Revolution of 1905, and was the scene of the mutiny on the warship Potemkin, when sailors protesting against the serving of rotten meat eventually threw the officers overboard.

E   35°   F   G   H   40°

European Russia

The port of Murmansk remains ice free throughout the winter thanks to the Gulf Stream, whereas St. Petersburg 600 miles (965 km) to the south on the Baltic Sea is ice-bound between December and May.

ARCTIC OCEAN

Karskoye More

Novaya Zemlya

Barents Sea

Ostrov Vaygach

Ostrov Kolguyev

RUSSIAN FEDERATION (Ural Mountains)

Arctic Circle

Vorkuta

Usa

Pechora

Ukhta

Syktyvkar

Mezen

Pinega

Murmansk

Kol'skiy Poluostrov

Beloye More

Arkhangel'sk

Severnaya Dvina

Kotlas

NORWAY

SWEDEN

FINLAND

Onezhskoye Ozero

Onega

Petrozavodsk

Ladozhskoye Ozero

Vologda

Cherepovets

Rybinskoye Vdkhr.

Tver

Novgorod

Velikiye Luki

Smolensk

Norwegian Sea

Arctic Circle

Gulf of Bothnia

Gulf of Finland

Baltic Sea

ESTONIA

Sankt Petersburg

Pskov

LATVIA

LITHUANIA

BELARUS

0 km 400
0 miles 400

The Ural Mountains form the traditional boundary between Europe and Asia, extending some 1550 miles (2500 km). They were formed over 280 million years ago as the East European and Siberian plates moved together.

From August 1942 to February 1943 German armies laid siege to Volgograd, formerly known as Stalingrad. The Germans themselves were eventually surrounded and lost almost 250,000 men.

Caviar is the processed eggs, or roe, of sturgeon that live in the Caspian Sea and Volga River. Overfishing and poaching in recent years have seen the price of the finest Caviar rise to around US $4000 for 2.2 lbs (1 kg).

Running from the Black Sea to the Caspian Sea the Caucasus Mountains include Mt El'brus, which at 18,511 ft (5642 m) is the highest point in Europe, and still uplifting at the rate of 0.4 inches (10 mm) every year.

KAZAKHSTAN

UZBEKISTAN

TURKMENISTAN

Aral Sea

Perm'
Izhevsk
Naberezhnyye Chelny
Ufa
Orenburg
Orsk
Ural'skiye Gory
Nizhniy Novgorod
Cheboksary
Kazan'
Ul'yanovsk
Tol'yatti
Samara
Balakovo
Saransk
Penza
Ryazan'
Tambov
Saratov
Mikhaylovka
Volgograd
Astrakhan'
Volga
Caspian Sea
Makhachkala
Orël
Voronezh
Belgorod
Bryansk
Rostov-na-Donu
Krasnodar
Stavropol'
Cherkessk
Nal'chik
Vladikavkaz
Grozny
Elista
Kuma
Don
Donets
Sea of Azov
Sochi
Black Sea
El'brus
5642 m
Caucasus
GEORGIA
ARMENIA
AZERBAIJAN
TURKEY
IRAN
IRAQ
UKRAINE

IRAN

50°
70°
40°
60°

North & West Asia

ARCTIC

Franz Josef Land

Severnaya Zemlya

Svalbard (Norway)

Novaya Zemlya

Kara Sea

Norwegian Sea

North Cape

Barents Sea

Nor

Arctic Circle

RUSSIAN

West Siberian

Centr

Ob'

Ural Mountains

Plain

Irtysh

Ob'

Yenisey

Chulym

Gulf of Bothnia

Lake Onega

Northern Dvina

Lake Ladoga

Volga

S

Irtysh

Ishim

North Sea

Baltic Sea

Central Russian Upland

Volga

A

KALININGRAD (Russ. Fed.)

EUROPE

Don

KAZAKHSTAN

Otero Zaysan

S

Aral Sea

Lake Balkhash

Ili

Danube

Black Sea

Caucasus

Caspian Sea

UZBEKISTAN

Tien Shan

GEORGIA

KYRGYZSTAN

ARMENIA

AZERB.

TURKMEN.

Amu Darya

TURKEY

Lake Van

TAJIKISTAN

Mediterranean Sea

SYRIA

IRAQ

IRAN

AFGHANISTAN

Tibetan Plateau

LEBANON

Euphrates

Himalaya

ISRAEL

JORDAN

Tigris

KUWAIT

Ganges

Nile

BAHRAIN

The Gulf

Tropic of Cancer

QATAR

U.A.E.

Red Sea

SAUDI ARABIA

OMAN

Arabian Sea

Bay of Bengal

AFRICA

YEMEN

Gulf of Aden

Socotra (Yemen)

A B C D

NAVIGATOR
137
62 **94-95** 134
106

O C E A N

120°   140°   160°   180°   80°

1

Ozero
Taymyr

Laptev Sea

New Siberian Islands

East Siberian
Sea

Wrangel Island

 berian Lowland

Anabar   Olenek   Lena   Yana

Indigirka

Kolyma

Long Strait

Chukchi
Sea

Bering Strait

erian Plateau

F E D E R A T I O N

Arctic Circle

Velikaya

2

60°

b   e   r   i   a

Chona   Vitim   Lena   Amga

Lake
Baikal

Sea of
Okhotsk

Kamchatka

Bering
Sea

Amur   Zeya

Aleutian Islands

I   **A**

Argun

Sakhalin

Kurile Islands

3

40°

(administered by
Russian Federation,
claimed by Japan.)

obi

Sea of
Japan

P A C I F I C

Yellow River

East
China
Sea

O C E A N

Yangtze

Tropic of Cancer

4

20°

South
China
Sea

0 km   800

0 miles   800

120°   140°   160°   180°

E   **F**   **G**   **H**

5

Russia & Kazakhstan

ARCTIC

NORWAY

DENMARK

SWEDEN

GERMANY

Arctic Circle

Barents Sea

Zemlya Franza Iosifa

KALININGRAD
(part of Russian Federation)

FINLAND

Murmansk

POLAND

LAT. EST.
LITH.

Pskov

Sankt-Peterburg

BELARUS

Novgorod

Arkhangel'sk

Novaya Zemlya

Karskoye Mor

UKRAINE

Cherepovets

MOSCOW

Bryansk

Vologda

Yaroslavl'

Vorkuta

MOLDOVA

Tula

Ryazan'

Nizhniy
Novgorod

Kirov

Syktyvkar

Salekhard

Nori

Voronezh

Kazan'

Perm'

Zapadno-
Sibirskaya

R U

Rostov-
na-Donu

Izhevsk

Serov

Ravnina

F E D

Volgograd

Samara

Ufa

Yekaterinburg

Nizhnevartovs

Sochi

Ural'sk

Orenburg

Chelyabinsk

Ob'

Stavropol'

Nal'chik

Astrakhan'

Rudnyy

Kostanay

Petropavlovsk

Omsk

Krasnoya

Groznyy

GEORGIA

Orsk

Tomsk

ARM.

Makhachkala

Aktau

Kokshetau

ASTANA

Novosibirsk

AZ.

Caspian Sea

K A Z A K H S T A N

Pavlodar

Barnaul

Kemerov

Aral
Sea

Karaganda

Semipalatinsk

Novokuznet

TURKMENISTAN

Zhezkazgan

Ust'-
Kamenogors

Kyzylorda

Balkhash

IRAN

UZBEKISTAN

Shymkent

Ozero
Balkhash

Taraz

Taldykorgan

Almaty

KYRGYZSTAN

CHINA

OCEAN

Ostrov Vrangelya

80° 180° 70°

160° *Vostochno-Sibirskoye More* 60°

Pevek

Severnaya Zemlya

140°

Anadyr'

Bering Sea

180°

120°

Novosibirskiye Ostrova Ambarchik

170°

1

Ostrov Taymyr

100°

More Laptevykh

Ozero Taymyr Tiksi

Ossora

2

Lena Ust'-Kamchatsks

Poluostov Kamchatka

160°

Olenëk

Verkhoyanskiy Khrebet

Magadan

Petropavlovsk-Kamchatskiy

ednesibirskoye Ploskogor'ye

Okhotsk

50°

3

I A N Suntar Yakutsk

Sea of Okhotsk

i b i r (*Siberia*)

Lena

A T I O N

Sakhalin

Kuril'skiye Ostrova

Kansk Bratsk

Komsomol'sk-na-Amure

150°

4

Ozero Baykal Skovorodno

Yuzhhno-Sakhalinsk

Irkutsk Chita Blagoveshchensk

Khabarovsk

40°

Ulan-Ude

Amur

C H I N A

JAPAN

Vladivostok

◆ The Trans-Siberian Railroad, completed in 1916, runs 5866 miles (9440 km) between Moscow and Vladivostok. Crossing eight time zones, the journey takes eight days.

0 km 500

0 miles 500

130°

5

ONGOLIA

100° 110° 120° 150°

F F G H

Turkey & the Caucasus

ROMANIA

Black Sea

BULGARIA

◆ An average of 50,000 commercial ships pass through the Bosporus a year, along with thousands of ferries and smaller passenger boats. The strait is three times busier than the Suez Canal and four times as busy as the Panama Canal.

Edirne
Kırklareli
Sinop
GREECE
Tekirdağ
Zonguldak
Küre Dağları
Kastamonu
Samsur
Çanakkale Boğazı (Dardanelles)
Bosporus
İstanbul
Karabük
Çanık Dağları
Ör
Bursa
İzmit
Adapazarı
Çankırı
Kızıl Irmak
Marmara Denizi
Çanakkale
Balıkesir
Eskişehir
ANKARA
Çorum
Tokat
Siv
Kırıkkale
Ayvalık
Lésvos
Manisa
Kütahya
T U R
Chíos
İzmir
Uşak
Afyon
Nevşehir
Kayseri
Sámos
Aydın
Tuz Gölü
Niğde
Kahra
maras
Muğla
Denizli
İsparta
Konya
Bodrum
Ereğli
Osmaniye
Antalya
Toros Dağları
Tarsus
Adana
Dalaman
Mersin
Gaziant
İskenderun
Antalya Körfezi
Megísti
Antakya
Ródos
TURKISH REPUBLIC OF NORTHERN CYPRUS
(recognized only by Turkey)
Kárpathos
Girne (Kyrenia)
Gazimağusa (Famagusta)
NICOSIA
Mediterranean Sea
Paphos
Larnaca
Limassol
CYPRUS
LEBANON

RUSSIAN FEDERATION

◆ An earthquake struck Armenia in 1988, killing 55,000 people and devastating the country's infastructure.

Caspian Sea

Gagra
Sokhumi
Och'amch'ire
C a u c a s u s
P'ot'i
GEORGIA
K'ut'aisi
Bat'umi
T'BILISI
Rust'avi
Quba
Hopa
Kura
Gänca
Mingäçevir
Sumqayıt
BAKU
abzon
Rize
Gyumri
Vanadzor
AZERBAIJAN
Kars
ARMENIA
Sevana Lich
Nagornyy Karabakh
ŏğu *Karadeniz Dağları*
YEREVAN
Aras
Xankändi
Erzincan
Erzurum
Büyükağrı Dağı (Mount Ararat) 5137m ▲
Naxçıvan
AZERBAIJAN
Aras
Länkäran
Eläzığ
Muş
Van Gölü
Van
Tigris
◆ Azerbaijan has substantial oil reserves located in and around the Caspian Sea. They were some of the earliest oilfields in the world to be exploited.
alatya
Siirt
iyaman
Diyarbakır
Batman
Mardin
I R A N
Şanlıurfa
◆ The salty water of Lake Van inhibits all animal life except the Darekh, a small fish that has adapted to the harsh conditions.

◆ Atatürk Dam, one of the largest dams in the world, was completed in 1990. The reservoir behind the dam covers an area of 315 sq miles (816 sq km) and often requires interruptions in the flow of the Euphrates River to maintain water levels.

S Y R I A
I R A Q

0 km   200
0 miles   200

The Near East

The Euphrates is 1700 miles (2470 km) long and drains an area of 171,000 sq mi (443,000 sq km). Although less than 30 percent of the river's drainage basin is in Turkey, about 95 percent of the river's water originates in the Turkish highlands.

Lebanon only has one permanent river, the Nahr el Litani, which runs for 110 miles (175 km).

Manufactured by a secret process, Damascus steel was much prized in the preindustrial era as an extremely hard metal used for high quality sword blades.

TURKEY

IRAQ

SYRIA

LEBANON

CYPRUS

Tigris

Al Jazirah

Al Qāmishlī

Al Ḥasakah

Dayr az Zawr

Euphrates

Ar Raqqah

Buḥayrat al Asad

Ḥalab

A'zāz

Idlib

Orontes

Ḥamāh

Ḥimṣ

Tudmur

Anti Lebanon

Lebanon

DAMASCUS

Baalbek

Zahle

Al Lādhiqīyah

Ṭarṭūs

Tripoli

BEIRUT

Saida

Mediterranean Sea

35°

40°

35°

0 km   100

0 miles   100

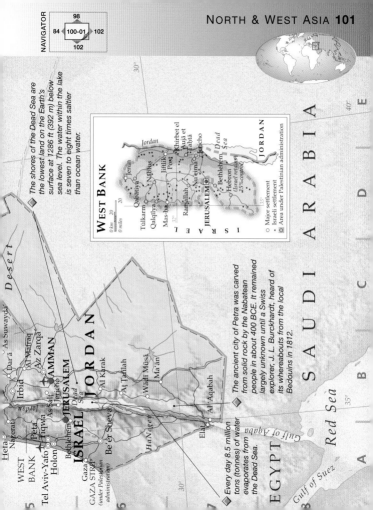

The shores of the Dead Sea are the lowest land on the Earth's surface at 1286 ft (392 m) below sea level. The water within the lake is seven to eight times saltier than ocean water.

The ancient city of Petra was carved from solid rock by the Nabatean people in about 400 BCE. It remained largely unknown until a Swiss explorer, J. L. Burckhardt, heard of its whereabouts from the local Bedouins in 1812.

Every day 8.5 million tons (tonnes) of water evaporates from the Dead Sea.

WEST BANK

Major settlement
Israeli settlement
Area under Palestinian administration

The Middle East

In the 10th century, the Grand Vizier of Persia took his entire library with him wherever he went. The 117,000 volume library was carried by camels trained to walk in alphabetical order.

Four thousand years ago Babylonian law laid down a minimum wage for every class of workers in the kingdom.

Saudi Arabia contains the world's largest oil reserves. The region can produce over 8 million barrels of oil every day.

Ar Rub' al Khali, also known as the Empty Quarter, is the largest uninterrupted sand desert in the world, with sand dune ridges up to 25 miles (40 km) long.

The name "Red Sea" is derived from the extensive blooms of algae that occasionally occur. These change color when they die, turning the sea's normally intense blue-green waters a deep red.

Every Muslim must make at least one pilgrimage to Mecca during their lifetime. Muslims regard the small shrine called the Ka'ban, located near the center of the Great Mosque in Mecca, as the most sacred place on Earth.

Gulf of Oman
Tropic of Cancer
Sharjah
MUSCAT
Suhar
Al Rustaq
Nazwa
Ramlat
Al Wahibah
Jazirat
Maşīrah
Khalij
Maşīrah
Duqm
Ṣawqirah
'Juzur al Ḥalāniyāt

O M A N

Arabian
Sea

Dubayy
QATAR
MANAMA
Al Hufūf
ABU DHABI
DOHA
U.A.E.

Ar Rub' al Khali
(Empty Quarter)

Şalālah

INDIAN

OCEAN

Arabian
Peninsula

SAUDI ARABIA

Ra's Xaafuun

50°

Sanāw

Al Mukallā
Suquṭrā
(Soqotra)
(to Yemen)

Sayḥūt
Ḥaḍramawt
Say'ūn
Wuday'ah
Ramlat
as Sab'atayn
Najrān
Ḥaraḍ
Laylā
As Sulayyil
Ar Rub' al Khāli

RIYADH
Al Madār ar Rimāl

SANA
Adan
Gulf of Aden

S O M A L I A

Sa'dah
Ta'izz
Abhā
Jīzān
Jazā'ir
Farasān

Makkah
(Mecca)
At Tā'if
Al Hudaydah

DJIBOUTI

E T H I O P I A

Al Madīnah

Jiddah

Red

Sea

SUDAN

EGYPT

ERITREA

20°

10°

5

6

7

8

Central Asia

KAZAKHSTAN

*Aral
Sea*

◇ Since 1960, the Aral Sea has shrunk
by 40 percent, becoming extremely
saline and consequently losing all
but one of it's once-abundant
fish species.

U s t y u r t
P l a t e a u

Turan
Lowland

Syr Darya

UZBEKISTAN

Nukus

Keneurgench
Dashkhovuz

Urganch

Türtkül'

Uchquduq

Zarafshon

Caspian

Turkmenbashi

TURKMENISTAN

Nawoiy

Aydar

Cheleken

Nebitdag
Gazandzhyk

Gyzylarbat

T u r a n

G a r a g u m y

Bukhoro

Samarqan

Seydi

Chardzhev

Qarshi

Bakharden
Geok-Tepe

Byuzmeyin

ASHGABAT

Garagumy

Sayat

Amu Darya

Kerki

Mary Bayramaly

Sea

Kaaka

Tły Kanal

Tedzhen

Sheberghan

Āqcha

Murgab

Mazar-e Shar
Meymaneh

◇ The desert of Kara Kum (Garagumy) occupies
over 70 percent of Turkmenistan, severely limiting
human settlement across much of the country.

Bālā Morghāb

Gushgy

Darya-ye Morghāb

AFGHANISTAN

I R A N

Herāt

Harīrūd

◇ The Karakum Canal, the world's longest irrigation
canal, stretches some 683 miles (1100 km) and
is known as the "River of Life" as it irrigates
large areas of arid land.

Farāh

Gereshk

Kalāt

Zaranj

Dasht-e Mārgow

Kandahār

Daryā-ye Helmand

0 km   200

0 miles   200

70°   80°

Ozero Balkhash

K A Z A K H S T A N   1

BISHKEK

Kara-Balta   Tokmak   Tyup
Talas   Karakol   *Ozero*
HKENT Chirchiq   **KYRGYZSTAN** *Issyk-Kul* *Tien Shan*
Namangan   2
Angren   Audijon   Dzhalal-Abad   Naryn   *Kokshaal-Tau*
Olmaliq   Qŭqon   40°
Khŭjand   Farghona
Sŭlyukta Khaydarkan   Osh
Zeravshan *Surkhob*

◆ Mount Communism was so named for being
the highest point in the former Soviet Union,
rising to 24,590 ft (7495 m).

USHANBE   **TAJIKSTAN**   *Pamirs*
Norak   Dangara   Murghob
pa   Kulob Khŏrugh   C H I N A   3
lm   Farkhor *Pamir*
Kŭnduz   Fevzàbad   *Pamir*

Baghlān
Hindu Kush
mtī   ◆ Until recent years, people living in remote areas of
le   Asadābād   Afghanistan were immunized against smallpox by
rikār   having dried powdered scabs from victims of the
BUL   Jalālābād   disease blown up their noses. This treatment was   4
                       invented by the Chinese in the 11th century, and is
Ghazni   thought to be the oldest form of vaccination.
Gardēz

◆ Despite an area of 251,771 sq miles (652,090 sq km),
Afghanistan has a limited road network and no
railroads whatsoever, making access to much
of the country extremely difficult.

AKISTAN   5
        I N D I A
70°   80°   30°

F   F   G   H

South & East Asia

Black Sea

Caspian Sea

Aral Sea

Syr Darya

Lake Balkhash

Irtysh

Yenisey

Uvs Nuur

Lake Baikal

Hovsgol Nuur

MONGOLI

Altai Mountains

Tien Shan

A S I A

Iranian Plateau

Hindu Kush

Takla Makan Desert

Altun Shan

Kunlun Mountains

Plateau of Tibet

C H I N

Gobi

Yellow River

The Gulf

Gulf of Oman

PAKISTAN

Sutlej

Indus

Thar Desert

Himalayas

Yamuna

Ganges

Brahmaputra

NEPAL

▲ Mount Everest 8848m

BHUTAN

Mekong

Salween

Red River

20°

Rann of Kuchchh

Gulf of Khambhat

INDIA

Deccan

Western Ghats

Eastern Ghats

BANGLADESH

MYANMAR (BURMA)

Irrawaddy

VIETNA

LAOS

H

Arabian Sea

Mekong

THAILAND

Laccadive Islands (to India)

Bay of Bengal

Andaman Islands (to India)

Andaman Sea

CAMBO

Tônle S

Gulf of Thailand

MALDIVES

Gulf of Mannar

SRI LANKA

Nicobar Islands (to India)

MAL

SINGA

Equator

Sumatra

INDIAN

OCEAN

0 km   1000

0 miles   1000

40°

60°

80°

100°

40°

1

2

3

4

5

20°

80°

100°

20°
140°
160°
40°
20°

Amur

Vegan

Khingan Range

Manchuria
Plain

Liao He

Sakhalin

Lake Khanka

Hokkaido

1

Yellow

**NORTH
KOREA**

**SOUTH
KOREA**

JAPAN

Sea of
Japan

20°

Great Plain of China

*Yellow
Sea*

Korea Strait

Shikoku

Kyushu

East China
Sea

Ryukyu Islands

2

Tak‍shan Strait

TAIWAN

Philippine

Sea

PACIFIC

3

acel Islands
(puted)

Luzon Strait

Luzon

**Northern
Marianas Is.**
(to US)

OCEAN

uth China
Sea

PHILIPPINES

Guam
(to US)

M i c r o n e s i a

3

Sprat ly
slands
disputed)

Palawan

*Sulu
Sea*

Mindanao

Equator

4

UNEL

A

*Celebes
Sea*

Halmahera

M e l a n e s i a

Bismarck Archipelago

*Solomon
Islands*

rneo

Moluccas

Seram

Pegunungan Maoke

New Guinea

*Solomon
Sea*

NDONESIA

Celebes

Banda Sea

Arafura

5

*Flores
Sea*

Lesser Sunda Islands

Timor

EAST TIMOR
*(under UN Transitional
Authority from Feb 2000)*

*Coral
Sea*

140°
160°

E
F
G
H

Western China & Mongolia

◆ The Altai Mountains provide one of the last refuges for the endangered snow leopard. There are thought to be only 600 animals left in the wild.

◆ The Turpan Depression is the lowest and hottest place in China. Temperatures can exceed 117°F (47°C) around the lake of Aydingkol Hu, which lies 505 ft (154 m) below sea level.

◆ Although forming around 20 percent of China's landmass, Tibet is sparsely populated, supporting only 1 percent of China's 1.3 billion population.

RUSSIAN FE

KAZAKHSTAN

MONG

KYRGYZSTAN

TAJIKISTAN

AFGH.

PAKISTAN

INDIA

NEPAL

BHUTAN

Ozero Issyk-Kul'

Ulaangom
Olgiy
Altay
Hovd
Altay
Bayanhongo

Karamay
Kuytun
Yining
Shihezi
ÜRÜMQI
Qitai
Turpan
Hami
Xingxingxia
Ejin

Tien Shan
Bosten Hu
Korla
Ruoqiang
Lop Nur
GANSU
Qilian Sha

Kashi
Yengisar
Shache
Yecheng
(claimed by India)
Moyu
Qira

Tarim He
Tarim Basin
XINJIANG UYGUR
ZIZHIQU
Taklimakan
Shamo
Altun Shan
Qaidam Pendi
Golmud
Dula
Qinghai

Karakoram Range
Kashmir
JAMMU AND KASHMIR
AKSAI CHIN
(administered by China, claimed by India)
Qingzang Gaoyuan
(Plateau of Tibet)
C H I
QINGHAI
Bayan Har S
Yushu

DEMCHOK/DÊMQOG
(administered by China, claimed by India)
Zanda
Gar
Rutog
XIZANG ZIZHIQU
(Tibet)
Tanggula Shan
Tongtian He
Mekong
Qamdo

Himalayas
Tangra
Yumco
Nyima
Siling Co
Nam Co
Damxung
Nagqu
Amdo
Nyainqêntanglha Shan

Lhaze
LHASA
Gyangzê

Mount Everest
8848m

ARUNACHAL PRADESH
(claimed by China)

Gurbantünggüt Shamo
Ulungur Hu
Hovsgol Nuur
Uvs Nuur
Hyargas Nuur
Har Us Nuur
Hangayn Nuru
Tsetse
Möro

Zapadnyy Sayan
Yenisey

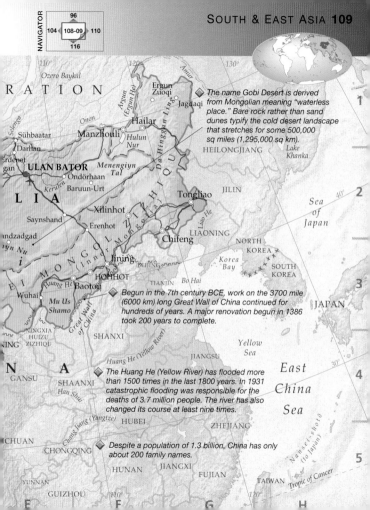

RATION

110°

Ozero Baykal

Selenge

Sühbaatar

Darhan

Ondret
gan

Onon

Manzhouli

ULAN BATOR

Ondörhaan

Kerulen

Baruun-Urt

LIA

Saynshand

andzadgad

iyn Nuu
i

EI

Wuhai

Mu Us
Shamo

NINGXIA
HUIZU
ZIZHIQU

ING

GANSU

N

SHAANXI

Han Shui

CHUAN

CHONGQING

YUNNAN

GUIZHOU

Argun (Ergun He)

Ergun
Zuoqi

Hailar

Hulun
Nur

Menengiyn
Tal

Xilinhot

Erenhot

Jining

HOHHOT

Baoton

Huang He

Great Wall
of China

SHANXI

Huang He (Yellow River)

Jagdaqi

HEILONGJIANG

Tongliao

Liao He

Chifeng

JILIN

LIAONING

BEIJING

TIANJIN

Bo Hai

Korea
Bay

NORTH
KOREA

JIANGSU

Yellow
Sea

A

Chang Jiang (Yangtze)

HUBEI

HUNAN

JIANGXI

Amur

Lake
Khanka

Sea
of
Japan

40°

SOUTH
KOREA

JAPAN

30°

East
China
Sea

Nansei-shotō
(to Japan)

FUJIAN

TAIWAN

Tropic of Cancer

110°

120°

◆ The name Gobi Desert is derived from Mongolian meaning "waterless place." Bare rock rather than sand dunes typify the cold desert landscape that stretches for some 500,000 sq miles (1,295,000 sq km).

◆ Begun in the 7th century BCE, work on the 3700 mile (6000 km) long Great Wall of China continued for hundreds of years. A major renovation begun in 1386 took 200 years to complete.

◆ The Huang He (Yellow River) has flooded more than 1500 times in the last 1800 years. In 1931 catastrophic flooding was responsible for the deaths of 3.7 million people. The river has also changed its course at least nine times.

◆ Despite a population of 1.3 billion, China has only about 200 family names.

Eastern China & Korea

◆ Whereas European languages such as English or French use an alphabet of 26 letters, the Chinese language uses a system of over 50,000 characters or symbols.

◆ The "Yongle dadian," an encyclopedia of the Chinese Ming dynasty, had 22,937 chapters in 10,000 volumes. More than 2000 Chinese scholars worked on the book for 5 years before it was finished.

◆ Tangshan, China, suffered the deadliest earthquake of the 20th century on July 28, 1976. One quarter of the population was killed or seriously injured, with an estimated death toll of 242,000 people.

◆ Tiananmen Square in Beijing is the largest public square in the world covering an area of 100 acres (40.5 hectares).

RUSSIAN FEDERATION

MONGOLIA

NEI MONGOL (Inner Mongolia)

XINJIANG UYGUR ZIZHIQU

Ozero Baykal

Amur (Heilong Jiang)

Shilka

Argun (Ergun He)

Onon

Selenga

Xiao Hinggan Ling

Lake Khanka

Sea of Japan

Qiqihar

HEILONGJIANG

HARBIN

JILIN

Mudanjiang

Jilin

Changchun

Hunjiang

Fushun

CHANGCHUN

LIAONING

SHENYANG

Fuxin

Jinzhou

Anshan

Benxi

Dandong

NORTH KOREA

Chongjin

Hamhung

Hŭich'ŏn

P'YONGYANG

Namp'o

Korea Bay

Bo Hai

Dalian

Sea of Japan

SOUTH KOREA

SEOUL

Taegu

Taejŏn

Pusan

HEBEI

BEIJING

TIANJIN

Datong

Shijiazhuang

TAIYUAN

Handan

JINAN

SHANDONG

Qingdao

Zibo

Great Wall

Huang He (Yellow)

Qilian Shan

Qinghai Hu

Qaidam Pendi

YINCHUAN

NINGXIA

He

E

D

C

B

A

45°

40°

Ostrov Iturup

Ostrov Shikotan

Kurile Islands (administered by the Russian Federation, claimed by Japan)

Kurile Islands

Ostrov Kunashir

Nemuro

Kushiro

Sea of Okhotsk

Abashiri

Hokkaidō

Ostrov Sakhalin

La Pérouse Strait

Asahikawa

Obihiro

Tomakomai

Wakkanai

Rebun-tō

Rishiri-tō

Sapporo

Otaru

Hakodate

Okushiri-tō

Hachinohe

Morioka

Honshū

Sendai

Fukushima

Iwaki

Aomori

Akita

Niigata

Sado

Shinano-gawa

Sea of Japan

JAPAN

CHINA

RUSSIAN FEDERATION

NORTH KOREA

135°

140°

145°

130°

40°

5

△ At 33.4 miles (53.8 km), 14.3 miles (23.3 km) of which lie under the Tsugaru Strait, the Seikan Tunnel is the longest tunnel in the world. Construction began in 1964 and took 24 years to complete.

△ The Toyota Motor Co. Ltd was first established in 1937 as a spin-off from Toyoda Automatic Loom Works. The company now produces 4.5 million cars a year equivalent to one every six seconds.

Liancourt Rocks

The same family has occupied the Imperial Throne of Japan for the last 1300 years. The present-day emperor, Akihito, is the 125th in succession.

On August 12, 1990, Typhoon Winona, combined with the summer holiday rush, created the longest traffic jam in Japan's history, an 84-mile long tailback involving about 15,000 vehicles.

The longest bridge in the world is the Akashi Kaikyo Bridge linking Honshu and Shikoku, with a central span of 6352 ft (1991 m), the total length shore to shore is 12,831 ft (3,911 m) or 2.4 miles (3.9 km).

Yokohama
Nagoya
Okazaki
Hamamatsu
Hachijō-jima
Aoga-shima

Izu-shotō

Philippine Sea

PACIFIC

OCEAN

Matsue
Tottori
Hamada
Okayama
Kurashiki
Hiroshima
Yamaguchi
Shimonoseki
Kitakyūshū
Fukuoka
Saeki
Nagasaki
Kumamoto
Miyazaki
Kagoshima

Kōbe
Ōsaka
Kyōto
Wakayama
Shingū

Tokushima
Kōchi
Nakamura
Shikoku

Ōita
Matsuyama

Kyūshū

Amakusa-nada

Tanega-shima
Yaku-shima

Ōsumi-shotō

*Ichiki
Iki*

Gotō-rettō

Tsushima

Korea Strait

KOREA

Bingo-ko

Ōsumi-shotō

East China Sea

Tokuno-shima
Amami-O-shima

Ryūkyū-rettō

Okinawa
Naha

0 km   200
0 miles   200

30°

25°

30°

35°

130°   135°   140°   E

A   B   C   D

Southern India & Sri Lanka

70°

Mumbai   Kalyān   Nānded
(Bombay)   Nizāmābād

Pune   Decca

Solāpur   Krishna

1 ◆ The Mumbai (Bombay) movie industry, known as
Bollywood, makes around 800 films each year,
compared to America's 100, making it the most
prolific film-producing country in the world.

Hyderābā

I N D I

Karnātaka

Belgaum   Hubli   Kurno

Pānāji

Dāvangere   Anantapur

A r a b i a n

Bangalore   Ve

Mangalore   Mysore

2   *S e a*

Ta͟

Salem   *Nā*

Amīndīvi Is.

Lakshadweep
(part of India)

Calicut

Coimbatore   Tiruch
           rapī

Kavaratti I.

Ernākulam

Kalpeni I.

Cochin   Madur

3 ◆ The word ghats, literally "stairs that
descend to a river," refers to the
stair-like appearance of the slopes
of the Western Ghats mountain
range, as they descend to
the coastal plain.

Minicoy I.

Trivandrum

Nāgercoil   Ma

*Ihavandippolhu
Atoll*

MALDIVES

4 ◆ There are over 1300 islands in the Maldives
but only about 200 are inhabited. All the
islands are low lying, none rising more
than 6 ft (1.8m) above sea level.

✈
● MALE'

Kolhumadulu Atoll

0 km   300

0 miles   300

5   0°

I N D I A N

Huvadhu Atoll

70°

90°

B a y
o f
B e n g a l

Eastern Ghats

Visākhapatnam

Rājahmundry

Vijayawada

gole

'lore

hennai
(Madras)
chīpuram

dicherry

k Strait

fna

SRI LANKA

Trincomalee

Batticaloa

Kandy

OLOMBO

alle

Matara

MYANMAR
(BURMA)

Mouths of the
Irrawaddy

Andaman Is.
(part of India)

North Andaman

Middle Andaman

Port Blair

South Andaman

Little Andaman

Andaman
Sea

10°

Nicobar Is.
(part of India)

Great Nicobar

Indira
Point

Sumatera

INDONESIA

OCEAN

Equator   0°

90°

The Indian cobra is often displayed
by snake charmers. The cobras
appear to respond to the music
played by the charmer, but, like
all snakes, they are deaf and
only follow the movements of
the charmer.

The world's largest tea producer,
Sri Lanka has over 8500 sq miles
(22,000 sq km) of land under
tea cultivation, yielding about
240,000 tons (tonnes) a year,
and accounting for over 20
percent of world exports.

The Ninetyeast Ridge takes its name
from the line of longitude it follows.
At around 2600 miles (4200 km), it
is the world's longest and straightest
undersea ridge.

1

2

3

4

5

F   F   G   H

North India, Pakistan & Bangladesh

60°

(claimed by In

The Karakoram Highway was finally completed in 1978 after 24,000 workers had toiled for almost 20 years. The road climbs to 16,000 ft (4890 m) at the Khunjerab Pass.

Hindu Kush

K2 8611m

Karakoram Ra

(A "line of control" was agreed between India and Pakistan in 1972)

Mardān

Peshāwar

AFGHANISTAN

ISLĀMĀBĀD

Jamu & Kashmīr

Rāwalpindi

Jhelum

Punjab

Gujrāt

Gujrānwāla

Amritsar

Sargodha

Lahore

Jalandha

Toba Kākar Range

Faisalābād

Ludhiāna

Chandigarh

Quetta

Okāra

30°

Dera Ghāzi Khān

Multān

Chāgai Hills

Bahāwalpur

Delhi

P A K I S T A N

NEW DELHI

Shikārpur

Rahīmyār Khān

Bīkāner

Med

Central Makrān Range

Lārkāna

Indus

Thar Desert

Jaipur

Āgra

Sukkur

Rājasthān

Nawābshāh

Jodhpur

Ajmer

Gwalior

Hyderābād

Kota

Karāchi

Indus

Tropic of Cancer

I

Mouths of the Indus

Rann of Kachchh

0 km   200

0 miles   200

Gāndhidhām

Ahmadābād

Bh

Gulf of Kachchh

Gujarāt

Indore

Madh

Jāmnagar

Rājkot

Vadodara

A r a b i a n

Narmada

Porbandar

Bhāvnagar

Nāg

S e a

Sūrat

Mahārāshtr

20°

Gulf of Khambhāt

Damān

On January 26, 2001 a massive earthquake devastated the Gujarat region of India, costing some 25,000 lives.

Nāshik

Nānde

Mumbai (Bombay)

Kalyān

Nizāmā

✕✕✕ *Ceasefire Line*

Pune

Solāpur

70°

XINJIANGUYGUR
ZIZHIQU

AI CHIN
ninistered by China,
ed by India)

CHOK/DÉMQOG
ninistered by China,
ed by India)

XIZANG ZIZHIQU
(Tibet)

C H I N A QINGHAI

◆ The northern ranges of the Himalayas contain the highest
   mountains in the world, with average heights of more than
   23,000 ft (7000 m) and many peaks higher
   than 26,000 ft (8000m).

◆ Cerrapunji, 4232 ft (1290 m) above sea level, has an average annual
   rainfall of 503 inches (1279 cm), although this is monsoon rain and
   the winter is a virtual drought. The highest ever seasonal rainfall
   was 901 inches (2290 cm).

◆ In the kingdom of Bhutan, all
   citizens officially become a
   year older on New Year's Day.

H i m a l a y a s

ARUNACHAL PRADESH
(claimed by China)

reilly

NEPAL

Mount Everest
8848m ▲
●KATHMANDU ●THIMPHU
Gangtok BHUTAN

Uttar
Pradesh

●Lucknow

Kānpur

Vārānasi Patna
●Birātnagar
Saidpur Guwāhāti
Dispur ●Kohima
Jamālpur Sylhet Imphāl
BANGLADESH

Allahābād
Gaya Rājshāhi
Bihār

IA Dhanbād West DHAKA
Rānchī Bengal Comilla
Jabalpur Khulna
adesh Calcutta Chittagong
Raipur (Kolkata)

MYANMAR
(BURMA)

Tropic of Cancer

Mouths of the Ganges

Orissa
●Cuttack Bay
of
Visākhapatnam Bengal

Mahānadi

Eastern Ghats

rangal

◆ The heaviest hailstones
   on record, weighing about
   2.25 lbs (1 kg), are
   reported to have killed 92
   people in the Gopalganj
   area of Bangladesh on
   April 14, 1986.

Mainland Southeast Asia

Around 70 percent of the world's teak grows in the hills of northern Myanmar. However overexploitation means that supplies may soon be exhausted.

The Anopheles mosquito, which carries the malaria parasite Plasmodium, is estimated to have been responsible for half of all human deaths not caused by war.

A M

Qui Nhon

Nha Trang

Stœng Trĕng

Da Lat

Kâmpŏng Cham

Ho Chi Minh

Phumĭ Kŏng

Samraông

Batdâmbâng

Sễ Săn

Sê San

Srêpôk

Swãy Riêng

Can Tho

Kâmpŏng Chhnăng

Mekong

Rach Gia

PHNOM PENH

C A M B O D I A

Mouths of the Mekong

Tônlé Sap

Kâmpôt

Kâmpóng Saôm

Ayutthaya

Chon Buri

Pattaya

Ko Chang

BANGKOK

Ratchaburi

Gulf of Thailand

Ko Phangan

Ko Samui

Nakhon Si Thammarat

Chumphon

Songkhla

Pattani

Yala

Hat Yai

Surat Thani

Trang

Ko Phuket

Phuket

Ratchaburi

Tavoy

Mergui

Isthmus of Kra

Mergui Archipelago

Andaman Sea

Nicobar Islands (part of India)

South China Sea

Malay Peninsula

M A L A Y S I A

Strait of Malacca

I N D O N E S I A

Sumatra

I N D I A N   O C E A N

◆ Following years of conflict it is estimated that around 3 million landmines remain buried in the soils of Cambodia.

◆ Bangkok has some of the worst traffic jams in the world. In July 1992, after a monsoon storm, it took 11 hours for one jam to clear.

◆ The world's smallest mammal is the bumblebee bat of Thailand, weighing less than 0.09 oz (2.5g).

0 km   200
0 miles   200

5

6

7

8

A   B   C   D   E

Maritime Southeast Asia

MYANMAR
(BURMA)

THAILAND

LAOS

VIETNAM

Gulf of
Tongking

Hainan Dao
(to China)

CAMBODIA

Paracel Islands
*(disputed by China, Taiwan
and Vietnam)*

S o u t h   C h i n a
S e a

0 km   400
0 miles   400

*Andaman
Sea*

*Gulf of
Thailand*

Isthmus of Kra

Spratly Islands
*(disputed by China,
Malaysia, Philippines,
Taiwan and Vietnam)*

◆ *The Rafflesia plant has the largest flower in
the world. The bloom, 3 ft (90 cm) in diameter,
attracts insects by imitating the foul
smell of rotting flesh.*

*Nicobar Islands
(to India)*

George
Town

Bandaaceh

Kota Bharu

Kuala Terengganu

Kota Kinabalu

**BANDAR SERI
BEGAWAN
BRUNEI**

Strait of Malacca

Medan

Taiping

Ipoh

Kuantan

Klang

KUALA LUMPUR

Pematangsiantar

*Danau
Toba*

Seremban

M A L A Y S I A

Sibu

Sarawak

Sibolga

Pulau Simeulue

Johor Bahru

Kuching

*Pegunungan
Muller*

Equator

Pulau Nias

SINGAPORE

Pontianak

Kapuas

Kalimantan

B o r n e o

*Sumatera
(Sumatra)*

Padang

Pekanbaru

Samarinda

Pulau Siberut

Jambi

Batang Hari

Selat Karimata

Balikpapan

*Kepulauan
Mentawai*

Bangka

Palembang

Banjarmasin

Barisan, Pegunungan

*Pulau
Belitung*

I N D O N E S I A

Bengkulu

*Java
Sea*

Selat Sunda

Bandarlampung

Cirebon

Tegal

Pekalongan

JAKARTA

Semarang

Ma...

Bogor

Kudus

Surabaya

Sukabumi

Bandung

Cilacap

Magelang

*Java
(Java)*

Yogyakarta

Surakarta

Denpasar

Madiun

Kediri

Malang

Mataram

Jember

*INDIAN
OCEAN*

◆ *In August 1883 a devastating volcanic
eruption destroyed most of the island of
Krakatau and triggered a tsunami that
claimed around 33,000 lives.*

Philippine

Sea

Luzon Strait

Babuyan Channel

Tuguergarao
Ilagan
Luzon

Dagupan
Cabanatuan
Lucena
Naga
Legaspi

NILA

angas

oro

Mindoro

Calbayog
Tacloban

Roxas City
Iloilo
Bacolod
City
Cebu
Butuan

Puerto
Princesa

Cadiz

Cagayan de Oro

Iligan

Mindanao

Davao

Zamboanga

General
Santos

Sulu Archipelago

Kepulauan
Talaud

au

Celebes Sea

Manado

Gorontalo

Gulf of
Tomini

alu

Sulawesi
(Celebes)

Kepulauan
Banggai

Kepulauan
Sula

Kendari

Parepare

Pulau
Buton

Ujungpandang

Banda Sea

es Sea

Tenggara

Flores

Pulau Alor

Kepulauan
Wetar

Pulau
Leti

Sumba

Savu Sea

Kupang

Timor

Timor Sea

◆ The Philippines take their name from Philip II
of Spain, who was king when the islands were
colonized during the 16th century.

PHILIPPINES

PACIFIC

Yap

OCEAN

◆ Indonesia is the world's largest archipelago
with almost 14,000 islands stretching 3100
miles (5000 km) between the Indian
and Pacific oceans.

Babeldaob

PALAU

Kepulauan
Santang

Davao Gulf

Bohol Sea

Northern
Mariana
Islands
(to US)

Guam (to US)

MICRONESIA

Molucca Sea

Pulau Morotai
Pulau
Halmahera

Maluku
Sea

Halmahera

Wahai

Ambon

Pulau
Buru

Pulau
Seram

Ceram Sea

Seram

Laut
(Moluccas)

Sorong
Jazirah
Doberai

Kepulauan
Kai

Kepulauan
Tanimbar

Pulau Yamdena

Arafura Sea

Pulau
Biak

Jayapura

Sungai Mamberano

Pegunungan Maoke

Irian Jaya

New Guinea

Kepulauan
Aru

Digul

Sungai Digul

Torres Strait

AUSTRALIA

Equator

PAPUA

NEW

GUINEA

DILI

EAST TIMOR
(under UN Transitional
Authority from Feb 2000)

N   E   S   I   A

The Indian Ocean

The prize of £20,000 offered in 1714 by the Board of Longitude in London was eventually won in 1763 by John Harrison with his No.4 Marine Chronometer which, for the first time allowed mariners to accurately determine their longitude.

Lake Baikal

Yellow River

Tropic of Cancer

Hong Kong (Xianggang)

South China Sea

Borneo

East Indies

Singapore

Equator

Sumatra

Java

ASIA

Mekong

Gulf of Thailand

Andaman Sea

Java

Investi

Yenisey

Ob'

Yangtze

Brahmaputra

Irrawaddy

Fan

Bay of Bengal

Andaman Islands (to India)

Nicobar Islands (to India)

Mentawai

Cocos Basin

Ganges

Calcutta (Kolkata)

Ganges Fan

Sri Lanka

Colombo

Ceylon Plain

Mid-Indian

Himalayas

Lake Balkhash

Indus

Karachi

Mumbai (Bombay)

Arabian Sea

Laccadive Islands (to India)

MALDIVES

Laccadive Plateau

Chagos Trench

Mid

Aral Sea

Indus Fan

Gulf of Oman

Arabian Basin

Carlsberg Ridge

Chagos-Laccadive Ridge

Iranian Plateau

Murray Ridge

Owen Fracture Zone

Caspian Sea

Volga

The Gulf

Dubai

Mina Qabus

Socotra

SEYCHELLES

Somali Basin

Mid

Black Sea

Caucasus

Kuwait

Arabian Peninsula

Aden

Gulf of Aden

Horn of Africa

(to Yemen)

Mascarene

Tigris

Euphrates

Red Sea

Ethiopian Highlands

Equator

Mombasa

Aldabra

AFRICA

Tropic of Cancer

AUSTRALASIA

Tropic of Capricorn

Exmouth
Plateau

Perth
Basin

Fremantle
Naturaliste
Plateau

Wharton
Basin

Broken Ridge

East Indiaman Ridge

Ninety-East Ridge

S o u t h e a s t   I n d i a n   R i d g e

Diamantina Fracture Zone

I N D I A N

O C E A N

Osborn
Plateau

S O U T H E R N

O C E A N

A N T A R C T I C A

South Indian Basin

Limit of winter pack ice

Limit of summer pack ice

Antarctic Circle

◆ Every cubic mile (4.3 cu km) of
seawater holds over 150 million
tons (tonnes) of minerals.

Amsterdam Island

Île St-Paul

Crozet
Basin

Kerguelen Plateau

Banzare
Seamounts

Kerguelen

French Southern &
Antarctic Territories
(to France)

Crozet
Islands

Heard & Mcdonald Islands
(to Australia)

◆ The largest animal ever seen alive was a 113.5 ft (35 m),
170-ton (tonne) female blue whale.

MAURITIUS

Réunion
(to France)

Farafangana

Madagascar
Basin

Southwest Indian Ridge

E n d e r b y   P l a i n

Atlantic
Basin

Prince Edward
Islands
(to South Africa)

Antarctic Circle

Madagascar
(to France)

Madagascar
Plateau

Natal
Basin

Mascarene
Plain

Mozambique
Channel

Durban

Davie Ridge

0 km   1500
0 miles   1500

Australasia & Oceania

Philippine Sea

Wake Island
(to US)

20°

Northern Mariana Islands
(to US)

MARSHALL ISLANDS

Saipan

Mid-Pacific Mountains

Philippine Basin

Guam
(to US)

Mariana Trench

Ratak Chain

M
i
c
r
o
n
e
s
i
a

Philippines

Yap

Yap Trench

MICRONESIA

Caroline Islands

Ralik Chain

Babeldaob

Chuuk

Pohnpei

Kosrae

Sulu
Sea

PALAU

M e l a n e

Nauru

NAURU

Banaba

Celebes
Sea

Banda
Sea

Bismarck Archipelago

PAPUA NEW
GUINEA

Bismarck Sea

s
i
a

SOLOMON
ISLANDS

TUVA

Borneo

Equator

Mount Wilhelm
4509m

New Guinea

Bougainville
Island

Solomon Islands

Celebes

Solomon
Sea

Guadalcanal

Santa Cruz
Islands

W

Timor

Arafura
Sea

Torres Strait

Coral
Sea

VANUATU

North Fiji
Basin

Flores

Espiritu Santo

Malekula

Efate

Vani

Vit
Lev

Timor
Sea

Gulf of
Carpentaria

Arnhem
Land

Cape
York
Peninsula

Coral Sea
Islands
(to Australia)

New Caledonia
(to France)

Ashmore &
Cartier Islands
(to Australia)

Great Barrier Reef

New Caledonia

So

Fiji

INDIAN
OCEAN

AUSTRALIA

Great
Sandy
Desert

Macdonnell
Ranges

Simpson
Desert

Great Dividing Range

New Caledonia Ridge

Norfolk
Ridge

Norfolk Islan
(to Australia)

20°

Tropic of Capricorn

Gibson
Desert

Uluru
(Ayers Rock)

L. Eyre North

Grey Range

Darling

Lord Howe
Island
(to Australia)

North
Fiji Rise

North
Island

Great
Victoria
Desert

L. Torrens

Murray

Mount Kosciuszko
2228m

Lord Howe Rise

NEW
ZEALAND

Nullarbor Plain

Great Australian Bight

Kangaroo
Island

Bass
Strait

*Tasman
Sea*

South Island

Cape Leeuwin

South
Australian
Basin

Tasmania

Tasman Basin

Auckland Islands
(to New Zealand)

Sou
3744m

Antip
Is

100°

40°

120°

140°

*Tasman
Plateau*

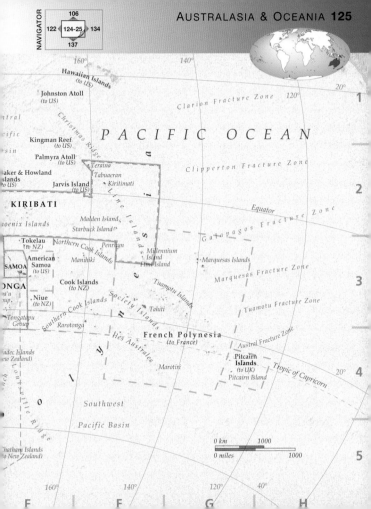

160° 140° 120° 20°

Hawaiian Islands
(to US)

1

Johnston Atoll
(to US)

Clarion Fracture Zone

PACIFIC OCEAN

Christmas Ridge

Kingman Reef
(to US)

Palmyra Atoll
(to US)

Clipperton Fracture Zone

Baker & Howell
Islands
(to US)

Teraina
Tabuaeran
Kiritimati

Jarvis Island
(to US)

2

Line Islands

KIRIBATI

Equator

Phoenix Islands

Malden Island
Starbuck Island

Galapagos Fracture Zone

Marquesas Fracture Zone

Tokelau
(to NZ)

Northern Cook Islands

Penrhyn

Manihiki

Millennium
Island
Flint Island

Marquesas Islands

SAMOA

American
Samoa
(to US)

3

TONGA

Cook Islands
(to NZ)

Niue
(to NZ)

Society Islands

Tahiti

Tuamotu Islands

Tuamotu Fracture Zone

Tongatapu
Group

Southern Cook Islands

Rarotonga

Îles Australes

French Polynesia
(to France)

Austral Fracture Zone

Kermadec Islands
(to New Zealand)

Marotiri

Pitcairn
Islands
(to UK)

Pitcairn Island

Tropic of Capricorn

20°

Southwest
Pacific Basin

Chatham Islands
(to New Zealand)

0 km   1000
0 miles   1000

5

160° 140° 120° 40°

E F F G H

The Southwest Pacific

130°   140°   150°   160°   170°

Guam ✈ HAGÅTÑA

MARSHALL ISLANDS

(US unincorporated territory)

Marianas Trench

Micronesia

Ratak Chain

Ralik Chain

Majuro

1

10°

Caroline Islands

OREOR ✈   Yap

Chuuk Is.   Pohnpei
PALIKIR ✈

PALAU

MICRONESIA

Kosrae

2

0°   Equator

◆ The Pitohui bird has a poison on its feathers and skin similar to the poison arrow tree frog, making it the only known example of a poisonous bird.

BAI
Tar

PAPUA NEW GUINEA

NAURU

Ban

INDONESIA

Bismarck Archipelago   *New Ireland*

▲ Mt Wilhelm
4509m

Madang

New Guinea

Bougainville I.

Melanesia

3

Lae

New Britain

New Georgia Islands

PORT MORESBY ✈

Solomon Sea

HONIARA ✈   Santa Cruz Is.

10°   *Arafura Sea*

Torres Strait

SOLOMON ISLANDS

4

Gulf of Carpentaria

Arnhem Land

Coral Sea

VANUATU

Banks Is

◆ Found only in the rain forest of New Guinea, Queen Alexandra's Birdwing, with a wingspan of 11 inches (280 mm), is the largest butterfly in the world.

Coral Sea Islands
(Australian external territory)

PORT-VILA ✈

20°

New Caledonia
(French overseas territory)

Îles Loyauté

5

AUSTRALIA

Great Barrier Reef

NOUMÉA

130°   140°   150°   160°   170°

A   B   C   D

180°   *170°*   *160°*   *150°*

International Date Line

P A C I F I C   O C E A N

1

10°

◈ *In 1994 the International Date Line was repositioned around Kiribati territory bringing Millennium Island 14 hours ahead of GMT, making it the first landfall for sunrise at the dawn of the new millennium.*

Kingman Reef   **Palmyra Atoll**
(administered by US)   *(administered by US)*

Teraina
Tabuaeran

Baker & Howland Is.
(administered by US)   **Jarvis I.**   *Kiritimati*
(administered by US)

L i n e   I s l a n d s

Equator   *0°*

2

Tungaru (*rt Islands*)

K I R I B A T I

Phoenix Islands

◈ *Samoa is home to the world's smallest spider, the Patu marplesi, which spans a mere 0.0017 inches (0.04mm).*

3

VALU

● **FONGAFALE** ✈

Tokelau
(NZ overseas territory)

Vostok I.   *Millennium I.*   *10°*

American Samoa   *Northern Cook Is.*
(US unincorporated territory)

Flint I.

P o   l   y   n   e   s   i   a

Wallis & Futuna
(French overseas territory)   **SAMOA**
ÁPIA ✈   ✈ **PAGO PAGO**

French Polynesia
(French overseas territory)
Îles de la Société

4

IJI

Vanua Levu

Vava'u Group

Cook Islands
(in free assoc. with NZ)

✈ **PAPEETE**

Tahiti

ity ● **SUVA** ✈
ou

Ha'apai Group

Niue
(in free assoc. with NZ)
✈ **ALOFI** *Southern Cook Is.*

TONGA

● **NUKU'ALOFA**

AVARUA ✈

International Date Line

Rarotonga

Tropic of Capricorn

0 km   500
0 miles   500

5

20°

180°   *170°*

Western Australia

◈ On Christmas Day, 1974, Cyclone Tracy devastated Darwin with winds of up to 175 mph (280km/h) resulting in 66 deaths, thousands of injuries and 95 percent of the city destroyed.

◈ One of the largest states in the world, with an area of more than 975,000 sq miles (2.5 million sq km), Western Australia covers a third of the Australian continent.

Arafura Sea

Croker Island

Melville Island

Bathurst Island

Darwin

Clarence Strait

DARWIN

Arnhem Land

Katherine

Dalj Waters

Top Springs Roadhouse

Pine Creek

Victoria River

Kununurra

Halls Creek

Tennant Creek

Tanami Desert

NORTHERN TERRITORY

Macdonnell Ranges

Timor Sea

Cape Londonderry

Wyndham

Joseph Bonaparte Gulf

Kimberley Plateau

Fitzroy Crossing

Great Sandy Desert

Lake Mackay

Bonaparte Archipelago

Heywood Islands

King Sound

Fitzroy River

Percival Lakes

Lake

Broome

WESTERN

Eighty Mile Beach

Marble Bar

INDIAN

OCEAN

Port Hedland

Dampier

Fortescue River

Onslow

Hamersley Range

Ashburton

Exmouth Gulf

Exmouth

A   B   C   D   E

INDONESIA

Bali

Pulau Lombok

Java

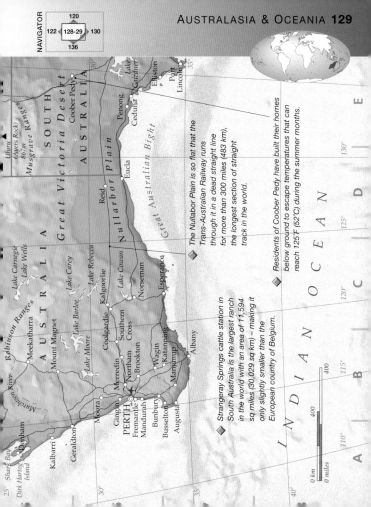

Uluru
(Ayers Rock)
867m
Musgrave Ranges

S O U T H

Coober Pedy

A U S T R A L I A

Great Victoria Desert

Penong
Ceduna

N u l l a r b o r   P l a i n

Eucla

Great Australian Bight

Reid

Elliston
Port
Lincoln

Lake
Gairdner

Kalbarri
Shark Bay
Dirk Hartog
Island

Murchison River

Northam

Robinson Ranges

Lake Carnegie
Lake Wells

A U S T R A L I A

Meekatharra
Mount Magnet

Lake Barlee

Lake Moore

Coolgardie

Southern
Cross

Lake Carey

Lake Rebecca

Kalgoorlie

Lake Cowan

Norseman

Esperance

Geraldton

Moora

Gingin
PERTH
Fremantle
Mandurah

Merredin
Northam
Brookton

Wagin
Katanning
Manjimup

Bunbury
Busselton
Augusta

Albany

I N D I A N

O C E A N

0 km   400
0 miles   400

25°

30°

35°

40°

35°

115°

120°

125°

130°

110°

A   B   C   D   E

Eastern Australia

The venom of the Sea Wasp, Marine Stinger, or Box Jellyfish can kill a person in between 30 seconds and four minutes.

Australia's Great Barrier Reef is the world's largest area of coral islands and reefs, running for about 1,240 miles (2,000 km) along the coast of Queensland.

Koalas feed only on nutrient-poor eucalypt leaves and consequently have evolved a low-energy lifestyle based around sleeping for 20 hours each day.

PAPUA NEW GUINEA

INDONESIA

Coral Sea

Coral Sea Islands
(to Australia)

Great Barrier Reef

Great Barrier Reef

Torres Strait

Cape York

Cape York Peninsula

Princess Charlotte Bay

Cooktown

Port Douglas

Cairns

Tully

Hinchinbrook Island

Townsville

Bowen

Whitsunday Group

Mackay

Charters Towers

Clermont

Emerald

Rockhampton

Barcaldine

Great Dividing Range

Mitchell River

Gilbert River

Normanton

Gregory Range

Hughenden

Winton

Longreach

QUEENSLAND

Flinders River

Burketown

Selwyn Range

Cloncurry

Mount Isa

Gulf of Carpentaria

Wellesley Islands

Groote Eylandt

Barkly Tableland

Arnhem Land

Arafura Sea

Wessel Islands

DARWIN

Pine Creek

Katherine

Daly Waters

Top Springs Roadhouse

Tennant Creek

Tanami Desert

NORTHERN TERRITORY

Alice Springs

Macdonnell Range

Tropic of Capricorn

AUSTRALIA

BRISBANE
Gold
Surfers Paradise
Coast
Murwillumbah
Dalby
Toowoomba
Grafton
Coffs Harbour
Port Macquarie
St.
George
Goondiwindi
Moree
Walgett
Armidale
Tamworth
Newcastle
Gosford
SYDNEY
Wollongong
Cunnamulla
Bourke
Nyngan
Dubbo
Parramatta
CANBERRA
AUSTRALIAN
CAPITAL TERRITORY
Cooma
Wilcannia
Ivanhoe
Cootamundra
Wagga
Wagga
Mount
Kosciuszko
2228m
South East Point
Flinders Island
Broken
Hill
Mildura
Bendigo
MELBOURNE
Traralgon
Launceston
Burnie
Marrawah
Devonport
HOBART
Lake
Callabonna
Ouyen
Horsham
Ballarat
Geelong
Warrnambool
Portland
Mount Gambier
King Island
Bass Strait
Banks Strait
TASMANIA
Marree
Lake
Blanche
Lake
Frome
Peterborough
Crystal Brook
Gawler
ADELAIDE
Lake
Eyre South
Lake
Torrens
Lake
Gairdner
Port
Augusta
Whyalla
Port
Lincoln
Kangaroo Island
Coober
Pedy
Penong
Ceduna

Tarcoola

SOUTH AUSTRALIA

Great
Victoria
Desert

N E W   S O U T H   W A L E S

V I C T O R I A

Darling River

Lachlan River

Murray River

Murrumbidgee River

Barwon River

Paroo River

Bogan River

Great   Dividing   Range

Grey   Range

Barrier Range

Flinders   Ranges

Eyre
Peninsula

Spencer Gulf

T a s m a n

S e a

Bass   Strait

◆ The Platypus lives in an aquatic
environment, suckles its young
like a mammal, lays eggs, and
has webbed feet and a bill
resembling that of a duck.

◆ Huge truck rigs known as
Road Trains, which can reach
up to 175 ft (53.5 m) in length,
carry freight across the vast
distances of the Australian interior.
They often have as many as three
trailers, weighing more than
100 tons (tonnes) in total.

0 km   400
0 miles   400

30°

40°

30°

40°

130°

140°

150°

160°

A | B | C | D | E

5

6

7

8

New Zealand

The lizardlike tuatara is found on some of the islands and rocky stacks off New Zealand. It is the sole remaining representative of the reptilian order Rhynchocephalia, which first evolved before the dinosaurs. It has a third 'eye' on the top of its head which is sensitive to light.

Ninety Mile Beach is in fact only about 60 miles long. Nevertheless, this still makes it one of the longest sandy beaches in the world.

Around AD 130 something in the order of 33 billion tons (tonnes) of pumice was ejected in a massive volcanic eruption that left a 20,000 sq mile (51,800 sq km) debris field and created an enormous caldera that subsequently became Lake Taupo.

More than 55 million sheep thrive in New Zealand's mild climate, outnumbering the human population by 15 to 1.

Tasman Sea

North Island

NEW ZEALAND

Three Kings Islands

Te Kao

Kaitaia

North Cape

Great Exhibition Bay

Kaikohe

Paihia

Whangarei

Ruawai

Warkworth

Takapuna

Auckland

Waiuku

Hamilton

Cambridge

Te Kuiti

Taumarunui

Stratford

New Plymouth

Hawera

Wanganui

Palmerston North

Woodville

Manukau

Great Barrier Island

Hauraki Gulf

Whitianga

Tauranga

Whakatane

Rotorua

Taupo

Lake Taupo

Turangi

Dannevirke

Napier

Hastings

Waipawa

Bay of Plenty

Opotiki

East Cape

Ruatoria

Tokomaru

Tolaga

Gisborne

Wairoa

Hawke Bay

North Taranaki Bight

South Taranaki Bight

Cape Farewell

WELLINGTON

Cape Palliser

South Island

Blenheim

Kaikoura

Richmond Range

Richmond Range

Pegasus Bay

Rangiora

Christchurch

Banks Peninsula

New Zealand has always been a leader in progressive social legislation. In 1893 it was the first country to grant women the right to vote.

PACIFIC

OCEAN

The royal albatross colony on Otago Peninsula is the only mainland nesting site for these birds in the world. Soaring on wings up to 9.6' (3 m) across, breeding pairs mate for life and have been known to live for over 60 years.

Seddonville

Westport

Reefton

Greymouth

Hokitika

Otira

Hurunui

Ashburton

Canterbury Bight

Timaru

Studholme

Oamaru

SOUTHERN ALPS

Fox Glacier

Mt Cook 3744m

Mayfield

Fairlie

Otago Peninsula

Dunedin

Haast

Lake Wanaka

Wanaka

Queenstown

Alexandra

Lake Wakatipu

Roxburgh

Milford

Sound

Lake Te Anau

Te Anau

Manapouri

Gore

Balclutha

The Kakapo is a nocturnal flightless parrot that lives in burrows. When in danger, its main form of defense is to remain perfectly still, which made it an easy target for predators such as the dogs, cats, rats, and ferrets that were introduced in the 19th century. Consequently it is in danger of extinction; in 1998 there were only 57 birds left in the wild.

Riverton

Invercargill

Waiau

Stewart Island

South West Cape

Foveaux Strait

Halfmoon Bay

Fiordland

Though still the highest peak in New Zealand, at 12,394 ft (3744 m), a massive rock fall in 1991 reduced the height of the mountain by 66 ft (20 m).

0 km   100
0 miles   100

42°
44°
46°
48°

166° 168° 170° 172° 174° 176° 178°

The Pacific Ocean

◆ *Challenger Deep in the Mariana Trench is 35,838 ft (10,923 m), or almost 7 miles (11 km), below the surface of the Pacific. At this depth water pressures is around 16,000 lbs/sq inch (1,127 kg/cm sq).*

Arctic Circle

Ob' Yenisey Lena Bering Strait

Aleutian Islands
Aleutian Basin
Bering Sea
Aleutian Trench
Chinook Trough

1

ASIA Gobi Vladivostok Sea of Okhotsk Kurile Islands Kurile Trench Northwest Pacific Basin Mendocino

Yellow River Osaka Tokyo
Shanghai Yellow Sea Nagoya **Japan** Midway Island
Yangtze East China Sea Northern Mariana Islands (to US) Wake Island (to US) Johnston Atoll (to US)
Hong Kong (Xianggang) Kyushu Ryukyu Islands Hawaiian Ridge

2 Tropic of Cancer Taiwan Philippine Sea Guam (to US) *Pacific Mountains* **PAC**

Manila Philippines Philippine Basin 11,034m Challenger Deep **MARSHALL ISLANDS** Central Pacific Basin Kingman Reef (to US)
South China Sea **MICRONESIA** Caroline Islands *Micronesia* Baker & Howland Is. (to US) Jarvi (to U)
Singapore Celebes PALAU Ontong Java Rise Melanesian Basin
Equator Sumatra Borneo Celebes Sea *Melanesia* **NAURU** **KIRIBATI**

3 Java Sea Banda Sea New Guinea **TUVALU** Tokelau (to NZ)
Jakarta Java Flores Timor **SOLOMON ISLANDS** Wallis & Futuna (to France) **SAMO Americ**
Timor Sea Arafura Sea Coral Sea **VANUATU** (to Australia) **FIJI** Samoa (to US)
INDIAN Great Barrier Reef New Caledonia (to France) **TONGA** C Se
Tropic of Capricorn **AUSTRALIA** Great Dividing Range Kermadec Islands (to NZ) Niue (to NZ)
OCEAN Lord Howe Rise Norfolk Island (to Australia)

4 Great Australian Bight Murray Sydney
South Australian Basin Tasman Sea North Island Chatham Islar (to NZ)
0 km 2000 Tasmania Hobart **New Zealand**
0 miles 2000 South Island Campbell Plateau International Dateline

◆ *Manua Loa on the Big Island of Hawaii rises 33,132 ft (10,098 m) from the ocean floor to it's peak 13,677 ft (4169 m) above the surface of the Pacific Ocean, and contains around 9,700 cubic miles (39,731 cu km) of rock.*

5 Pacific Antar

Antarctic Circle **ANTARCTICA**

A B C D

Anchorage

Hudson Bay

NORTH AMERICA

Rocky Mountains

Gulf of Alaska

Vancouver

Cascadia Basin

San Francisco

Arctic Circle

Labrador Sea

ATLANTIC OCEAN

◆ Pacific giant kelp can grow up to 18 inches (45 cm) a day, and may eventually reach up to 197 ft (60 m) or 34 times the height of the average man.

Zone

urray Fracture Zone

Long Beach

Molokai Fracture Zone

Hawaiian Islands
o US)

Tropic of Cancer

Gulf of Mexico

Greater Antilles

Lesser Antilles

IC OCEAN

yra
to US)

Clarion Fracture Zone

Clipperton Fracture Zone

Middle America Trench

Caribbean Sea

Panama City

imati
istmas Island)

ia

Clipperton Island
(to France)

Guatemala Basin

◆ The Pacific Equatorial Counter Current flows eastward toward South America, carrying up to 40 million tons (tonnes) of warm water with it every second.

Galapagos Fracture Zone

Gallego Rise

Galapagos Islands
(to Ecuador)

Marquesas Islands

Marquesas Fracture Zone

Tiki Basin

Bauer Basin

Galapagos Rise

Callao

SOUTH

un
ahiti

French Polynesia
(to France)

Austral Fracture Zone

Mendaña Fracture Zone

*Sala y Gomez
(to Chile)*

Isla San Ambrosio
(to Chile)

AMERICA

Tropic of Capricorn

es Australes

Îles Gambier

Pitcairn Islands
(to UK)

Easter Island
(to Chile)

Easter Fracture Zone

Isla San Félix
(to Chile)

Gulf of California

East Pacific Rise

hwest
cific
sin

Agassiz Fracture Zone

Islas Juan Fernández
(to Chile)

Valparaiso

Chile Rise

Chile Basin

Parana

Eltanin Fracture Zone

Mornington Abyssal Plain

Cape Horn

Limit of winter pack ice

Southeast Pacific Basin

Bellingshausen Plain

Drake Passage

Peter I Island
(to Norway)

Amundsen Plain

Limit of summer pack ice

Antarctic Circle

136 POLAR REGIONS
Antarctica

NAVIGATOR
134 | 136 | 122
134
48
134

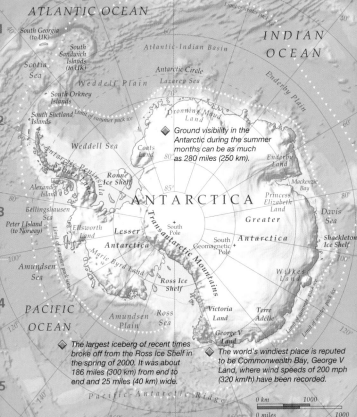

ATLANTIC OCEAN

INDIAN OCEAN

1

South Georgia (to UK)

South Sandwich Islands (to UK)

Scotia Sea

Atlantic-Indian Basin

Antarctic Circle

Lazarev Sea

Enderby Plain

Weddell Plain

South Orkney Islands

South Shetland Islands

Limit of summer pack ice

Dronning Maud Land

2

Weddell Sea

Coats Land

Enderby Land

Antarctic Peninsula

Ronne Ice Shelf

◆ Ground visibility in the Antarctic during the summer months can be as much as 280 miles (250 km).

Mackenzie Bay

Alexander Island

Bellingshausen Sea

Peter I Island (to Norway)

Ellsworth Land

ANTARCTICA

South Pole

Princess Elizabeth Land

Davis Sea

Shackleton Ice Shelf

3

Lesser Antarctica

Transantarctic Mountains

South Geomagnetic Pole

Greater Antarctica

Wilkes Land

Amundsen Sea

Marie Byrd Land

Ross Ice Shelf

Limit of summer pack ice

PACIFIC OCEAN

Amundsen Plain

Ross Sea

Victoria Land

Terre Adélie

4

George V Land

Limit of winter pack ice

◆ The largest iceberg of recent times broke off from the Ross Ice Shelf in the spring of 2000. It was about 186 miles (300 km) from end to end and 25 miles (40 km) wide.

◆ The world's windiest place is reputed to be Commonwealth Bay, George V Land, where wind speeds of 200 mph (320 km/h) have been recorded.

Pacific-Antarctic Ridge

0 km 1000
0 miles 1000

A B C D

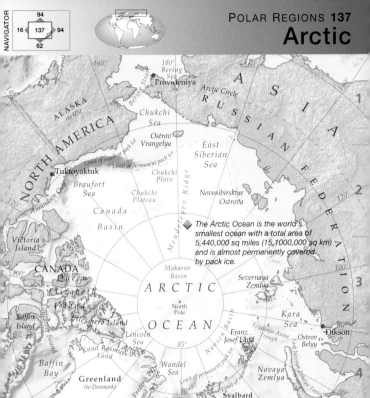

160°

180°

Bering Strait

Providéniya

Arctic Circle

A S I A

RUSSIAN

60°

1

ALASKA
(to US)

Chukchi
Sea

East
Siberian
Sea

FEDERATION

NORTH AMERICA

Ostrov
Vrangelya

Limit of summer pack ice

Limit of permanent pack ice

Tuktoyaktuk

Chukchi
Plain

Novosibirskiye
Ostrova

120°

2

Beaufort
Sea

Chukchi
Plateau

Menteleyev Ridge

◇ The Arctic Ocean is the world's
smallest ocean with a total area of
5,440,000 sq miles (15,1000,000 sq km)
and is almost permanently covered
by pack ice.

100°

Amundsen Gulf

Canada
Basin

Makarov
Basin

Severnaya
Zemlya

Victoria
Island

CANADA

Queen

ARCTIC

North
Pole

Kara
Sea

Dikson

3

Elizabeth

Lincoln

Fram Basin

OCEAN

85°

Nansen Basin

Franz
Josef Land

Ostrov
Belyy

Baffin
Island

Ellesmere Island

Knud Rasmuss
Land

Wandel
Sea

Limit of permanent pack ice

Novaya
Zemlya

East Novaya Zemlya Trough

Baffin
Bay

Greenland
(to Denmark)

Kong Frederik

Limit of summer

Svalbard
(to Norway)

60°

4

◇ The Arctic Lion's Main is the
world's largest jellyfish, 7 ft
(2.1 m) in diameter. Its main
body trails tentacles up to
180 ft (55 m) in length.

Spitsbergen

Longyearbyen

Bjørnøya
(to Norway)

Barents
Sea

Greenland
Sea

North Cape

Murmansk

0 km   500

Kola
Peninsula

Archangel

5

0 miles   500

Jan Mayen
(to Norway)

Denmark Strait

20°

Norwegian
Sea

Iceland
Plateau

North

EUROPE

40°

FINLAND

The

Country
Factfiles

Franz Josef Land
(to Russia)

Svalbard
(to Norway)

Jan Mayen
(to Norway)

Greenland
(Denmark)

NUUK

Gulf of
St. Lawrence

Labrador

Baffin
Bay

Baffin Island

Hudson

ARCTIC

North
Pole +

OCEAN

Queen Elizabeth
Islands

Bay

Lake
Superior

C A N A D A

ASIA

Great Bear
Lake

Reindeer Lake

Lake Winnipeg

Great Slave Lake

Lake Athabasca

Mackenzie

Arctic Circle

Yukon

ALASKA

R o c k y   M o u n

Rocky Mountains

Snake

PACIFIC

OCEAN

North & Central America

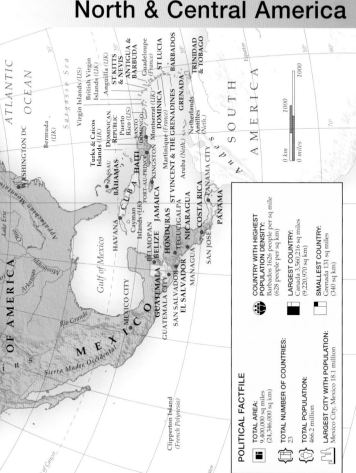

ATLANTIC OCEAN

Sargasso Sea

WASHINGTON DC

Bermuda (UK)

Virgin Islands (US)
British Virgin Islands (UK)
Anguilla (UK)
ST KITTS & NEVIS
ANTIGUA & BARBUDA
Guadeloupe (France)
ST LUCIA
BARBADOS
TRINIDAD & TOBAGO

Turks & Caicos Islands (UK)

DOMINICAN REPUBLIC
Puerto Rico (US)
SANTO DOMINGO
Montserrat (UK)
DOMINICA
Martinique (France)
ST VINCENT & THE GRENADINES
GRENADA
Netherlands Antilles (Neth.)
Aruba (Neth.)

NASSAU
BAHAMAS
HAITI
PORT-AU-PRINCE
KINGSTON

SOUTH AMERICA

Andes

Appalachian Mountains

Lake Erie
Lake Ohio

CUBA
HAVANA
Cayman Islands (UK)
JAMAICA

BELIZE
BELMOPAN
HONDURAS
TEGUCIGALPA
GUATEMALA
GUATEMALA CITY
SAN SALVADOR
EL SALVADOR
MANAGUA
NICARAGUA
SAN JOSE
COSTA RICA
PANAMA CITY
PANAMA

Gulf of Mexico

MEXICO CITY

Mississippi

Arkansas

Rio Grande

M E X I C O

Sierra Madre Occidental

Clipperton Island (French Polynesia)

Equator

Tropic of Cancer

0 km   1000
0 miles   1000

POLITICAL FACTFILE

TOTAL AREA:
9,400,000 sq miles
(24,346,000 sq km)

TOTAL NUMBER OF COUNTRIES:
23

TOTAL POPULATION:
466.2 million

LARGEST CITY WITH POPULATION:
Mexico City, Mexico 18.1 million

COUNTRY WITH HIGHEST POPULATION DENSITY:
Barbados 1626 people per sq mile
(628 people per sq km)

LARGEST COUNTRY:
Canada 3,560,216 sq miles
(9,220,970 sq km)

SMALLEST COUNTRY:
Grenada 131 sq miles
(340 sq km)

Equator

ATLANTIC OCEAN

Caribbean Sea

40°

60°

80°

20°

20°

Equator

BRASÍLIA

B R A Z I L

São Francisco
Represa de Sobradinho

Tocantins

Xingu

Araguaia

Amazon

Madeira

Amazon Basin

Río Negro

Juruá

Purus

Madre de Dios

Beni

BOLIVIA

SUCRE

LA PAZ

Lake Titicaca

P E R U

A n d e s

LIMA

Marañón

Napo

Putumayo

Caquetá

ECUADOR

QUITO

COLOMBIA

BOGOTÁ

Magdalena

Cauca

Meta

Guaviare

Orinoco

VENEZUELA

CARACAS

Guiana Highlands

GUYANA

GEORGETOWN

SURINAME

PARAMARIBO

CAYENNE

French Guiana
(France)

Isthmus of Panama

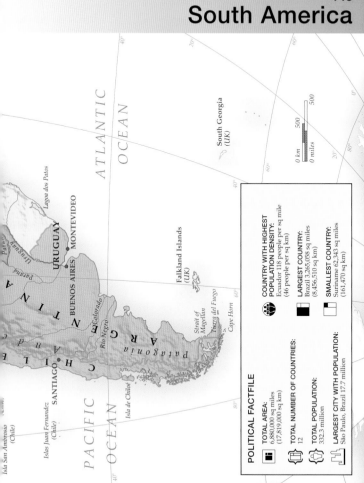

ATLANTIC

OCEAN

PACIFIC

OCEAN

South Georgia
(UK)

URUGUAY
MONTEVIDEO
BUENOS AIRES

Lagoa dos Patos

Paraná

Uruguay

Paraná

Falkland Islands
(UK)

Colorado

Río Negro

Strait of Magellan

Tierra del Fuego

Cape Horn

A R G E N T I N A

C H I L E

Patagonia

Andes

SANTIAGO

Isla de Chiloé

Islas Juan Fernández
(Chile)

Isla San Ambrosio
(Chile)

0 km   500

0 miles   500

POLITICAL FACTFILE

TOTAL AREA:
6,880,000 sq miles
(17,819,000 sq km)

TOTAL NUMBER OF COUNTRIES:
12

TOTAL POPULATION:
332.3 million

LARGEST CITY WITH POPULATION:
São Paulo, Brazil 17.7 million

COUNTRY WITH HIGHEST POPULATION DENSITY:
Ecuador 118 people per sq mile
(46 people per sq km)

LARGEST COUNTRY:
Brazil 3,265,058 sq miles
(8,456,510 sq km)

SMALLEST COUNTRY:
Suriname 62,343 sq miles
(161,470 sq km)

ATLANTIC
OCEAN

E U R O P E

Black Sea

A S I A

The Gulf

Tropic of Cancer

Arabian Peninsula

Syrian Desert

Mediterranean Sea

Red Sea

ERITREA
ASMARA

DJIBOUTI

SOMALIA

ADDIS ABABA

ETHIOPIA

Shebeli

Blue Nile

White Nile

CAIRO

Nile

KHARTOUM

SUDAN

Madeira
(Portugal)

Islas Canarias
(Spain)

Ceuta
(Spain)
Melilla
(Spain)

RABAT

MOROCCO

Atlas Mountains

ALGERIA

TUNIS
TUNISIA

TRIPOLI

Libyan
Desert

L I B Y A

EGYPT

S a h a r a

Tibesti

CHAD

NDJAMENA

CENTRAL AFRICAN
REPUBLIC

CAMEROON

LAÂYOUNE

WESTERN
SAHARA
(disputed)

Tropic of Cancer

NOUAKCHOTT

MAURITANIA

M A L I

N I G E R

NIAMEY

Niger

OUAGADOUGOU
BURKINA

NIGERIA

ABUJA

PORTO-NOVO

BENIN
TOGO
LOMÉ

GHANA

ACCRA

DAKAR

SENEGAL

BANJUL
GAMBIA

BISSAU
GUINEA-BISSAU

CONAKRY
GUINEA

BAMAKO

FREETOWN
SIERRA LEONE

MONROVIA
LIBERIA

CÔTE
D'IVOIRE
(IVORY COAST)

YAMOUSSOUKRO

ALGIERS

Senegal

ALGERIE

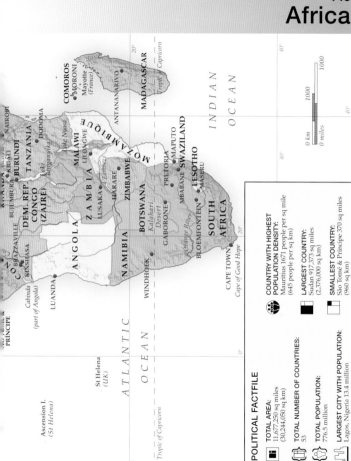

COMOROS
MORONI
Mayotte
(France)

MADAGASCAR

ANTANANARIVO

Tropic of Capricorn

INDIAN

OCEAN

RWANDA
KIGALI
BUJUMBURA
BURUNDI
NAIROBI
DODOMA
TANZANIA
Lake Nyasa
MALAWI
LILONGWE
Lake Tanganyika
DEM. REP.
CONGO
(ZAIRE)
ZAMBIA
LUSAKA
HARARE
ZIMBABWE
Zambezi
MOZAMBIQUE
MAPUTO
MBABANE SWAZILAND
PRETORIA
LESOTHO
MASERU

CONGO
BRAZZAVILLE
KINSHASA
*Cabinda
(part of Angola)*
LUANDA
ANGOLA
NAMIBIA
WINDHOEK
BOTSWANA
*Kalahari
Desert*
GABORONE
BLOEMFONTEIN
SOUTH
AFRICA
CAPE TOWN
Cape of Good Hope
Orange River

SÃO TOMÉ &
PRÍNCIPE

St Helena
(UK)

ATLANTIC

OCEAN

Tropic of Capricorn

Ascension I.
(St Helena)

0 km   1000
0 miles   1000

POLITICAL FACTFILE

TOTAL AREA:
11,677,250 sq miles
(30,244,050 sq km)

TOTAL NUMBER OF COUNTRIES:
53

TOTAL POPULATION:
776.5 million

LARGEST CITY WITH POPULATION:
Lagos, Nigeria 13.4 million

**COUNTRY WITH HIGHEST
POPULATION DENSITY:**
Mauritius 1671 people per sq mile
(645 people per sq km)

LARGEST COUNTRY:
Sudan 917,373 sq miles
(2,376,000 sq km)

SMALLEST COUNTRY:
São Tomé & Príncipe 370 sq miles
(960 sq km)

REYKJAVÍK **ICELAND**

Arctic Circle

Norwegi *Sea*

Faeroe Islands
(Denmark)

Shetland Islands

Outer
Hebrides
British
Isles

Orkney Islands

OSLO

North
Sea

**REPUBLIC
OF
IRELAND**
DUBLIN

**UNITED
KINGDOM**

DENMARK
COPENHAGEN

LONDON

AMSTERDAM

NETH.
THE
HAGUE

BERLIN

Channel Is.
(UK)

BELGIUM
BRUSSELS

GERMANY

LUXEMBOURG

PRA

PARIS
Loire

LUXEMBOURG

CZECH REP

FRANCE

LIECH. BRA
VIEN

BERN

AUST

SWITZERLAND

SLOV

LJUBLJANA

Bay of Biscay

ZAG

CROATI

ATLANTIC

Duero

MONACO

SAN MARINO

SAR
BO
&

OCEAN

PORTUGAL

Tagus

MADRID

ANDORRA

VATICAN CITY

Corsica

ROME

IT

Madeira
(Portugal)

LISBON

SPAIN

Guadalquivir

Ebro

Garonne

Rhine

Balearic Islands

Sardinia

Gibraltar
(UK)

Ceuta
(Spain)

Melilla
(Spain)

M e d i t e r r a

Sicily

Canary Islands
(Spain)

Atlas *M o u n t a i n s*

AFRICA

VALLETTA

MALT

POLITICAL FACTFILE

TOTAL AREA:
4,809,200 sq miles
(12,456,000 sq km)

TOTAL NUMBER OF COUNTRIES:
43

TOTAL POPULATION:
582.5 million

LARGEST CITY WITH POPULATION:
Paris, France 9.6 million

**COUNTRY WITH HIGHEST
POPULATION DENSITY:**
Monaco 42,503 people per sq mile
(16,410 people per sq km)

LARGEST COUNTRY:
European Russia 1,527,341 sq miles
(3,955,818 sq km)

SMALLEST COUNTRY:
Vatican City, Italy 0.17 sq miles
(0.44 sq km)

20° 40° 60° 80° 60°

NORWAY

FINLAND

Ob

Irtysh

80°

Northern Dvina

Lake Onega

R U S S I A N

Lake Ladoga

F E D E R A T I O N

HELSINKI

CKHOLM

TALLINN

ESTONIA

MOSCOW

LATVIA

RIGA

Ural

50°

THUANIA

VILNIUS

Volga

NINGRAD

MINSK

ss.Fed.)

BELARUS

Aral Sea

WARSAW

LAND

KIEV

Don

UKRAINE

Dnieper

VAKIA

MOLDOVA

APEST

Caspian Sea

NGARY

CHISINAU

ROMANIA

Caucasus

40°

LGRADE

BUCHAREST

GO.

Danube

Black Sea

A

VIA

SOFIA

BULGARIA

S

SKOPJE

TURKEY

60°

ANA

I

BANIA

A

GREECE

0 km   1000

ATHENS

0 miles   1000

Crete

Cyprus

40° 30°

ARCTIC OCEAN

Franz Josef Land

Severnaya Zemlya

Kara Sea

Laptev Sea

EUROPE

RUSSIAN FEDERATI

Ob

Yenisey

Irtysh

Lake Baikal

Black Sea

ANKARA

ASTANA

KAZAKHSTAN

TURKEY
GEORGIA
TBILISI

ULAN BATOR

MONGOL

Tropic of Cancer

CYPRUS
NICOSIA

ARMENIA
YEREVAN
AZERBAIJAN
BAKU

Aral Sea
Lake Balkhash

UZBEKISTAN

BISHKEK

BEIRUT
LEBANON
SYRIA
DAMASCUS
AMMAN

TURKMENISTAN
ASHGABAT

TASHKENT

KYRGYZSTAN

JERUSALEM
ISRAEL
JORDAN

BAGHDAD
TEHRAN

DUSHANBE
TAJIKISTAN

IRAQ
IRAN

KABUL

CHIN

KUWAIT
KUWAIT

ISLAMABAD

BAHRAIN
MANAMA

AFGHANISTAN

RIYADH
QATAR
DOHA
ABU DHABI

PAKISTAN
NEW
DELHI

NEPAL
KATHMANDU

THIMPHU
BHUTAN

Red Sea

**SAUDI
ARABIA**

U.A.E
MUSCAT

Indus

DHAKA
BANGLADESH

SANA

OMAN

Ganges

**MYANMAR
(BURMA)**

VII
HA
L

YEMEN

*Arabian
Sea*

INDIA

RANGOON

VIEN
THAI

AFRICA

*Socotra
(Yemen)*

BANGKOK
CAMB

*Bay of
Bengal*

Equator

*Laccadive
Islands
(India)*

*Andaman &
Nicobar Islands
(India)*

MALE

COLOMBO

MALDIVES

**SRI
LANKA**

KUALA LUMPUR

SINGAPO

INDIAN OCEAN

Aleutian Islands

Sea Of Okhotsk

Kurile Islands

Tropic of Cancer

POLITICAL FACTFILE

TOTAL AREA:
16,838,365 sq miles
(43,608,000 sq km)

TOTAL NUMBER OF COUNTRIES:
48

TOTAL POPULATION:
3778.6 million

LARGEST CITY WITH POPULATION:
Tokyo, Japan 26.4 million

**COUNTRY WITH HIGHEST
POPULATION DENSITY:**
Singapore 15,285 people per sq mile
(5902 people per sq km)

LARGEST COUNTRY:
Asiatic Russia 5,065,471 sq miles
(13,119,582 sq km)

SMALLEST COUNTRY:
Maldives 116 sq miles
(300 sq km)

NORTH
KOREA

JAPAN

PYONGYANG
SEOUL

TOKYO

SOUTH
KOREA

Ryukyu Islands

TAIPEI

TAIWAN

PACIFIC

OCEAN

MANILA

PHILIPPINES

Equator

BANDAR
SERI BEGAWAN

BRUNEI

ONESIA

OCEANIA

0 km   1000

0 miles   1000

DILI

Pante Makasa
(East Timor)

EAST TIMOR

Australasia & Oceania

Philippine Sea

Wake Island (to US)

Northern Mariana Islands (US)

MARSHALL ISLAND

Guam (US) ○ HAGÅTÑA

Mi

MAJU

PALIKIR

Caroline Islands

MICRONESIA

BAIR

OREOR
Babeldaob

NAURU

Melane

NAURU

PALAU

PAPUA NEW GUINEA

TUVA

FONGA

SOLOMON ISLANDS

Equator

A S I A

PORT MORESBY

HONIARA

VANUATU

PORT-VILA

Ashmore & Cartier Islands (Australia)

Coral Sea Islands (Australia)

New Caledonia (France)

NOUMÉA

INDIAN OCEAN

Great Dividing Range

AUSTRALIA

Norfolk Island (Australia)

Lake Eyre North

Darling

Lord Howe Island (Australia)

Lake Torrens
Lake Gairdner

NEW ZEALAND

Tropic of Capricorn

Murray

CANBERRA

WELLINGTO

Tasman Sea

Tasmania

Auckland Islands (New Zealand)

Australasia & Oceania

POLITICAL FACTFILE

TOTAL AREA:
3,376,700 sq miles (8,745,750 sq km)

TOTAL NUMBER OF COUNTRIES:
14

TOTAL POPULATION:
28.6 million

LARGEST CITY WITH POPULATION:
Sydney, Australia 3.7 million

COUNTRY WITH HIGHEST POPULATION DENSITY:
Nauru 1381 people per sq mile (548 people per sq km)

LARGEST COUNTRY:
Australia 2,941,282 sq miles (7,617,930 sq km)

SMALLEST COUNTRY:
Nauru 8 sq miles (21 sq km)

Johnston Atoll
(US)

er & Howland
Islands
(US)

Jarvis Island
(US)

KIRIBATI

Phoenix Islands

PACIFIC

OCEAN

Equator

Tokelau
(NZ)

SAMOA
APIA

American
Samoa
(US)

Marquesas Islands

PAGO PAGO

Cook Islands
(NZ)

PAPEETE

ONGA

Niue
(NZ)

Society Islands

UKU'ALOFA

AVARUA

French Polynesia
(France)

Îles Australes

madec Islands
ew Zealand)

Pitcairn
Islands
(UK)

Tropic of Capricorn

International Dateline

uatham Islands
(New Zealand)

0 km   1000

0 miles   1000

Key to factfile maps

FOREWORD

THIS FACTFILE is intended as a guide to a world that is continually changing as political fashions and personalities come and go. Nevertheless, all the material in these factfiles has been researched from the most up-to-date and authoritative sources to give an incisive portrait of the geographical, political, and economic characteristics that make each country so unique.

KEY TO MAP SYMBOLS

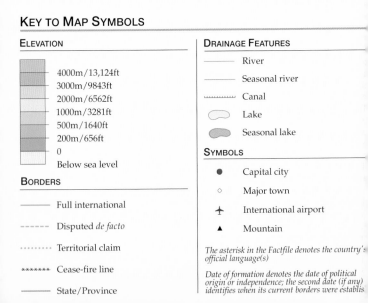

ELEVATION

4000m/13,124ft
3000m/9843ft
2000m/6562ft
1000m/3281ft
500m/1640ft
200m/656ft
0
Below sea level

BORDERS

— Full international

----- Disputed *de facto*

········· Territorial claim

×××××× Cease-fire line

— State/Province

DRAINAGE FEATURES

—— River

—— Seasonal river

·········· Canal

Lake

Seasonal lake

SYMBOLS

● Capital city

○ Major town

✈ International airport

▲ Mountain

The asterisk in the Factfile denotes the country's official language(s)

Date of formation denotes the date of political origin or independence; the second date (if any) identifies when its current borders were establis

Afghanistan

Landlocked in southwestern Asia, about three-quarters of Afghanistan is inaccessible terrain. In 1996 the *taliban*, a hard-line Muslim militia, imposed a strict Islamic regime.

GEOGRAPHY
Predominantly mountainous. Highest range is the Hindu Kush. Mountains are bordered by fertile plains. Desert plateau in the south.

CLIMATE
Harsh continental. Hot, dry summers. Cold winters with heavy snow, especially in Hindu Kush.

PEOPLE & SOCIETY
Soviet forces invaded (1979–89) to support communist government against Islamic guerrillas. Sectarian differences between Sunnis and Shi'as became acute under the *taliban* regime. The health system collapsed. Women in Afghanistan enjoy few rights, being denied health care, education, and employment. Many Afghans are nomadic sheep farmers and most live in extreme poverty. US-led anti-terrorist attacks began in 2001.

THE ECONOMY
Economy has collapsed. The largest sector, agriculture, has been damaged. Illicit opium trade is the main currency earner.

◆ **INSIGHT:** *The UN estimates that it will take 100 years to remove the ten million landmines laid in the country*

FACTFILE

OFFICIAL NAME: Islamic State of Afghanistan
DATE OF FORMATION: 1919
CAPITAL: Kábul
POPULATION: 22.7 million
TOTAL AREA: 251,772 sq miles (652,090 sq km)

DENSITY: 90 people per sq mile
LANGUAGES: Persian*, Pashtu*, other
RELIGIONS: Sunni Muslim 84%, Shi'a Muslim 15%, other 1%
ETHNIC MIX: Pashto 52%, Tajik 21%, Hazara 19%, Uzbek 5%, other 3%
GOVERNMENT: *Taliban* (not recognized)
CURRENCY: Afghani = 100 puls

Albania

Lying at the southeastern end of the Adriatic Sea, Albania held its first multiparty elections in 1991. The flood of ethnic Albanian refugees from Kosovo in 1999 strained the country severely.

GEOGRAPHY

Narrow coastal plain. Interior is mostly hills and mountains. Forest and scrub cover over 40% of the land.

CLIMATE

Mediterranean coastal climate, with warm summers and cool winters. Mountains receive heavy rains or snows in winter.

PEOPLE & SOCIETY

Last eastern European country to move toward Western economic liberalism – pace of change remains a sensitive issue. Mosques and churches have reopened in what was once the world's only officially atheist state. Greek minority in the south suffers much discrimination.

◆ **INSIGHT:** *The Albanians' name for their nation, Shqipërisë, means "Land of the Eagle"*

THE ECONOMY

Oil and gas reserves plus high growth rate have potential to offset rudimentary infrastructure and lack of foreign investment.

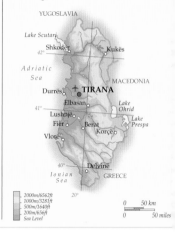

YUGOSLAVIA

Lake Scutari

Shkodër • Kukës

42°

Adriatic Sea

MACEDONIA

Durrës • ★ TIRANA

Elbasan

41° • Lushnjë *Lake Ohrid*

Fier • Berat *Lake Prespa*

Vlorë Korçë

40° Delvinë

Ionian Sea GREECE

20°

2000m/6562ft
1000m/3281ft
500m/1640ft
200m/656ft
Sea Level

0   50 km
0   50 miles

FACTFILE

OFFICIAL NAME: Republic of Albania
DATE OF FORMATION: 1913
CAPITAL: Tirana
POPULATION: 3.1 million
TOTAL AREA: 10,579 sq miles (27,400 sq km)
DENSITY: 293 people per sq mile

LANGUAGES: Albanian, Greek
RELIGIONS: Sunni Muslim 70%, Greek Orthodox 20%, Roman Catholic 10%
ETHNIC MIX: Albanian 86%, Greek 12%, other (inc. Macedonian) 2%
GOVERNMENT: Multiparty republic
CURRENCY: Lek = 100 qindars

Algeria

Africa's second largest country, Algeria achieved independence from France in 1962. Today, its military-dominated government faces a severe challenge from Islamic extremists.

GEOGRAPHY
85% of the country lies within the Sahara. Fertile coastal region with plains and hills rises in the southeast to the Atlas Mountains.

CLIMATE
Coastal areas are warm and temperate, with most rainfall during the mild winters. The south is very hot, with negligible rainfall.

PEOPLE & SOCIETY
Algerians are predominantly Arab, under 30 years of age and urban. Most indigenous Berbers consider the mountainous Kabylia region in the northeast to be their homeland. The Sahara sustains just 500,000 people, mainly oil workers and Tuareg nomads with goat and camel herds, who move between the irrigated oases. In recent years, political violence has claimed the lives of 3,000 people.

THE ECONOMY
Oil and gas exports. Political turmoil has led to exodus of skilled foreign labor. Limited agriculture.

INSIGHT: *The world's highest sand dunes are located in the deserts of east central Algeria*

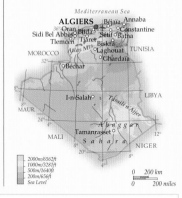

FACTFILE

OFFICIAL NAME: Democratic and Popular Republic of Algeria
DATE OF FORMATION: 1962
CAPITAL: Algiers
POPULATION: 31.5 million
TOTAL AREA: 919,590 sq miles (2,381,740 sq km)

DENSITY: 34 people per sq mile
LANGUAGES: Arabic*, Berber, French
RELIGIONS: Sunni Muslim 99%, Christian and Jewish 1%
ETHNIC MIX: Arab 75%, Berber 24%, European 1%
GOVERNMENT: Multiparty republic
CURRENCY: Dinar = 100 centimes

Andorra

A tiny landlocked principality, Andorra lies high in the eastern Pyrenees between France and Spain. It held its first full elections in 1993. Tourism is the main source of income.

GEOGRAPHY
High mountains, with six deep, glaciated valleys that drain into the River Valira as it flows into Spain.

CLIMATE
Cool, wet springs followed by dry, warm summers. Mountain snows linger until March.

PEOPLE & SOCIETY
Immigration is strictly monitored and restricted by quota to French and Spanish nationals seeking employment in Andorra. A referendum in 1993 ended 715 years of semi-feudal status but Andorran society remains conservative. Divorce is illegal.

INSIGHT: *Andorra's coprincipality status dates from the 13th century. The "princes" are the President of France and the Bishop of Urgel in Spain.*

THE ECONOMY
Tourism and duty-free sales dominate the economy. Strict banking secrecy laws and low consumer taxes promote investment and commerce. France and Spain effectively decide economic policy. Dependence on imported food and raw materials.

FACTFILE

OFFICIAL NAME: Principality of Andorra

DATE OF FORMATION: 1278

CAPITAL: Andorra la Vella

POPULATION: 66,824

TOTAL AREA: 179 sq miles (465 sq km)

DENSITY: 373 people per sq mile

LANGUAGES: Catalan, Spanish, other

RELIGIONS: Roman Catholic 94%, other 6%

ETHNIC MIX: Spanish 46%, Andorran 28%, French 8%, other 18%

GOVERNMENT: Parliamentary democracy

CURRENCY: Euro = 100 cents

Angola

Located in southwest Africa, Angola has suffered almost continuous civil war following independence from Portugal in 1975. In 1998 hopes for peace faded as fighting was renewed.

GEOGRAPHY
Most of the land is hilly and grass-covered. Desert in the south. Mountains in the center and north.

CLIMATE
Varies from temperate to tropical. Rainfall decreases north to south. Coast is cooler and dry.

PEOPLE & SOCIETY
Civil war was fought by two groups. UNITA cast itself as sole representative of the Ovimbundu, in order to attack ruling Kimbundu-dominated MPLA. In 1991–92, MPLA abandoned Marxist rule and held free elections. UNITA lost, and resumed civil war. Up to 500,000 people died as a result. Renewed fighting in 1999 after massacre of an entire village.

◆ **INSIGHT:** *Angola has some of the richest alluvial diamond deposits*

THE ECONOMY
Potentially one of Africa's richest countries, but civil war has hampered economic development. Oil and diamonds are exported.

2000m/6562ft
1000m/3281ft
500m/1640ft
200m/656ft
Sea Level

0   200 km
0   200 miles

FACTFILE

OFFICIAL NAME: Republic of Angola
DATE OF FORMATION: 1975
CAPITAL: Luanda
POPULATION: 12.9 million
TOTAL AREA: 481,351 sq miles
(1,246,700 sq km)
DENSITY: 27 people per sq mile

LANGUAGES: Portuguese, other
RELIGIONS: Roman Catholic 50%, other 30%, Protestant 20%
ETHNIC MIX: Ovimbundu 37%, Kimbundu 25%, Bakongo 13%, other 25%
GOVERNMENT: Presidential regime
CURRENCY: Kwanza = 100 lwei

Antarctica

The circumpolar continent of Antarctica is almost entirely covered by ice, some up to 1.2 miles (2 km) thick. It also contains 90% of the Earth's fresh water reserves.

GEOGRAPHY

The bulk of Antarctica's ice is contained in the Greater Antarctic Ice Sheet – a huge dome that rises steeply from the coast and flattens to a plateau in the interior.

CLIMATE

Powerful winds create a storm belt around the continent, which brings cloud, fog, and blizzards. Winter temperatures can fall to –112°F (–80°C).

PEOPLE & SOCIETY

No indigenous population. Scientists and logistical staff work at the 40 permanent, and as many as 100 temporary, research stations. A few Chilean settler families live on King George Island. Tourism is mostly by cruise ship to the Antarctic Peninsula. Tourist numbers had reached 9400 by the year 2001.

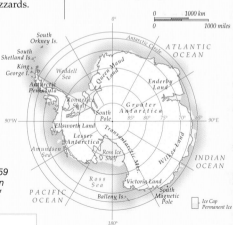

Territorial Claims:
Chilean claim
Argentinian claim
Brazilian zone of interest
British claim
Norwegian undefined limit
Australian claim
French claim
New Zealand claim

The Antarctic Treaty of 1959 holds all territorial claims in abeyance in the interest of international cooperation

0   1000 km
0   1000 miles

Antarctic Circle
ATLANTIC OCEAN
South Orkney Is.
South Shetland Is.
King George I.
Weddell Sea
Queen Maud Land
Enderby Land
Antarctic Peninsula
Ronne Ice Shelf
South Pole
Greater Antarctica
85° 80° 75° 70° 65° 90°E
90°W
Ellsworth Land
Lesser Antarctica
Transantarctic Mts.
Wilkes Land
Amundsen Sea
Ross Ice Shelf
INDIAN OCEAN
Ross Sea
Victoria Land
South Magnetic Pole
PACIFIC OCEAN
Balleny Is.
180°

Ice Cap
Permanent Ice

FACTFILE

DATE OF FORMATION: 1961
TOTAL AREA: 5,366,790 sq miles
(13,900,000 sq km)

INSIGHT: *If the ice sheets of Antarctica were to melt, the world's oceans would rise by as much as 200–210 ft (60–65 m)*

Antigua & Barbuda

A former colony of Spain, France, and Britain, Antigua and Barbuda lies at the outer edge of the Leeward Islands group in the Caribbean, and includes the uninhabited islet of Redonda.

GEOGRAPHY

Mainly low-lying limestone and coral islands with some higher volcanic areas. Antigua's coast is indented with bays and harbors.

CLIMATE

Tropical, moderated by trade winds and sea breezes. Humidity and rainfall are low for the region.

PEOPLE & SOCIETY

Population almost entirely of African origin, with small communities of Europeans and South Asians. Women's status has risen as a result of greater access to education. Wealth disparities are small and unemployment is low. Politics have been dominated for the past 30 years by the Bird family.

◆ **INSIGHT:** In 1865, Redonda was "claimed" by an eccentric Englishman as a kingdom for his son

THE ECONOMY

Tourism is the main source of revenue and the biggest provider of jobs. Fishing and sea-island cotton industries are expanding.

FACTFILE

OFFICIAL NAME: Antigua & Barbuda
DATE OF FORMATION: 1981
CAPITAL: St John's
POPULATION: 66,422
TOTAL AREA: 170 sq miles
(440 sq km)
DENSITY: 391 people per sq mile

LANGUAGES: English*, English Creole
RELIGIONS: Anglican 44.5%, other Protestant 42.2%, Roman Catholic 10.2%, Rastafarian 0.7%, other 2%
ETHNIC MIX: African 95%, other 5%
GOVERNMENT: Parliamentary democracy.
CURRENCY: E. Caribbean $ = 100 cents

Argentina

Argentina occupies most of the southern half of South America. Its politics have been characterized by periods of military rule. In 1983, however, it returned to multiparty democracy.

GEOGRAPHY

Andes in the west form a natural border with Chile. East of the Andes are heavily wooded plains (*Gran Chaco*) and treeless but fertile Pampas plains. Bleak and arid Patagonia in the south.

CLIMATE

Andes are semiarid in the north and snowy in the south. Pampas have a mild climate with summer rains.

PEOPLE & SOCIETY

People are largely of European descent; over one third are of Italian origin. Indigenous peoples are now in a minority, living mainly in Andean regions or in the *Gran Chaco*. More than 85% of Argentinians are urban dwellers, with 40% living in the capital.

◆ **INSIGHT:** *The Tango originated in the poorer quarters of Buenos Aires at the end of the 19th century*

THE ECONOMY

Rich and varied agricultural base. Important oil and gas reserves are still underexploited. Skilled labor force.

4000m/13124ft
3000m/9843ft
2000m/6562ft
1000m/3281ft
200m/656ft
Sea Level

0   400 km
0   400 mil

FACTFILE

OFFICIAL NAME: Argentine Republic
DATE OF FORMATION: 1816
CAPITAL: Buenos Aires
POPULATION: 37 million
TOTAL AREA: 1,056,636 miles (2,736,690 sq km)
DENSITY: 35 people per sq mile

LANGUAGES: Spanish*, Italian, English, German, French, Indian languages
RELIGIONS: Roman Catholic 90%, Jewish 2%, Protestant 2%, other 6%
ETHNIC MIX: European 85%, Mestizo 14%, Indian 1%
GOVERNMENT: Presidential democracy
CURRENCY: Argentine peso

Armenia

The smallest of the former USSR's republics, Armenia lies landlocked in the Lesser Caucasus Mountains. Since 1988, the confrontation with Azerbaijan has dominated national life.

GEOGRAPHY
Rugged and mountainous, with expanses of semidesert and a large lake in the east, Sevana Lich.

CLIMATE
Continental climate, with little rainfall in the lowlands. The winters are often bitterly cold.

PEOPLE & SOCIETY
There is a strong commitment to Christianity, and to Armenian culture. Minority groups are well integrated. War with Azerbaijan over the enclave of Nagorno Karabakh has meant that 100,000 Armenians living in Azerbaijan have been forced to return home to live in poverty. In 1988, 25,000 people died in an earthquake in the west.

◆ INSIGHT: *In the 4th century, Armenia became the first country to adopt Christianity as its state religion*

THE ECONOMY
Few natural resources, though lead, copper, and zinc are mined. Main agricultural products are wine, tobacco, olives, and rice. Well-developed machine-building and manufacturing – includes textiles, and bottling of mineral water.

3000m/9843ft
2000m/6562ft
1000m/3281ft
500m/1640ft

FACTFILE

OFFICIAL NAME: Republic of Armenia
DATE OF FORMATION: 1991
CAPITAL: Yerevan
POPULATION: 3.5 million
TOTAL AREA: 11,506 sq miles (29,800 sq km)
DENSITY: 304 people per sq mile

LANGUAGES: Armenian*, Azerbaijani, Russian, Kurdish
RELIGIONS: Armenian Apostolic 94%, other 6%
ETHNIC MIX: Armenian 93%, Azerbaijani 3%, Russian 2%, other 2%
GOVERNMENT: Multiparty republic
CURRENCY: Dram = 100 louma

Australia

The world's sixth-largest country. European settlement, mainly from Britain, began 200 years ago. Today, Australia's international focus has shifted away from Europe toward Asia.

GEOGRAPHY

An island continent located between the Indian and Pacific oceans. The variety of landscapes include tropical rain forests, the arid plateaus, ridges, and vast deserts of the "red center," the lowlands and river systems draining into Lake Eyre, rolling tracts of pastoral land, and magnificent beaches around much of the coastline. In the far east are the mountains of the Great Dividing Range. Famous natural features include Uluru (Ayers Rock) and the Great Barrier Reef.

CLIMATE

The interior, west, and south are arid and very hot in summer. Central desert areas can reach 120°F (50°C). The north is hot throughout the year, and humid during the summer monsoon. East, southeast, and south-west coastal areas are temperate.

PEOPLE & SOCIETY

The first settlers arrived in Australia at least 40,000 years ago. Today, Aborigines make up around 1% of the population. European settlement began in 1788, and was dominated by British and Irish immigrants, some of whom were convicts. Immigration drives after 1945 brought many Europeans to Australia. Since 1970s, 50% of immigrants have been Asian. The multicultural nature of modern Australian society is encouraged. Aborigines are the exception in an otherwise integrated society, and are marginalized both economically and socially. Wealth disparities are small. A referendum set for late 1999 on the question of replacing the British monarch with an elected president was defeated by a 55% majority. The issue of an Australian republic is still a matter for discussion.

FACTFILE

OFFICIAL NAME: Commonwealth of Australia
DATE OF FORMATION: 1901
CAPITAL: Canberra
POPULATION: 18.9 million
TOTAL AREA: 2,941,282 sq miles (7,617,930 sq km)

DENSITY: 6.4 people per sq mile
LANGUAGES: English, Greek, Italian.
RELIGIONS: Roman Catholic 26%, Anglican 24%, other 50%
ETHNIC MIX: European 95%, Asian 4% Aboriginal and other 1%
GOVERNMENT: Parliamentary democracy
CURRENCY: Australian $ = 100 cents

Australia

💲 THE ECONOMY

Efficient mining and agricultural industries. Successful tourist industry. Concentration on Asian markets during the 1990s, which grew to account for 0% of trade. Hit hard by the 1997 Asian financial crisis which tipped rapid regional growth into recession. Japan remains Australia's most important trading partner. In order to compete in Asia, the economy has been undergoing massive structural adjustment. Investment in booming Southeast Asian economies.

◆ **INSIGHT:** *Sydney has the world's largest suburban area, a conurbation so vast that the city is twice as large as Beijing and six times the size of Rome*

Austria

Bordering eight countries in the heart of Europe, Austria was created in 1918 after the collapse of the Habsburg empire. It briefly became part of Germany between 1938 and 1955.

GEOGRAPHY
Mainly mountainous. Alps and foothills cover the west and south. Lowlands in the east are part of the Danube River basin.

CLIMATE
Temperate continental climate. The western Alpine regions have colder winters and more rainfall.

PEOPLE & SOCIETY
Austrian society is homogeneous. Although all Austrians speak German, they consider themselves ethnically distinct from Germans. Minorities are few; there are a small number of Hungarians, Slovenes, and Croats, plus refugees from conflict in former Yugoslavia. Some of the population are beginning to challenge patriarchal and class-conscious social values. Austria's legislation reflects its strong environmental concerns.

THE ECONOMY
Large manufacturing base, despite lack of energy resources. The skilled labor force is key to the production of high-tech exports. Strong tourism sector. Raw materials.

INSIGHT: *Many of the world's grea composers were Austrian, including Mozart, Haydn, Schubert, and Strauss*

FACTFILE
OFFICIAL NAME: Republic of Austria
DATE OF FORMATION: 1918
CAPITAL: Vienna
POPULATION: 8.2 million
TOTAL AREA: 31,942 miles (82,730 sq km)
DENSITY: 257 people per sq mile

LANGUAGES: German*, Croatian, Slovene, Hungarian (Magyar)
RELIGIONS: Roman Catholic 78%, Protestant 5%, Muslim 2%, other (inc. Jewish) 6%, non-religious 9%
ETHNIC MIX: German 93%, other 7%
GOVERNMENT: Parliamentary democracy
CURRENCY: Euro = 100 cents

Azerbaijan

Situated on the western coast of the Caspian Sea, Azerbaijan was the first Soviet republic to declare independence in 1991. Border disputes with Armenia dominated the 1990s.

GEOGRAPHY
Caucasus Mountains in west, including Naxçıvan enclave south of Armenia. Flat, low-lying terrain on the coast of the Caspian Sea.

CLIMATE
Continental with pronounced seasonal extremes. Low rainfall, with peak months during summer.

PEOPLE & SOCIETY
Azerbaijanis now form a large majority. Thousands of Armenians, Russians, and Jews have left as a result of rising nationalism among Azerbaijanis. Racial hostility against those who remain is increasing. Influx of half a million Azerbaijani refugees fleeing war with Armenia over the disputed enclave of Nagorno Karabakh. Decline in the political status of women. Once effective social security system has collapsed.

THE ECONOMY
Oil and gas have considerable potential. War is a major drain on state resources. Market reforms attract foreign interest.

◆ **INSIGHT:** *The fire-worshipping Zoroastrian faith originated in Azerbaijan in the 6th century BC*

FACTFILE

OFFICIAL NAME: Republic of Azerbaijan
DATE OF FORMATION: 1991
CAPITAL: Baku
POPULATION: 7.7 million
TOTAL AREA: 33,436 sq miles (86,600 sq km)
DENSITY: 230 people per sq mile

LANGUAGES: Azerbaijani*, Russian, Armenian, other
RELIGIONS: Shi'aithna Muslim 61%, Sunni Muslim 26%, other 13%
ETHNIC MIX: Azeri 83%, Armenian 6%, Russian 5%, Daghestani 3%, other 3%
GOVERNMENT: Multiparty republic
CURRENCY: Manat = 100 gopik

Bahamas

Located off the Florida coast in the western Atlantic, the Bahamas comprises an archipelago of some 700 islands and 2400 cays, only 30 of which are inhabited.

GEOGRAPHY

Long, mainly flat coral formations with a few low hills. Some islands have pine forests, lagoons, and mangrove swamps.

CLIMATE

Subtropical. Hot summers, and mild winters. Heavy rainfall, especially in summer. Hurricanes can strike from July–December.

PEOPLE & SOCIETY

Over half the population live on New Providence. The tourist industry employs 40% of the work force. The remainder of the population are engaged in traditional fishing and agriculture, or in administration. Close ties with US were strained in 1980s, with senior government members implicated in narcotics corruption. In 1993, tough policies instituted to deter settling of Haitian refugees.

THE ECONOMY

Tourism accounts for half of all revenues. Major financial services sector includes banking and insurance.

INSIGHT: *Six tourists per inhabitant visit the Bahamas every year*

FACTFILE

OFFICIAL NAME: The Commonwealth of the Bahamas
DATE OF FORMATION: 1973
CAPITAL: Nassau
POPULATION: 307,000
TOTAL AREA: 3865 sq miles (10,010 sq km)

DENSITY: 79 people per sq mile
LANGUAGES: English*, English Creole
RELIGIONS: Baptist 32%, Anglican 20%, Catholic 19%, other 29%,
ETHNIC MIX: Black African 85%, other 15%
GOVERNMENT: Parliamentary democracy
CURRENCY: Bahamian $ = 100 cents

Bahrain

Bahrain is an archipelago of 33 islands between the Qatar peninsula and the Saudi Arabian mainland. Only three of the islands are inhabited. It was the first Gulf emirate to export oil.

GEOGRAPHY

All islands are low-lying. The largest, Bahrain island, is mainly sandy plains and salt marshes.

CLIMATE

Summers are hot and humid. Winters are mild. Low rainfall.

PEOPLE & SOCIETY

Largely Muslim population is divided between Shi'a majority and Sunni minority. Ruling Sunni class hold the best jobs in bureaucracy and business. Shi'ites tend to do menial work. Al-Khalifa family has ruled since 1783. Regime is autocratic and political dissent is not tolerated. Bahrain is the most liberal of the Gulf states. Women have access to education and jobs.

◆ **INSIGHT:** *The road causeway linking Bahrain Island to Saudi Arabia's eastern province was completed in 1986*

THE ECONOMY

Main exports are refined petroleum and aluminum products. As oil reserves run out, gas is of increasing importance. Bahrain is also the Arab world's major offshore banking center.

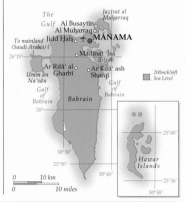

FACTFILE

OFFICIAL NAME: State of Bahrain
DATE OF FORMATION: 1971
CAPITAL: Manama
POPULATION: 617,000
TOTAL AREA: 262 sq miles (680 sq km)
DENSITY: 2354 people per sq mile

LANGUAGES: Arabic*, English, Urdu
RELIGIONS: Muslim (mainly Shi'a) 99%, other 1%
ETHNIC MIX: Bahrani 70%, Iranian, Indian, Pakistani 24%, other Arab 4%, European 2%
GOVERNMENT: Monarchy
CURRENCY: Manat = 100 gopik

Bangladesh

Bangladesh lies at the north end of the Bay of Bengal.
It seceded from Pakistan in 1971 and, after much
political instability, returned to democracy in 1991.

GEOGRAPHY

Mostly flat alluvial plains and
deltas of the Brahmaputra and Ganges
rivers. Southeast coasts are fringed
with mangrove forests.

CLIMATE

Hot and humid. During the
monsoon, water level can rise 20 feet
(six meters) above sea level, flooding
two-thirds of the country.

PEOPLE & SOCIETY

Bangladesh has suffered from
a cycle of floods, cyclones, famine,
political corruption and military
coups. Although over half of the
population still live below the
poverty line, living standards have
improved in the past decade.

INSIGHT: *Average rainfall in the
Sylhet region of NE Bangladesh is
around 13 ft (4 m) a year*

THE ECONOMY

Heavily dependent on foreign
aid. Agriculture is vulnerable to
unpredictable climate. Bangladesh
accounts for 80% of world jute fiber
exports. Expanding textile industry.

FACTFILE

OFFICIAL NAME: People's Republic of
Bangladesh
DATE OF FORMATION: 1971
CAPITAL: Dhaka
POPULATION: 129.2 million
TOTAL AREA: 51,702 sq miles
(133,910 sq km)

DENSITY: 565 people per sq mile
LANGUAGES: Bangla*, Urdu, Chakma,
Marma (Margh), other
RELIGIONS: Muslim (mainly Sunni) 87%,
Hindu 12%, other 1%
ETHNIC MIX: Bengali 98%, other 2%
GOVERNMENT: Parliamentary democracy
CURRENCY: Taka = 100 paisa

Barbados

Barbados is the most easterly of the Caribbean islands. Once solely inhabited by Arawak Indians, Barbados was first colonized by British settlers in the 1620s.

GEOGRAPHY
Encircled by coral reefs. Fertile and predominantly flat, with a few gentle hills to the north.

CLIMATE
Moderate tropical climate. Sunnier and drier than its more mountainous neighbors.

PEOPLE & SOCIETY
Some latent tension between white community, who control politics and much of the economy, and majority black population, but violence is rare. Increasing social mobility has enabled black Bajans to enter the professions. Despite political stability and good welfare and education services, emigration is high, notably to the US and UK.

◆ **INSIGHT:** *Barbados retains a strong British influence and is referred to by its neighbors as "Little England"*

THE ECONOMY
Sugar is the traditional cash crop. Well-developed tourist industry employs almost 40% of the work force. Financial services and information processing are important new growth sectors.

FACTFILE
OFFICIAL NAME: Barbados
DATE OF FORMATION: 1966
CAPITAL: Bridgetown
POPULATION: 270,000
TOTAL AREA: 169 sq miles (430 sq km)
DENSITY: 1598 people per sq mile

LANGUAGES: English*, English Creole
RELIGIONS: Anglican 40%, Pentecostal 8%, Methodist 7%, Roman Catholic 4%, other 24%, nonreligious 17%
ETHNIC MIX: Black African 90%, other 10%
GOVERNMENT: Parliamentary democracy
CURRENCY: Barbados $ = 100 cents

Belarus

Formerly known as White Russia, Belarus lies landlocked in eastern Europe. It reluctantly became independent of the USSR in 1991. There are few resources other than agriculture.

GEOGRAPHY

Mainly plains and low hills. The Dnieper and Dvina rivers drain the eastern lowlands. Vast Pripet Marshes in the southwest.

CLIMATE

Extreme continental climate. Long, sub-freezing, but mainly dry winters, and hot summers.

PEOPLE & SOCIETY

Only 2% of people are non-Slav, so ethnic tension is minimal. The entire population has a right to Belorussian citizenship, although only 11% are fluent in Belorussian. The slowest of the ex-Soviet states to implement political reform, a post-Soviet constitution was not adopted until 1994. Wealth is held by a small ex-communist elite. Fallout from 1986 Chornobil' nuclear disaster in Ukraine seriously affected Belorussians' health and environment.

THE ECONOMY

Food processing and heavy industries stagnate while politicians argue over market reforms. Low unemployment but high inflation.

INSIGHT: *The number of cancer and leukaemia cases is 10,000 above the pre-Chornobil' annual average*

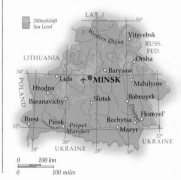

FACTFILE

OFFICIAL NAME: Republic of Belarus
DATE OF FORMATION: 1991
CAPITAL: Minsk
POPULATION: 10.2 million
TOTAL AREA: 80,154 sq miles (207,600 sq km)
DENSITY: 127 people per sq mile

LANGUAGES: Belorussian*, Russian
RELIGIONS: Russian Orthodox 60%, Roman Catholic 8%, other (including Protestant, Muslim, Jewish) 32%
ETHNIC MIX: Belorussian 78%, Russian 13%, Polish 4%, Ukranian 3%, other 2%
GOVERNMENT: Presidential regime
CURRENCY: Rouble = 100 kopeks

Belgium

Belgium lies in northwestern Europe. Its history has been marked by tensions between the majority Flemish and minority French-speaking communities since the 1830s.

GEOGRAPHY

Low-lying coastal plain covers two-thirds of the country. Land becomes hilly and forested in the southeast (Ardennes) region.

CLIMATE

Maritime climate with Gulf stream influences. Temperatures are mild, with heavy cloud cover and rain. More rainfall and weather fluctuations on coast.

PEOPLE & SOCIETY

Since 1970, Flemish-speaking regions have become more prosperous than those of the minority French-speakers (Walloons), overturning the traditional roles and increasing friction. In order to contain tensions, Belgium began to move toward federalism in 1980. Both groups now have their own governments and control most of their own affairs.

THE ECONOMY

Variety of industrial exports, including steel, glassware, cut diamonds, and textiles. Attractive location for foreign multinationals.

INSIGHT: *The Ardennes, in the southeast of the country, are famous for their forests, cuisine, and lakes. Rivers dissect the region.*

FACTFILE

OFFICIAL NAME: Kingdom of Belgium
DATE OF FORMATION: 1830
CAPITAL: Brussels
POPULATION: 10.2 million
TOTAL AREA: 12,672 sq miles (32,820 sq km)
DENSITY: 805 people per sq mile

LANGUAGES: French*, Dutch*, Flemish
RELIGIONS: Roman Catholic 88%, other (Protestant, Muslim, Jewish) 12%
ETHNIC MIX: Flemish 58%, Walloon 33%, Italian 2%, other European 6%, Moroccan 1%
GOVERNMENT: Parliamentary democracy
CURRENCY: Euro = 100 cents

Belize

Belize lies on the eastern shore of the Yucatan Peninsula. Formerly called British Honduras, Belize was the last Central American country to gain its independence, in 1981.

GEOGRAPHY
Almost half the land area is forested. Low mountains in south-east. Flat swampy coastal plains.

CLIMATE
Tropical. Very hot and humid, with May–December rainy season.

PEOPLE & SOCIETY
Spanish-speaking *mestizos* now outnumber black Creoles for the first time. Huge influx of migrants from other states in the region in the past decade. This has caused some tension. Newcomers provide manpower for agriculture, but have put pressure on social services. The Creoles have traditionally dominated society, but high levels of emigration to the US have weakened their influence.

◆ **INSIGHT:** *Belize's barrier reef is the second largest in the world*

THE ECONOMY
Agriculture, tourism and remittances from Belizeans living abroad are economic mainstays. Citrus fruit concentrates, lobsters, shrimp, and textiles are exported.

FACTFILE

OFFICIAL NAME: Belize
DATE OF FORMATION: 1981
CAPITAL: Belmopan
POPULATION: 200,000
TOTAL AREA: 8803 sq miles (22,800 sq km)
DENSITY: 23 people per sq mile

LANGUAGES: English*, English Creole, Spanish, Maya, Garifuna
RELIGIONS: Roman Catholic 62%, Anglican 12%, Methodist 6%, other 20%
ETHNIC MIX: Mestizo 44%, Creole 30%, Maya 11%, Garifuna 7%, other 8%
GOVERNMENT: Parliamentary democracy
CURRENCY: Taka = 100 paisa

Benin

Benin stretches north from the West African coast. In 1990, it became one of the pioneers of African democratization, ending 17 years of one-party Marxist-Leninist rule.

GEOGRAPHY
Long, sandy coastal region. Numerous lagoons lie just behind the shoreline. Forested plateaus inland. Mountains in the northwest.

CLIMATE
Hot and humid in the south. Two rainy seasons. Hot, dusty harmattan winds blow during the December–February dry season.

PEOPLE & SOCIETY
Around 50 ethnic groups. Fon people in the south dominate politics. Other major groups are Adja and Yoruba. In the far north, Fulani follow a nomadic lifestyle. Tension between north and south, partly reflecting Muslim–Christian divide, and partly because south is more developed. Women hold positions of power in retail trade. Substantial differences in wealth reflect strongly hierarchical society.

THE ECONOMY
Mostly subsistence farming. Cash crops include cotton, cocoa beans, and coffee. Some oil and limestone are produced. France is the main aid donor.

INSIGHT:
Benin trains many doctors, but more of them work in France than in Benin

500m/1640ft
200m/656ft
Sea Level

0   100 km
0   100 miles

FACTFILE
OFFICIAL NAME: Republic of Benin
DATE OF FORMATION: 1960
CAPITAL: Porto-Novo
POPULATION: 6.1 million
TOTAL AREA: 42,710 sq miles (110,620 sq km)
DENSITY: 143 people per sq mile

LANGUAGES: French*, Fon, Bariba, Yoruba, Adja, Houeda, Fulani
RELIGIONS: Traditional beliefs 70%, Muslim 15%, Christian 15%
ETHNIC MIX: Fon 47%, Adja 12%, Bariba 10%, other 31%
GOVERNMENT: Presidential regime
CURRENCY: CFA franc = 100 centimes

Bhutan

Perched in the eastern Himalayas between India and China lies the landlocked kingdom of Bhutan. It is largely closed to the outside world, to protect its culture and environment.

GEOGRAPHY

Low, tropical southern strip rising through fertile central valleys to high Himalayas in the north. Two-thirds of the land is forested.

CLIMATE

South is tropical, north is alpine, cold and harsh. Central valleys warmer in east than west.

PEOPLE & SOCIETY

The king is absolute monarch, head of both state and government. Most people originate from Tibet, and are devoutly Buddhist. A quarter are Hindu Nepalese, who settled in the south. Bhutan has 20 languages. In 1988, Dzongkha (a Tibetan dialect native to just 16% of the people) was made the official language and Nepali was banned. Many southerners have been deported as illegal immigrants, creating fierce ethnic tensions.

THE ECONOMY

Reliant upon aid from, and trade with, India. 80% of people farm their own plots of land and herd cattle and yaks. Development of cash crops for Asian markets.

INSIGHT: *To protect traditional Bhutanese values, television was banned in the country until 1999*

4000m/13124ft	
3000m/9843ft	
2000m/6562ft	
1000m/3281ft	
500m/1640ft	
200m/656ft	
Sea Level	

0   50 km
0   50 miles

FACTFILE

OFFICIAL NAME: Kingdom of Bhutan
DATE OF FORMATION: 1865
CAPITAL: Thimphu
POPULATION: 2.1 million
TOTAL AREA: 18,147 sq miles (47,000 sq km)
DENSITY: 116 people per sq mile

LANGUAGES: Dzongkha*, Nepali, other
RELIGIONS: Mahayana Buddhist 70%, Hindu 24%, other 6%
ETHNIC MIX: Bhute 50%, Nepalese 35%, other 15%
GOVERNMENT: Constitutional monarchy
CURRENCY: Ngultrum = 100 chetrum

Bolivia

Bolivia lies landlocked high in central South America. Mineral riches once made it the region's wealthiest state. Today, it is the poorest nation in the whole of South America.

GEOGRAPHY

A high windswept plateau, the *altiplano*, lies between two Andean mountain ranges. Semiarid grasslands to the southeast; dense tropical forests to the north.

CLIMATE

Altiplano has extreme tropical climate, with night frost in winter. North and east are hot and humid.

PEOPLE & SOCIETY

Discrimination of the indigenous majority is prevalent at most levels of society. Political process and economy remain under the control of a few wealthy families of Spanish descent. Most Bolivians are poor subsistence farmers or miners.

◆ **INSIGHT:** *La Paz is the world's highest capital city, at 13,385 feet (3631 m) above sea level*

THE ECONOMY

Gold, silver, zinc, and tin are mined. Recently discovered oil and natural gas deposits. Overseas investors remain deterred by social problems of extreme poverty, and the influence of cocaine barons.

FACTFILE

OFFICIAL NAME: Republic of Bolivia
DATE OF FORMATION: 1903
CAPITAL: La Paz (administrative);
Sucre (judicial)
POPULATION: 8.3 million
TOTAL AREA: 418,682 sq miles
(1,084,390 sq km)

DENSITY: 20 people per sq mile
LANGUAGES: Spanish*, Quechua*,
Aymará*, Tupi-Guaraní
RELIGIONS: Catholic 93%, other 7%
ETHNIC MIX: Quechua 37%, Aymara 32%,
mixed 13%, European 10%, other 8%
GOVERNMENT: Presidential democracy
CURRENCY: Boliviano = 100 centavos

Bosnia & Herzegovina

Dominating southeast Europe, Bosnia and Herzegovina was the focus of the bitter ethnic conflict which surrounded the dissolution of the former Yugoslavian regime.

GEOGRAPHY
Hills and mountains, with narrow river valleys. Lowlands in the north. Mainly deciduous forest covers about half of the total area.

CLIMATE
Continental. Hot summers and cold, often snowy winters.

PEOPLE & SOCIETY
Civil war between rival ethnic groups. Ethnic Bosnians (mainly Muslim) form the largest group, with large minorities of Serbs and Croats. Communities have been destroyed or uprooted ("ethnic cleansing") as Serbs and Croats established separate ethnic areas. The UN and NATO have been involved as peacekeepers.

◆ **INSIGHT:** *By 1995, over two million people were homeless and a further million had fled the country*

THE ECONOMY
Before 1991, Bosnia was home to five of former Yugoslavia's largest companies. It has the potential to become a thriving market economy with a strong manufacturing base.

FACTFILE

OFFICIAL NAME: The Republic of Bosnia and Herzegovina
DATE OF FORMATION: 1992
CAPITAL: Sarajevo
POPULATION: 4 million
TOTAL AREA: 19,741 sq miles (51,130 sq km)

DENSITY: 203 people per sq mile
LANGUAGES: Serbian*, Croatian*, other
RELIGIONS: Muslim 40%, Serbian Orthodox 31%, other 29%
ETHNIC MIX: Bosnian 44%, Serb 31%, Croat 17%, other 8%
GOVERNMENT: Multiparty republic
CURRENCY: Dinar = 100 para

Botswana

Once the British protectorate of Bechuanaland, Botswana lies landlocked between Namibia, Zambia, Zimbabwe and South Africa. Diamonds provide it with a prosperous economy.

GEOGRAPHY
Lies on vast plateau, high above sea level. Hills in the east. Kalahari Desert in center and southwest. Swamps and salt-pans elsewhere and in Okavango Basin.

CLIMATE
Dry and prone to drought. Summer wet season, April–October. Winters are warm, with cold nights.

PEOPLE & SOCIETY
Tswana make up 75% of the population. San, or Kalahari Bushmen, the first inhabitants, have been marginalized. 72% of people live in rural areas. Traditional forms of authority such as the village *kgotla*, or parliament, remain important.

◆ INSIGHT: *Water, Botswana's most precious resource, is honoured in the name of the currency – pula*

THE ECONOMY
Diamonds are the leading export. Also deposits of copper, nickel, coal, salt, soda ash. Beef is exported to Europe. Tourism aimed at wealthy wildlife enthusiasts.

FACTFILE

OFFICIAL NAME: Republic of Botswana
DATE OF FORMATION: 1966
CAPITAL: Gaborone
POPULATION: 1.6 million
TOTAL AREA: 218,814 sq miles (566,730 sq km)
DENSITY: 7 people per sq mile

LANGUAGES: English*, Tswana, Shona, San, Khoikhoi, Ndebele
RELIGIONS: Traditional beliefs 50%, Christian (mostly Protestant) 30%, other (inc. Muslim) 20%
ETHNIC MIX: Tswana 98%, other 2%
GOVERNMENT: Presidential democracy
CURRENCY: Pula = 100 thebe

Brazil

Covering almost half of South America, Brazil is the site of the world's largest and ecologically most important rain forest. The country has immense natural and economic resources.

GEOGRAPHY

Covering over one-third of Brazil's total land area, the rain forest grows around the massive Amazon River and its delta. Apart from the basin of the River Plate to the south, the rest of the country consists of highlands. The mountainous north is part forested and part desert. The coastal plain in the southeast has swampy areas. The Atlantic coastline is 1240 miles (2000 km) long.

CLIMATE

Brazil's share of the Amazon Basin, occupying half the country, has a model tropical, equatorial climate. Temperatures are high, with almost no seasonal variation. The Brazilian plateau has far greater ranges of temperature and rainfall. The north-east is very dry, and suffers from frequent droughts. The south has hot summers and cool winters.

PEOPLE & SOCIETY

Diverse population includes native Indians, blacks, European immigrants, and people of mixed race. Amerindians suffer prejudice from most other peoples in Brazil. Shanty towns in the cities attract poor migrants from the northeast. Urban crime, violent land disputes, and unchecked Amazonia development tarnish image as a modern nation. Catholicism and the family unit remain strong.

THE ECONOMY

Hyperinflation, poor planning, and corruption frustrate efforts to harness undoubted potential: vast mineral reserves, diverse industry and agriculture. One of the largest exporters of coffee, sugar, and orange juice.

Equato

COLOM

PER

FACTFILE

OFFICIAL NAME: Fed. Republic of Brazil
DATE OF FORMATION: 1822
CAPITAL: Brasília
POPULATION: 170 million
TOTAL AREA: 3,265,058 sq miles (8,456,510 sq km)
DENSITY: 52 people per sq mile

LANGUAGES: Portuguese*, German, Italian, English, Spanish, Polish
RELIGIONS: Roman Catholic 89%, Protestant 6%, other 5%
ETHNIC MIX: White 66%, mixed 22%, Black 12%
GOVERNMENT: Presidential democracy
CURRENCY: Real = 100 centavos

Brazil

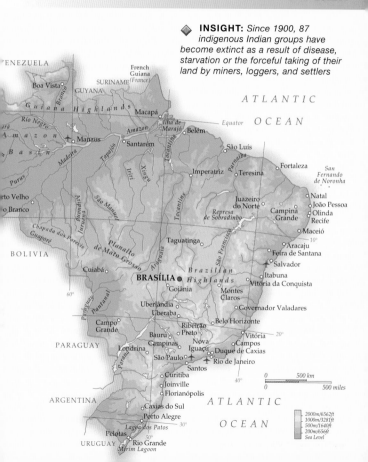

INSIGHT: Since 1900, 87 indigenous Indian groups have become extinct as a result of disease, starvation or the forceful taking of their land by miners, loggers, and settlers

VENEZUELA

Boa Vista

GUYANA

SURINAME

French Guiana *(France)*

Guiana Highlands

Rio Branco

Macapá

ATLANTIC

Rio Negro

Ilha de Marajó

Amazon

Equator

OCEAN

Amazon Basin

Manaus

Santarém

Belém

São Luís

Madeira

Tapajós

Irirí

Xingu

Tocantins

Parnaíba

Teresina

Fortaleza

San Fernando de Noronha

Imperatriz

Purus

orto Velho

o Branco

São Manuel

Juruena

Aripuanã

Juazeiro do Norte

Natal

João Pessoa

Olinda

Recife

Chapada dos Parecis

Guaporé

Planalto de Mato Grosso

Represa de Sobradinho

Campina Grande

Maceió

BOLIVIA

São Francisco

Taguatinga

Aracaju

10°

Feira de Santana

Salvador

Araguaia

Cuiabá

Brazilian Highlands

Itabuna

Vitória da Conquista

BRASÍLIA

Goiânia

Montes Claros

Paraguay

Pantanal

Uberlândia

Governador Valadares

Uberaba

Campo Grande

Belo Horizonte

Ribeirão Preto

Vitória

20°

Bauru

Campinas

Nova Iguaçu

Campos

Londrina

Paraná

São Paulo

Duque de Caxias

PARAGUAY

Santos

Rio de Janeiro

Curitiba

Joinville

0   500 km

Florianópolis

0   500 miles

40°

ARGENTINA

ATLANTIC

Caxias do Sul

Porto Alegre

Lagoa dos Patos

30°

OCEAN

Pelotas

50°

Rio Grande

2000m/6562ft
1000m/3281ft
500m/1640ft
200m/656ft
Sea Level

URUGUAY

Mirim Lagoon

Brunei

Lying on the northwestern coast of the island of Borneo, Brunei is surrounded and divided in two by the Malaysian state of Sarawak. It has been independent since 1984.

GEOGRAPHY

Mostly dense lowland rain forest and mangrove swamps, with some mountains in the southeast.

CLIMATE

Tropical. Six-month rainy season with very high humidity.

PEOPLE & SOCIETY

Malays benefit from positive discrimination. Many in Chinese community are stateless. Since a failed rebellion in 1962, Brunei has been ruled by decree of the Sultan. In 1990, "Malay Muslim Monarchy" was introduced, promoting Islamic values as state ideology. Women, less restricted than in some Muslim states, are obliged to wear headscarves but not the veil.

◆ **INSIGHT:** *The Sultan spent US $450 million building the world's largest palace at Bandar Seri Begawan*

THE ECONOMY

Oil and natural gas reserves have brought one of the world's highest standards of living. Massive overseas investments. Major consumer of high-tech hi-fi, video equipment, Western designer clothes.

FACTFILE

OFFICIAL NAME: The Sultanate of Brunei
DATE OF FORMATION: 1984
CAPITAL: Bandar Seri Begawan
POPULATION: 328,000
TOTAL AREA: 2034 sq miles (5270 sq km)

DENSITY: 161 people per sq mile
LANGUAGES: Malay, English, Chinese
RELIGIONS: Muslim 66%, Buddhist 14%, Christian 10%, other 10%
ETHNIC MIX: Malay 67%, Chinese 16%, indigenous 6%, other 11%
GOVERNMENT: Monarchy
CURRENCY: Brunei $ = 100 cents

Bulgaria

Located in southeastern Europe, Bulgaria was under communist rule from 1947 to 1989. Since then, the country has made slow progress toward political and economic stability.

GEOGRAPHY
Mountains run east–west across centre and along southern border. Danube plain in north, Thracian plain in southeast. Black Sea to the east.

CLIMATE
Warm summers and snowy winters, especially in mountains. East winds bring seasonal extremes.

PEOPLE & SOCIETY
Government has sought to assimilate separate ethnic groups, thereby suppressing cultural identities. Large exodus of Bulgarian Turks in 1989. Recent privatization program has left many Turks landless and prompted further emigration. Gypsies suffer discrimination at all levels of society. Women have equal rights in theory, but society remains patriarchal. The ruling party, consisting mainly of ex-communists, has resisted change.

THE ECONOMY
Political and technical delays hinder privatization program. Good agricultural production, including grapes for well-developed wine industry, and tobacco.

INSIGHT: *For many years, shaking the head implied "yes" in Bulgaria whilst a nod meant "no"*

FACTFILE

OFFICIAL NAME: Republic of Bulgaria
DATE OF FORMATION: 1908
CAPITAL: Sofia
POPULATION: 8.2 million
TOTAL AREA: 42,683 sq miles (110,550 sq km)
DENSITY: 192 people per sq mile

LANGUAGES: Bulgarian*, Turkish, Macedonian, Romany, Armenian
RELIGIONS: Bulgarian Orthodox 85%, Muslim 13%, other 2%
ETHNIC MIX: Bulgarian 85%, Turkish 9%, Macedonian 3%, Romany 3%
GOVERNMENT: Multiparty republic
CURRENCY: Lev = 100 stotinki

Burkina

Known as Upper Volta until 1984, the West African state of Burkina has been ruled by military dictators for most of its postindependence history. It is now a multiparty state.

GEOGRAPHY
The north of country is covered by the Sahara. The south is largely savannah. The three main rivers are the Black, White, and Red Voltas.

CLIMATE
Tropical. Dry, cool weather November–February. Erratic rain March–April, mostly in southeast.

PEOPLE & SOCIETY
No ethnic group is dominant, but the Mossi, from around Ouagadougou, have always played an important part in government. The people from the west are much more ethnically mixed. Extreme poverty has led to a strong sense of egalitarianism. The extended family is important, and reaches from villages into towns and cities. Women wield considerable influence and power within this system, but most are still denied access to education.

THE ECONOMY
Based on agriculture – cotton is most valuable cash crop – but not self-sufficient in food. Gold is the leading non-agricultural export.

INSIGHT: *Droughts and poor soils mean that many must migrate to Ghana and Côte d'Ivoire for work*

FACTFILE
OFFICIAL NAME: Burkina Faso
DATE OF FORMATION: 1960
CAPITAL: Ouagadougou
POPULATION: 11.9 million
TOTAL AREA: 105,714 sq miles (273,800 sq km)
DENSITY: 113 people per sq mile

LANGUAGES: French*, Mossi, Fulani, Tuareg, Dyula, Songhai
RELIGIONS: Traditional beliefs 55%, Muslim 35%, Roman Catholic 9%, other Christian 1%
ETHNIC MIX: Mossi 50%, other 50%
GOVERNMENT: Multiparty republic
CURRENCY: CFA franc = 100 centimes

Burundi

Small, densely populated and landlocked, Burundi lies just south of the Equator, on the Nile–Congo watershed in Central Africa. Ethnic tensions are the main factor in politics.

GEOGRAPHY

Hilly with high plateaus in center and savannah in the east. Great Rift Valley on western side.

CLIMATE

Temperate, with high humidity. Heavy and frequent rainfall, mostly October–May. Highlands have frost.

PEOPLE & SOCIETY

Burundi's postindependence history has been dominated by ethnic conflict – with repeated large-scale massacres – between majority Hutu and the Tutsi, who control the army. Over 120,000 people, mostly Hutu, have been killed since 1992. Twa pygmies are not involved in the conflict. Most people are subsistence farmers.

> **INSIGHT:** *Burundi's birth rate is one of the highest in Africa. On average women have seven children*

THE ECONOMY

Overwhelmingly agricultural economy. Small quantities of gold and tungsten. Potential of oil in Lake Tanganyika. Burundi has 5% of the world's nickel reserves.

FACTFILE

OFFICIAL NAME: Republic of Burundi
DATE OF FORMATION: 1962
CAPITAL: Bujumbura
POPULATION: 6.7 million
TOTAL AREA: 9903 sq miles (25,650 sq km)
DENSITY: 677 people per sq mile

LANGUAGES: Kirundi*, French*, Swahili, other
RELIGIONS: Roman Catholic 60%, traditional beliefs 39%, Muslim 1%
ETHNIC MIX: Hutu 85%, Tutsi 14%, Twa 1%
GOVERNMENT: Military–based regime
CURRENCY: Franc = 100 centimes

Cambodia

Located on the Indochinese Peninsula in Southeast Asia, Cambodia has emerged from two decades of civil war and invasion from Vietnam. Rice is the principal crop.

GEOGRAPHY
Mostly low-lying basin. Tônlé Sap (Great Lake) drains into the Mekong River. Forested mountains and plateau east of the Mekong.

CLIMATE
Tropical. High temperatures throughout the year. Heavy rainfall during May–October monsoon.

PEOPLE & SOCIETY
Under Pol Pot's Marxist Khmer Rouge regime between 1975 and 1979, over one million Cambodians died. Half a million more went into exile in Thailand. Effects of revolution and civil war are still felt and are reflected in the world's highest rate of orphans and widows. Free elections held under UN supervision in 1993 brought fragile stability, and the Khmer Rouge discontinued its armed struggle after the death of Pol Pot in 1998.

THE ECONOMY
Economy is still recovering from civil war. Loss of skilled workers as result of Khmer Rouge anti-bourgeois atrocities in 1970s. Modest trade in rubber and timber.

◆ **INSIGHT:** *Cambodia has many impressive temples, dating from when the country was the center of the Khmer empire*

FACTFILE

OFFICIAL NAME: Kingdom of Cambodia
DATE OF FORMATION: 1953
CAPITAL: Phnom Penh
POPULATION: 11.2 million
TOTAL AREA: 68,154 sq miles (176,520 sq km)
DENSITY: 164 people per sq mile

LANGUAGES: Khmer*, French, other
RELIGIONS: Theravada Buddhism 95%, other 5%
ETHNIC MIX: Khmer 94%, Chinese 4%, Vietnamese 1%, other 1%
GOVERNMENT: Constitutional monarchy
CURRENCY: Riel = 100 sen

Cameroon

Situated on the central West African coast, Cameroon was effectively a one-party state for 30 years. Multiparty elections were held in 1992, returning the former ruling party to power.

GEOGRAPHY

Over half the land is forested: equatorial rainforest in north, ever-green forest and wooded savannah in south. Mountains in the west.

CLIMATE

South is equatorial, with plentiful rainfall, declining inland. Far north is beset by drought.

PEOPLE & SOCIETY

Around 230 ethnic groups; no single group is dominant. Bamileke is the largest, but it has never held political power. Some tension between more affluent south and poorer north, albeit diminished by the ethnic diversity. Rivalry between majority French and minority English speakers.

◆ **INSIGHT:** *Cameroon's name derives from the Portuguese word* camarões – *after the shrimp fished by the early European explorers*

THE ECONOMY

Moderate oil reserves. Very diversified agricultural economy – timber, cocoa, coffee, rubber. Self-sufficient in food. Growing national debt owing to failure to adjust to falling oil revenues.

FACTFILE

OFFICIAL NAME: Republic of Cameroon
DATE OF FORMATION: 1961
CAPITAL: Yaoundé
POPULATION: 15.1 million
TOTAL AREA: 179,691 sq miles (465,400 sq km)
DENSITY: 84 people per sq mile

LANGUAGES: English*, French*, Fang, Bulu, Yaunde, Duala, Mbum
RELIGIONS: Catholic 35%, Traditional 25%, Muslim 22%, Protestant 18%
ETHNIC MIX: Highlanders 31%, Equatorial Bantu 19%, other 50%
GOVERNMENT: Presidential democracy
CURRENCY: CFA franc = 100 centimes

Canada

Canada extends from its long border with the US to the Arctic Ocean. The political relationship of French-speaking Québec with the rest of the country remains a key constitutional issue.

GEOGRAPHY

The world's third-largest country, stretching north to Cape Colombia on Ellesmere Island, south to Lake Erie, and across five time zones from the Pacific seaboard to Newfoundland. Arctic tundra and islands in the far north give way southward to forests, interspersed with lakes and rivers, and then the vast Canadian Shield, which covers over half the area of Canada. Rocky Mountains in west, beyond which are the Coast Mountains, islands, and fjords. Fertile lowlands in the east.

CLIMATE

Ranges from polar and sub-polar in the north, to cool in the south. Winters in the interior are colder and longer than on the coast, with temperatures well below freezing and deep snow; summers are hotter. Pacific coast has the warmest winters.

PEOPLE & SOCIETY

More than 65% of the population live along the narrow strip of land near the US border, fostering shared cultural values. Social differences, however, include wider welfare provision and Commonwealth membership. The Québécois wish to preserve their culture and language from further Anglicization, and demand to be recognized as a "distinct society." The government welcomes ethnic diversity among immigrants, promoting a policy which encourages each group to maintain its own culture. Land claims made by the indigenous peoples were settled in recent years. Nunavut, an Inuit-governed territory which covers nearly a quarter of Canada's land area, was created from a portion of the Northwest Territories in 1999. Women are well represented at most levels of business and government.

FACTFILE

OFFICIAL NAME: Canada
DATE OF FORMATION: 1867
CAPITAL: Ottawa
POPULATION: 31.1 million
TOTAL AREA: 3,560,216 sq miles (9,220,970 sq km)
DENSITY: 9 people per sq mile

LANGUAGES: English*, French*, Chinese, Italian, German, Cree, Inuktitut
RELIGIONS: Roman Catholic 47%, Protestant 41%, non-religious 12%
ETHNIC MIX: British origin 44%, French origin 25%, other 27%, Indian/Inuit 4%
GOVERNMENT: Parliamentary democracy
CURRENCY: Canadian $ = 100 cents

Canada

💲 THE ECONOMY

Wide-ranging resources, providing exports, cheap energy, and raw materials for manufactures, underpin high standard of living. At the end of the 1980s, many of Canada's welfare programs were cut back, and the defense budget was sharply reduced. Growth resumed after 1993 and strengthened toward the end of the decade. Manufactured exports have increasing competition since the mid-1980s, while prices for its primary exports fell. Better productivity and rise of high-tech industries have increased levels of unemployment.

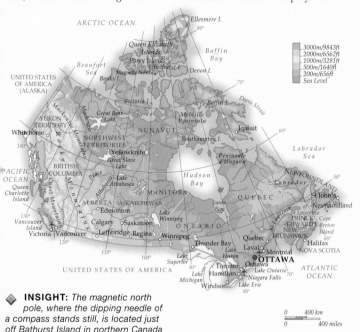

⬛	3000m/9843ft
⬛	2000m/6562ft
⬛	1000m/3281ft
⬛	500m/1640ft
⬛	200m/656ft
	Sea Level

◈ INSIGHT: *The magnetic north pole, where the dipping needle of a compass stands still, is located just off Bathurst Island in northern Canada*

0   400 km
0   400 miles

Cape Verde

Off the west coast of Africa, in the Atlantic Ocean, lies the group of islands that make up Cape Verde, a Portuguese colony until it gained independence in 1975.

GEOGRAPHY
Ten main islands and eight smaller islets, all of volcanic origin. Mostly mountainous, with steep cliffs and rocky headlands.

CLIMATE
Warm, and very dry. Subject to droughts that can sometimes last for years at a time.

PEOPLE & SOCIETY
Most people are of mixed Portuguese-African origin; the rest are largely African, descended from slaves or from more recent immigrants from the mainland. 50% of the population live on Santiago. Roman Catholicism and the extended family are strong. Some ethnic tension exists between the islands.

INSIGHT: *Poor soils and lack of surface water mean that Cape Verde needs to import 90% of its food*

THE ECONOMY
Most people are subsistence farmers. Fish is the main export. Only minerals produced are salt, and volcanic rock for cement.

2000m/6562ft
1000m/3281ft
500m/1640ft
200m/656ft
Sea Level

Santo Antão
Mindelo
São Vicente
Santa Luzia
São Nicolau
Ilhas de Barlavento
Sal
Sal Rei
Boa Vista

ATLANTIC
OCEAN

Ilhas de Sotavento
Maio
Tarrafil
Brava
São Filipe
Santiago (São Tiago)
Fogo
●PRAIA

0   50 km
0   50 miles

FACTFILE
OFFICIAL NAME: Republic of Cape Verde
DATE OF FORMATION: 1975
CAPITAL: Praia
POPULATION: 428,000
TOTAL AREA: 1556 sq miles (4030 sq km)

DENSITY: 275 people per sq mile
LANGUAGES: Portuguese*, Creole
RELIGIONS: Roman Catholic 97%, other 2%, Protestant 1%
ETHNIC MIX: Creole (Mestiç) 60%, African 30%, other 10%
GOVERNMENT: Multiparty republic
CURRENCY: Escudo = 100 centavos

Central African Republic

The Central African Republic is a landlocked country lying between the basins of the Chad and Congo rivers. Its arid north sustains less than 2% of the population.

GEOGRAPHY

Comprises a low plateau, covered by scrub or savannah. Equatorial rain forests in the south. One of Africa's great rivers, the Ubangi, forms the border with Dem. Rep. Congo (Zaire).

CLIMATE

The south is equatorial; the north is hot and dry. Rain occurs all year round, with heaviest falls between July and October.

PEOPLE & SOCIETY

Baya and Banda are largest ethnic groups, but Sango, spoken by minority river peoples in the south, is the *lingua franca*. Most political leaders since independence have come from the south. Women, as in other non-Muslim African countries, have considerable power. Large number of ethnic groups helps limit disputes.

THE ECONOMY

Dominated by subsistence farming. Exports include gold, diamonds, cotton, and timber. Country is self-sufficient in food production. Poor infrastructure.

◆ **INSIGHT:** *The country was severely depopulated in previous centuries by the impact of the Arab and European slave trades*

1000m/3281ft
500m/1640ft
200m/656ft
Sea Level

0   200 km
0   200 miles

FACTFILE

OFFICIAL NAME: Central African Republic
DATE OF FORMATION: 1960
CAPITAL: Bangui
POPULATION: 3.6 million
TOTAL AREA: 240,532 sq miles (622,980 sq km)

DENSITY: 15 people per sq mile
LANGUAGES: French*, Sango, Banda
RELIGIONS: Traditional beliefs 60%, Christian 35%, Muslim 5%
ETHNIC MIX: Baya 34%, Banda 27%, Mandjia 21%, Sara 10%, other 8%
GOVERNMENT: Multiparty republic
CURRENCY: CFA franc = 100 centimes

Chad

Landlocked in north central Africa, Chad has had a turbulent history since independence from France in 1960. Intermittent periods of civil war followed a military coup in 1975.

GEOGRAPHY

Mostly plateaux sloping west-wards to Lake Chad. Northern third is Sahara. Tibesti Mountains in north rise to 10,826 ft (3300 m).

CLIMATE

Three distinct zones: desert in north, semiarid region in center and tropics in south.

PEOPLE & SOCIETY

Half the population live in southern fifth of the country. Northern third has only 100,000 people, mainly Muslim Toubeu nomads. Political strife between Muslims in north and Christians in south. Recent attempts have been made to introduce a multi-party system, after 30 years of military and one-party rule.

◆ **INSIGHT:** *Lake Chad is slowly drying up – it is now estimated to be just 20% of the size it was in 1970*

THE ECONOMY

One of Africa's poorest states. Vast majority of people involved in subsistence agriculture, notably cotton and cattle herding. Recent discovery of large oil deposits.

3000m/9843ft
2000m/6562ft
1000m/3281ft
500m/1640ft
200m/656ft
Sea Level

LIBYA

Tibesti

Sahara

NIGER

Lake Chad
Bol
Abéché

NIGERIA
Mongo

SUDAN

NDJAMENA

Bongor
Fianga
CENTRAL
AFRICAN
REPUBLIC

Benoy
Sarh

CAMEROON
Moundou
Doba

0   200 km

0   200 miles

FACTFILE

OFFICIAL NAME: Republic of Chad
DATE OF FORMATION: 1960
CAPITAL: Ndjamena
POPULATION: 7.7 million
TOTAL AREA: 496,177 sq miles (1,259,200 sq km)
DENSITY: 16 people per sq mile

LANGUAGES: French*, Sara, Maba
RELIGIONS: Muslim 50%, Traditional beliefs 43%, Christian 7%
ETHNIC MIX: Nomads (Tuareg and Toubou) 38%, Sara 30% other 17%, Arab 15%
GOVERNMENT: Presidential democracy
CURRENCY: CFA franc = 100 centimes

Chile

Chile extends in a ribbon down the west coast of South America. It returned to elected civilian rule in 1989 after a referendum rejected its military dictator, General Pinochet.

GEOGRAPHY
Pampas (broad grassy plains) between coastal uplands and Andes. Atacama Desert in north. Deep sea channels, lakes and fjords in south.

CLIMATE
Arid in the north. Hot, dry summers and mild winters in the centre. Higher Andean peaks have glaciers and year-round snow. Very wet and stormy in the south.

PEOPLE & SOCIETY
Most people are of European stock, and are highly urbanized. Indigenous Indians live exclusively in south. Poor housing and pollution are problems in Santiago. General Pinochet's dictatorship was brutally repressive, but the business and middle classes prospered. Growth has continued under civilian rule, but many Chileans live in poverty.

THE ECONOMY
World's biggest copper producer. Growth in foreign investment due to political stability. Exports include wine, fishmeal, fruits, and salmon.

4000m/13124ft	
3000m/9843ft	
2000m/6562ft	
1000m/3281ft	
Sea Level	

```
PERU
BOLIVIA
Arica
Iquique
Antofagasta
PACIFIC
OCEAN
Viña del Mar
Valparaíso    SANTIAGO
Rancagua
Talcahuano    Talca
Concepción    Chillán
              Temuco
Valdivia
Puerto Montt
Isla de Chiloé
              ARGENTINA
Punta Arenas
Strait of Magellan
Cape Horn

72°  68°  20°
28°
32°
76°  40°
44°
48°
68°  52°
56°
```

0   300 km
0   300 miles

◆ **INSIGHT:** Chile's Atacama Desert is the driest place on Earth

FACTFILE
OFFICIAL NAME: Republic of Chile
DATE OF FORMATION: 1818
CAPITAL: Santiago
POPULATION: 15.2 million
TOTAL AREA: 289,112 sq miles (748,800 sq km)
DENSITY: 52.5 people per sq mile

LANGUAGES: Spanish*, Indian languages
RELIGIONS: Roman Catholic 80%, other and non-religious 20%
ETHNIC MIX: Mixed and European 90%, Indian 10%
GOVERNMENT: Presidential democracy
CURRENCY: Peso = 100 centavos

China

Covering a vast area of eastern Asia, China is bordered by 14 countries. From the founding of Communist China in 1949, until his death in 1976, Mao Zedong dominated the nation.

GEOGRAPHY

A land of huge physical diversity, China has a long Pacific coastline to the east. Two-thirds of China is uplands. The southwestern mountains include Tibet, the world's highest plateau; in the northwest, the Tien Shan Mountains separate the arid Tarim and Dzungarian basins. The rolling hills and plains of the low-lying east are home to two-thirds of the population.

CLIMATE

China is divided into two main climatic regions. The north and west are semiarid or arid, with extreme temperature variations. The south and east are warmer and more humid, with year-round rainfall. Winter temperatures vary with latitude, but are warmest on the subtropical southeast coast. Summer temperatures are more uniform, rising above 70°F (21°C).

PEOPLE & SOCIETY

Most people are Han Chinese. The rest of the population belong to one of 55 minority nationalities, or recognized ethnic groups. Many of these groups have a disproportionate political significance as they live in strategic border areas. A policy of re-settling Han Chinese in remote regions is deeply resented and has led to uprisings in Xinjiang and Tibet. The government has relaxed the one-child family policy for minorities after some small groups were brought close to extinction. Han Chinese still face controls. Chinese society is patriarchal in practice, and generations tend to live together. However, economic change is breaking down the social controls of the Mao era. Divorce and unemployment are rising; materialism has replaced the puritanism of the past. A resurgence of religious belief has occurred in recent years.

FACTFILE

OFFICIAL NAME: People's Republic of China

DATE OF FORMATION: 1912

CAPITAL: Beijing

POPULATION: 1.28 billion

TOTAL AREA: 3,600,927 sq miles (9,326,410 sq km)

DENSITY: 355 people per sq mile

LANGUAGES: Mandarin*, other

RELIGIONS: Non-religious 59%, other 33%, Buddhist 6%, Muslim 2%

ETHNIC MIX: Han 93%, other 5%, Zhaung 1%, Hui 1%

GOVERNMENT: One-party state

CURRENCY: Yuan = 10 jiao = 100 fen

THE ECONOMY

China has been moving rapidly toward a market-oriented economy since the 1980s. Growth has had to be curbed on several occasions to control inflation. There are vast mineral reserves, and the industrial sector faces increasingly diversification. Rising unemployment has led to migration to the cities. An abundance of resources is unevenly distributed, and the transportation system is poor. Privatization of the debt-ridden state sector is a major task. China is self-sufficient in food; irrigation helps farmers to feed 20% of the world's population using only 7% of its farmland. Since 1997 Hong Kong has been the major financial center.

INSIGHT: *China has the world's oldest continuous civilization. Its recorded history began 4000 years ago, with the Shang dynasty*

4000m/13124ft	
3000m/9843ft	
2000m/6562ft	
1000m/3281ft	
500m/1640ft	
200m/656ft	
Sea Level	

0   400 km
0   400 miles

Colombia

Lying in northwest South America, Colombia has coastlines on both the Caribbean and the Pacific. It is primarily noted for its coffee, emeralds, gold, and narcotics-trafficking.

GEOGRAPHY
The densely forested and almost uninhabited east is separated from the western coastal plains by the Andes, which divide into three ranges (*cordilleras*) with intervening valleys.

CLIMATE
Coastal plains are hot and wet. The highlands are much cooler. The equatorial east has two wet seasons.

PEOPLE & SOCIETY
Most Colombians are of mixed blood. Native Indians are concentrated in the southwest and Amazonia. Recent constitutional reform has given them a greater political voice. The government began peace talks with right-wing rebels for the first time in 6 years in 1999.

◆ **INSIGHT:** *Colombia is the world's leading producer of emeralds*

THE ECONOMY
Healthy and diversified export sector – especially coffee and coal. Considerable growth potential, but drugs-related violence and corruption deter foreign investors.

▨	3000m/9843ft
▨	2000m/6562ft
▨	1000m/3281ft
▨	500m/1640ft
	Sea Level

0   200 km
0   200 miles

FACTFILE

OFFICIAL NAME: Republic of Colombia
DATE OF FORMATION: 1819
CAPITAL: Bogotá
POPULATION: 42.3 million
TOTAL AREA: 401,042 sq miles (1,038,700 sq km)
DENSITY: 105.5 people per sq mile

LANGUAGES: Spanish*, Indian languages, English Creole
RELIGIONS: Catholic 95%, other 5%
ETHNIC MIX: Mestizo 58%, White 20%, European-African 14%, Black African 4%, Black Amerindian 3%, other 1%
GOVERNMENT: Presidential democracy
CURRENCY: Peso = 100 centavos

Comoros

Off the east African coast, between Mozambique and
Madagascar, lies the archipelago republic of the Comoros,
comprising three main islands and a number of smaller islets.

GEOGRAPHY
Main islands are of volcanic
origin and are heavily forested.
The remainder are coral atolls.

CLIMATE
Hot and humid all year round,
especially on the coasts. November to
May is hottest and wettest period.

PEOPLE & SOCIETY
The Comoros have absorbed a
diversity of people over the years,
including Africans, Arabs, Polynesians,
and Persians. There have also been
Portuguese, Dutch, French, and Indian
immigrants. Ethnic tension is rarely
a problem. Wealth is concentrated
among political and business elite.
Schools are equipped to teach only
basic literacy, hygiene, and agricultural
skills. The country is politically
unstable – frequent coup attempts
have been made during 1990s.

THE ECONOMY
One of the world's poorest
countries. 80% of people are farmers.
Vanilla and cloves are main cash
crops. Lack of basic infrastructure.

INSIGHT: *The Comoros is the
world's largest producer of ylang-
ylang – an extract from trees used
in manufacturing perfumes*

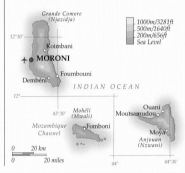

FACTFILE

OFFICIAL NAME: Federal Islamic
Republic of the Comoros
DATE OF FORMATION: 1975
CAPITAL: Moroni
POPULATION: 694,000
TOTAL AREA: 861 sq miles
(2230 sq km)

DENSITY: 806 people per sq mile
LANGUAGES: Arabic*, French*, Comoran
RELIGIONS: Muslim (mainly Sunni) 98%,
Roman Catholic 1%, other 1%
ETHNIC MIX: Comorian 97%,
Makua 2%, other (inc. French) 1%
GOVERNMENT: Military-based regime
CURRENCY: Franc = 100 centimes

Congo

Astride the Equator in west central Africa, this former French colony emerged from 20 years of Marxist-Leninist rule in 1990. Democracy has since been overtaken by feuds and violence.

GEOGRAPHY
Mostly forest- or savannah-covered plateaus, drained by the Ubangi and Congo river systems. Narrow coastal plain is lined with sand dunes and lagoons.

CLIMATE
Hot, tropical. Temperatures rarely fall below 86°F (30°C). Two wet and two dry seasons. Rainfall is heaviest south of the Equator.

PEOPLE & SOCIETY
One of the most tribally conscious nations in Africa. Four main ethnic groups: Bakongo, Sangha, Teke, and Mboshi. Main tensions between Bakongo in the north and Mboshi in the south. Middle class is sustained by oil wealth. Schools are run according to the French system and are still subject to inspection from Paris. Multiparty elections held in 1992.

THE ECONOMY
Oil is main source of revenue. Cash crops include sugar, coffee, cocoa, and palm oil. Substantial industrial base. Large foreign debt.

◆ **INSIGHT:** *In 1970, Congo became the first African country to declare itself a communist state*

FACTFILE
OFFICIAL NAME: The Republic of the Congo
DATE OF FORMATION: 1960
CAPITAL: Brazzaville
POPULATION: 2.9 million
TOTAL AREA: 131,853 sq miles (341,500 sq km)

DENSITY: 22 people per sq mile
LANGUAGES: French*, Kongo, other
RELIGIONS: Traditional 50%, Catholic 25%, Protestant 23%, Muslim 2%
ETHNIC MIX: Bakongo 48%, Sangha 20%, Teke 17%, Mboshi 12%, other 3%
GOVERNMENT: Military-based regime
CURRENCY: CFA franc = 100 centimes

Congo, Dem. Rep. (Zaire)

Straddling the Equator in central Africa, the Democratic Republic of the Congo is one of Africa's largest countries. It achieved independence from Belgium in 1960. Named Zaire between 1971-98.

GEOGRAPHY

Rain forested basin of River Congo occupies 60% of the land area. High mountain ranges and lakes stretch down the eastern border.

CLIMATE

Tropical and humid. Distinct wet and dry seasons south of the Equator. The north is mainly wet.

PEOPLE & SOCIETY

12 main ethnic groups and around 190 smaller ones. The original inhabitants, Forest Pygmies, are now a marginalized group. Ethnic tensions contained until 1990, when outbreaks of ethnic violence led to civil war. Cease-fire agreed upon in 1999.

◆ **INSIGHT:** *The tropical rain forests of Dem. Rep. Congo comprise almost 6% of the world's, and 50% of Africa's, remaining woodlands*

THE ECONOMY

25 years of mismanagement have brought economy near to collapse. Hyperinflation. Minerals, including copper and diamonds, provide 85% of export earnings.

▨ 2000m/6562ft
▨ 1000m/3281ft
▨ 500m/1640ft
▨ 200m/656ft
▨ Sea Level

0   200 km
0   200 miles

FACTFILE

OFFICIAL NAME: Democratic Republic of the Congo
DATE OF FORMATION: 1960
CAPITAL: Kinshasa
POPULATION: 51.7 million
TOTAL AREA: 875,520 sq miles (2,267,600 sq km)

DENSITY: 59 people per sq mile
LANGUAGES: French*, Kiswahili, Tshiluba, Kikongo, Lingala
RELIGION: Traditional 50%, Christian 50%
ETHNIC MIX: Bantu and Hamitic 45%, other 55%
GOVERNMENT: Military-based regime
CURRENCY: Congolese Franc

Costa Rica

Costa Rica is the most stable country in Central America. Its neutrality in foreign affairs is long-standing, but it has strong ties with the US. The national army was abolished in 1949.

GEOGRAPHY

Coastal plains of swamp and savannah rise to a fertile central plateau, which leads to a mountain range with active volcanic peaks.

CLIMATE

Hot and humid in coastal regions. Temperate central uplands. High annual rainfall.

PEOPLE & SOCIETY

Population has a mixture of Spanish, African, and native Indian ancestry. Costa Rica's long democratic tradition, developed public health system and high literacy rates are unrivaled in the region. Plantation-owning families and the US are influential in politics.

◆ **INSIGHT:** *Costa Rica's constitution is the only one in the world to forbid national armies*

THE ECONOMY

Traditionally agricultural, but mining and manufacturing are developing rapidly. Bananas, beef, and coffee are the leading exports. Tourist numbers have increased considerably in recent years.

3000m/9843ft	
2000m/6562ft	
1000m/3281ft	
500m/1640ft	
200m/656ft	
Sea Level	

FACTFILE

OFFICIAL NAME: Republic of Costa Rica

DATE OF FORMATION: 1821

CAPITAL: San José

POPULATION: 4 million

TOTAL AREA: 19,714 miles (51,060 sq km)

DENSITY: 203 people per sq km

LANGUAGES: Spanish*, English Creole, Bribri, Cabecar

RELIGIONS: Roman Catholic 76%, other (inc. Protestant) 24%

ETHNIC MIX: Mestizo and European 96%, Black 2%, Indian 1% Chinese 1%

GOVERNMENT: Presidential democracy

CURRENCY: Colón = 100 centimos

Côte d'Ivoire (Ivory Coast)

One of the larger nations along the coast of West Africa, the Côte d'Ivoire remains under the influence of its former colonial ruler, France, from which it gained independence in 1960.

GEOGRAPHY

Sandy coastal strip backed by a largely rain forested interior, and a savannah plateau in the north.

CLIMATE

High temperatures all year round. South has two wet seasons; north has one, with lower rainfall.

PEOPLE & SOCIETY

More than 60 ethnic groups. President Houphouët-Boigny, who ruled from independence until 1993, promoted his own group, the Baoule. Succession of Konan Bedic, another Baoule, has annoyed other tribes. The extended family keeps laborers who migrate to the cities in contact with their native villages.

◆ **INSIGHT:** *The Basilica of Our Lady of the Peace in Yamoussoukro is the second largest church in the world.*

THE ECONOMY

Cash crops include cocoa, coffee, palm oil, bananas, and rubber. Teak, mahogany and ebony in rain forests. Offshore oil and gas reserves.

1000m/3281ft
500m/1640ft
200m/656ft
Sea Level

0   100 km
0   100 miles

FACTFILE

OFFICIAL NAME: Republic of Côte d'Ivoire
DATE OF FORMATION: 1960
CAPITAL: Yamoussoukro
POPULATION: 14.8 million
TOTAL AREA: 122,780 sq miles (318,000 sq km)

DENSITY: 121 people per sq mile
LANGUAGES: French*, Akran, other
RELIGIONS: Traditional beliefs 63%, Muslim 25%, Christian 12%
ETHNIC MIX: Baoule 23%, Bété 18%, Senufo 15%, other 44%
GOVERNMENT: Multiparty republic
CURRENCY: CFA franc = 100 centimes

Croatia

A former Yugoslav republic, incorporating the historic regions of Istra, Dalmatia, and Slavonia. Postindependence fighting thwarted plans to capitalize on its location along the Adriatic.

GEOGRAPHY

Rocky, mountainous Adriatic coastline is dotted with islands. Interior is a mixture of wooded mountains and broad valleys.

CLIMATE

The interior has a temperate continental climate. Mediterranean climate along the Adriatic coast.

PEOPLE & SOCIETY

Turbulence was triggered by long-held ethnic hostilities. Open warfare between Croats and Serbs began in 1990. Some areas with local Serb majorities, such as Eastern Slavonia, achieved de facto autonomy, after fierce fighting in 1992. Destruction was widespread; thousands of people were made homeless.

◆ **INSIGHT:** *The Croatian language uses the Roman alphabet, while Serbian employs Cyrillic (Russian) script*

THE ECONOMY

Economy was severely strained by fighting and influx of refugees. Potential for renewed success in manufacturing, tourism. Exports to the West have grown, despite conflict.

FACTFILE

OFFICIAL NAME: Republic of Croatia

DATE OF FORMATION: 1991

CAPITAL: Zagreb

POPULATION: 4.5 million

TOTAL AREA: 21,829 sq miles (56,538 sq km)

DENSITY: 206 people per sq mile

LANGUAGES: Croatian*, Serbian*

RELIGIONS: Roman Catholic 76%, Orthodox Catholic 11%, Muslim 1%, other 12%

ETHNIC MIX: Croat 78%, Serb 12%, Yugoslav 2%, Muslim 1%, other 7%

GOVERNMENT: Parliamentary democracy

CURRENCY: Kuna = 100 para

Cuba

A former Spanish colony, Cuba is the largest island in the Caribbean and the only Communist country in the Americas. It has been led by Fidel Castro since 1959.

GEOGRAPHY

Mostly fertile plains and basins. Three mountainous areas. Forests of pine and mahogany cover one quarter of the country.

CLIMATE

Subtropical. Hot all year round, and very hot in summer. Heaviest rainfall in the mountains. Hurricanes can strike in the fall.

PEOPLE & SOCIETY

Castro's regime has reduced once extreme wealth disparities, given education a high priority and established an efficient health service. Political dissent, however, is not tolerated. A dramatic fall in living standards since the late 1980s has led 30,000 Cubans to flee by boat to the US, to seek asylum. About 70% of Cubans are of Spanish descent, and ethnic tension is minimal.

THE ECONOMY

Main product is sugar. Cuba's economy is in crisis following the loss of its patron and supplier, the former USSR. Recent reforms have allowed small-scale enterprise and use of US dollar. The 30-year-old US trade embargo continues.

INSIGHT: *Most modern cars in Cuba are imported, along with computers, in exchange for sugar in a special trading deal with Japan*

FACTFILE

OFFICIAL NAME: Republic of Cuba
DATE OF FORMATION: 1902
CAPITAL: Havana
POPULATION: 11.2 million
TOTAL AREA: 42,803 sq miles (110,860 sq km)
DENSITY: 262 people per sq mile

LANGUAGES: Spanish*, English, French, Chinese
RELIGIONS: Non-religious 49%, Roman Catholic 40%, Atheist 6%, other 5%
ETHNIC MIX: White 66%, European-African 22%, Black 12%
GOVERNMENT: One-party state
CURRENCY: Peso = 100 centavos

Cyprus

Cyprus lies south of Turkey in the eastern Mediterranean. Since 1974, it has been partitioned between the Turkish-occupied north and the Greek south.

GEOGRAPHY

Mountains in the center-west give way to a fertile plain in the east, flanked by hills to the northeast.

CLIMATE

Mediterranean. Summers are hot and dry. Winters are mild, with snow in the mountains.

PEOPLE & SOCIETY

Majority of the population is Greek Christian. Since the 16th century, a minority community of Turkish Muslims has lived in the north of the island. In 1974 Turkish troops occupied the north, which was proclaimed the Turkish Republic of Northern Cyprus, but is recognized only by Turkey. Wage levels are on average three times higher in the south, where the tourist industry is booming. Unemployment levels in the north, meanwhile, are rising.

THE ECONOMY

In the south, tourism is the key industry. Shipping and light manufacturing also important. In the north, the main exports are citrus fruits and live animals.

◆ **INSIGHT:** *The buffer zone dividing Cyprus is manned by UN forces, at an estimated cost of $100m a year*

FACTFILE

OFFICIAL NAME: Republic of Cyprus
DATE OF FORMATION: 1974
CAPITAL: Nicosia
POPULATION: 786,000
TOTAL AREA: 3567 sq miles (9,240 sq km)
DENSITY: 220 people per sq mile

LANGUAGES: Greek*, Turkish, other
RELIGIONS: Greek Orthodox 73%, Muslim 23%, other 4%
ETHNIC MIX: Greek 77%, Turkish 18%, other 5%
GOVERNMENT: Presidential democracy
CURRENCY: Cypriot £/Turkish lira

Czech Republic

Once part of Czechoslovakia in Central Europe, the Czech Republic became independent in 1993, after peacefully dissolving its federal union with Slovakia.

GEOGRAPHY
Landlocked in Eastern Europe. Bohemia, the western territory, is a plateau surrounded by mountains. Moravia, in the east, is characterized by hills and lowlands.

CLIMATE
Cool, sometimes cold winters, and warm summer months, which bring most of the annual rainfall.

PEOPLE & SOCIETY
Secular and urban society, with high divorce rates. Czechs make up the vast majority of the population, while the next largest group is of Moravians. The 300,000 Slovaks left after partition are now permitted dual citizenship. Ethnic tensions are few, but there is some hostility towards Romanian immigrants. A new commercial elite is emerging alongside ex-communist entrepreneurs.

THE ECONOMY
Traditional heavy industries (machinery, iron, car-making) have been successfully privatized. Large tourism revenues. Skilled labor force. Rising unemployment.

◆ **INSIGHT:** *Over 15 million tourists, mainly from Europe and the US, visit Prague each year*

1000m/3281ft
500m/1640ft
200m/656ft
Sea Level

0   50 km
0   50 miles

FACTFILE

OFFICIAL NAME: Czech Republic
DATE OF FORMATION: 1993
CAPITAL: Prague
POPULATION: 10.2 million
TOTAL AREA: 30,449 sq miles (78,864 sq km)
DENSITY: 335 people per sq mile

LANGUAGES: Czech*, Slovak, Romany, other
RELIGIONS: Catholic 39%, Atheist 38%, Protestant 3%, Hussites 2%, other 18%
ETHNIC MIX: Czech 81%, Moravian 13%, Slovak 6%
GOVERNMENT: Parliamentary democracy
CURRENCY: Koruna = 100 halura

Denmark

Denmark occupies the Jutland peninsula and over 400 islands in southern Scandinavia. Greenland and the Faeroe Islands are self-governing associated territories.

GEOGRAPHY

Fertile farmland covers two-thirds of the terrain, which is among the flattest in the world. About 100 islands are inhabited.

CLIMATE

Damp, temperate climate with mild summers and cold, wet winters. Rainfall is moderate.

PEOPLE & SOCIETY

Prosperous population maintains traditions of tolerance and welfare provision. High rates of divorce and cohabiting mean that almost 40% of children are brought up by unmarried couples or single parents. Over 75% of women now work in part-time or full-time jobs. Denmark provides the best state child support in Europe.

◆ **INSIGHT:** *Denmark is Europe's oldest kingdom – the monarchy dates back to the 10th century*

THE ECONOMY

Few natural resources but a diverse manufacturing base. The skilled work force is a key to high-tech industrial success. Bacon, ham, and dairy products are exported.

FACTFILE

OFFICIAL NAME: Kingdom of Denmark
DATE OF FORMATION: 960
CAPITAL: Copenhagen (København)
POPULATION: 5.3 million
TOTAL AREA: 16,359 sq miles (42,370 sq km)
DENSITY: 324 people per sq mile

LANGUAGES: Danish*, other
RELIGIONS: Evangelical Lutheran 89%, Roman Catholic 1%, other 10%
ETHNIC MIX: Danish 96%, Faeroese and Inuit 1%, other (inc. Scandanavian) 3%
GOVERNMENT: Parliamentary democracy
CURRENCY: Krone = 100 øre

Djibouti

A city state with a desert hinterland, Djibouti lies in northeast Africa on a strait linking the Red Sea and the Indian Ocean. Once known as French Somaliland, it became independent in 1977.

GEOGRAPHY

Mainly low-lying desert and semidesert, with a volcanic mountain range in the north.

CLIMATE

Hot all year round, with June–August temperatures reaching 109°F (45°C). Very low rainfall.

PEOPLE & SOCIETY

Dominant ethnic groups are the Issas in the south, and the nomadic Afars in the north. Tensions between them developed into a guerrilla war in 1991. Smaller tribal groups make up the rest of the population, together with French and other European expatriates, and Arabs. Population was swelled by 20,000 Somali refugees in 1992. France exerts considerable influence in Djibouti, supporting it financially and maintaining a naval base and a military garrison.

THE ECONOMY

Djibouti's major asset is its port in a key Red Sea location.

INSIGHT: *Chewing the leaves of the mildly narcotic Qat shrub is an age-old social ritual in Djibouti*

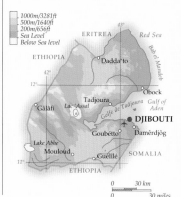

FACTFILE

OFFICIAL NAME: Republic of Djibouti
DATE OF FORMATION: 1977
CAPITAL: Djibouti
POPULATION: 638,000
TOTAL AREA: 8949 sq miles (23,180 sq km)
DENSITY: 71 people per sq mile

LANGUAGES: Arabic*, French*, Somali, Afar, other
RELIGIONS: Muslim (mainly Sunni) 94%, Christian 6%
ETHNIC MIX: Issa 60%, Afar 35%, other 5%
GOVERNMENT: Presidential democracy
CURRENCY: Franc = 100 centimes

Dominica

Renowned as the Caribbean island that resisted European colonization until the 18th century, when it was controlled first by the French, and then, until 1978, by the British.

GEOGRAPHY
Mountainous and densely forested. Volcanic activity has given the land very fertile soils, hot springs, geysers, and black sand beaches.

CLIMATE
Tropical, cooled by constant trade winds. Heavy annual rainfall. Tropical depressions and hurricanes are likely June–November.

PEOPLE & SOCIETY
Population mainly of African origin. Small community of Carib Indians – the last remaining in the Caribbean – on the east coast. Most people live in extended families. Politicians tend to come from professional classes, usually doctors or lawyers. For 15 years until 1995, Dominica was governed by Eugenia Charles, the first female prime minister in the Caribbean.

THE ECONOMY
Bananas and tourism are the economic mainstays. Current preferential access to EU and US markets now threatened by moves to deregulate the banana trade.

◆ **INSIGHT:** *Dominica is known as the "Nature Island" due to its spectacular flora and fauna*

FACTFILE
OFFICIAL NAME: Commonwealth of Dominica
DATE OF FORMATION: 1978
CAPITAL: Roseau
POPULATION: 73,000
TOTAL AREA: 290 sq miles (750 sq km)
DENSITY: 252 people per sq mile

LANGUAGES: English*, French Creole, Carib, Cocoy
RELIGIONS: Roman Catholic 77%, Protestant 15%, other 8%
ETHNIC MIX: Black 91%, Mixed 6%, Indian 2%, other 1%
GOVERNMENT: Parliamentary democracy
CURRENCY: E. Caribbean $ = 100 cents

Dominican Republic

The Dominican Republic occupies the eastern two-thirds of the island of Hispaniola in the Caribbean. Frequent coups and a strong US influence mark its recent past.

GEOGRAPHY

Highlands and rain forested mountains – including highest peak in Caribbean, Pico Duarte – interspersed with fertile valleys. Extensive coastal plain in the east.

CLIMATE

Hot and humid close to sea level, cooler at altitude. Heavy rainfall, especially in the northeast.

PEOPLE & SOCIETY

White landowners and the military hold political power. Mixed-race majority control commerce and form bulk of the professional middle classes. Many of the poor are black. White and mixed-race women are starting to enter the professions. Widespread poverty and high unemployment have led some Dominicans to emigrate to the USA, or become drug-traffickers.

THE ECONOMY

Mining – mainly of nickel and gold – and sugar are major sectors. Hidden economy based on trans-shipment of narcotics to the US. Recent dramatic growth in tourism.

INSIGHT: *Santo Domingo is the oldest city in the Americas. It was founded in 1496 by the brother of Christopher Columbus*

FACTFILE

OFFICIAL NAME: Dominican Republic
DATE OF FORMATION: 1865
CAPITAL: Santo Domingo
POPULATION: 8.5 million
TOTAL AREA: 18,679 sq miles (48,380 sq km)
DENSITY: 455 people per sq mile

LANGUAGES: Spanish*, French Creole
RELIGIONS: Roman Catholic 92%, other and non-religious 8%
ETHNIC MIX: Mixed 75%, White 15%, Black 10%
GOVERNMENT: Presidential democracy
CURRENCY: Peso = 100 centavos

East Timor

This new nation occupies the eastern half of the island of Timor, colonised from 1520 by the Portuguese. Invaded by Indonesia in 1975, it declared independence in 1999.

GEOGRAPHY

A narrow coastal plain gives way to forested highlands. Timor's mountain backbone rises to 9715 ft (2963 m).

CLIMATE

Tropical. Heavy rain in wet season (December–March), then dry and hot, particularly in the north.

PEOPLE & SOCIETY

The Portuguese departure in 1975 left warring factions exposed to invasion by Indonesia, which soon proclaimed East Timor its 27th province and ruthlessly suppressed any resistance. Indonesian settlers became numerous in the 1990s. In August 1999 the Timorese voted overwhelmingly for independence. Massacres and destruction by pro-Indonesian militias followed. A UN administration (UNTAET) was set up to oversee independence by late 2001.

THE ECONOMY

East Timor's economy has crippling short-term problems; towns and communications need rebuilding after extensive damage during the upheavals of 1999. Coffee is the main cash crop, corn the staple food.

◆ **INSIGHT:** *Once dependent on sandalwood, the economy could be transformed by oil under the Timor Sea*

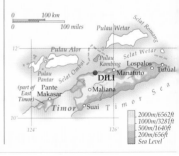

FACTFILE

OFFICIAL NAME: East Timor
DATE OF FORMATION: 2001
CAPITAL: Dili
POPULATION: 750,000
TOTAL AREA: 5756 sq miles
(14,874 sq km)
DENSITY: 130 people per sq mile

LANGUAGES: Tetum, Bahasa Malay, Portuguese
RELIGIONS: Roman Catholic 90%, other (inc. Muslim) 10%
ETHNIC MIX: Various Papuan groups 78%, Indonesian 20%, Chinese 2%
GOVERNMENT: Multiparty republic
CURRENCY: US dollar = 100 cents

Ecuador

Once part of the Inca heartland, Ecuador sits high on South America's western coast. Its territory includes the beautiful Galápagos Islands, 610 miles (970 km) to the west.

GEOGRAPHY

Broad coastal plain, inter-Andean central highlands, dense jungle in upper Amazon basin.

CLIMATE

The climate is hot and moist on the coast, cool in the Andes, and hot equatorial in the Amazon basin.

PEOPLE & SOCIETY

Most people live in coastal lowlands or Andean highlands. Many have migrated from over-farmed Andean valleys to main port and commercial center, Guayaquil. Strong and unified Indian movement backed by Catholic Church. Amazonian Indians are successfully pressing for recognition of land rights.

◆ **INSIGHT:** *Darwin's study on the Galápagos Islands in 1856 played a major part in his theory of evolution*

THE ECONOMY

The world's biggest banana producer, and a net oil exporter. Commercial agriculture is the main employer. Fishing industry. Ecotourism on Galápagos Islands.

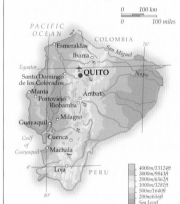

FACTFILE

OFFICIAL NAME: Republic of Ecuador
DATE OF FORMATION: 1830
CAPITAL: Quito
POPULATION: 12.6 million
TOTAL AREA: 106,887 sq miles (276,840 sq km)
DENSITY: 118 people per sq mile

LANGUAGES: Spanish*, Quechua* and eight other Indian languages
RELIGIONS: Roman Catholic 93%, Protestant, Jewish and other 7%
ETHNIC MIX: Mestizo (Euro-Indian) 55%, Indian 25%, Black 10%, White 10%
GOVERNMENT: Presidential democracy
CURRENCY: Sucre = 100 centavos

Egypt

Occupying the northeast corner of Africa, Egypt is bisected by the highly fertile Nile valley. Its essentially pro-Western, military-backed regime is being challenged by Islamic fundamentalists.

GEOGRAPHY
Fertile Nile valley separates arid Libyan Desert from smaller semiarid eastern desert. Sinai peninsula has mountains in south.

CLIMATE
Summers are very hot, but winters are cooler. Rainfall is negligible, except on the coast.

PEOPLE & SOCIETY
Continuously inhabited for more than 8000 years, with a tradition of religious and ethnic tolerance. Most Egyptians are Arabs, Bedouins, and Nubians. Small colonies of Greeks and Armenians live in the larger towns. Women play full part in education system, politics, and economy. Government is fighting Islamic terrorist groups, whose acts of violence have included attacks on politicians, police, and tourists.

THE ECONOMY
Oil and gas are main sources of revenue. Tolls from the Suez Canal. Successful tourist industry is threatened by security fears.

INSIGHT: *Egypt has been a major tourist destination since the 1880s*

FACTFILE

OFFICIAL NAME: Arab Republic of Egypt

DATE OF FORMATION: 1936

CAPITAL: Cairo

POPULATION: 68.5 million

TOTAL AREA: 384,343 sq miles (995,450 sq km)

DENSITY: 178 people per sq mile

LANGUAGES: Arabic*, French, English, Berber, Greek, Armenian

RELIGIONS: Muslim (mainly Sunni) 94%, Coptic Christian and other 6%

ETHNIC MIX: Eastern Hamitic 90%, other (Greek, Armenian, Nubian) 10%

GOVERNMENT: Presidential democracy

CURRENCY: Pound = 100 piastres

El Salvador

El Salvador is Central America's smallest state. A 12-year war between US-backed government troops and left-wing guerrillas ended in 1992 with a UN-brokered peace agreement.

GEOGRAPHY

El Salvador is a narrow coastal belt backed by two mountain ranges. Located within a seismic zone, there are more than 20 volcanic peaks. Central plateau.

CLIMATE

Tropical coastal belt is very hot, with seasonal rains. Cooler, temperate climate in highlands.

PEOPLE & SOCIETY

Population is largely *mestizo*; ethnic tensions are few. The civil war was fought over gross economic disparities, which still exist despite some reform. 75,000 people died during the war, many of whom were unarmed civilians. Around 500,000 more were displaced – mainly rural peasant families. In 1992, left-wing movement gave up its arms and joined in a formal political process.

THE ECONOMY

Civil war caused $2 billion-worth of damage. Huge amounts of foreign aid needed for survival. Over-dependence on coffee, which accounts for 90% of exports.

INSIGHT: *Named for the Saviour, Jesus Christ, El Salvador is the most densely populated of the Central American republics*

FACTFILE

OFFICIAL NAME: Republic of El Salvador
DATE OF FORMATION: 1856
CAPITAL: San Salvador
POPULATION: 6.3 million
TOTAL AREA: 8000 sq miles
(20,720 sq km)
DENSITY: 788 people per sq mile

LANGUAGES: Spanish*, Nahua
RELIGIONS: Roman Catholic 80%, Evangelical 18%, other 2%
ETHNIC MIX: Mestizo (Euro-Indian) 94%, Indian 5%, White 1%
GOVERNMENT: Presidential democracy
CURRENCY: Salvadorean Colón (100 centavos) & US dollar

Equatorial Guinea

 Comprises the mainland territory of Río Muni and five islands on the west coast of central Africa, just north of the equator. In 1993, the first free elections were held.

GEOGRAPHY

Islands are mountainous and volcanic. The mainland is lower, with mangrove swamps along coast.

CLIMATE

Bioco is extremely wet and humid. The mainland is only marginally drier and cooler.

PEOPLE & SOCIETY

The mainland is sparsely populated. Most people are Fang, a people who also inhabit Cameroon and northern Gabon, and who dominate the country's politics. The dictatorship left the ruling Mongomo clan with most of the wealth. Bioco is populated mostly by Bubi and a minority of Creoles known as *Fernandinos*. The extended family is strong and maintained its solidarity despite disruptive social pressure during the years of dictatorship.

THE ECONOMY

Isla da Bioco generates the most income. Main exports are tropical timber and cocoa. Oil and gas reserves yet to be fully exploited.

◆ **INSIGHT:** *Some 100,000 people now live outside the country, having fled its dictatorial regimes*

2000m/6562ft
1000m/3281ft
500m/1640ft
200m/656ft
Sea Level

FACTFILE

OFFICIAL NAME: Republic of Equatorial Guinea
DATE OF FORMATION: 1968
CAPITAL: Malabo
POPULATION: 453,000
TOTAL AREA: 10,830 sq miles (28,050 sq km)

DENSITY: 42 people per sq mile
LANGUAGES: Spanish*, Fang, other
RELIGIONS: Roman Catholic 89%, other 11%
ETHNIC MIX: Fang 85%, Bubi 4%, other 11%
GOVERNMENT: Presidential regime
CURRENCY: CFA franc = 100 centimes

Eritrea

Eritrea effectively seceded from Ethiopia in 1991, following a destructive and bloody 30-year war for independence. A border war began again in 1998, with heavy losses on both sides.

GEOGRAPHY

Mostly consists of rugged mountains, bush, and the Danakil Desert, which falls below sea level.

CLIMATE

Warm in the mountains; desert areas are hot. Droughts from July onwards are common.

PEOPLE & SOCIETY

Strong sense of nationhood forged by the war. Over 80% of people are subsistence farmers. Elections expected in 1997 have not yet taken place. Until multiparty elections are held, the country is being run by core of EPLF leaders who conducted military campaign. Border dispute with Ethiopia erupted in 1998.

◆ **INSIGHT:** *75% of Eritreans are dependent upon aid for all, or part, of their annual food supply*

THE ECONOMY

Legacy of disruption and destruction from war. Susceptible to drought and famine. Most of the population live at subsistence level. Potential for mining of gold, copper, silver, and zinc. Possible foreign earnings from oil exports.

2000m/6562ft
1000m/3281ft
500m/1640ft
200m/656ft
Sea Level
Below Sea Level

FACTFILE

OFFICIAL NAME: State of Eritrea
DATE OF FORMATION: 1993
CAPITAL: Asmara
POPULATION: 3.9 million
TOTAL AREA: 45,405 sq miles
(117,600 sq km)
DENSITY: 86 people per sq mile

LANGUAGES: Tigrinya*, Arabic*, Tigre, Afar, Bilen, Kunama, Nara
RELIGIONS: Christian 45%, Muslim 45%, other 10%
ETHNIC MIX: Tigray 50%, Kunama 40%, Afar 4%, Saho 3%, other 3%
GOVERNMENT: Transitional regime
CURRENCY: Ethiopian birr = 100 cents

Estonia

Traditionally the most Western-oriented of the Baltic states, Estonia is the smallest and most developed of the three and has the highest standard of living of any former Soviet republic

GEOGRAPHY

Estonia's terrain is flat, boggy, and partly forested, with over 1500 islands. Lake Peipus forms much of the eastern border with Russia.

CLIMATE

Maritime, with some continental extremes. Harsh winters, with cool summers and damp springs.

PEOPLE & SOCIETY

The Estonians are related linguistically and ethnically to the Finns. Friction between ethnic Estonians and the large Russian minority has led to reassertion of Estonian culture and language, as well as job discrimination. Some postindependence political upheaval reflects disenchantment with free-market economics. Families are small; divorce rates are high. The country was the first amongst the Baltic states to abolish the death penalty.

THE ECONOMY

Agricultural machinery, electric motors, and ships are the leading manufactures. There is also a strong timber industry. Increased trade links with Finland and Germany.

INSIGHT: *Estonia is a popular tourist destination for Finns, who come for the water and winter sports, architectural heritage, and nature tours*

FACTFILE

OFFICIAL NAME: Republic of Estonia
DATE OF FORMATION: 1991
CAPITAL: Tallinn
POPULATION: 1.4 million
TOTAL AREA: 17,423 sq miles (45,125 sq km)
DENSITY: 80 people per sq mile

LANGUAGES: Estonian*, Russian
RELIGIONS: Evangelical Lutheran 56%, Russian Orthodox 25%, other 19%
ETHNIC MIX: Estonian 62%, Russian 30%, other 8%
GOVERNMENT: Parliamentary democracy
CURRENCY: Kroon = 100 cents

Ethiopia

Located in northeast Africa, the former empire of Ethiopia was a Marxist regime from 1974–91. Now a free-market democracy, it has suffered a series of economic, civil, and natural crises.

GEOGRAPHY

Great Rift Valley divides mountainous northwest region from desert lowlands in northeast and southeast. Ethiopian Plateau is drained mainly by the Blue Nile.

CLIMATE

Moderate with summer rains. Highlands are warm, with night frost and snowfalls on the mountains.

PEOPLE & SOCIETY

76 Ethiopian nationalities speak 86 languages. Oromo are the largest group. In 1995, the first multiparty elections were held, ending four years of rule by a transitional government, and beginning a new nine-state federation.

INSIGHT: *Solomon and the Queen of Sheba are said to have founded the Kingdom of Abyssinia (Ethiopia) c.1000 BC*

THE ECONOMY

The world's second poorest nation. Most people are subsistence farmers. Despite war-damaged infrastructure and periodic serious droughts, agricultural and industrial output are growing as the country moves toward a market economy.

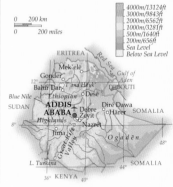

4000m/13124ft
3000m/9843ft
2000m/6562ft
1000m/3281ft
500m/1640ft
200m/656ft
Sea Level
Below Sea Level

0   200 km
0   200 miles

ERITREA
Mek'ele
Gonder
Bahir Dar
Lake Tana Hāyk'
Blue Nile
Desē
Gulf of Aden
DJIBOUTI
ADDIS ABABA
Ethiopian Highlands
Debre Zeyit
Dirē Dawa
Harēr
SUDAN
Nazrēt
SOMALIA
Jima
Great Rift Valley
O g a d ē n
L. Turkana
KENYA
SOMALIA

FACTFILE

OFFICIAL NAME: Federal Democratic Republic of Ethiopia

DATE OF FORMATION: 1993

CAPITAL: Addis Ababa

POPULATION: 62.6 million

TOTAL AREA: 428,571 sq miles (1,110,000 sq km)

DENSITY: 179 people per sq mile

LANGUAGES: Amharic*, English, Arabic

RELIGIONS: Orthodox 40%, Muslim 40%, Traditional beliefs 15%, other 5%

ETHNIC MIX: Oromo 40%, Amhara 25%, Sidamo 9%, other 26%

GOVERNMENT: Multiparty republic

CURRENCY: Birr = 100 cents

Fiji

A volcanic archipelago in the southern Pacific Ocean, comprising two large islands and 880 islets. From 1874 to 1970, Fiji was a British colony. Tensions exist between urban and rural Fijians.

GEOGRAPHY
Main islands are mountainous, fringed by coral reefs. Remainder are limestone and coral formations.

CLIMATE
Tropical. High temperatures year round. Cyclones are a hazard.

PEOPLE & SOCIETY
The British introduced workers from India in the late 19th century, and by 1946 their descendants outnumbered the Native Fijian population. In 1987, the Indian-dominated government was overthrown by Native Fijians. Many Indo-Fijians left the country. Civilian rule returned in 1990, and a new constitution discriminating against Indo-Fijians was introduced.

◆ INSIGHT: *Both Fijians and Indians practice fire-walking; Indians walk on hot embers, Fijians on heated stones*

THE ECONOMY
Well-diversified economy based on sugar production, gold mining, timber and commercial fishing. Tourists are returning after a drop in numbers after the coups.

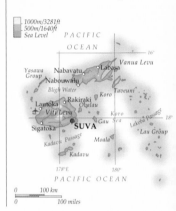

□ 1000m/3281ft
□ 500m/1640ft
□ Sea Level

PACIFIC OCEAN

Yasawa Group
Nabavatu • Labasa   Vanua Levu
Nabouwalu
Bligh Water   Koro   Taveuni
Lautoka • Rakiraki
Viti Levu   Ovalau   Koro
Sigatoka   Gau   Sea   Lakeba Passage
Kadavu Passage   Moala   Lau Group
Kadavu

SUVA

178°E   180°

PACIFIC OCEAN

0   100 km
0   100 miles

FACTFILE
OFFICIAL NAME: Republic of Fiji
DATE OF FORMATION: 1970
CAPITAL: Suva
POPULATION: 817,000
TOTAL AREA: 7054 sq miles (18,270 sq km)
DENSITY: 116 people per sq mile

LANGUAGES: English*, Fijian*, Hindi, Urdu, Tamil, Telugu
RELIGIONS: Hindu 38%, Methodist 37%, Catholic 9%, Muslim 8%, other 8%
ETHNIC MIX: Melanesian 48%, Indian 46%, other 6%
GOVERNMENT: Multiparty republic
CURRENCY: Fiji $ = 100 cents

Finland

Finland's language and national identity have been influenced by both its Scandinavian and Russian neighbours. Once closely associated with the USSR, Finland is now a member of the EU.

GEOGRAPHY
South and centre are flat, with low hills and many lakes. Uplands and low mountains in the north. 60% of the land area is forested.

CLIMATE
Long, harsh winters with frequent snowfalls. Short, warmer summers. Rainfall is low, and decreases northwards.

PEOPLE & SOCIETY
More than half the population live in the five districts around Helsinki. The Swedish minority live mainly in the Åland Islands in the southwest. The Sami (Lapps) lead a seminomadic existence above the Arctic Circle. Over 50% of women go out to work, continuing a long tradition of equality between the sexes. Families tend to be closeknit, although divorce rates are high.

THE ECONOMY
Wood-based industries account for 40% of exports. Strong engineering and electronics sectors.

◆ **INSIGHT:** *Finland has Europe's largest inland waterway system*

FACTFILE
OFFICIAL NAME: Republic of Finland
DATE OF FORMATION: 1917
CAPITAL: Helsinki
POPULATION: 5.2 million
TOTAL AREA: 117,609 sq miles (304,610 sq km)
DENSITY: 44 people per sq mile

LANGUAGES: Finnish*, Swedish, Lappish
RELIGIONS: Evangelical Lutheran 89%, Finnish Orthodox/Catholic 2%, other 9%
ETHNIC MIX: Finnish 93%, other (including Sami) 7%
GOVERNMENT: Parliamentary democracy
CURRENCY: Euro = 100 cents

France

Straddling Western Europe from the English Channel to the Mediterranean Sea, France was Europe's first modern republic and is now one of the world's leading industrial powers.

GEOGRAPHY
Broad plain covers northern half of the country. Tall mountain ranges in the east and southwest, with a mountainous plateau in the center.

CLIMATE
Three main climates: temperate and damp northwest; continental east; and Mediterranean south.

PEOPLE & SOCIETY
Strong French national identity coexists with pronounced regional differences, including local languages. Long tradition of absorbing immigrants (European Jews, North African Muslims, economic migrants from Southern Europe). Catholic Church is no longer central to daily life.

◆ **INSIGHT:** *The French wine industry predates the Roman occupation, beginning at around 600 BC*

THE ECONOMY
Steel, chemicals, electronics, heavy engineering, and aircraft typify a strong and diversified export sector. World leader in cosmetics, perfumes, and quality wines.

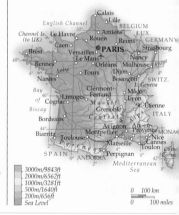

3000m/9843ft
2000m/6562ft
1000m/3281ft
500m/1640ft
200m/656ft
Sea Level

0   100 km
0   100 miles

FACTFILE
OFFICIAL NAME: The French Republic
DATE OF FORMATION: 1685
CAPITAL: Paris
POPULATION: 59.1 million
TOTAL AREA: 212,393 sq miles (550,100 sq km)
DENSITY: 278 people per sq mile

LANGUAGES: French*, Provençal, German, Breton, Catalan, Basque
RELIGIONS: Catholic 88%, Muslim 8%, Protestant 2%, Jewish 1%, Buddhist 1%
ETHNIC MIX: French 90%, North African 6%, German 2%, other 2%
GOVERNMENT: Multiparty republic
CURRENCY: Euro = 100 cents

Gabon

Gabon is a former French colony straddling the Equator on Africa's west coast. Independent since 1960, it returned to multiparty politics in 1990, after 22 years of one-party rule.

GEOGRAPHY

Low plateaus and mountains lie beyond the coastal strip. Two-thirds of the land is covered by rain forest.

CLIMATE

Hot and tropical, with little distinction between seasons. Cold Benguela Current cools the coast.

PEOPLE & SOCIETY

Some 40 different languages are spoken. The Fang, who live mainly in the north, are the largest ethnic group, but have yet to gain control of the government. Oil wealth has led to growth of an affluent middle class. Menial jobs are done by immigrant workers. Education follows the French system. With almost half its population living in towns, Gabon is one of Africa's most urbanized countries. The government is encouraging population growth.

THE ECONOMY

Oil is the main source of revenue. Tropical hardwoods are being exploited. Cocoa beans, coffee, and rice grown for export.

◆ **INSIGHT:** *Libreville was founded as a settlement for freed French slaves in 1849*

FACTFILE

OFFICIAL NAME: The Gabonese Republic
DATE OF FORMATION: 1960
CAPITAL: Libreville
POPULATION: 1.2 million
TOTAL AREA: 99,486 sq miles (257,670 sq km)
DENSITY: 12 people per sq mile

LANGUAGES: French*, Fang, other
RELIGIONS: Christian (Catholic) 55%, traditional beliefs 40%, Muslim 1%, other 4%
ETHNIC MIX: Fang 35%, Eshira 25%, other Bantu 29%, French 2%, other 9%
GOVERNMENT: Multiparty republic
CURRENCY: CFA franc = 100 centimes

Gambia

Gambia is a narrow state on the west coast of Africa, surrounded on three sides by Senegal. It was renowned for its stability until its government was overthrown in a coup in 1994.

GEOGRAPHY

Located on the narrow strip of land bordering the River Gambia. Long, sandy beaches are backed by mangrove swamps along the river. Savannah and tropical forests higher up.

CLIMATE

Subtropical, with wet, humid months July–October and warm, dry season November–May.

PEOPLE & SOCIETY

Little tension between various ethnic groups. Creole community, known as the Aku, is small but socially prominent. People are increasingly leaving rural areas for the towns, where average incomes are four times higher. Each year seasonal immigrants from neighboring states come to farm peanuts. Women are very active as traders.

THE ECONOMY

80% of the labor force is involved in agriculture. Peanuts are the principal crop. The fisheries sector is being improved. Growth in tourism is now halted by political instability. Smuggling problems. Most donor aid, suspended after the 1994 coup, has largely resumed.

INSIGHT: *Overfishing in the waters off the Gambia and Senegal, mainly by distant nations, is a growing problem*

FACTFILE

OFFICIAL NAME: Republic of The Gambia
DATE OF FORMATION: 1965
CAPITAL: Banjul
POPULATION: 1.3 million
TOTAL AREA: 3861 sq miles (10,000 sq km)
DENSITY: 337 people per sq mile

LANGUAGES: English*, other
RELIGIONS: Sunni Muslim 90%, Christian 9%, indigenous beliefs 1%
ETHNIC MIX: Mandingo 42%, Fulani 18%, Wolof 16%, Jola 10%, Serahuli 9%, other 5%
GOVERNMENT: Multiparty republic
CURRENCY: Dalasi = 100 butut

Georgia

Located on the eastern shore of the Black Sea, Georgia has been torn by civil war and ethnic disputes since achieving independence from the Soviet Union in 1991.

GEOGRAPHY

Kura valley lies between Caucasus Mountains in the north and Lesser Caucasus range in south. Lowlands along the Black Sea coast.

CLIMATE

Subtropical along the coast, changing to continental extremes at high altitudes. Rainfall is moderate.

PEOPLE & SOCIETY

Paternalistic society, with strong family, cultural, and literary traditions. Georgians are the majority group. An uneasy truce followed the 1990–93 civil war, and the political scene remained volatile. In 1994, another civil war was fought, as ethnic Abkhazians attempted to secede from Georgia. More than 300,000 people have been displaced by the conflicts. Around one in five Georgians live in poverty, but a small, wealthy elite is found in the capital.

THE ECONOMY

Food processing and wine production are the main industries. Economy has broken down due to war and severance of links with other former Soviet republics.

◆ **INSIGHT:** *Western Georgia was the land of the legendary Golden Fleece of Greek mythology*

▨	3000m/9843ft
▨	2000m/6562ft
▨	1000m/3281ft
▨	500m/1640ft
▨	200m/656ft
	Sea Level

0   100 km
0   100 miles

📖 FACTFILE

OFFICIAL NAME: Republic of Georgia
DATE OF FORMATION: 1991
CAPITAL: Tbilisi
POPULATION: 5 million
TOTAL AREA: 26,911 sq miles
(69,700 sq km)
DENSITY: 186 people per sq mile

LANGUAGES: Georgian*, Russian, other
RELIGIONS: Georgian Orthodox 65%, Muslim 11%, Russian Orthodox 10%, Armenian Orthodox 8%, unknown 6%
ETHNIC MIX: Georgian 70%, Armenian 8%, Azeri 6%, Russian 6%, other 10%
GOVERNMENT: Presidential democracy
CURRENCY: Lari

Germany

Europe's strongest economic and industrial power, Germany was divided into a democratic west and a communist east in 1945. It was reunified in 1990, after the fall of the east's regime.

GEOGRAPHY
Coastal plains in the north, rising to rolling hills of central region. Alpine region in the south.

CLIMATE
Damp, temperate in northern and central regions. Continental extremes in mountainous south.

PEOPLE & SOCIETY
Social and economic differences reflect former East–West divisions. Some prosperous Western Germans resent added taxes since reunification. Far-right political groups have emerged. Immigrant "guest workers" – mainly Turks – face citizenship problems and occasional racial attacks. Strong feminist and Green movements.

◆ **INSIGHT:** *Germany's rivers and canals carry as much freight as its busy toll-free roads*

THE ECONOMY
Massive exports of electronics, heavy engineering, chemicals, and cars. Postwar "miracle" powered by efficiency and good labor relations.

FACTFILE
OFFICIAL NAME: Federal Republic of Germany
DATE OF FORMATION: 1990
CAPITAL: Berlin
POPULATION: 82.2 million
TOTAL AREA: 134,949 sq miles (349,520 sq km)

DENSITY: 609 people per sq mile
LANGUAGES: German*, Sorbian, other
RELIGIONS: Protestant 36%, Catholic 35%, Muslim 2%, other 27%
ETHNIC MIX: German 92%, other 8%
GOVERNMENT: Parliamentary democracy
CURRENCY: Euro = 100 cents

Ghana

The heartland of the ancient Ashanti kingdom, Ghana in West Africa was once known as the Gold Coast. It has experienced intermittent periods of military rule since independence in 1957.

GEOGRAPHY

Mostly low-lying. The west is covered in rain forest. The world's third largest artificial lake – Lake Volta – was created by damming the White Volta River.

CLIMATE

Tropical. There are two wet seasons in the south, but the north is drier, and has just one.

PEOPLE & SOCIETY

Around 75 cultural-linguistic groups. The largest is the Akan, who include the Ashanti and Fanti peoples. Over 100 languages and dialects are spoken. Southern peoples are richer and more urban than those of the north. There are few tribal tensions. Family ties are strong. Multiparty elections in 1992 and 1996 confirmed and consolidated former military leader Jerry Rawlings in power.

THE ECONOMY

Produces 15% of the world's cocoa. Hardwood trees such as maple and sapele. Gold, bauxite, diamonds, and manganese are major exports.

INSIGHT: *Ghana was the first British colony in Africa to gain independence*

FACTFILE

OFFICIAL NAME: Republic of Ghana
DATE OF FORMATION: 1957
CAPITAL: Accra
POPULATION: 20.2 million
TOTAL AREA: 88,810 sq miles (230,020 sq km)
DENSITY: 227 people per sq mile

LANGUAGES: English*, Akan, Mossi, Ewe, Ga, Twi, Fanti, Gurma, other
RELIGIONS: Christian 43%, traditional beliefs 38%, Muslim 11%, other 8%
ETHNIC MIX: Ashanti and Fanti 52%, Moshi 16%, Ewe 12%, Ga 8%, other 12%
GOVERNMENT: Presidential democracy
CURRENCY: Cedi = 100 pesewas

Greece

The Balkan state of Greece is bounded on three sides by the Mediterranean, Aegean, and Ionian seas. It has a strong seafaring tradition, with some of the world's richest shipowners.

GEOGRAPHY
Mountainous peninsula with over 2000 islands. Large central plain along the mainland's Aegean coast.

CLIMATE
Mainly Mediterranean with dry, hot summers. Alpine climate in northern mountain areas.

PEOPLE & SOCIETY
Postwar industrial development altered the dominance of agriculture and seafaring. The rural exodus to industrial cities has been stemmed but over half the population now live in the two largest cities. Age-old culture and Greek Orthodox Church balance social mobility. Civil marriage and divorce only became legal in 1982.

◆ **INSIGHT:** *Classical sights have made tourism one of the most important industries in Greece*

THE ECONOMY
High inflation and poor investment work against strong economic sectors: tourism, shipping, agriculture. Thriving black economy.

2000m/6562ft
1000m/3281ft
500m/1640ft
200m/656ft
Sea Level

0   100 km
0   100 miles

FACTFILE
OFFICIAL NAME: Hellenic Republic
DATE OF FORMATION: 1913
CAPITAL: Athens
POPULATION: 10.6 million
TOTAL AREA: 50,521 sq miles (130,850 sq km)
DENSITY: 210 people per sq mile

LANGUAGES: Greek*, Turkish, Albanian, Macedonian
RELIGIONS: Greek Orthodox 98%, Muslim 1%, other 1%
ETHNIC MIX: Greek 98%, other 2%
GOVERNMENT: Presidential democracy
CURRENCY: Euro = 100 cents

Grenada

The southernmost Windward Island of Grenada became a focus of attention in 1983, when the US, with token Caribbean backing, mounted an invasion to sever links with Castro's Cuba.

GEOGRAPHY

Volcanic in origin, with densely forested central mountains. Its territory also includes the islands of Carriacou and Petite Martinique.

CLIMATE

Tropical, tempered by trade winds. Hurricanes are a hazard in the July–November wet season.

PEOPLE & SOCIETY

Grenadians are mainly of African origin; their traditions remain strong, especially on Carriacou. Inter-ethnic marriage has reduced tensions between the groups. Extended families, often headed by women, are the norm. The invasion ousted the Marxist regime and restored democracy.

◆ **INSIGHT:** *Known as "the spice island of the Caribbean," it is the world's second largest nutmeg producer*

THE ECONOMY

Nutmeg, the most important crop, is currently affected by low world prices. Mace, cocoa, saffron, and cloves are also grown. Tourism has developed in the past decade.

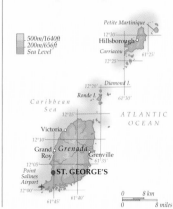

500m/1640ft
200m/656ft
Sea Level

Petite Martinique
12°30'
Hillsborough
Carriacou
61°25'
12°25'

Diamond I.
12°20'
Ronde I.
61°30'

Caribbean Sea
12°15'

ATLANTIC OCEAN

Victoria
12°10'

Grand Roy
Grenada
Grenville
61°35'
12°05'
ST. GEORGE'S
Point Salines Airport
12°00'
61°45'   61°40'

0   8 km
0   8 miles

FACTFILE

OFFICIAL NAME: Grenada
DATE OF FORMATION: 1974
CAPITAL: St George's
POPULATION: 99,500
TOTAL AREA: 131 sq miles
(340 sq km)
DENSITY: 760 people per sq mile

LANGUAGES: English*, English Creole
RELIGIONS: Roman Catholic 68%, Anglican 17%, other 15%
ETHNIC MIX: Black African 82%, mulatto 13%, Indian 3%, other 2%
GOVERNMENT: Parliamentary democracy
CURRENCY: East Caribbean $ = 100 cents

Guatemala

The largest and most populous nation on the Central American isthmus, Guatemala returned to civilian rule in 1986, after 32 years of violent and repressive military rule.

GEOGRAPHY
Narrow Pacific coastal plain. Central highlands with volcanoes. Short coast on the Caribbean Sea. Tropical rain forests in the north.

CLIMATE
Tropical, hot and humid in coastal regions and north. More temperate in central highlands.

PEOPLE & SOCIETY
Indians form a majority, but power, wealth and land is controlled by a *ladino* elite. Highland Indians were the victims of the military's indiscriminate campaign against guerrilla groups 1978–84. Since civilian rule, the level of violence has diminished, but extreme poverty is still widespread.

◆ **INSIGHT:** *Guatemala, which means "land of trees," was the center of the ancient Maya civilization*

THE ECONOMY
Agriculture is the key sector. Sugar, coffee, beef, bananas, and cardamom are top exports. Political stability has revived tourism.

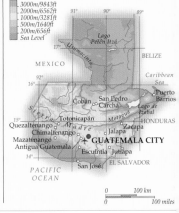

FACTFILE
OFFICIAL NAME: Republic of Guatemala
DATE OF FORMATION: 1838
CAPITAL: Guatemala City
POPULATION: 11.4 million
TOTAL AREA: 41,864 sq miles (108,430 sq km)
DENSITY: 272 people per sq mile

LANGUAGES: Spanish*, Quiché, Mam, Kekchí, Cakchiquel, Mayan
RELIGIONS: Roman Catholic 66%, Protestant 33%, other 1%
ETHNIC MIX: Amerindian 60%, Mestizo 30%, other 10%
GOVERNMENT: Presidential democracy
CURRENCY: Quetzal = 100 centavos

Guinea

Facing the Atlantic Ocean, on the west coast of Africa, Guinea became the first French colony in Africa to gain independence, in 1958. The country was under military rule from 1984 to 1995.

GEOGRAPHY
Coastal plains and mangrove swamps in west rise to forested or savannah highlands in the south. Semidesert in the north.

CLIMATE
Tropical, with a wet season April–October. Heavy annual rainfall. Hot *harmattan* wind blows from Sahara during dry season.

PEOPLE & SOCIETY
Malinke and Fulani make up most of the population, but traditional rivalries between them have allowed coastal peoples such as the Soussou to dominate politics. Daily life revolves around the extended family. Women acquired influence under Marxist party rule between 1958 and 1984, but the Muslim revival since then has reversed the trend. The first multiparty elections were held in 1995.

THE ECONOMY
Two-thirds of people are farmers. Cash crops are palm oil, bananas, pineapples, and rice. Gold, diamond, and bauxite reserves.

INSIGHT: *The colors of Guinea's flag represent the three words of the country's motto: work (red), justice (yellow), and solidarity (green)*

- 1000m/3281ft
- 500m/1640ft
- 200m/656ft
- Sea Level

FACTFILE

OFFICIAL NAME: Republic of Guinea
DATE OF FORMATION: 1958
CAPITAL: Conakry
POPULATION: 7.4 million
TOTAL AREA: 94,926 sq miles (245,860 sq km)
DENSITY: 78 people per sq mile

LANGUAGES: French*, Fulani, Malinke, Soussou, Kissi, other
RELIGIONS: Muslim 65%, traditional beliefs 33%, Christian 2%
ETHNIC MIX: Fila 30%, Malinke 30%, Soussou 15%, Kissi 10%, other 15%
GOVERNMENT: Multiparty republic
CURRENCY: Franc = 100 centimes

Guinea-Bissau

Known as Portuguese Guinea during its days as a colony, Guinea-Bissau is situated on Africa's west coast, bordered by Senegal to the north and Guinea to the south and east.

GEOGRAPHY

Low-lying, apart from savannah highlands in northeast. Rain forests and swamps are found along coastal areas.

CLIMATE

Tropical, with wet season May–November and dry season December–April. Hot harmattan wind blows during dry season.

PEOPLE & SOCIETY

The largest ethnic group is the Balante, who live in the south. Though less than 2% of the population, the mixed Portuguese-African *mestiços* dominate the top ranks of government and bureaucracy. Most people live and work on small family farms, grouped in self-contained villages. The bulk of the urban population live in the capital, Bissau. After 20 years of single-party rule, the first multiparty elections were held in 1994.

THE ECONOMY

Mostly subsistence farming – maize, sweet potatoes, cassava. Main cash crops are cashews, peanuts and palm kernels. Lack of sufficiency in rice staple. Offshore oil as yet untapped. Fisheries and timber potential.

INSIGHT: *In 1974, Guinea-Bissau became the first Portuguese colony to gain independence*

200m/656ft
Sea Level

FACTFILE

OFFICIAL NAME: Republic of Guinea-Bissau
DATE OF FORMATION: 1974
CAPITAL: Bissau
POPULATION: 1.2 million
TOTAL AREA: 10,570 sq miles (28,120 sq km)

DENSITY: 114 people per sq mile
LANGUAGES: Portuguese*, other
RELIGIONS: Indigenous beliefs 52%, Muslim 40%, Christian 8%
ETHNIC MIX: Balanta 25%, Fula 20%, Mandinka & Mandyako 23%, other 32%
GOVERNMENT: Presidential democracy
CURRENCY: Peso = 100 centavos

Guyana

On the northeast coast of the continent, Guyana is South America's only English-speaking country. Independence from the UK was achieved in 1966, and it became a republic in 1970.

GEOGRAPHY

Mainly artificial coast, reclaimed by dikes and dams from swamps and tidal marshes. Forests cover 85% of the interior, rising to savannah uplands and mountains.

CLIMATE

Tropical. Coast cooled by sea breezes. Lowlands are hot, wet and humid. Highlands are a little cooler.

PEOPLE & SOCIETY

Population is largely descended from Africans brought over during the slave trade, or from South Asian laborers who arrived after slavery was abolished. Racial tensions exist between the two groups. Politics were characterized by favoritism toward the Afro-Guyanese until the 1992 elections. The presidential election of 1997 was rejected by the opposition. A new constitution was drafted in 1999.

THE ECONOMY

Free-market economics have improved prospects. Bauxite, gold, rice, and diamonds are produced.

INSIGHT: *Guyana means "land of many waters" – it has 994 miles (1600 km) of rivers*

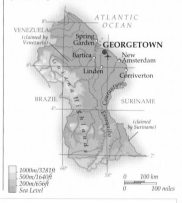

■ 1000m/3281ft	
■ 500m/1640ft	
■ 200m/656ft	0 100 km
Sea Level	0 100 miles

FACTFILE

OFFICIAL NAME: Cooperative Republic of Guyana

DATE OF FORMATION: 1966

CAPITAL: Georgetown

POPULATION: 861,000

TOTAL AREA: 76,003 sq miles (196,850 sq km)

DENSITY: 11 people per sq mile

LANGUAGES: English*, Creole, Hindi, Urdu, Indian languages

RELIGIONS: Christian 57%, other 43%

ETHNIC MIX: East Indian 52%, Black African 38%, Amerindian 4%, other 6%

GOVERNMENT: Presidential democracy

CURRENCY: Guyana $ =100 cents

Haiti

Formerly a Spanish colony, Haiti shares the Caribbean island of Hispaniola with the Dominican Republic. At independence in 1804, it became the world's first black republic.

GEOGRAPHY
Predominantly mountainous, with forests and fertile plains.

CLIMATE
Tropical, with rain throughout the year. Humid in coastal areas, much cooler in the mountains.

PEOPLE & SOCIETY
Most Haitians are of African descent. A few have European roots, primarily French. The rigid class structure maintains vast disparities of wealth. The majority of the population live in extreme poverty; Haiti is the poorest country in the Americas. In recent years, the combination of political oppression and a collapsing economy led thousands to seek asylum in the US or the neighboring Dominican Republic. In 1994, US-led troops reinstated the elected president, who was ousted by the military in 1991.

THE ECONOMY
Few natural resources. In 1994, after 3 years of UN sanctions, the country's economic links were restored and foreign aid resumed.

INSIGHT: *Haiti's independence was achieved after a slave rebellion led by Toussaint l'Ouverture in 1791*

FACTFILE

OFFICIAL NAME: Republic of Haiti
DATE OF FORMATION: 1804
CAPITAL: Port-au-Prince
POPULATION: 8.2 million
TOTAL AREA: 10,641 sq miles (27,560 sq km)
DENSITY: 771 people per sq mile

LANGUAGES: French*, French Creole*, English
RELIGIONS: Roman Catholic 80%, Protestant 16%, other 4%
ETHNIC MIX: Black African 95%, mulatto and European 5%
GOVERNMENT: Multiparty republic
CURRENCY: Gourde = 100 centimes

Honduras

Straddling the Central American isthmus, Honduras has a very short Pacific coast. It returned to democratic civilian rule in 1984, after a succession of military governments.

GEOGRAPHY
Narrow plains along both coasts, with a mountainous interior, cut by river valleys. Tropical forests, swamps, and lagoons in the east.

CLIMATE
Tropical coastal lowlands are hot and humid, with May–October rains. Interior is cooler and drier.

PEOPLE & SOCIETY
The majority of the population is mestizo. *Garifuna* (black) people on the Caribbean coast maintain their own language and culture. Indians inhabit the east and remote mountain areas; their land rights are often violated. Rural poverty and strong Roman Catholicism mean that the family is a powerful unifying force. Women's status is low. Land reform, and high unemployment are main issues facing the government.

THE ECONOMY
Second poorest country in the region. Bananas are a traditional cash crop – production is dominated by two US companies. Coffee, timber, and livestock are also exported.

INSIGHT: *Honduran currency is named after a Lenca Indian chief who was the main leader of resistance to the Spanish conquest in the 16th century*

FACTFILE

OFFICIAL NAME: Republic of Honduras
DATE OF FORMATION: 1838
CAPITAL: Tegucigalpa
POPULATION: 6.5 million
TOTAL AREA: 43,200 sq miles (111,890 sq km)
DENSITY: 150 people per sq mile

LANGUAGES: Spanish*, English Creole, Garifuna, Indian languages
RELIGIONS: Roman Catholic 97%, Protestant minority 3%
ETHNIC MIX: Mestizo 90%, Indian 4%, Black African 5%, White 1%
GOVERNMENT: Presidential democracy
CURRENCY: Lempira = 100 centavos

Hungary

Hungary is bordered by seven states at the heart of Central Europe. Recent reforms to its economic and political policies have brought it closer to EU and NATO membership.

GEOGRAPHY
Landlocked. Fertile plains in east and northwest; west and north are hilly. The River Danube bisects the country from north to south.

CLIMATE
Continental, with wet springs, late but very hot summers, and cold, cloudy winters. The transition between seasons tends to be sudden.

PEOPLE & SOCIETY
Ethnically homogeneous and stable society, showing signs of stress since the transfer to a market economy. Most homes are overcrowded, due to a severe housing shortage. Since 1989, a middle class has emerged, but life for the unemployed and unskilled is harder than under communism. Hungary has the highest suicide rate in the world. Concern over treatment of Hungarian nationals in neighboring states.

THE ECONOMY
Unemployment and weak banking sector hamper moves to open economy. Heavy industries and agriculture remain strong. Growing tourism and services.

INSIGHT: *The Hungarian language is Asian in origin and has features not found in any other Western language*

500m/1640ft
200m/656ft
Sea Level

0   50 km
0   50 miles

FACTFILE
OFFICIAL NAME: Republic of Hungary
DATE OF FORMATION: 1918
CAPITAL: Budapest
POPULATION: 10 million
TOTAL AREA: 35,652 sq miles (92,340 sq km)
DENSITY: 280 people per sq mile

LANGUAGES: Hungarian (Magyar)*, German, Slovak, other
RELIGIONS: Catholic 64%, Calvinist 20%, non-religious 7%, other 9%
ETHNIC MIX: Magyar 90%, German 2%, Romany 1%, Slovak 1%, other 6%
GOVERNMENT: Parliamentary democracy
CURRENCY: Forint = 100 filler

Iceland

Europe's westernmost country, Iceland has a strategic location in the north Atlantic, straddling the Mid-Atlantic Ridge. Its spectacular landscape is largely uninhabited.

GEOGRAPHY

Grassy coastal lowlands, with fjords in the north. Central plateau of cold lava desert, geothermal springs, and glaciers. Around 200 volcanoes, with numerous geysers and solfataras.

CLIMATE

Its location in the middle of the Gulf Stream moderates the climate. Mild winters and brief, cool summers.

PEOPLE & SOCIETY

Prosperous and homogeneous society includes only 4000 foreign residents. High social mobility, free health care and heating (using geothermal power). Longevity rates are among the highest in the world. Equivocal attitude toward Europe accompanies increasing US influence. Strong emphasis on education and literacy. Low crime rate, but concerns over alcohol-related violence.

THE ECONOMY

Fish or fish products make up 80% of exports. Developing light industry produces knitwear, textiles, paint. Ecotourism potential.

INSIGHT: *Iceland has the world's oldest parliament, the Althing, which was founded in AD 930*

FACTFILE

OFFICIAL NAME: Republic of Iceland
DATE OF FORMATION: 1944
CAPITAL: Reykjavík
POPULATION: 281,000
TOTAL AREA: 38,706 sq miles (100,250 sq km)
DENSITY: 7 people per sq mile

LANGUAGES: Icelandic*, other
RELIGIONS: Evangelical Lutheran 93%, other Christian 1%, non-religious 6%
ETHNIC MIX: Icelandic (Norwegian-Celtic descent) 94%, Danish 1%, other 5%
GOVERNMENT: Parliamentary democracy
CURRENCY: Krona = 100 aurar

India

India is the world's second most populous country. The birth rate has recently been falling, but even at its current level India's population will probably overtake China's by 2030.

GEOGRAPHY

Separated from the rest of Asia by the Himalayan mountain range, India forms a subcontinent. As well as the Himalayas, there are two other main geographical regions, the Indo-Gangetic plain, which lies between the foothills of the Himalayas and the Vindhya Mountains, and the central-southern Deccan plateau. The Ghats are smaller mountain ranges located on the east and west coasts.

CLIMATE

Varies greatly according to latitude, altitude and season. Most of India has three seasons: hot, wet, and cool. In summer, temperatures in the north can reach 104°F (40°C). The monsoon breaks in June and peters out in September to October. In the cool season, the weather is mainly dry. The climate in the warmer south is less variable than in the north.

PEOPLE & SOCIETY

Cultural and religious pressures encourage large families. Despite a major birth control program, the decrease in population growth has been marginal. Today, nationwide awareness campaigns aim to promote the idea of smaller families. India's planners consider the rise in the population the most significant break on development. The overwhelming majority of Indians are Hindu. Each Hindu belongs to one of thousands of castes and subcastes. Hindus are born into their caste, which determines who they can marry and their future status and occupation. Various attempts to reform the system have met with violent opposition. At least 30% of all Indians live in extreme poverty. Over 100,000 people live on the streets of Mumbai. A dispute over control of Kashmir continues to sour relations with Pakistan.

FACTFILE

OFFICIAL NAME: Republic of India
DATE OF FORMATION: 1947
CAPITAL: New Delhi
POPULATION: 1.013 billion
TOTAL AREA: 1,147,948 sq miles (2,973,190 sq km)
DENSITY: 882 people per sq mile

LANGUAGES: Hindi*, English*, other
RELIGIONS: Hindu 83%, Muslim 11%, Christian 2%, Sikh 2%, Buddhist 1%, other 1%
ETHNIC MIX: Indo-Aryan 72%, Dravidian 25%, Mongoloid and other 3%
GOVERNMENT: Parliamentary democracy
CURRENCY: Rupee = 100 paisa

THE ECONOMY

Undergoing radical changes from protectionist mixed economy to free market. Reforms lowering trade barriers and increasing foreign investment. New high-tech industries. Principal exports are clothing, gems, jewelry, and engineering products.

INSIGHT: *India's national animal, the tiger, was chosen by the Mohenjo-Daro civilization as their emblem, 4000 years ago*

5000m/16405ft
4000m/13124ft
3000m/9843ft
2000m/6562ft
1000m/3281ft
500m/1640ft
200m/656ft
Sea Level

A 'line of control' was agreed between India and Pakistan in 1972

Aksai Chin – administered by China, claimed by India
Demchok/Dêmqog – administered by China, claimed by India

Much of Arunáchal Pradesh is claimed by China

Srinagar
Jammu & Kashmir
Amritsar
Jalandhar
Ludhiāna
Chandigarh
Meerut
Delhi
NEW DELHI
Bareilly
Jodhpur
Jaipur
Āgra
Lucknow
Kānpur
Gwalior
Kota
Varānasi
Patna
Shiliguri
NEPAL
BHUTAN
CHINA
Brahmaputra
MYANMAR (BURMA)
Assam
Imphāl
BANGLADESH
Dhanbād
Rānchī
Calcutta (Kolkata)
Haora
Mouths of the Ganges
Ahmadābād
Indore
Bhōpāl
Jabalpur
Jamshedpur
Cuttack
Jāmnagar
Rājkot
Vadodara
Surat
Nāgpur
Mahānadi
Narmada
Rann of Kachchh
Gulf of Kachchh
Gulf of Khambhāt
Kalyān
Mumbai (Bombay)
Pune
Nānded
Solāpur
Hyderābād
Deccan
Godāvari
Krishna
Visākhapatnam
Bay of Bengal
Arabian Sea
Hubli
Pānaji
Western Ghats
Eastern Ghats
Chennai (Madras)
Bangalore
Salem
Mysore
Coimbatore
Cochin
Madurai
Lakshadweep (Laccadive Is.)
INDIAN OCEAN
Andaman Islands
North Andaman
Middle Andaman
South Andaman
Port Blair
Little Andaman
Nicobar Islands
Indira Point
Great Nicobar
PAKISTAN
Thar Desert
Himalaya
Ganges
Indus

0   200 km
0   200 miles

Indonesia

Formerly known as the Dutch East Indies, Indonesia is the world's largest archipelago. Its 13,677 islands stretch 3000 miles (5000 km) eastward from the Indian to the Pacific oceans.

GEOGRAPHY

Indonesia is highly mountainous with numerous tropical swamps. The land is covered with dense rain forest, especially on New Guinea, where it remains largely unexplored. There are more than 200 volcanoes in the region, many of which are still active. The land masses of Java, Bali, Sumatra, Lombok, and Borneo were once joined together by dry land, which has since been submerged by rising sea levels. Some of the islands are large enough to have formed coastal lowlands.

CLIMATE

The climate of Indonesia is predominantly tropical monsoon. Variations relate mainly to differences in latitude and physical structure; hilly areas are cooler overall. Rain falls throughout the year, often in thunderstorms, but there is a relatively dry season from June to September.

THE ECONOMY

Varied resources, especially energy. Cheap and plentiful labor pool. Bureaucracy and corruption remains rife. Major debt burden and the continuing economic recession has led to collapse of investor confidence.

4000m/13124ft
3000m/9843ft
2000m/6562ft
1000m/3281ft
500m/1640ft
Sea Level

FACTFILE

OFFICIAL NAME: Republic of Indonesia
DATE OF FORMATION: 1945
CAPITAL: Jakarta
POPULATION: 212.1 million
TOTAL AREA: 699,447 sq miles (1,811,570 sq km)
DENSITY: 303 people per sq mile

LANGUAGES: Bahasa Indonesia*, 250 (est.) languages or dialects
RELIGIONS: Sunni Muslim 87%, Christian 9%, Hindu 2%, other 2%
ETHNIC MIX: Javanese 45%, Sundanese 14%, Madurese 8%, other 33%
GOVERNMENT: Multiparty republic
CURRENCY: Rupiah = 100 sen

PEOPLE & SOCIETY

The basic Melanesian–Malay ethnic division disguises a diverse society. Bahasa Indonesia, the national language, coexists with at least 250 other spoken languages or dialects. Attempts by the Javanese political elite to suppress local cultures have been vigorously opposed, especially by the East Timorese (who recently founded a separate state), the Aceh of northern Sumatra, and the Papuans of Irian Jaya. Religious and interethnic hostility is increasing. There have been clashes between Christians and Muslims in many areas, and discrimination against ethnic Chinese has encouraged vicious attacks on their businesses. Gender equality is enshrined in law, and women are active in public life.

◆ **INSIGHT:** *Indonesia has a very youthful population; almost 45% of its people are under 20 years of age*

Iran

Since the 1979 Islamic fundamentalist revolution led by
Ayatollah Khomeini, the Middle Eastern country of Iran
has become the world's largest theocracy.

GEOGRAPHY
High desert plateau with large
salt pans in the east. West and north are
mountainous. Coastal land bordering
Caspian Sea is rainy and forested.

CLIMATE
Desert climate. Hot summers,
and bitterly cold winters. Area around
the Caspian Sea is more temperate.

PEOPLE & SOCIETY
Many ethnic groups, including
Persians, Azerbaijanis, and Kurds.
Large number of refugees, mainly
from Afghanistan. Since the 1979
Islamic revolution, Iran's political
life has been dominated by militant
Islamic idealism. The Mullahs' belief
that adherence to religious values
is more important than economic
welfare has resulted in declining
living standards. Role of women
in public life is restricted.

THE ECONOMY
One of the world's biggest oil
producers. Government restricts
contact with the West, blocking
acquisition of vital technology.
High unemployment and inflation.

INSIGHT: *More than a hundred
offences carry the death penalty*

3000m/9843ft
2000m/6562ft
1000m/3281ft
500m/1640ft
200m/656ft
Sea Level

0   200 km
0   200 miles

FACTFILE
OFFICIAL NAME: Islamic Republic of Iran
DATE OF FORMATION: 1906
CAPITAL: Tehran
POPULATION: 67.7 million
TOTAL AREA: 631,659 sq miles
(1,636,000 sq km)
DENSITY: 107 people per sq mile

LANGUAGES: Farsi (Persian)*, other
RELIGIONS: Shi'a Muslim 95%,
Sunni Muslim 4%, other 1%
ETHNIC MIX: Persian 50%, Azeri 20%,
Lur and Bakhtiari 10%, Kurd 8%,
Arab 2%, other 10%
GOVERNMENT: Islamic theocracy
CURRENCY: Rial = 100 dinars

Iraq

Oil-rich Iraq is situated in the central Middle East. Since the removal of the monarchy in 1958, it has experienced domestic political turmoil and numerous international conflicts.

GEOGRAPHY

Mainly desert. The rivers Tigris and Euphrates water fertile regions and create the southern marshland. Mountains along northeast border.

CLIMATE

Deserts of south have hot, dry summers and mild winters. North has dry summers, but winters can be harsh in the mountains. Rainfall is low.

PEOPLE & SOCIETY

Population is mainly Arab and Kurdish, with small minorities of Turks and Persians. In 1979, President Saddam Hussein led the country in an inconclusive war with Iran (1980–88). In 1990, Hussein's invasion of Kuwait precipitated the Gulf War against UN forces. In later years, failure to co-operate with UN weapons inspectors have led to punitive air strikes and sustained economic sanctions.

THE ECONOMY

Gulf War and resulting UN sanctions had a devastating effect on the economy. Iraq was unable to sell its oil on the international market.

INSIGHT: *As Mesopotamia, Iraq was the site where the Sumerians established the world's first civilization*

3000m/9843ft
2000m/6562ft
1000m/3281ft
500m/1640ft
200m/656ft
Sea Level

0   100 km
0   100 miles

FACTFILE

OFFICIAL NAME: Republic of Iraq
DATE OF FORMATION: 1932
CAPITAL: Baghdad
POPULATION: 23.1 million
TOTAL AREA: 168,869 sq miles (437,370 sq km)
DENSITY: 137 people per sq mile

LANGUAGES: Arabic*, Kurdish, Turkish, Farsi (Persian)
RELIGIONS: Shi'a ithna Muslim 63%, Sunni Muslim 33%, other 4%
ETHNIC MIX: Arab 79%, Kurdish 16%, Persian 3%, Turkoman 2%
GOVERNMENT: One-party state
CURRENCY: Dinar = 1,000 fils

Ireland

Lying in the Atlantic Ocean, off the west coast of Britain, the Irish state occupies about 85% of the island of Ireland, with the remainder (Northern Ireland) being part of the UK.

GEOGRAPHY

Low mountain ranges along an irregular coastline surround an inland plain punctuated by lakes, undulating hills and peat bogs.

CLIMATE

The Gulf Stream accounts for the mild and wet climate. Snow is rare, except in the mountains.

PEOPLE & SOCIETY

Although homogeneous in ethnicity and Catholic religion, the population show signs of change. The younger Irish question Vatican teachings on birth control, divorce, and abortion. Traditionally a migrant nation, there is now net immigration. The Good Friday peace agreement was reached over Northern Ireland in 1998, though this has yet to be successfully implemented. The Northern Irish Assembly was established in 1998.

THE ECONOMY

High unemployment tarnishes high-tech export successes and trade surplus. The work force is highly educated. Efficient agriculture and food-processing industries.

◆ **INSIGHT:** *Currently, about 20,000 people speak Irish Gaelic as their everyday language*

FACTFILE

OFFICIAL NAME: Republic of Ireland
DATE OF FORMATION: 1922
CAPITAL: Dublin
POPULATION: 3.7 million
TOTAL AREA: 26,598 sq miles (68,890 sq km)
DENSITY: 139 people per sq mile

LANGUAGES: English*, Irish Gaelic*
RELIGIONS: Roman Catholic 88%, Anglican 3%, Jewish 1%, Presbyterian 1%, other/non-religious 7%
ETHNIC MIX: Irish 95%, other (mainly British) 5%
GOVERNMENT: Parliamentary democracy
CURRENCY: Euro = 100 cents

Israel

Created as a new state in 1948, the Middle East nation of
Israel lies on the east coast of the Mediterranean. Following
wars with its Arab neighbors, it has extended its boundaries.

GEOGRAPHY
Coastal plain. Desert in the
south. In the east lie the Great Rift
valley and the Dead Sea – the lowest
point on the Earth's surface.

CLIMATE
Summers are hot and dry. Wet
season, March–November, is mild.

PEOPLE & SOCIETY
Large numbers of Jews settled
in Palestine before Israel was founded
in 1948. After World War II, there was
a massive increase in immigration.
Sephardic Jews from the Middle East
and Mediterranean are now in the
majority, but Ashkenazi Jews from
Central Europe still dominate
business and politics. Palestinians
in Gaza and Jericho gained limited
autonomy in 1994. Recently, tensions
between the two ethnic groups have
escalated into widespread conflict.

THE ECONOMY
High unemployment and
inflation. Major exporter of mineral
salts. Important banking sector.

INSIGHT: *All Jews worldwide
have the right of Israeli citizenship*

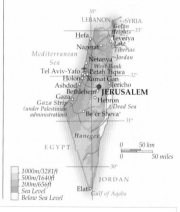

1000m/3281ft
500m/1640ft
200m/656ft
Sea Level
Below Sea Level

0   50 km
0   50 miles

FACTFILE

OFFICIAL NAME: State of Israel
DATE OF FORMATION: 1948
CAPITAL: Jerusalem
POPULATION: 6.2 million
TOTAL AREA: 7849 sq miles
(20,330 sq km)
DENSITY: 790 people per sq mile

LANGUAGES: Hebrew*, Arabic, Yiddish,
German, Russian, Polish, Romanian,
Persian, English
RELIGIONS: Jewish 82%, Muslim 14%,
Christian 2%, other 2%
ETHNIC MIX: Jewish 82%, Arab 18%
GOVERNMENT: Parliamentary democracy
CURRENCY: New shekel = 100 agorot

Italy

The Italian peninsula was home to the Roman Empire, one of the greatest ancient civilizations. The south has two famous volcanoes, Vesuvius and Etna.

GEOGRAPHY
The Appennino form the backbone of a rugged peninsula, extending from the Alps into the Mediterranean Sea. Alluvial plain in the north.

CLIMATE
Mediterranean in the south. Seasonal extremes in the mountains and on the northern alluvial plain.

PEOPLE & SOCIETY
Ethnically homogeneous, but with a gulf between the prosperous, industrial north and the poorer, agricultural south. Strong regional identities persist, especially on the islands of Sicily and Sardinia. Allegiance to the family survives the lessened influence of Church.

◆ **INSIGHT:** *Italy was a collection of dukedoms, monarchies, and city states before it became unified in 1871*

THE ECONOMY
World leader in industrial and product design, as well as textiles. Strong tourism and agriculture sectors. Large public sector debt.

FACTFILE

OFFICIAL NAME: Italian Republic
DATE OF FORMATION: 1871
CAPITAL: Rome
POPULATION: 57.3 million
TOTAL AREA: 113,536 sq miles (294,060 sq km)
DENSITY: 505 people per sq mile

LANGUAGES: Italian*, German, French, Rhaeto-Romanic, Sardinian
RELIGIONS: Roman Catholic 83%, Protestant 1%, Jewish 1%, other 15%
ETHNIC MIX: Italian 94%, Sardinian 2%, other 4%
GOVERNMENT: Parliamentary democracy
CURRENCY: Euro = 100 cents

Jamaica

First colonized by the Spanish and then by the English, the Caribbean island of Jamaica achieved independence in 1962. It remains an influential force in Caribbean politics.

GEOGRAPHY

Mainly mountainous, with lush tropical vegetation. Inaccessible limestone area in the northwest. Low, irregular coastal plains are broken by hills and plateaus.

CLIMATE

Tropical. Hot and humid at sea level, with temperate mountain areas. Hurricanes are likely June–November.

PEOPLE & SOCIETY

Ethnically diverse, but tensions result from vast disparities in wealth, rather than race. Economic and political life dominated by a few wealthy, long-established families. Many women hold senior positions in public life. Armed crime, much of it drugs-related, is a problem. Large areas of Kingston, which have their own *patois*, are ruled by Dons, gang leaders who administer their own violent justice.

THE ECONOMY

Major producer of bauxite (aluminum ore). Tourism well developed. Light industry and data processing for US companies. Sugar, coffee, and rum are exported.

INSIGHT: *Jamaica's Rastafarians look to the late emperor of Ethiopia, Haile Selassie, as their spiritual leader, and Africa as their spiritual home*

FACTFILE

OFFICIAL NAME: Jamaica
DATE OF FORMATION: 1962
CAPITAL: Kingston
POPULATION: 2.6 million
TOTAL AREA: 4,181 sq miles (10,830 sq km)
DENSITY: 622 people per sq mile

LANGUAGES: English*, English Creole, Hindi, Spanish, Chinese
RELIGIONS: Christian 55%, other and non-religious 45%
ETHNIC MIX: Black 75%, mulatto 13%, Euro/Chinese 11%, Indian 1%
GOVERNMENT: Parliamentary democracy
CURRENCY: Jamaican $ = 100 cents

Japan

Japan is located off the East Asian coast and comprises four principal islands and over 3000 smaller ones. A powerful economy, it has an emperor as ceremonial head of state.

GEOGRAPHY

The terrain is predominantly mountainous, with fertile coastal plains; over two-thirds is woodland. There is no single continuous mountain range; the mountains divide into many small land blocks separated by lowlands and dissected by numerous river valleys. The islands lie on the Pacific "Ring of Fire," and earthquakes and volcanic eruptions are frequent. The Pacific coast is vulnerable to *tsunamis* – tidal waves triggered by submarine earthquakes.

CLIMATE

Generally temperate oceanic. Spring is warm and sunny, while summer is hot and humid, with high rainfall. In western Hokkaidó and northwest Honshú, winters are very cold, with heavy snowfall. Freak storms and damaging floods in recent years have raised concern over global climate changes.

PEOPLE & SOCIETY

One of the most racially homogeneous societies in the world. Its sense of order is reflected in the phenomenon of the lifetime employer. People define themselves by the company they work for, not the job they do. Employers organize social activities and even encourage and approve marriages. Women mostly play a traditional role running the home; some, however, are beginning to take up long-term careers. Social form remains very important. Respect for elders and social and business superiors is strongly ingrained. There is little tradition of generation rebellion, but the youth market is powerful and current fashions place teenagers at their center. The education system is highly pressurized Nongraduates have difficulty reaching management level jobs, so competition for university places is intense.

FACTFILE

OFFICIAL NAME: Japan
DATE OF FORMATION: 1945
CAPITAL: Tokyo
POPULATION: 1.013 billion
TOTAL AREA: 145,374 sq miles (376,520 sq km)
DENSITY: 871 people per sq mile

LANGUAGES: Japanese*, Korean, Chinese
RELIGIONS: Shinto and Buddhist 76%, Buddhist 16%, other (inc. Christian) 8%
ETHNIC MIX: Japanese 99%, other (mainly Korean) 1%
GOVERNMENT: Parliamentary democracy
CURRENCY: Yen = 100 sen

Japan

THE ECONOMY
The world's most competitive producer of high-tech electronic products and cars. Talent for developing ideas from EU and the US. Once-revolutionary management and production methods. Global spread of business, especially to the EU and the US. Commitment to long-term research and development. The trade surplus is a source of international tension. Japan suffered from an economic crisis in 1998 which threatened the global economy.

◆ **INSIGHT:** *The Japanese are among the world's most avid newspaper readers, with daily sales exceeding 70 million copies*

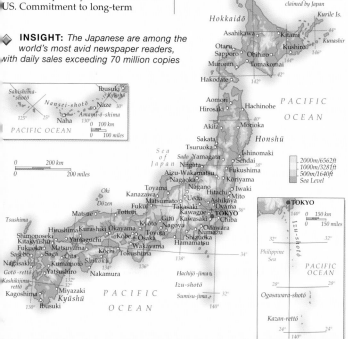

Jordan

The kingdom of Jordan lies east of Israel, and also borders the Palestinian-controlled West Bank. It was a key player in Middle East politics during the reign of the late King Hussein.

GEOGRAPHY

Mostly desert plateaus, with occasional salt pans. Lowest parts lie along eastern shore of Dead Sea and East Bank of the River Jordan.

CLIMATE

Hot, dry summers. Cool, wet winters. Areas below sea level very hot in summer, and warm in winter.

PEOPLE & SOCIETY

A predominantly Muslim country with a strong national identity, Jordan's population has Bedouin roots. There is a Christian minority and a large Palestinian population who moved to Jordan from Israeli-occupied territory. Jordan legally includes the West Bank and East Jerusalem, but gave up its claim to the West Bank to the PLO in 1988. The monarchy's power base lies among the rural tribes, which also provide the backbone of the military.

THE ECONOMY

Phosphates, chemicals, and fertilizers are principal exports. Skilled, educated work force.

INSIGHT: *The Nabataean ruins at the ancient city of Petra attract thousands of tourists every year*

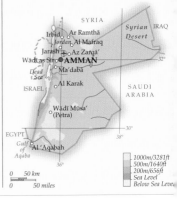

1000m/3281ft	
500m/1640ft	
200m/656ft	
Sea Level	
Below Sea Level	

0   50 km
0   50 miles

FACTFILE

OFFICIAL NAME: Hashemite Kingdom of Jordan
DATE OF FORMATION: 1946
CAPITAL: Amman
POPULATION: 6.7 million
TOTAL AREA: 34,335 sq miles (88,930 sq km)

DENSITY: 195 people per sq km
LANGUAGES: Arabic*, other
RELIGIONS: Muslim (mainly Sunni) 92%, other (mostly Christian) 8%
ETHNIC MIX: Arab 98%, Armenian 1%, Circassian 1%
GOVERNMENT: Constitutional monarchy
CURRENCY: Dinar = 1000 fil

Kazakhstan

Mineral-rich Kazakhstan was the last of the former Soviet republics to declare independence. It has the potential to become the major Central Asian economic power.

GEOGRAPHY
Mainly steppe. Volga delta and Caspian Sea in the west. Central plateau. Inhospitable Altai mountains in the east. Semidesert in the south.

CLIMATE
Dry continental. Temperature variations between desert south and northern steppes are large. Winters are mildest near the Caspian Sea.

PEOPLE & SOCIETY
Kazakhs only just outnumber Russians in a multiethnic society. Stable relations with Russia, plus an increased international profile, preserve relative harmony, though ethnic tensions are growing steadily. Few Kazakhs maintain a nomadic lifestyle, but Islam and loyalty to the three Hordes (clan federations) remain strong. First presidential elections with choice of candidates in 1999.

THE ECONOMY
Vast mineral resources, notably gas, oil, coal, uranium, and gold. Increasing foreign investment, but living standards have fallen with market reforms to date.

INSIGHT: *The Soviet Union's space program was based at Baykonyr, in south Kazakhstan*

3000m/9843ft	
2000m/6562ft	
1000m/3281ft	
500m/1640ft	
200m/656ft	
Sea Level	
Below Sea level	

0   400 km
0   400 miles

FACTFILE

OFFICIAL NAME: Republic of Kazakhstan
DATE OF FORMATION: 1991
CAPITAL: Astana
POPULATION: 16.2 million
TOTAL AREA: 1,049,150 sq miles (2,717,300 sq km)
DENSITY: 15 people per sq mile

LANGUAGES: Kazakh*, Russian, other
RELIGIONS: Muslim 50%, Russian Orthodox 13%, Protestant 1%, other 36%,
ETHNIC MIX: Kazakh 53%, Russian 30%, Ukrainian 4%, other 13%
GOVERNMENT: Presidential democracy
CURRENCY: Tenge = 100 tein

Kenya

Kenya straddles the Equator on Africa's east coast. Once a British colony, it became a multiparty democracy in 1992 and has been led by President Moi since 1978.

GEOGRAPHY
A central plateau is divided by the Great Rift Valley. North of the Equator is mainly semidesert. To the east lies a fertile coastal belt.

CLIMATE
The coast and the Great Rift Valley are hot and humid. The plateau interior is temperate. The northeastern desert is hot and dry. Rain usually falls April–May and October–November.

PEOPLE & SOCIETY
Kenya's 70 ethnic groups share about 40 languages. The rural majority has strong clan and family links. One of the world's highest population growth rates, coupled with high poverty, has exacerbated the recent ethnic violence.

◆ INSIGHT: *Kenya has more than 40 game reserves and national parks, and two marine parks*

THE ECONOMY
Tourism is the leading foreign exchange earner. Tea and coffee are grown as cash crops. There is a large and diversified manufacturing sector.

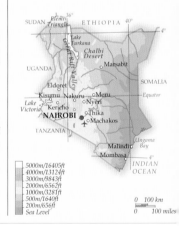

5000m/16405ft	
4000m/13124ft	
3000m/9843ft	
2000m/6562ft	
1000m/3281ft	
500m/1640ft	
200m/656ft	
Sea Level	

0   100 km
0   100 miles

FACTFILE
OFFICIAL NAME: Republic of Kenya
DATE OF FORMATION: 1963
CAPITAL: Nairobi
POPULATION: 30.1 million
TOTAL AREA: 218,907 sq miles (566,970 sq km)
DENSITY: 138 people per sq mile

LANGUAGES: Swahili*, English, Kikuyu, Luo, Kamba, other
RELIGIONS: Christian 60%, traditional beliefs 25%, Muslim 6%, other 9%
ETHNIC MIX: Kikuyu 21%, Luhya 14%, Luo 13%, Kamba 11%, other 41%
GOVERNMENT: Presidential democracy
CURRENCY: Shilling = 100 cents

Kiribati

Part of the British colony of the Gilbert and Ellice Islands, the Gilberts adopted the name Kiribati at independence in 1979. The state comprises 33 islands in the mid-Pacific Ocean.

GEOGRAPHY

Kiribati consists of three groups of tiny, very low-lying coral atolls scattered across 1,930,000 sq miles (5 million sq km) of ocean. Most of the islands have central lagoons.

CLIMATE

Central islands have a maritime equatorial climate. Those to north and south are tropical, with constant high temperatures. There is little rainfall.

PEOPLE & SOCIETY

Local people still refer to themselves as Gilbertese. Apart from the inhabitants of the island of Banaba, who employed anthropologists to establish their racial distinction, almost all people are Micronesian. Most are poor subsistence farmers. The islands are effectively ruled by traditional chiefs, though there is a party system based on the British model.

THE ECONOMY

Until 1980, when deposits ran out, phosphate from Banaba provided 80% of exports. Since then, coconuts, copra, and fish have become the main exports, but the islands are still heavily dependent on foreign aid.

◆ **INSIGHT:** *In 1981, the UK paid A$10 million to Banabans for the destruction of their island by mining*

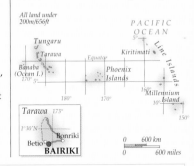

All land under 200m/656ft

PACIFIC OCEAN

Tungaru
Tarawa
Banaba (Ocean I.)
170° 5°
Equator
Kiritimati
Phoenix Islands
Line Islands
170°
180°
160°
Millennium Island
10°
150°

Tarawa 173°
1°30'N
Bonriki
Betio
BAIRIKI

0   600 km
0   600 miles

FACTFILE

OFFICIAL NAME: Republic of Kiribati
DATE OF FORMATION: 1979
CAPITAL: Bairiki (Tarawa Atoll)
POPULATION: 91,985
TOTAL AREA: 274 sq miles (710 sq km)
DENSITY: 336 people per sq mile

LANGUAGES: English*, Kiribati, other
RELIGIONS: Catholic 53%, Kiribati Protestant 39%, other 8%
ETHNIC MIX: Micronesian 98%, other 2%
GOVERNMENT: Non-party democracy
CURRENCY: Australian $ = 100 cents

North Korea

North Korea occupies the northern half of the Korean peninsula. Established as an independent communist republic in 1948, it remains largely isolated from the outside world.

GEOGRAPHY
Mostly mountainous, with fertile plains in the southwest.

CLIMATE
Continental. Warm summers and cold winters, especially in the north, where snow is common.

PEOPLE & SOCIETY
People live severely regulated lives. Divorce is nonexistent and extramarital sex is highly frowned upon. Women form 57% of the work force, but are also expected to run the home. Children are looked after in state-run crèches. The Korean Worker's Party is the only legal political party. Clashes between the navy and that of South Korea in 1999 marred plans to resume reunification talks.

◆ INSIGHT: *Telephones and private cars are forbidden in North Korea*

THE ECONOMY
The economy suffered badly in the 1990s, following the demise of aid from China and the former Soviet Union. The current famine means massive international aid is required to stave off starvation.

- 2000m/6562ft
- 1000m/3281ft
- 500m/1640ft
- 200m/656ft
- Sea Level

RUSS FED.

CHINA

Ch'ongjin
Kanggye
Huich'on
Sinŭiju
Hamhung
Iwŏn
Kimch'aek
Korea Bay
Hŭngnam
Wŏnsan
●PYONGYANG
Sea of Japan
Namp'o
Haeju
Kaesŏng
SOUTH KOREA
Yellow Sea

0 50 km
0 50 miles

FACTFILE

OFFICIAL NAME: Democratic People's Republic of Korea
DATE OF FORMATION: 1948
CAPITAL: Pyongyang
POPULATION: 24 million
TOTAL AREA: 46,490 sq miles (120,410 sq km)

DENSITY: 516 people per sq mile
LANGUAGES: Korean*, Chinese
RELIGIONS: Traditional beliefs 16%, Ch'ondogyo 14%, Buddhist 2%, nonreligious 68%
ETHNIC MIX: Korean 100%
GOVERNMENT: One-party state
CURRENCY: Won = 100 chon

South Korea

South Korea occupies the southern half of the Korean peninsula Under US sponsorship, it was separated from the communist North in 1948, and is now a successful capitalist economy.

GEOGRAPHY
Over 80% is mountainous and two-thirds is forested. The flattest and most populous parts lie along the west coast and in the extreme south.

CLIMATE
There are four distinct seasons. Winters are dry, and bitterly cold. Summers are hot and humid.

PEOPLE & SOCIETY
Inhabited by a single ethnic group for the last 2000 years. Family life is a central and clearly defined part of Korean society. Women's role is traditional. Since the Korean War (1950–53), North and South Korea have remained mutually hostile; recent plans for reunification talks marred by clashes between navies.

◆ **INSIGHT:** *Over 60% of Koreans are named Kim, Lee, or Park*

THE ECONOMY
World's biggest shipbuilder. High demand from China for Korean goods, especially cars. Electronics and household appliances are important.

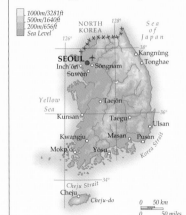

▨	1000m/3281ft
▨	500m/1640ft
▨	200m/656ft
▨	Sea Level

NORTH KOREA

Sea of Japan

128°
126°
38°

SEOUL
Inch'ŏn • Sŏngnam
Suwŏn

Kangnŭng
Tonghae

Yellow Sea

Taejŏn
Kunsan
Taegu
36°
Ulsan

Kwangju
Masan
Pusan
Mokp'o
Yŏsu

Korea Strait

34°
Cheju Strait
Cheju
Cheju-do

0   50 km
0   50 miles

FACTFILE

OFFICIAL NAME: Republic of Korea
DATE OF FORMATION: 1948
CAPITAL: Seoul
POPULATION: 46.8 million
TOTAL AREA: 38,119 sq miles (98,730 sq km)
DENSITY: 1,228 people per sq mile

LANGUAGES: Korean*, Chinese
RELIGIONS: Mahayana Buddhist 47%, Protestant 38%, Catholic 11%, Confucian 3%, other 1%
ETHNIC MIX: Korean 100%
GOVERNMENT: Presidential democracy
CURRENCY: Won = 100 chon

Kuwait

Kuwait lies at the northwest extreme of the Gulf, dwarfed by its neighbors Iraq, Iran, and Saudi Arabia. It was a British protectorate until 1961, when full independence was granted.

GEOGRAPHY
Terrain is low-lying desert. The lowest land is in the north. Cultivation is only possible along the coast.

CLIMATE
Summers are very hot and dry. Winters are cooler, with some rain and occasional frost at night.

PEOPLE & SOCIETY
An oil-rich monarchy, ruled by the Al-Sabah family. Oil wealth has attracted workers from India, Pakistan, and other Arab states. In 1990, Iraq invaded Kuwait, claiming the state as its 19th province. A US-led alliance, backed by the UN, ousted Iraqi forces following a short war in 1991. Many foreign workers were expelled after the war, in an attempt to ensure a Kuwaiti majority. Although Kuwait is a fundamentalist Sunni Muslim society, women have considerable freedom.

THE ECONOMY
Oil and gas production has been restored to pre-invasion levels. Skilled labor, raw materials, and food are imported. Vulnerability to Iraqi attack deters Western industrial investment.

◆ **INSIGHT:** *During the Gulf War, 800 of Kuwait's 950 oil wells were deliberately fired*

FACTFILE

OFFICIAL NAME: State of Kuwait
DATE OF FORMATION: 1961
CAPITAL: Kuwait City
POPULATION: 2 million
TOTAL AREA: 6880 sq miles (17,820 sq km)
DENSITY: 291 people per sq mile

LANGUAGES: Arabic*, English, other
RELIGIONS: Sunni & Shi'a Muslim 75%, Christian, Hindu and other 15%, other Muslim 10%
ETHNIC MIX: Kuwaiti 45%, other Arab 35%, South Asian 9%, other 11%
GOVERNMENT: Constitutional monarchy
CURRENCY: Dinar = 1000 fils

Kyrgyzstan

A small and very mountainous landlocked state in Central Asia. The least urbanized of the ex-Soviet republics, it was among the last to develop its own cultural nationalism.

GEOGRAPHY

The mountainous spurs of the Tien Shan range contain glaciers, alpine meadows, forests, and narrow valleys. Semidesert in the west.

CLIMATE

Varies from permanent snow and cold deserts at high altitudes, to hot deserts in low regions.

PEOPLE & SOCIETY

Ethnic Kyrgyz majority status dates only from the late 1980s, and is due to their higher birth rate. There is considerable tension between the Kyrgyz and other groups, particularly the Uzbeks. A large Russian community no longer wields power, but is seen as necessary for the transfer of skills. The trend in politics is toward greater Islamicization. Concerns over rising crime rate and opium poppy cultivation accompany political reforms.

THE ECONOMY

Dominated by the state and the tradition of collective farming. Small quantities of commercially exploitable coal, oil, and gas. Great hydroelectric power potential.

◆ **INSIGHT:** *Kyrgyz folklore is based around the 1000-year-old poem,* Manas, *which takes a week to recite*

📘 FACTFILE

OFFICIAL NAME: Kyrgyz Republic
DATE OF FORMATION: 1991
CAPITAL: Bishkek
POPULATION: 4.7 million
TOTAL AREA: 76,640 sq miles (198,500 sq km)
DENSITY: 61 people per sq mile

LANGUAGES: Kyrgyz*, Russian, Uzbek
RELIGIONS: Sunni Muslim 70%, Russian Orthodox 30%
ETHNIC MIX: Kyrgyz 57%, Russian 19%, Uzbek 13%, Tatar 2%, Ukranian 2%, other 7%
GOVERNMENT: Presidential democracy
CURRENCY: Som = 100 teen

Laos

A former French colony, independent in 1953, Laos lies landlocked in Southeast Asia. Heavily bombed during the Vietnam War, it has been under communist rule since 1975.

GEOGRAPHY

Largely forested mountains, broadening in the north to a plateau. Lowlands along the Mekong valley.

CLIMATE

Monsoon rains September–May. The rest of the year is hot and dry.

PEOPLE & SOCIETY

There are over 60 ethnic groups. Lowland Laotians (Lao Loum) live along the Mekong River and are wet-rice farmers. Upland Laotians (Lao Theung) and mountain-top Laotians (Lao Soung) practice slash-and-burn farming. Government efforts to halt this traditional farming method, which can destroy forests and watersheds, have been resisted.

◆ **INSIGHT:** *In the early 1990s, Laos and Thailand built a "Friendship Bridge" across the Mekong at Vientiane*

THE ECONOMY

One of the world's 20 least-developed nations. The government began to introduce market-oriented reforms in 1986. Potential for timber, mining, and garment manufacturing.

FACTFILE

OFFICIAL NAME: Lao People's Democratic Republic
DATE OF FORMATION: 1953
CAPITAL: Vientiane
POPULATION: 5.4 million
TOTAL AREA: 89,112 sq miles (230,800 sq km)

DENSITY: 61 people per sq mile
LANGUAGES: Lao*, Miao, Yao, other
RELIGIONS: Buddhist 85%, other (including Anmist) 15%
ETHNIC MIX: Lao Loum 56%, Lao Theung 34%, Lao Soung 9%, other 1%
GOVERNMENT: One-party state
CURRENCY: Kip = 100 cents

Latvia

Latvia lies on the east coast of the Baltic Sea, between Estonia and Lithuania. Like its Baltic neighbors, it became independent from Moscow in 1991. It retains a large Russian population.

GEOGRAPHY

A flat coastal plain which is deeply indented by the Gulf of Riga. Poor drainage creates many bogs and swamps in the forested interior.

CLIMATE

Temperate, with warm summers and cold winters. There is steady rainfall throughout the year.

PEOPLE & SOCIETY

Latvians make up only half the population, and are a minority in Riga. Latvia is the most urbanized of the three Baltic states, with more than 70% of the population living in cities and towns. Delicate relations with Russia are dictated by a large Russian minority, and energy and infrastructure investment dating from the Soviet period. The status of women is on a par with that in most of western Europe. The divorce rate is high.

THE ECONOMY

Transportation and defense equipment lead strong industrial sector. Developed paper-making industry. Good ports. Russia remains the main trading partner, though foreign investment is rising.

INSIGHT: *Latvia's flag is said to represent a sheet stained with the blood of a 13th-century Latvian hero*

FACTFILE

OFFICIAL NAME: Republic of Latvia
DATE OF FORMATION: 1991
CAPITAL: Riga
POPULATION: 2.4 million
TOTAL AREA: 24,938 sq miles (64,589 sq km)
DENSITY: 96 people per sq mile

LANGUAGES: Latvian*, Russian
RELIGIONS: Lutheran 55%, Catholic 24%, Russian Orthodox 9%, other 12%
ETHNIC MIX: Latvian 52%, Russian 34%, Belorussian 5%, Ukrainian 4%, other 5%
GOVERNMENT: Presidential democracy
CURRENCY: Lat = 100 santimi

Lebanon

Lebanon is dwarfed by its two powerful neighbors, Syria and Israel. Civil war threatened to break up the state in 1975, but a peace agreement was brokered by Saudi Arabia in 1989.

GEOGRAPHY
Behind a narrow coastal plain, two parallel mountain ranges run the entire length of the country, separated by the fertile El Beqaa valley.

CLIMATE
Winters are mild and summers are hot, with high coastal humidity. Snow falls on high ground in winter.

PEOPLE & SOCIETY
The population is split between Christians and Muslims, but retains a strong sense of national identity. Although in the minority, Christians have been the traditional rulers. In 1975, civil war broke out between the two groups. A settlement, which gave the Muslims more power, was reached in 1989. Elections in 1992 brought hope of greater stability. A huge economic gulf exists between the poor and a small, immensely rich elite.

THE ECONOMY
Opportunity to regain position as Arab center for banking and services now the war is ended. Potentially a major producer of wine and fruit.

INSIGHT: *The Cedar of Lebanon has been the nation's symbol for more than 2000 years*

FACTFILE
OFFICIAL NAME: Republic of Lebanon
DATE OF FORMATION: 1944
CAPITAL: Beirut
POPULATION: 3.3 million
TOTAL AREA: 3949 sq miles (10,230 sq km)
DENSITY: 836 people per sq mile

LANGUAGES: Arabic*, French, Armenian, English
RELIGIONS: Muslim (mainly Shi'a) 70%, Christian (mainly Maronite) 30%
ETHNIC MIX: Arab 94%, Armenian 4%, other 2%
GOVERNMENT: Multiparty republic
CURRENCY: Pound = 100 piastres

Lesotho

The landlocked kingdom of Lesotho is entirely surrounded by – and economically dependent on – South Africa, which provides all its land transportation links with the outside world.

GEOGRAPHY
A high mountainous plateau, cut by valleys and ravines. The Maluti range runs through the center. The Drakensberg range lies to the east.

CLIMATE
Temperate. Summers are hot with torrential rain storms. Snow is frequent in the mountains in winter.

PEOPLE & SOCIETY
Almost everyone is Basotho, although there are some South Asians, Europeans, and Taiwanese. A strong sense of national identity has tended to minimize ethnic tensions. Many men work as migrant laborers in South Africa, leaving 72% of households, and most of the farms, run by women.

◆ INSIGHT: *Lesotho has one of the highest literacy rates in Africa, and the highest female literacy rate – 93%*

THE ECONOMY
Few natural resources. Heavy reliance on the incomes of its migrant workers. Subsistence farming is the main activity. Exports include wool, mohair, and livestock.

3000m/9843ft
2000m/6562ft
1000m/3281ft

0   50 km
0   50 miles

FACTFILE
OFFICIAL NAME: Kingdom of Lesotho
DATE OF FORMATION: 1966
CAPITAL: Maseru
POPULATION: 2.2 million
TOTAL AREA: 11,718 sq miles
(30,350 sq km)
DENSITY: 188 people per sq mile

LANGUAGES: English*, Sesotho*, Zulu
RELIGIONS: Christian 90%, traditional beliefs 10%
ETHNIC MIX: Sotho 97%, European and Asian 3%
GOVERNMENT: Constitutional monarchy
CURRENCY: Loti = 100 lisente

Liberia

Liberia, Africa's oldest republic, faces the Atlantic Ocean. Today Liberia is struggling to recover from a civil war which reduced it to a state of anarchy between 1990 and 1996.

GEOGRAPHY
A coastline of beaches and mangrove swamps rises to forested plateaus and highlands inland.

CLIMATE
High temperatures. Except in the extreme southeast, there is only one wet season, from May to October.

PEOPLE & SOCIETY
The key social distinction has been between Americo-Liberians – descendants of freed slaves – and the indigenous tribal peoples. However, political assimilation and intermarriage have eased tensions. Inter-tribal tension is now a problem. A civil war has ravaged the country since 1990, with private armies competing for power.

◆ **INSIGHT:** Liberia is named after the people liberated from slavery who arrived from the US in the 1800s

THE ECONOMY
Civil war has led to the collapse of the economy – there is very little commercial activity. Only 1% of the land is suitable for cultivation. There are an estimated one billion tonnes of iron-ore reserves at Mount Nimba.

FACTFILE
OFFICIAL NAME: Republic of Liberia
DATE OF FORMATION: 1847
CAPITAL: Monrovia
POPULATION: 3.2 million
TOTAL AREA: 37,189 sq miles (96,320 sq km)
DENSITY: 86 people per sq mile

LANGUAGES: English*, Kpelle, Bassa Vai, Grebo, Kru, Kissi, Gola
RELIGIONS: Christian 68%, traditional beliefs 18%, Muslim 14%,
ETHNIC MIX: Indigenous tribes 95%, Americo-Liberians 5%
GOVERNMENT: Multiparty republic
CURRENCY: Liberian $ = 100 cents

Libya

Situated on the Mediterranean coast of North Africa, Libya is a Muslim dictatorship, politically marginalized by the West for its terrorist links. UN sanctions were recently suspended.

GEOGRAPHY

Apart from the coastal strip and a mountain range in the south, Libya is desert or semidesert. Natural oases provide the agricultural land.

CLIMATE

Hot and arid. The coastal area has a temperate climate, with mild, wet winters, and hot, dry summers.

PEOPLE & SOCIETY

Most Libyans are of Arab and Berber origin. A revolution in 1969 brought Colonel Gadaffi to power. He represents independence, Islamic faith, belief in communal lifestyle, and hatred of urban rich. Revolution wiped out private enterprise and middle classes. Jews and European settlers were banished. Since then, Libya has changed from being largely a nation of nomads and livestock herders to 70% city-dwellers.

THE ECONOMY

90% of export earnings come from oil, which is subject to fluctuating world prices. Dates, olives, peaches, and grapes are grown in the oases.

◆ **INSIGHT:** *Libya's sulfur-free oil gives out little pollution when burned*

2000m/6562ft	
1000m/3281ft	
500m/1640ft	
200m/656ft	
Sea Level	
Below Sea Level	

0   200 km
0   200 miles

FACTFILE

OFFICIAL NAME: The Great Socialist People's Libyan Arab Jamahiriya
DATE OF FORMATION: 1951
CAPITAL: Tripoli
POPULATION: 5.6 million
TOTAL AREA: 679,358 sq miles (1,759,540 sq km)

DENSITY: 8 people per sq mile
LANGUAGES: Arabic*, Tuareg
RELIGIONS: Muslim (mainly Sunni) 97%, other 3%
ETHNIC MIX: Arab and Berber 95%, other 5%
GOVERNMENT: One-party state
CURRENCY: Dinar = 1000 dirhams

Luxembourg

Making up part of the plateau of the Ardennes in Western Europe, Luxembourg is one of Europe's richest states. A tax haven and banking center, it is also home to key EU institutions.

GEOGRAPHY
Dense Ardennes forests in the north, with a low, open plateau to the south. Undulating terrain throughout.

CLIMATE
The climate is moist, with warm summers and mild winters. Snow is common only in the Ardennes.

PEOPLE & SOCIETY
Society is peaceable, despite a large proportion of foreigners (half the work force and one third of the residents). Integration has been straightforward; most are fellow Western Europeans and Catholics, mainly from Italy and Portugal. Very low unemployment and high salaries promote stability.

◆ **INSIGHT:** *Luxembourg's capital, Luxembourg, is home to over 980 investment funds and some 200 banks*

THE ECONOMY
Traditional industries such as steelmaking have given way in recent years to a thriving banking and service sector. Its tax-haven status attracts foreign companies.

500m/1640ft
200m/656ft
Sea Level

Clervaux

50°

GERMANY

Ettelbruck

Echternach

Mersch

BELGIUM

● LUXEMBOURG

Pétange

Differdange
Esch-sur-Alzette
Dudelange

49°30'

FRANCE

6°30'

6°

| 0 | 10 km |
| 0 | 10 miles |

FACTFILE
OFFICIAL NAME: Grand Duchy of Luxembourg
DATE OF FORMATION: 1867
CAPITAL: Luxembourg
POPULATION: 431,000
TOTAL AREA: 998 sq miles (2585 sq km)

DENSITY: 432 people per sq mile
LANGUAGES: Letzeburgish*, French*, German*, Italian, Portuguese, other
RELIGIONS: Catholic 97%, other 3%
ETHNIC MIX: Luxemburger 73%, foreign residents 27%
GOVERNMENT: Parliamentary democracy
CURRENCY: Euro = 100 cents

Macedonia

Landlocked in the southern Balkans, Macedonia was troubled by the sanctions placed on its northern trading partners in the mid-1990s, and by violent conflict with ethnic Albanians in 2001.

GEOGRAPHY
Mainly mountainous or hilly, with deep river basins in the center. Plains in the northeast and southwest.

CLIMATE
Continental climate with wet springs and dry autumns. Heavy snowfalls in northern mountains.

PEOPLE & SOCIETY
Slav Macedonians comprise two-thirds of the population. Officially 20% are Albanian, although Albanians claim they account for 40%, a figure which has since risen to include Albanian refugees fleeing Kosovo. The Greek government is hostile toward the state because it suspects it may try to absorb northern Greece. Social structures remain essentially socialist. Macedonians are mostly Eastern Orthodox, with some Muslims; ethnic Albanians are mostly Muslim.

THE ECONOMY
Serbian sanctions paralyze exports, but foreign aid and grants boost the foreign exchange reserves. Growing private sector. Thriving black market in the capital.

INSIGHT: *Ohrid is the deepest lake in Europe at 964 ft (294 m)*

FACTFILE
OFFICIAL NAME: Former Yugoslav Republic of Macedonia
DATE OF FORMATION: 1991
CAPITAL: Skopje
POPULATION: 2 million
TOTAL AREA: 9929 sq miles (25,715 sq km)

DENSITY: 201 people per sq mile
LANGUAGES: Macedonian, Serbian & croatian (no official language)
RELIGIONS: Christian 74%, Muslim 26%
ETHNIC MIX: Macedonian 67%, Albanian 23%, Turkish 4%, Serb 2%, other 4%
GOVERNMENT: Multiparty republic
CURRENCY: Denar = 100 deni

Madagascar

Lying off the west African coast in the Indian Ocean, the former French colony of Madagascar is the world's fourth largest island. Free elections in 1993 ended 18 years of socialist government.

GEOGRAPHY
More than two thirds of the country forms a savannah-covered plateau, which drops sharply to a narrow coastal belt in the east.

CLIMATE
Tropical, and often hit by cyclones. Monsoons affect the east coast. The southwest is much drier.

PEOPLE & SOCIETY
People are Malay-Indonesian in origin, intermixed with later migrants from the African mainland. The main ethnic division is between the Merina of the central plateau and the poorer *côtier* (coastal) peoples. The Merina were the country's historic rulers, and remain the social and political elite.

◆ **INSIGHT:** *80% of Madagascar's plants and many of its animal species are found nowhere else*

THE ECONOMY
Over 80% of people are farmers. Coffee is the most important cash crop. World's largest producer of vanilla. Shrimp are a valuable export.

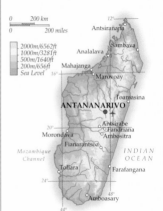

2000m/6562ft	
1000m/3281ft	
500m/1640ft	
200m/656ft	
Sea Level	

FACTFILE

OFFICIAL NAME: Democratic Republic of Madagascar
DATE OF FORMATION: 1960
CAPITAL: Antananarivo
POPULATION: 15.9 million
TOTAL AREA: 224,532 sq miles (581,540 sq km)

DENSITY: 71 people per sq mile
LANGUAGES: Malagasy*, French*
RELIGIONS: Traditional beliefs 52%, Christian 41%, Muslim 7%
ETHNIC MIX: Merina 26%, Betsimisaraka 15%, Betsileo 12%, other 47%
GOVERNMENT: Presidential democracy
CURRENCY: Franc = 100 centimes

Malawi

A former British colony, Malawi lies landlocked in southeast Africa, bordering the Great Rift Valley. Its name means "the land where the sun is reflected in the water like fire."

GEOGRAPHY
Lake Nyasa takes up one fifth of the landscape. Highlands lie west of the lake. Much of the land is covered by forests and savannah.

CLIMATE
Mainly subtropical. The south is hot and humid. Highlands are cooler.

PEOPLE & SOCIETY
There are few ethnic tensions as most people share a common Bantu origin. However, tensions between north and south have arisen in recent years. Northerners are increasingly disaffected by their lack of political representation. Many Asians are involved in the retail trade. Multi-party politics was introduced in 1993.

◆ **INSIGHT:** *Lake Nyasa is 353 miles (568 km) in length and contains at least 500 species of fish*

THE ECONOMY
Tobacco accounts for 76% of export earnings. Tea and sugar production. Coal, bauxite reserves.

2000m/6562ft	
1000m/3281ft	
500m/1640ft	
200m/656ft	
Sea Level	

FACTFILE
OFFICIAL NAME: Republic of Malawi
DATE OF FORMATION: 1964
CAPITAL: Lilongwe
POPULATION: 10.9 million
TOTAL AREA: 36,324 sq miles (94,080 sq km)
DENSITY: 300 people per sq mile

LANGUAGES: English*, Chewa*, other
RELIGIONS: Protestant 55%, Roman Catholic 20%, Muslim 20%, traditional beliefs 5%
ETHNIC MIX: Bantu 99%, other 1%
GOVERNMENT: Presidential democracy
CURRENCY: Kwacha = 100 tambala

Malaysia

Comprising the three separate territories of Malaya, Sarawak, and Sabah, Malaysia stretches over 1240 miles (2000 km) from peninsular Malaysia to the northeastern end of Borneo.

GEOGRAPHY
Almost three-quarters of the land is tropical rain forest or swamp forest. A central mountain chain, the Banjaran Titiwangsa, divides peninsular Malaysia (Malaya), separating a narrow eastern coastal belt from fertile western plains and sheltered beaches and bays. The territories of Sarawak and Sabah share the island of Borneo with Brunei and Indonesia, and are characterized by swampy coastal plains rising to mountains on the border with Indonesia.

CLIMATE
Warm equatorial. Rainfall is heavy throughout the year, but with distinct rainy seasons from March to May and from September to November. Coastal areas are subject to the alternating southwest and northeast monsoon winds.

INSIGHT: *Malaysia is Southeast Asia's major tourist destination, with over six million visitors a year, and tourism is now Malaysia's third largest foreign exchange earner*

FACTFILE
OFFICIAL NAME: Federation of Malaysia
DATE OF FORMATION: 1965
CAPITAL: Kuala Lumpur
POPULATION: 22.2 million
TOTAL AREA: 126,853 sq miles (328,550 sq km)
DENSITY: 175 people per sq mile

LANGUAGES: Malay*, Chinese*, Tamil
RELIGIONS: Muslim 53%, Buddhist 19% Chinese faiths 12%, Christian 7%, traditional beliefs 2%, other 7%
ETHNIC MIX: Malay 47%, Chinese 32%, Indian 8%, other 13%
GOVERNMENT: Paliamentary democracy
CURRENCY: Ringgit = 100 cents

Malaysia

PEOPLE & SOCIETY

The key distinction in Malaysian society is between the indigenous Malays, termed the "Bumiputras" (literally, sons of the soil), and the Chinese. The Malays form the larger group, accounting for just under half of the population. However, the smaller Chinese population has traditionally controlled most economic activity. Malays have been favored in the education system and job market since the 1970s, in order to address this imbalance. There are estimated to be more than one million Indonesian and Filipino immigrants in Malaysia, attracted by its abor shortages and a dearth of employment in their own countries. Gender discrimination was only outlawed in 2001. In an attempt to promote Islamic tradition, Muslim women are encouraged to wear veils.

THE ECONOMY

Rapid growth since late 1980s, largely state-directed and underpinned by a push for foreign investment and privatization of state assets. Successful car and electronics industries – Malaysia is the world's biggest producer of disk drives. Heavy industries such as steel. Leading producer of rubber, palm oil, pepper, tin, and tropical hardwoods. High level of debt. Vulnerable to international capital movements. Shortage of skilled labor. Asian finanical crisis of 1997 forced Malaysia to adopt economic austerity measures, and revise its plan for full industrialization.

Malta

The Maltese archipelago lies midway between Europe and Africa. Controlled throughout its history by successive colonial powers, it gained independence from the UK in 1964.

GEOGRAPHY

The main island of Malta has low hills and a ragged coastline with numerous harbors, bays, sandy beaches, and rocky coves. The island of Gozo is more densely vegetated.

CLIMATE

Mediterranean climate. There are many hours of sunshine all year round, with very little rainfall.

PEOPLE & SOCIETY

Over the centuries, the Maltese have been subject to Arab, Sicilian, Spanish, French, and English influences. Today, the population is socially conservative and devoutly Roman Catholic, on a percentage basis more so than virtually any other nation. Divorce is illegal. Many young Maltese go abroad to find work – notably to the US and Australia – as opportunities for them on the islands are few.

THE ECONOMY

Tourism is the chief source of income. Offshore banking potential. Schemes have been set to attract foreign high-tech industry. Almost all requirements have to be imported.

◆ **INSIGHT:** *The Maltese language has Phoenician origins but features Arabic etymology and intonation*

FACTFILE

OFFICIAL NAME: Republic of Malta
DATE OF FORMATION: 1964
CAPITAL: Valletta
POPULATION: 389,000
TOTAL AREA: 124 sq miles (320 sq km)
DENSITY: 3137 people per sq mile

LANGUAGES: Maltese*, English
RELIGIONS: Roman Catholic 98%, other and nonreligious 2%
ETHNIC MIX: Maltese (mixed Arab, Sicilian, Norman, Spanish, Italian, English) 96%, other 4%
GOVERNMENT: Parliamentary democracy
CURRENCY: Lira = 100 cents

Marshall Islands

Under US rule as part of the UN Trust Territory of the Pacific Islands until independence in 1986, the Marshall Islands comprise a group of 34 widely scattered atolls.

GEOGRAPHY

Narrow coral rings with sandy beaches enclosing lagoons. Those in the south have thicker vegetation. Kwajalein is the world's largest atoll.

CLIMATE

Tropical oceanic, cooled year-round by northeast trade winds.

PEOPLE & SOCIETY

Majuro, the capital city and commercial center, is home to almost half the population. Tensions are high due to poor living conditions. Life on the outlying islands is still traditional, based around subsistence agriculture and fishing. Marshallese society is matrilineal: titles are chiefly handed down from the mother's side.

INSIGHT: *In 1954, Bikini Atoll was the site for the testing of the largest US H-bomb – the 18–22 megaton Bravo*

THE ECONOMY

Almost totally dependent on US aid and the rent paid by the US for its missile base on Kwajalein atoll. Revenue from Japan for the use of Marshallese waters for tuna-fishing. Copra and coconut oil are the only significant agricultural exports.

FACTFILE

OFFICIAL NAME: Republic of the Marshall Islands
DATE OF FORMATION: 1986
CAPITAL: Delap district
POPULATION: 68,126
TOTAL AREA: 70 sq miles (181 sq km)

DENSITY: 973 people per sq mile
LANGUAGES: English*, Marshallese*
RELIGIONS: Protestant 90%, Roman Catholic 8%, other 2%
ETHNIC MIX: Micronesian 97%, other Pacific islanders 3%
GOVERNMENT: Parliamentary democracy
CURRENCY: US $ = 100 cents

Mauritania

Two-thirds of Mauritania's territory is desert – the only productive land is that drained by the Senegal River. The country has taken a strongly Arab direction since 1964.

GEOGRAPHY
The Sahara, barren except for some scattered oases, covers the north. Savannah lands lie to the south.

CLIMATE
The climate is generally hot and dry, aggravated by the dusty harmattan wind. Summer rain in the south, virtually none in the north.

PEOPLE & SOCIETY
The Maures control political life and dominate the minority black population. Ethnic tension centers on the oppression of blacks by Maures. Tens of thousands of blacks are estimated to be in illegal slavery. Family solidarity among nomadic peoples is particularly strong.

◆ **INSIGHT:** *Slavery officially became illegal in Mauritania in 1980, but de facto slavery still persists*

THE ECONOMY
Agriculture and herding. Iron and copper mining. World's largest gypsum deposits. Some of the best fishing grounds in west Africa.

FACTFILE
OFFICIAL NAME: Islamic Republic of Mauritania
DATE OF FORMATION: 1960
CAPITAL: Nouakchott
POPULATION: 2.7 million
TOTAL AREA: 395,953 sq miles (1,025,520 sq km)

DENSITY: 7 people per sq mile
LANGUAGES: French*, Hassaniyah Arabic, Wolof
RELIGIONS: Sunni Muslim 100%
ETHNIC MIX: Maure 81%, Wolof 7%, Tukulor 5%, Soninka 3%, other 4%
GOVERNMENT: Multiparty republic
CURRENCY: Ouguiya = 5 khoums

Mauritius

The islands that make up Mauritius lie in the Indian Ocean east of Madagascar. They have enjoyed considerable economic success following recent industrial diversification and expansion.

GEOGRAPHY

The volcanic main island of Mauritius is ringed by coral reefs, and rises from the coast to a fertile central plateau. The outer islands – Rodriguez, the Agalega Islands, and the Cargados Carajos Shoals – lie some 311 miles (500 km) to the north.

CLIMATE

Warm and humid. Tropical storms are frequent December–March, the hottest and wettest months.

PEOPLE & SOCIETY

Most people are descendants of laborers brought over from India in the 19th century. A small minority of French descent form the wealthiest group, controlling the sugar industry. The literacy rate for the under-30s is 95%. Crime rates on the main island are fairly low; the outer islands are virtually crime free.

THE ECONOMY

Sugar, tourism, and clothing manufacture are main sources of income. Sugar accounts for 30% of exports. Potential as an offshore financial center is being developed.

INSIGHT: *The islands lie on the Mascarene Archipelago – once a land bridge between Asia and Africa*

FACTFILE

OFFICIAL NAME: Mauritius
DATE OF FORMATION: 1968
CAPITAL: Port Louis
POPULATION: 1.2 million
TOTAL AREA: 718 sq miles (1860 sq km)
DENSITY: 1671 people per sq mile

LANGUAGES: English*, French Creole, Hindi, Bhojpuri, Chinese
RELIGIONS: Hindu 52%, Catholic 26%, Muslim 17%, Protestant 2%, other 3%
ETHNIC MIX: Indo-Mauritian 68%, Creole 27%, other 5%
GOVERNMENT: Parliamentary democracy
CURRENCY: Rupee = 100 cents

Mexico

Increasingly considered a part of North rather than Central America, Mexico straddles the southern end of the continent. It was a Spanish colony for 300 years until independence in 1836

GEOGRAPHY

Coastal plains along the Pacific and Atlantic seaboards rise to a high arid central plateau. To the east and west are the Sierra Madre mountain ranges. Limestone lowlands form the projecting Yucatan peninsula.

CLIMATE

The plateau and high mountains are warm for much of year. The Pacific coast is tropical: storms occur mostly March–December. Northwest is dry.

THE ECONOMY

One of the world's largest oil producers. Exotic fruits and vegetables are grown as cash crops. Population growth is outstripping job creation. The North American Free Trade Agreement, signed with the US and Canada, came into force in 1994. US companies are poised to move into Mexico and enter competition with Mexican industry.

FACTFILE

OFFICIAL NAME: United States of Mexico
DATE OF FORMATION: 1936
CAPITAL: Mexico City
POPULATION: 98.9 million
TOTAL AREA: 736,945 sq miles
(1,908,690 sq km)
DENSITY: 134 people per sq mile

LANGUAGES: Spanish*, Mayan dialects
RELIGIONS: Roman Catholic 95%, Protestant 1%, other 4%
ETHNIC MIX: Mestizo 55%, indigenous Indian 20%, European 16%, other 9%
GOVERNMENT: Presidential democracy
CURRENCY: Peso = 100 centavos

Mexico

PEOPLE & SOCIETY

Most Mexicans are *mestizos* of mixed Spanish and Indian descent. Though Indian culture is promoted by the state, rural Indians are largely segregated from Hispanic society and most live in poverty. The situation dates back to the Spanish colonial period, and only recently has it been seriously challenged in the form of intermittent rebellions by landless Indians. The small black community is well integrated. Men remain dominant in business and few women take part in the political process. Mexico is a multiparty democracy in name; in practice, the PRI (Institutional Revolutionary Party) has retained power since 1929. Rural depopulation and high unemployment are major problems. The population of Mexico is growing faster than that of any other large country – between 1960 and 1980, the population doubled.

◆ **INSIGHT:** *More people emigrate from Mexico than any other state in the world. Hundreds of thousands of Mexicans cross into the US each year, many of them staying as illegal immigrants*

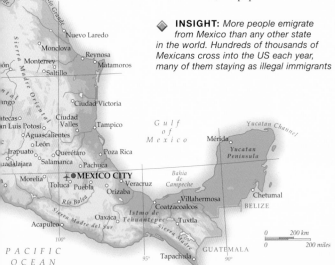

Micronesia

The Federated States of Micronesia, situated in the western Pacific, comprise 607 islands and atolls grouped into four main island states: Pohnpei, Kosrae, Chuuk, and Yap.

GEOGRAPHY
Mixture of high volcanic islands with forested interiors, and low-lying coral atolls. Some of the islands have coastal mangrove swamps.

CLIMATE
Tropical, with high humidity. There is very heavy rainfall outside the January–March dry season.

INSIGHT: *Chuuk's lagoon contains the sunken wrecks of over 100 WWII Japanese ships and 270 planes*

PEOPLE & SOCIETY
Once part of the US-administered UN Trust Territory of the Pacific Islands, Micronesia still relies on US aid, which funds food stamps, schools and hospitals. Most islanders live without electricity or running water. Society is traditionally matrilineal.

THE ECONOMY
Fishing and copra production are the mainstays. The construction industry is the largest private sector activity. Unemployment is high.

Philippine Sea

Yap

Ngulu

Sorol

Olimarao

Woleai

Namonuito

Lamotrek

Hall Is.

Murilo

Chuuk Is.

Weno

Pulusuk

Nama

Satawan

Pohnpei Is.

Oroluk

PALIKIR

Pohnpei

Mortlock Islands

Nukuoro

Kosrae

Caroline Islands

200m/656ft
Sea Level

0   200 km

0   200 miles

PACIFIC OCEAN

10°

140°   145°   150°   155°   160°

FACTFILE

OFFICIAL NAME: Federated States of Micronesia

DATE OF FORMATION: 1986

CAPITAL: Palikir (Pohnpei island)

POPULATION: 133,144

TOTAL AREA: 271 sq miles (702 sq km)

DENSITY: 491 people per sq mile

LANGUAGES: English*, Trukese, Pohnpeian, Mortlockese, other

RELIGIONS: Roman Catholic 50%, Protestant 48%, other 2%

ETHNIC MIX: Micronesian 100%

GOVERNMENT: Non-party republic

CURRENCY: US $ = 100 cents

Moldova

The smallest and most densely populated of the former Soviet republics, Moldova has strong ethnic, linguistic, and cultural links with Romania to the west.

GEOGRAPHY

The steppes and hilly plains are drained by Dniester and Prut rivers.

CLIMATE

Warm summers and relatively mild winters. Moderate rainfall is evenly spread throughout the year.

PEOPLE & SOCIETY

A shared heritage with Romania defines national identity, although in 1994 Moldovans voted against possible unification with Romania. Most of the population is engaged in intensive agriculture. The Slav peoples on the east bank of the River Dniester seek independence and have rejected autonomous status. The Gagauzi people also aspire to independence.

▶ **INSIGHT:** *Moldova's vast underground wine vaults contain entire "streets" of bottles built into rock quarries*

THE ECONOMY

Well-developed agricultural sector: wine, tobacco, cotton, food processing. Light manufacturing. Progress in establishing markets for exports. High unemployment.

FACTFILE

OFFICIAL NAME: Republic of Moldova
DATE OF FORMATION: 1991
CAPITAL: Chișinâu
POPULATION: 4.4 million
TOTAL AREA: 13,012 sq miles (33,700 sq km)
DENSITY: 338 people per sq mile

LANGUAGES: Moldovan*, Russian
RELIGIONS: Eastern Orthodox 98%, Jewish 2%
ETHNIC MIX: Moldovan (Romanian) 65%, Ukrainian 14%, Russian 13%, Gagauz 4%, other 4%
GOVERNMENT: Parliamentary democracy
CURRENCY: Leu = 100 bani

Monaco

Monaco is a tiny enclave on the Côte d'Azur whose destiny changed radically when the casino was opened in 1863. Modern Monaco has a jet set image and a thriving service sector.

GEOGRAPHY

A rocky promontory overlooking a narrow coastal strip that has been enlarged through land reclamation.

CLIMATE

Mediterranean. Summers are hot and dry; days with 12 hours of sunshine are not uncommon. Winters are mild and sunny.

PEOPLE & SOCIETY

Less than 20% of residents are Monégasques. Around half are French, the rest Italian, American, British, and Belgian. Nationals enjoy considerable privileges, including housing subsidies to protect them from Monaco's high property prices, and the right of first refusal before a job can be offered to a foreigner. Women have equal status but only acquired the vote in the constitutional changes of 1962.

THE ECONOMY

Tourism and gambling are the mainstays. Banking secrecy laws and tax-haven conditions are attractive to foreign investment. Monaco is almost totally dependent on imports due to its lack of natural resources.

◆ **INSIGHT:** *The Grimaldi princes have been Monaco's hereditary rulers for the past 700 years*

FACTFILE

OFFICIAL NAME: Principality of Monaco
DATE OF FORMATION: 1861
CAPITAL: Monaco
POPULATION: 31,693
TOTAL AREA: 0.75 sq miles (1.95 sq km)
DENSITY: 42,257 people per sq mile

LANGUAGES: French*, Italian, other
RELIGIONS: Roman Catholic 89%, Protestant 6%, other 5%
ETHNIC MIX: French 47%, Monégasque 17%, Italian 16%, other 20%
GOVERNMENT: Constitutional monarchy
CURRENCY: Euro = 100 cents

Mongolia

Landlocked between Russia and China, Mongolia is a vast and isolated country with a largely nomadic population. Over two-thirds of the country is part of the vast Gobi desert.

GEOGRAPHY

A mountainous steppe plateau in the north, with lakes in the north and west. The desert region of the Gobi dominates the south.

CLIMATE

Continental. Mild summers and long, dry, very cold winters, with heavy snowfall. Temperatures can drop as low as −22°F (−30°C).

PEOPLE & SOCIETY

Mongolia was unified by Genghis Khan in 1206 and was later absorbed into Manchu China. It became a communist People's Republic in 1924, and after 66 years of Soviet-style communist rule, introduced democracy in 1990. Most Mongolians still follow a traditional nomadic way of life, living in circular felt tents called gers. Others live on state-run farms. There is little indigenous ethnic tension.

THE ECONOMY

Rich in oil, coal, copper, and other minerals, which were barely exploited under communism. In the 1990s, there was a shift in agriculture away from traditional herding and toward a market economy.

◆ **INSIGHT:** *Horseracing, wrestling, and archery are the national sports. During the Nadam festival each July, competitions are held all over Mongolia*

FACTFILE

OFFICIAL NAME: Mongolia
DATE OF FORMATION: 1924
CAPITAL: Ulan Bator
POPULATION: 2.7 million
TOTAL AREA: 604,247 sq miles (1,565,000 sq km)
DENSITY: 4 people per sq mile

LANGUAGES: Khalkha Mongol*, Turkic, Russian, Chinese
RELIGIONS: Tibetan Buddhist 96%, Muslim 4%
ETHNIC MIX: Mongol 90%, Kazakh 4%, Chinese 2%, Russian 2%, other 2%
GOVERNMENT: Multiparty republic
CURRENCY: Tughrik = 100 möngös

Morocco

Morocco is a former French colony in northwest Africa. Since 1975 it has occupied the territory of Western Sahara, the future of which is yet to be determined by UN-supervised referendum.

GEOGRAPHY

Fertile coastal plain is interrupted in the east by the Rif Mountains. Atlas Mountain ranges to the south. Beyond lies the outer fringe of the Sahara.

CLIMATE

Ranges from temperate and warm in the north, to semiarid in the south. Cooler in the mountains.

PEOPLE & SOCIETY

About 35% of the population are descendants of original Berber inhabitants of northwest Africa, and live mainly in mountain villages. The Arab majority inhabits the lowlands. Disparities in wealth between urban and rural areas. High birth rate. The monarchy is powerful, and was headed by King Hassan II until his death in July 1999. The government is threatened by Islamic militants who fear the loss of an Arab identity.

THE ECONOMY

The world's main exporter of phosphates. Tourism and agriculture have great potential. Production of cannabis complicates closer EU links.

◆ **INSIGHT:** *Karueein University in Fès, founded in 859 CE, is the world's oldest existing educational institution*

Map

Mediterranean Sea
ATLANTIC OCEAN
Tanger, Ceuta (to Spain) Melilla (to Spain)
Tétouan
RABAT Kénitra — Oujda
Mohammedia Salé — Fès
Casablanca Meknès — 34°
Safi Khouribga
Beni Mellal
Marrakech
Essaouira
Agadir Ouarzazate ALGERIA
Anti Atlas — 30°
WESTERN SAHARA (Occupied by Morocco)
8° 0 100 km
12° 0 100 miles
4°

3000m/9843
2000m/6562
1000m/3281
500m/1640ft
200m/656ft
Sea Level

FACTFILE

OFFICIAL NAME: Kingdom of Morocco
DATE OF FORMATION: 1956
CAPITAL: Rabat
POPULATION: 28.4 million
TOTAL AREA: 172,316 sq miles (446,300 sq km)
DENSITY: 165 people per sq mile

LANGUAGES: Arabic*, Berber, French
RELIGIONS: Muslim (mainly Sunni) 99%, Christian 1%, Jewish 1%
ETHNIC MIX: Arab 70%, Berber 29%, European 1%
GOVERNMENT: Constitutional monarchy
CURRENCY: Dirham = 100 centimes

Mozambique

Mozambique lies on the southeast African coast. It was torn apart by a savage and devastating civil war between the Marxist government and a rebel faction between 1977 and 1992.

GEOGRAPHY

Largely a savannah-covered plateau. The coast is fringed by coral reefs and lagoons. The Zambezi River bisects the country from east to west.

CLIMATE

Tropical. The wet season is often March–October, but the rains frequently fail. Coastal temperatures are hottest.

PEOPLE & SOCIETY

Tensions in society are between northerners and southerners, rather than ethnic groups. Life is based around the extended family, which in some regions is matriarchal. Polygamy is fairly common. The government has faced the huge task of re-settling the one million war refugees. 90% of the population live in poverty.

◆ **INSIGHT:** *Maputo, the capital, has Africa's second largest harbor*

THE ECONOMY

Mozambique is almost entirely dependent on foreign aid. 85% of the population is engaged in agriculture.

■ 2000m/6562ft	
■ 1000m/3281ft	
■ 500m/1640ft	
■ 200m/656ft	
Sea Level	

FACTFILE

OFFICIAL NAME: Republic of Mozambique

DATE OF FORMATION: 1975

CAPITAL: Maputo

POPULATION: 19.7 million

TOTAL AREA: 302,737 sq miles (784,090 sq km)

DENSITY: 65 people per sq mile

LANGUAGES: Portuguese*, other

RELIGIONS: Traditional beliefs 60%, Christian 30%, Muslim 10%

ETHNIC MIX: Makua-Lomwe 47%, Thonga 23%, Malawi 12%, other 18%

GOVERNMENT: Multiparty republic

CURRENCY: Metical = 100 centavos

Myanmar (Burma)

Forming the eastern shores of the Bay of Bengal and the Andaman Sea in Southeast Asia, Myanmar has recently suffered extensive political repression and ethnic conflict.

GEOGRAPHY
The fertile Irrawaddy basin lies at the center. Mountains to the west, Shan plateau to the east. Tropical rain forest covers much of the land.

CLIMATE
Tropical. Hot summers, with high humidity, and warm winters.

PEOPLE & SOCIETY
The military, in power since 1962, rules Myanmar with little regard to human rights. Opposition is not tolerated. Minority groups maintain low-level guerrilla activity against the state. The 1990 election was won by an opposition democratic party. Its leader, Aung San Suu Kyi, was placed under house arrest. She was released in 1995.

◆ INSIGHT: *Myanmar is the world's biggest teak exporter, although reserves are diminishing rapidly*

THE ECONOMY
Under socialism, Burma has plunged from prosperity to poverty. There is a nationwide black market, on which prices are soaring. Main products are gems, teak, and rice.

INDIA · 25° · Myitkyina · CHINA · Irrawaddy
Monywa · Mandalay
Pakokku · Sagaing
Sittwe · Taunggyi · Shan Plateau · Mekong · LAOS
20° · 100°
Sandoway · Toungoo · THAILAND
Henzada · Prome
Bay of Bengal · Insein · Pegu
Bassein · Thaton
RANGOON ✈ · Moulmein
Mouths of the Irrawaddy · Kyaikkami
95°
Andaman Sea · Tavoy
15°
Mergui
Mergui Archipelago · Isthmus of Kra · 10°

4000m/13124ft
2000m/6562ft
1000m/3281ft
500m/1640ft
200m/656ft
Sea Level

0 —— 200 km
0 —— 200 miles

FACTFILE

OFFICIAL NAME: Union of Myanmar
DATE OF FORMATION: 1948
CAPITAL: Yangon (Rangoon)
POPULATION: 45.6 million
TOTAL AREA: 253,876 sq miles (657,540 sq km)
DENSITY: 180 people per sq mile

LANGUAGES: Burmese*, Karen, Shan, Chin, Kachin, Mon, Palaung, Wa
RELIGIONS: Buddhist 87%, Christian 6%, Muslim 4%, Hindu 1%, other 2%
ETHNIC MIX: Burman 68%, Shan 9%, Karen 6%, Rakhine 4%, other 13%
GOVERNMENT: Military-based regime
CURRENCY: Kyat = 100 pyas

Namibia

Located in southwestern Africa, Namibia became free of South African control in 1990, after years of uncertainty and guerrilla activity. The country has since moved away from apartheid.

GEOGRAPHY
The Namib Desert stretches along the coastal strip. Inland, a ridge of mountains rises to 8200 ft (2500 m). The Kalahari Desert lies in the east.

CLIMATE
Almost rainless. The coast is usually shrouded in thick fog, unless the hot, dry *berg* wind is blowing.

PEOPLE & SOCIETY
The largest ethnic group, the Ovambo, live mainly in the north. Whites, including a large German community, are centered around Windhoek. Ethnic strife, predicted at the time of independence, has not materialized. High illiteracy among blacks is due to the legacy of apartheid. Whites still control the economy.

◇ **INSIGHT:** *The Namib is the Earth's oldest, and one of its driest, deserts*

THE ECONOMY
Third wealthiest country in sub-Saharan Africa. Varied mineral resources, including uranium and diamonds. Rich offshore fishing grounds. Lack of skilled labor.

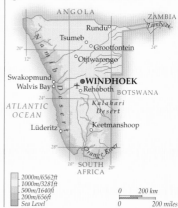

▓	2000m/6562ft
▓	1000m/3281ft
▓	500m/1640ft
▓	200m/656ft
	Sea Level

FACTFILE

OFFICIAL NAME: Republic of Namibia
DATE OF FORMATION: 1994
CAPITAL: Windhoek
POPULATION: 1.7 million
TOTAL AREA: 317,872 sq miles (823,290 sq km)
DENSITY: 5 people per sq mile

LANGUAGES: English*, Afrikaans, Ovambo, Kavango, German, other
RELIGIONS: Christian 90%, traditional beliefs 10%
ETHNIC MIX: Ovambo 50%, Kavango 9%, Herero 8%, Damara 8%, other 25%
GOVERNMENT: Presidential democracy
CURRENCY: Rand = 100 cents

Nauru

Nauru lies in the Pacific, northeast of Australia. Phosphate deposits made its citizens among the wealthiest in the world, but economic mismanagement left it facing ruin in the late 1990s.

GEOGRAPHY
A single low-lying coral atoll, with a fertile coastal belt. Coral cliffs encircle an elevated interior plateau.

CLIMATE
Equatorial, moderated by sea breezes. Occasional long droughts.

PEOPLE & SOCIETY
Native Nauruans are of mixed Micronesian and Polynesian origin. Most live in simple, traditional houses and spend their money on luxury cars and consumer goods. The government provides free welfare and education. A diet of imported processed foods has caused widespread obesity and diabetes. Mining is left to an imported labor force, mainly from Kiribati, who live in enclaves of male-only barracks and have few rights. Many of the young attend boarding schools in Australia and New Zealand.

THE ECONOMY
Phosphate, the only resource, is sold to Pacific Rim countries for use as a fertilizer. Deposits are near exhaustion. Huge investments in Australian and Hawaiian property.

◆ **INSIGHT:** *Phosphate mining has left 80% of the island uninhabitable*

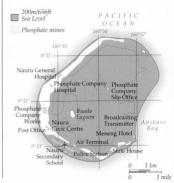

FACTFILE
OFFICIAL NAME: Republic of Nauru
DATE OF FORMATION: 1968
CAPITAL: No official capital
POPULATION: 11,000
TOTAL AREA: 8.1 sq miles (21 sq km)
DENSITY: 1358 people per sq mile

LANGUAGES: Nauruan*, English, other
RELIGIONS: Nauruan Congregational Church 60%, Christian 35%, other 5%
ETHNIC MIX: Nauruan 62%, other Pacific islanders 25%, Chinese/Vietnamese 8%, European 5%
GOVERNMENT: Non-party democracy
CURRENCY: Australian $ = 100 cents

Nepal

Nepal lies between India and China, on the southern shoulder of the Himalayan mountains. One of the world's poorest countries, its agricultural economy is heavily dependent on the monsoon.

GEOGRAPHY
Mainly mountainous. The area includes some of the highest mountains in the world, such as Everest. Flat, fertile river plains form the south.

CLIMATE
Warm monsoon season from July to October. The rest of the year is dry, sunny and mild. Winter temperatures in the Himalayas average 14°F (–10°C).

PEOPLE & SOCIETY
Few ethnic tensions, despite the variety of ethnic groups, including the Sherpas in the north, Terai peoples in the south, and the Newars, found mostly in the Kathmandu valley. Women's subordinate position is enshrined in the law. Hindu women are the most restricted. Nepal was ruled by an absolute monarchy until 1990; since then its politics have become increasingly turbulent.

THE ECONOMY
90% of the people work on the land. Crops include rice, maize, and millet. Dependent on foreign aid. Tourism is growing. There is great potential for hydroelectric power.

◆ **INSIGHT:** *Southern Nepal was the birthplace of Buddha (Prince Siddhartha Gautama), in 563 BC*

FACTFILE

OFFICIAL NAME: Kingdom of Nepal
DATE OF FORMATION: 1769
CAPITAL: Kathmandu
POPULATION: 23.9 million
TOTAL AREA: 52,818 sq miles (136,800 sq km)
DENSITY: 452 people per sq mile

LANGUAGES: Nepali*, Maithilli, other
RELIGIONS: Hindu 90%, Buddhist 5%, Muslim 3%, other 2%
ETHNIC MIX: Nepalese 52%, Maithili 11%, Tibeto-Burmese 10%, Bhojpuri 8%, other 19%
GOVERNMENT: Constitutional monarchy
CURRENCY: Rupee = 100 paisa

Netherlands

Astride the delta of five major rivers in northwest Europe, the Netherlands was one of the world's first confederative republics. The main port, Rotterdam, is also the world's largest.

GEOGRAPHY

Mainly flat, with 27% of the land below sea level and protected by dunes, dikes, and canals. There are a few low hills in the south and east.

CLIMATE

Mild, rainy winters and cool summers. Gales from the North Sea are common in fall and winter.

PEOPLE & SOCIETY

The Dutch see their country as the most tolerant in Europe. This reflects a long history of welcoming immigrants from former colonies and refugees seeking religious and political asylum. Its large urban concentration (89%) accounts for the high population density. The state does not try to impose a particular morality on its citizens. Laws concerning issues such as drug-taking, sexuality, and euthanasia, are among the world's most liberal.

THE ECONOMY

Diverse industrial sector exports metals, machinery, electronics, and chemicals. High-profile multinationals.

◆ **INSIGHT:** *A century ago there were 10,000 windmills in the Netherlands, compared with only 1000 today*

FACTFILE

OFFICIAL NAME: Kingdom of the Netherlands
DATE OF FORMATION: 1815
CAPITALS: Amsterdam, The Hague
POPULATION: 15.8 million
TOTAL AREA: 13,096 sq miles (33,920 sq km)

DENSITY: 1206 people per sq mile
LANGUAGES: Dutch*, Frisian, other
RELIGIONS: Catholic 36%, Protestant 27%, Muslim 3%, other 34%
ETHNIC MIX: Dutch 96%, Turkish 1%, Moroccan 1%, other 2%
GOVERNMENT: Parliamentary democracy
CURRENCY: Euro = 100 cents

New Zealand

Lying in the South Pacific, 990 miles (1600 km) southeast of Australia, New Zealand comprises the North and South Islands, separated by the Cook Strait, and many smaller islands.

GEOGRAPHY

North Island contains hot springs and geysers, and the bulk of the population. South Island is mostly mountainous, with eastern lowlands.

CLIMATE

Generally temperate and damp. The far north is almost subtropical, whereas southern winters are cold.

PEOPLE & SOCIETY

Maoris were the first settlers, 1200 years ago. Today's majority European population is descended mainly from British migrants who settled after 1840. Maoris' living and education standards are generally lower than average. The government is currently attempting to negotiate the settlement of Maori land claims.

◆ INSIGHT: *New Zealand women were the first to get the vote*

THE ECONOMY

Modern agricultural sector; New Zealand is the world's biggest exporter of meat, wool, cheese, and butter. Growing manufacturing industry. Healthy tourist industry.

2000m/6562ft
1000m/3281ft
500m/1640ft
200m/656ft
Sea Level

North Island

36°

Auckland
Manurewa
Tauranga
Hamilton
Rotorua
New
Plymouth
Taupo
Napier
Hastings
Palmerston
North
Lower Hutt
WELLINGTON
176°
Cook Strait

*Tasman
Sea*

40°

Blenheim

South Island

Christchurch

44°

Timaru
172°

Southern Alps

*PACIFIC
OCEAN*

Dunedin
Invercargill
Stewart Island
168°

0   200 km
0   200 miles

FACTFILE

OFFICIAL NAME: The Dominion of New Zealand

DATE OF FORMATION: 1926

CAPITAL: Wellington

POPULATION: 3.9 million

TOTAL AREA: 103,733 sq miles (268,670 sq km)

DENSITY: 38 people per sq mile

LANGUAGES: English*, Maori, other

RELIGIONS: Anglican 24%, Presbyterian 18%, Catholic 15%, other/nonreligious 42%

ETHNIC MIX: European 82%, Maori 9%, other (inc. Chinese/other islanders) 9%

GOVERNMENT: Parliamentary democracy

Nicaragua

Nicaragua lies at the heart of Central America. The Sandinista revolution of 1978 led to 11 years of civil war between the left-wing Sandinistas and the right-wing US-backed Contras.

GEOGRAPHY

Extensive forested plains in the east. Central mountain region with many active volcanoes. The Pacific coastlands are dominated by lakes.

CLIMATE

Tropical. The lowlands are hot all year round. The mountains are cooler. Prone to occasional hurricanes.

PEOPLE & SOCIETY

The isolated Atlantic regions, populated by Miskito Indians and blacks, gained limited independence in 1987. Elections in 1990 brought a right-wing pro-US party to power, but the Sandinistas remain a major political force in a country where poverty and unrest are rising.

◆ INSIGHT: *Lake Nicaragua is the only freshwater lake in the world to contain ocean animals*

THE ECONOMY

Coffee, sugar, and cotton are the main exports. All are affected by world price fluctuations. The economy is heavily dependent on foreign aid; the US is the largest donor.

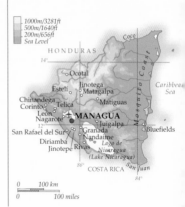

FACTFILE

OFFICIAL NAME: Republic of Nicaragua

DATE OF FORMATION: 1838

CAPITAL: Managua

POPULATION: 5.1 million

TOTAL AREA: 45,849 sq miles (118,750 sq km)

DENSITY: 111 people per sq mile

LANGUAGES: Spanish*, English Creole, Miskito

RELIGIONS: Roman Catholic 80%, Protestant Evangelicals 17%, other 3%

ETHNIC MIX: Mestizo 69%, White 14%, Black 8%, Indian 5%, Zambos 4%

GOVERNMENT: Presidential democracy

CURRENCY: Córdoba = 100 pence

Niger

Landlocked in the west of Africa, Niger is linked to the sea by the river Niger. It was ruled by one-party or military regimes until 1992, when a multiparty constitution was introduced.

GEOGRAPHY

The north and northeast regions are part of Sahara and Sahel. The Aïr mountains in the center rise high above the desert. Savannah lies to the south.

CLIMATE

High temperatures persist for most of the year at around 35°C (95°F). The north is virtually rainless.

PEOPLE & SOCIETY

Considerable tensions exist between Tuareg nomads in the north and groups in the south. Tuaregs have felt alienated from mainstream politics. A five-year rebellion by northern Tuaregs ended in 1995 with a peace agreement. A sense of community and egalitarianism among the southern peoples helps to combat economic difficulties. Niger is largely Islamic. Women have limited rights, and restricted access to education.

THE ECONOMY

Niger has vast uranium deposits. Frequent droughts and the southwest expansion of the Sahara are problems.

INSIGHT: *Niger's name is derived from the Tuareg word n'eghirren, which means "flowing water"*

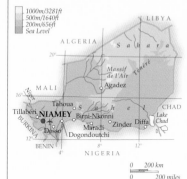

FACTFILE

OFFICIAL NAME: Republic of Niger
DATE OF FORMATION: 1960
CAPITAL: Niamey
POPULATION: 10.7 million
TOTAL AREA: 489,072 sq miles (1,266,700 sq km)
DENSITY: 22 people per sq mile

LANGUAGES: French*, Hausa, Djerma, Fulani, Tuareg, Teda
RELIGIONS: Muslim 84%, traditional beliefs 14%, Christian 1%, other 1%
ETHNIC MIX: Hausa 54%, Djerma 21%, Fulani 10%, Tuareg 9%, other 6%
GOVERNMENT: Multiparty republic
CURRENCY: CFA franc = 100 centimes

Nigeria

Nigeria in West Africa, a former UK colony, is a federation of 30 states. Dominated by military governments since 1966, the promised return to civilian rule came about in 1999.

GEOGRAPHY

Coastal area of beaches, swamps, and lagoons gives way to rain forest, and then to savannah on the high plateaus. Semidesert to the north.

CLIMATE

The south is hot, rainy and humid for most of the year. The arid north has one very humid wet season. The Jos plateau and highlands are cooler.

PEOPLE & SOCIETY

Some 250 ethnic groups: the largest are the Hausa, Yoruba, Ibo, and Fulani. Tensions between groups constantly threaten national unity, although they have largely been contained in recent years. Members of one group tend to blame those of another for their problems, rather than the political system. Except in the highly Islamic north, women are allowed economic independence.

THE ECONOMY

Oil has been the major economic mainstay since the 1970s, accounting for 90% of export earnings.

INSIGHT: *Nigeria is Africa's most populous state – one in every six Africans is Nigerian*

1000m/3281ft
500m/1640ft
200m/656ft
Sea Level

FACTFILE

OFFICIAL NAME: Federal Republic of Nigeria
DATE OF FORMATION: 1960
CAPITAL: Abuja
POPULATION: 111.5 million
TOTAL AREA: 351,648 sq miles (910,770 sq km)

DENSITY: 317 people per sq mile
LANGUAGES: English*, Hausa, Yoruba
RELIGIONS: Muslim 50%, Christian 40%, traditional beliefs 10%
ETHNIC MIX: Hausa 21%, Yoruba 21%, Ibo 18%, Fulani 11%, other 29%
GOVERNMENT: Multiparty republic
CURRENCY: Naira = 100 kobo

Norway

The Kingdom of Norway traces the rugged western coast of Scandinavia. Settlements are largely restricted to southern and coastal areas. Large oil and gas revenues bring prosperity.

GEOGRAPHY

The western coast is indented with numerous fjords and features tens of thousands of islands. Mountains and plateaus cover most of the country.

CLIMATE

Mild coastal climate. Inland, the east is more extreme, with warm summers and cold, snowy winters.

PEOPLE & SOCIETY

Fairly homogeneous, with some recent refugees from the Bosnian conflict. There is a strong family tradition despite the high divorce rate. Fair-minded consensus promotes female equality, boosted by the generous childcare provision. Wealth is more evenly distributed than in most developed countries.

INSIGHT: *Near Narvik, mainland Norway is only 4 miles (7 km) wide*

THE ECONOMY

Europe's largest producer and exporter of oil and gas. Metal, engineering, and chemical industries.

2000m/6562ft
1000m/3281ft
500m/1640ft
200m/656ft
Sea Level

Hammerfest
Karasjok
Tromsø
RUSS. FED.
FINLAND
Narvik
Bodø
Arctic Circle
Norwegian Sea
SWEDEN
Trondheim
Ålesund
Ørsta
Lillehammer
Bergen
Hønefoss
North Sea
OSLO
Drammen
Moss
Stavanger
Sandnes
Skien
Kristiansand
Skagerrak

0   200 km
0   200 miles

FACTFILE

OFFICIAL NAME: Kingdom of Norway
DATE OF FORMATION: 1905
CAPITAL: Oslo
POPULATION: 4.5 million
TOTAL AREA: 118,467 sq miles (306,830 sq km)
DENSITY: 38 people per sq mile

LANGUAGES: Norwegian* (Bokmal and Nynorsk), Lappish
RELIGIONS: Evangelical Lutheran 89%, Catholic 1%, other/nonreligious 10%
ETHNIC MIX: Norwegian 95%, Lapp 1%, other 4%
GOVERNMENT: Parliamentary democracy
CURRENCY: Krone = 100 øre

Oman

Situated on the eastern coast of the Arabian peninsula, Oman occupies a strategic position at the entrance to The Gulf. It is the least developed of the Gulf states, despite modest oil exports.

GEOGRAPHY

Mostly gravelly desert, with mountains in the north and south. Some narrow fertile coastal strips.

CLIMATE

Blistering heat in the west. Summer temperatures often climb above 113°F (45°C). Southern uplands receive rains June–September.

PEOPLE & SOCIETY

Most Omanis still live off the land, especially in the south. The majority are Ibadi Muslims who follow an appointed leader, the Imam. Ibadism is not opposed to freedom for women, and a few women hold positions of authority. Baluchis from Pakistan are the largest group of foreign workers.

INSIGHT: *Until the late 1980s, Oman was closed to all but business or official visitors*

THE ECONOMY

Oil accounts for most export revenue. Gas is set to eventually supplant oil. Other exports include fish, dates, limes and coconuts.

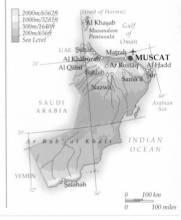

2000m/6562ft	
1000m/3281ft	
500m/1640ft	
200m/656ft	
Sea Level	

Strait of Hormuz
Al Khaşab
Musandam Peninsula
Gulf of Oman
UAE Şuḥār
Al Khabūrah Maţraḥ ○○ **MUSCAT**
24° Al Qābil ○ Ar Rustāq Al Hadd
Baḥlah ○ Şūr
Nazwā Samā'il
SAUDI
ARABIA 60°
Arabian Sea
20° *A r   R u b '   a l   K h ā l ī* INDIAN
OCEAN
YEMEN
52° Şalālah 56°
0   100 km
0   100 miles

FACTFILE

OFFICIAL NAME: Sultanate of Oman
DATE OF FORMATION: 1561
CAPITAL: Muscat
POPULATION: 2.5 million
TOTAL AREA: 82,031 sq miles (212,460 sq km)
DENSITY: 30 people per sq mile

LANGUAGES: Arabic*, Baluchi, other
RELIGIONS: Ibadi Muslim 75%, other Muslim and Hindu 25%
ETHNIC MIX: Arab 88%, Baluch 4%, Indian and Pakistani 3%, Persian 3%, African 2%
GOVERNMENT: Monarchy
CURRENCY: Rial = 1000 baizas

Pakistan

Once a part of British India, Pakistan was created in 1947 in response to demand for an independent, largely Muslim state. Bangladesh (former East Pakistan) gained independence in 1971.

GEOGRAPHY
The east and south is a great flood plain drained by the Indus. Hindu Kush range lies in the north. The west is semidesert plateau and mountains.

CLIMATE
Temperatures can soar to 122°F (50°C) in south and west, and fall to –4°F (–20°C) in the Hindu Kush.

PEOPLE & SOCIETY
The majority Punjabis control the bureaucracy and the army. Many tensions with minority groups. Vast gap between rich and poor. Strong family ties, reflected in dynastic and nepotistic political system. Border dispute with India over Kashmir recently escalated into violence.

◆ **INSIGHT:** *In 1988, Pakistan elected the first female prime minister in the Muslim world*

THE ECONOMY
Leading producer of cotton and rice, but unpredictable weather conditions often affect the crop. Oil and gas reserves. Inefficient and haphazard economic policies.

FACTFILE
OFFICIAL NAME: Islamic Republic of Pakistan
DATE OF FORMATION: 1947
CAPITAL: Islāmābād
POPULATION: 156.5 million
TOTAL AREA: 297,637 sq miles (770,880 sq km)

DENSITY: 526 people per sq mile
LANGUAGES: Urdu*, Punjabi, other
RELIGIONS: Sunni Muslim 77%, Shi'a Muslim 20%, Hindu 2%, Christian 1%
ETHNIC MIX: Punjabi 50%, Sindi 15%, Pashtu 15%, Mohajir 8%, other 12%
GOVERNMENT: Military-based regime
CURRENCY: Rupee = 100 paisa

Palau

The Palau archipelago, a group of over 300 islands, lies in the western Pacific Ocean. In 1994, it became an independent state, but continues to be heavily dependent on US aid.

GEOGRAPHY
Terrain varies from thickly-forested mountains to limestone and coral reefs. Babeldaob, the largest island, is volcanic, with many rivers and waterfalls.

CLIMATE
Hot and wet. Little variation in daily and seasonal temperatures. February–April is the dry season.

PEOPLE & SOCIETY
Palau was the last remaining US-administered UN Trust Territory of the Pacific Islands. Culturally, the population has been Americanized by the years of US administration, though the remote islands maintain a traditional way of life. Only nine islands are inhabited and two-thirds of the population live in Oreor. Society is matrilineal; women choose which males will be the clan chiefs.

THE ECONOMY
Subsistence level. Main crops are coconuts and cassava. Revenue from fishing licenses and tourism.

◆ **INSIGHT:** *Palau's reefs contain 1500 species of fish and 700 types of coral*

FACTFILE
OFFICIAL NAME: Republic of Palau
DATE OF FORMATION: 1994
CAPITAL: Oreor
POPULATION: 18,766
TOTAL AREA: 196 sq miles (508 sq km)
DENSITY: 96 people per sq mile

LANGUAGES: Palauan*, English*, Sonsorolese-Tobian, other
RELIGIONS: Roman Catholic 66%, Modekngei 34%
ETHNIC MIX: Micronesian 100%
GOVERNMENT: Non-party democracy
CURRENCY: US $ = 100 cents

Panama

Panama is the southernmost country in Central America. The collosal Panama Canal (which was under US-control until the year 2000) links the Pacific and Atlantic oceans.

GEOGRAPHY

Lowlands along both coasts, with savannah-covered plains and rolling hills. Mountainous interior. Swamps and rainforests in the east.

CLIMATE

Hot and humid, with heavy rainfall in the May–December wet season. Cooler at high altitudes.

PEOPLE & SOCIETY

A multiethnic society, dominated by people of Spanish origin. Indians live in remote areas. The Panama Canal and US military bases (the last of which closed in 1999) have given society a cosmopolitan outlook, but the Catholic extended family remains strong. In 1989, US troops arrested its dictator General Noriega and restored civilian rule.

THE ECONOMY

Important banking sector, plus related financial and insurance services. Earnings from merchant ships sailing under Panamanian flag. Banana and shrimp exports.

◆ **INSIGHT:** *The Panama Canal extends for 40 miles (64 km). Around 12,000 ships pass through it each year*

FACTFILE

OFFICIAL NAME: Republic of Panama
DATE OF FORMATION: 1903
CAPITAL: Panama City
POPULATION: 2.9 million
TOTAL AREA: 29,340 sq miles (75,990 sq km)
DENSITY: 99 people per sq mile

LANGUAGES: Spanish*, English Creole, Indian languages
RELIGIONS: Roman Catholic 86%, Protestant 6%, other 8%
ETHNIC MIX: Mestizo 60%, White 14%, Black 12%, Indian 8%, other 6%
GOVERNMENT: Presidential democracy
CURRENCY: Balboa = 100 centesimos

Papua New Guinea

A former Australian colony, Papua New Guinea occupies the eastern section of the island of New Guinea and several other island groups. Much of the country is still isolated.

GEOGRAPHY
Mountainous and forested mainland, with broad, swampy river valleys. 40 active volcanoes in the north. Around 600 outer islands.

CLIMATE
Hot and humid in lowlands, cooling towards highlands, where snow can fall on highest peaks.

PEOPLE & SOCIETY
Around 750 language groups (the highest number in the world) and even more tribes. The main social distinction is between lowlanders, who have frequent contact with the outside world, and the very isolated, but increasingly threatened, highlanders. Great tensions exist between highland tribes, and vendettas can often last several generations. Drought and a tsunami had their effect on the population over the past two years.

THE ECONOMY
Significant quantities of gold, copper, silver. Oil and natural gas reserves. Secessionist violence on Bougainville deters investors.

INSIGHT: *PNG is home to the only known poisonous birds; contact with the feathers produces skin blisters*

FACTFILE

OFFICIAL NAME: The Independent State of Papua New Guinea

DATE OF FORMATION: 1975

CAPITAL: Port Moresby

POPULATION: 4.8 million

TOTAL AREA: 174,849 sq miles (452,860 sq km)

DENSITY: 27 people per sq mile

LANGUAGES: Pidgin English*, Motu*, Papuan, 750 (est.) native languages

RELIGIONS: Christian 62%, indigenous beliefs 34%, other 4%

ETHNIC MIX: Melanesian/Mixed 100%

GOVERNMENT: Parliamentary democracy

CURRENCY: Kina = 100 toea

Paraguay

Landlocked in central South America, the former Spanish colony of Paraguay's post-independence history has included periods of military rule. Free elections were held in 1993.

GEOGRAPHY

The River Paraguay divides hilly and forested east from a flat alluvial plain with marsh and semidesert scrubland in the west.

CLIMATE

Subtropical. The *Gran Chaco* is generally hotter and drier. All areas experience floods and droughts.

PEOPLE & SOCIETY

Population mainly of mixed Spanish and native Indian origin. *Gran Chaco* is home to small groups of pure Guarani Indians, cattle-ranchers and Memmonites, a sect of German origin. Recent political troubles surround resignation of President Raul Cubas to avoid impeachment.

◆ **INSIGHT:** *The joint Paraguay-Brazil hydroelectric power project at Itaipú is the largest in the world*

THE ECONOMY

Agriculture employs 45% of the workforce. Soybeans and cotton are main exports. Electricity exporter – earnings cover oil imports. Growth is slow due to its remote position.

FACTFILE

OFFICIAL NAME: Republic of Paraguay
DATE OF FORMATION: 1935
CAPITAL: Asunción
POPULATION: 5.5 million
TOTAL AREA: 153,398 sq miles (397,300 sq km)
DENSITY: 36 people per sq mile

LANGUAGES: Spanish*, Guaraní*, Plattdeutsch (Low German)
RELIGIONS: Roman Catholic 96%, Protestant (inc. Mennonite) 4%
ETHNIC MIX: Mestizo 90%, indigenous Indian 2%, other 8%
GOVERNMENT: Presidential democracy
CURRENCY: Guaraní = 100 centimos

Peru

Once the heart of the Inca empire, before the Spanish conquest in the 16th century, Peru lies on the Pacific coast of South America, just south of the Equator.

GEOGRAPHY

Coastal plain rises to Andes mountains. Uplands, dissected by fertile valleys, lie east of Andes. Tropical forest in extreme east.

CLIMATE

Coast is mainly arid. Middle slopes of Andes are temperate; higher peaks are snow-covered. East is hot, humid, and very wet.

PEOPLE & SOCIETY

Populated mainly by Indians or mixed-race *mestizos*, but society is dominated by a small group of Spanish descendants. Indians, together with the small black community, suffer discrimination in the towns. In 1980, Sendero Luminoso guerrillas began an armed struggle against the government. Since then, over 25,000 people have died as a result of guerrilla, and army, violence.

THE ECONOMY

Abundant mineral resources. Rich fish stocks. Illegal export of coca leaves for cocaine production.

◆ **INSIGHT:** *Lake Titicaca is the world's highest navigable lake*

4000m/13124ft
2000m/6562ft
500m/1640ft
Sea Level

0   200 km

0   200 miles

FACTFILE

OFFICIAL NAME: Republic of Peru
DATE OF FORMATION: 1824
CAPITAL: Lima
POPULATION: 25.7 million
TOTAL AREA: 494,208 sq miles (1,280,000 sq km)
DENSITY: 52 people per sq mile

LANGUAGES: Spanish*, Quechua*, Aymará*, other Indian languages
RELIGIONS: Roman Catholic 95%, other 5%
ETHNIC MIX: Indigenous Indian 54%, Mestizo 32%, White 12%, other 2%
GOVERNMENT: Presidential democracy
CURRENCY: Nuevo sol = 100 centimos

Philippines

Lying in the western Pacific Ocean, the Philippines is the world's second largest archipelago. It comprises 7107 islands, of which 4600 are named and 1000 inhabited.

GEOGRAPHY

Larger islands are forested and mountainous. Over 20 active volcanoes. Frequent earthquakes.

CLIMATE

Tropical. Warm and humid all year round. Typhoons occur in the rainy season, June–October.

PEOPLE & SOCIETY

Over 100 ethnic groups. Most Filipinos are of Malay origin, and Christian. The Catholic Church is the dominant cultural force. It opposes state-sponsored family planning programs designed to curb accelerating population growth. Women have traditionally played a prominent part in society, and many enter the professions.

◆ **INSIGHT:** *The Philippines is the only Christian state in Asia*

THE ECONOMY

Peru is now open to outside investment. Agricultural productivity is rising. Power failures limit scope for expansion. Weak infrastructure.

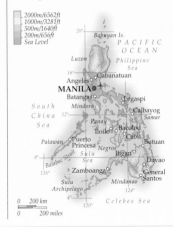

■	2000m/6562ft
■	1000m/3281ft
■	500m/1640ft
■	200m/656ft
	Sea Level

Babuyan Is.

PACIFIC OCEAN

Luzon

Philippine Sea

Cabanatuan

Angeles

MANILA

Batangas

Legaspi

Mindoro

Calbayog

Samar

South China Sea

Panay

Iloilo

Bacolod

Cebu

Butuan

Palawan

Puerto Princesa

Negros

Iligan

Davao

Balabac Strait

Sulu Sea

Zamboanga

Mindanao

General Santos

Sulu Archipelago

Celebes Sea

0   200 km

0   200 miles

FACTFILE

OFFICIAL NAME: Republic of the Philippines

DATE OF FORMATION: 1946

CAPITAL: Manila

POPULATION: 76 million

TOTAL AREA: 115,123 sq miles (298,170 sq km)

DENSITY: 660 people per sq mile

LANGUAGES: Pilipino*, English*, other

RELIGIONS: Roman Catholic 84%, Protestant 9%, Muslim 5%, other 2%

ETHNIC MIX: Malay 50%, Indonesian and Polynesian 30%, other 20%

GOVERNMENT: Presidential democracy

CURRENCY: Peso = 100 centavos

Poland

With its seven international borders, great size, and strategic location at the heart of Europe, Poland has always played an important role in international affairs.

GEOGRAPHY
Lowlands, part of the North European Plain, cover most of the country. The Carpathian Mountains run along the southern borders.

CLIMATE
Rainfall peaks during the hot summers. Cold winters with snow, especially in mountains.

PEOPLE & SOCIETY
Ethnic homogeneity masks a number of tensions. Secular liberals criticize the semiofficial status of the Catholic Church, and emerging wealth disparities are resented by those unaffected by free-market reforms. German minority presses for action on Green issues.

◆ **INSIGHT:** *Poland's eastern forests are home to Europe's largest remaining herds of European bison*

THE ECONOMY
High growth, with foreign investment linked to government privatization program. Heavy industries still dominate, but a service sector is quickly emerging.

■ 1000m/3281ft	
■ 500m/1640ft	
■ 200m/656ft	0 100 km
Sea Level	0 100 miles

FACTFILE
OFFICIAL NAME: Republic of Poland
DATE OF FORMATION: 1945
CAPITAL: Warsaw
POPULATION: 38.8 million
TOTAL AREA: 117,552 sq miles (304,460 sq km)
DENSITY: 330 people per sq mile

LANGUAGES: Polish*, German, other
RELIGIONS: Roman Catholic 93%, Eastern Orthodox 2%, other and nonreligious 5%
ETHNIC MIX: Polish 98%, German 1%, other 1%
GOVERNMENT: Parliamentary democracy
CURRENCY: Zloty = 100 groszy

Portugal

Portugal, with its long Atlantic coast, lies on the western side of the Iberian Peninsula, which it shares with Spain. It is the most westerly country on the European mainland.

GEOGRAPHY
The River Tagus bisects the country roughly east to west, dividing mountainous north from lower and more undulating south.

CLIMATE
North is cool and moist. South is warmer with dry, mild winters.

PEOPLE & SOCIETY
A homogeneous and stable society, which is losing some of its conservative traditions. A small, well-assimilated immigrant population, mainly from former colonies. Urban areas and the south are more socially progressive. The north is more responsive to traditional Catholic values. Family ties remain important.

◆ **INSIGHT:** *Portugal is the world's leading producer of cork, which comes from the bark of the cork oak*

THE ECONOMY
Agricultural exports include grain, vegetables, fruits, and wine, but farming methods are outdated. Strong banking and tourism sectors.

FACTFILE

OFFICIAL NAME: Republic of Portugal
DATE OF FORMATION: 1640
CAPITAL: Lisbon
POPULATION: 9.9 million
TOTAL AREA: 35,501 sq miles (91,950 sq km)
DENSITY: 279 people per sq mile

LANGUAGES: Portuguese*
RELIGIONS: Roman Catholic 97%, Protestant 1%, other 2%
ETHNIC MIX: Portuguese 99%, African 1%
GOVERNMENT: Parliamentary democracy
CURRENCY: Euro = 100 cents

Qatar

Projecting north from the Arabian peninsula into The Gulf, Qatar is a founder member of OPEC. Its plentiful reserves of oil and gas make it one of the wealthiest states in the region.

GEOGRAPHY
Flat, semiarid desert with sand dunes and salt pans. Vegetation is limited to small patches of scrub.

CLIMATE
Hot and humid. Temperatures in summer can soar to over 104°F (40°C). Rainfall is rare.

PEOPLE & SOCIETY
Only one in five Qataris is native-born. Most of the population are guest workers from the Indian subcontinent, Iran, and North Africa. Qataris were once nomadic Bedouins, but since the advent of oil wealth, they have become city-dwellers. As a result, the north is dotted with abandoned villages. Life is dominated by the ruling Al-Thani family.

◆ INSIGHT: *There are over 700 mosques in the capital, Doha*

THE ECONOMY
Steady supply of crude oil and huge gas reserves, plus related industries. Economy is heavily dependent on foreign workforce. All raw materials and most foods, except vegetables, are imported.

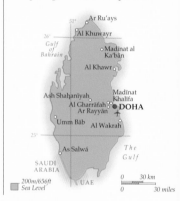

FACTFILE

OFFICIAL NAME: State of Qatar
DATE OF FORMATION: 1971
CAPITAL: Doha
POPULATION: 699,000
TOTAL AREA: 4247 sq miles (11,000 sq km)
DENSITY: 165 people per sq mile

LANGUAGES: Arabic*, Farsi (Persian), Urdu, Hindi, English
RELIGIONS: Muslim (mainly Sunni) 95%, other 5%
ETHNIC MIX: Arab 40%, Indian 18%, Pakistani 18%, Iranian 10%, other 14%
GOVERNMENT: Monarchy
CURRENCY: Riyal = 100 dirhams

Romania

Once dominated by the Ottoman, Russian, and Habsburg empires, Romania has been slowly converting to a free-market economy since the overthrow of its communist regime in 1989.

GEOGRAPHY
Carpathian Mountains encircle the Transylvanian plateau. Wide plains to the south and east. River Danube on southern border.

CLIMATE
Continental. Summers are hot and humid, winters are cold and snowy. Very heavy spring rains.

PEOPLE & SOCIETY
Since 1989, there has been a rise in Romanian nationalism, aggravated by the hardships brought by economic reform. Incidence of ethnic violence has also risen, particularly towards Hungarians and Romanies. Decrease in population in recent years due to emigration and falling birth rate.

◆ **INSIGHT:** *Transylvania is the home of Bram Stoker's terrifying fictional creation, Count Dracula*

THE ECONOMY
Pollution-spreading, outdated heavy industries and unmechanized agricultural sector. Wages have fallen since demise of communism. High number of small-scale foreign joint ventures. Tourism potential.

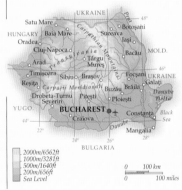

FACTFILE
OFFICIAL NAME: Romania
DATE OF FORMATION: 1947
CAPITAL: Bucharest
POPULATION: 22.3 million
TOTAL AREA: 88,934 sq miles (230,340 sq km)
DENSITY: 251 people per sq mile

LANGUAGES: Romanian*, Hungarian
RELIGIONS: Romanian Orthodox 87%, Roman Catholic 5%, Protestant 4%, Greek Catholic 1%, other 3%
ETHNIC MIX: Romanian 89%, Magyar 9%, Romany 1%, other 1%
GOVERNMENT: Multiparty republic
CURRENCY: Leu = 100 bani

Russian Federation

The Russian Federation is still the world's largest state, despite the breakup of the Soviet Union in 1991. It is currently struggling to capitalize on its diversity.

GEOGRAPHY

The Ural Mountains divide the European steppes and forests from the tundra and forests of Siberia. South-central deserts and mountains.

CLIMATE

Continental in European Russia. Elsewhere climate ranges from sub-arctic to Mediterranean and hot desert.

PEOPLE & SOCIETY

Ethnic Russians now make up 80% of the population, but there are many minority groups. 57 nationalities have territorial status, and a further 95 lack their own territory. The 1994 war with Chechnya indicated the potential for ethnic crisis. Wealth disparities, rising crime and black market activities have accompanied reforms. Extremist politicians have exploited standard-of-living and ethnic concerns.

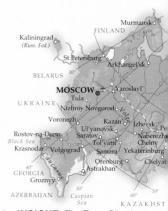

◆ **INSIGHT:** *The Trans-Siberian Railroad, which runs 5800 miles (9335 km) from Moscow to Vladivostok, is the longest in the world, passing through seven time zones*

FACTFILE

OFFICIAL NAME: Russian Federation
DATE OF FORMATION: 1991
CAPITAL: Moscow
POPULATION: 146.9 million
TOTAL AREA: 6,562,100 sq miles (16,995,800 sq km)
DENSITY: 22 people per sq mile

LANGUAGES: Russian*, other
RELIGIONS: Russian Orthodox 75%, other 25%
ETHNIC MIX: Russian 82%, Tatar 4%, Ukrainian 3%, Chuvash 1%, other 10%
GOVERNMENT: Presidential democracy
CURRENCY: Rouble = 100 kopeks

Russian Federation

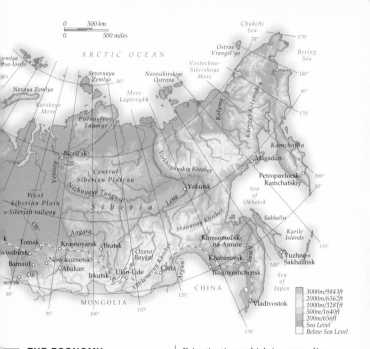

	3000m/9843ft
	2000m/6562ft
	1000m/3281ft
	500m/1640ft
	200m/656ft
	Sea Level
	Below Sea Level

$ THE ECONOMY

Lingering inefficiencies since transition to market economy sap Russia's obvious strengths: huge natural resources, in particular oil and gas, precious metals, timber, and hydrocarbons. Enormous engineering and scientific base.

Privatization, which is proceeding fast, and foreign investment could transform industry and agriculture. Many of the skills developed under communism are not relevant in an increasingly competitive economy. Organized crime syndicates own huge areas of the economy.

Rwanda

Rwanda lies just south of the Equator in east central Africa, far from the nearest port. Since independence from France in 1962, ethnic tensions have dominated politics.

GEOGRAPHY

A series of plateaus descend from the ridge of volcanic peaks in the west to the Akagera River on the eastern border. The Great Rift Valley also passes through this region.

CLIMATE

Tropical, though tempered by the altitude. Two wet seasons are separated by a dry season, from June to August. Heaviest rain in the west.

PEOPLE & SOCIETY

Rwandans live a subsistence existence. Traditional family and clan structures are strong. For over 500 years the cattle-owning Tutsi were politically dominant over the land-owning Hutu. In 1959, violent revolt led to a reversal of the roles. The two groups have since been waging a spasmodic war. In the most recent outbreak of violence, in 1994, over 200,000 people died.

THE ECONOMY

All economic activity has been completely disrupted due to the ethnic conflict. Rwanda has few resources, but assuming stability, it produces coffee. Possible oil and gas reserves. High transportation costs.

INSIGHT: *Rwanda is Africa's most densely populated country*

FACTFILE

OFFICIAL NAME: Republic of Rwanda
DATE OF FORMATION: 1962
CAPITAL: Kigali
POPULATION: 7.7 million
TOTAL AREA: 9633 sq miles (24,950 sq km)
DENSITY: 799 people per sq mile

LANGUAGES: Kinyarwanda*, French*, Kiswahili
RELIGIONS: Traditional beliefs 50%, Roman Catholic 45%, other 5%
ETHNIC MIX: Hutu 90%, Tutsi 8%, other (inc. Twa) 2%
GOVERNMENT: Transitional regime
CURRENCY: Franc = 100 centimes

St Kitts & Nevis

One of the Caribbean's most popular tourist destinations, St Kitts and Nevis lies in the northern part of the Leeward Islands. Nevis is the less developed of the two islands.

GEOGRAPHY
Volcanic in origin, with forested, mountainous interiors. Nevis has hot and cold springs.

CLIMATE
Tropical, tempered by trade winds. Little seasonal variation in temperature. Moderate rainfall.

PEOPLE & SOCIETY
Majority of the population is of African descent. Intermarriage has blurred other racial lines and eliminated ethnic tensions. For most people, the extended family is the norm. Wealth disparities are not great, but urban professionals enjoy a higher standard of living than rural sugar-cane farmers. Politics is based on the British system; funds are provided by professionals and the trade unions. The proposed Leeward Islands union is the main political issue.

THE ECONOMY
Sugar industry, currently UK-managed, has preferential access to EU and US markets. Successful and still expanding tourist industry.

INSIGHT: *Nevis has been renowned as a spa since the 18th century, and is known as the "Queen of the Caribbean"*

FACTFILE

OFFICIAL NAME: Federation of Saint Christopher and Nevis
DATE OF FORMATION: 1983
CAPITAL: Basseterre
POPULATION: 41,000
TOTAL AREA: 139 sq miles (360 sq km)

DENSITY: 295 people per sq mile
LANGUAGES: English*, English Creole
RELIGIONS: Anglican 33%, Methodist 29%, Moravian 9%, Catholic 7%, other 22%
ETHNIC MIX: Black 95%, mixed 5%
GOVERNMENT: Parliamentary democracy
CURRENCY: E. Caribbean $ = 100 cents

St Lucia

St Lucia is one of the most beautiful of the Caribbean Windward Islands. Ruled by the French and British at different times in its past, the island retains the character of both.

GEOGRAPHY
Volcanic and mountainous, with some broad fertile valleys. The Pitons, ancient lava cones, rise from the sea on the forested west coast.

CLIMATE
Tropical, moderated by trade winds. May–October wet season brings daily warm showers. Rainfall is highest in the mountains.

PEOPLE & SOCIETY
Population is a tension-free mixture of descendants of Africans, Europeans, and South Asians. Family life and the Church are important to most St Lucians. In rural areas women often head the households, and run much of the farming. There is growing local resistance to overdevelopment of the island by tourism. A proposed union with the other Windward Islands is the main political issue.

THE ECONOMY
Mainly agricultural, with some light industry. Bananas are biggest export. Successful tourist industry, but most resorts are foreign-owned.

INSIGHT: *St Lucia has two Nobel laureates, the most per capita in the world*

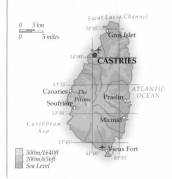

FACTFILE
OFFICIAL NAME: Saint Lucia
DATE OF FORMATION: 1979
CAPITAL: Castries
POPULATION: 156,260
TOTAL AREA: 236 sq miles (610 sq km)
DENSITY: 662 people per sq mile

LANGUAGES: English*, French Creole, Hindi, Urdu
RELIGIONS: Roman Catholic 90%, other 10%
ETHNIC MIX: Black 90%, Mulatto 6%, Asian 3%, White 1%
GOVERNMENT: Parliamentary democracy
CURRENCY: E. Caribbean $ = 100 cents

St Vincent & the Grenadines

The islands of St Vincent and the Grenadines form part of the Windward group in the Caribbean. St Vincent is mostly volcanic, while the Grenadines are flat, mainly bare, coral reefs.

GEOGRAPHY

St Vincent is mountainous and forested, with one of two active volcanoes in the Caribbean, La Soufrière. The Grenadines are 32 islands and cays fringed by beaches.

CLIMATE

Tropical, with constant trade winds. Hurricanes are likely during July–November wet season.

PEOPLE & SOCIETY

Population is racially diverse, but intermarriage has reduced tensions. Society is informal and relaxed, but family life is strongly influenced by the Anglican Church. Locals fear that their traditional lifestyle is being threatened by the expanding tourist industry.

▷ **INSIGHT:** *The islands' precolonial inhabitants, the Carib Indians, named them "Hairioun" – home of the blessed*

THE ECONOMY

Dependent on agriculture and tourism. Bananas are the main cash crop. Tourism, targeted at the jet-set and cruise-ship markets, is concentrated on the Grenadines.

📖 FACTFILE

OFFICIAL NAME: Saint Vincent and the Grenadines
DATE OF FORMATION: 1979
CAPITAL: Kingstown
POPULATION: 115,461
TOTAL AREA: 131 sq miles (340 sq km)

DENSITY: 880 people per sq mile
LANGUAGES: English*, English Creole
RELIGIONS: Anglican 42%, Methodist 20%, Catholic 19%, other 19%
ETHNIC MIX: Black 66%, Mulatto 19%, Asian 6%, White 4%, other 5%
GOVERNMENT: Parliamentary democracy
CURRENCY: E. Caribbean $ = 100 cents

Samoa

The southern Pacific islands of Samoa gained independence from New Zealand in 1962. Four of the nine volcanic islands are inhabited – Apolima, Manono, Sava'ai, and Upolu.

GEOGRAPHY

Comprises two large islands and seven smaller ones. The two largest islands have rain forested, mountainous interiors surrounded by coastal lowlands and coral reefs.

CLIMATE

Tropical, with high humidity. Cooler May–November. Hurricane season December–March.

PEOPLE & SOCIETY

Ethnic Samoans are the world's second largest Polynesian group, after the Maoris. Their way of life is communal and formalized. Extended family groups own 80% of the land. Each family has an elected chief, who looks after its political and social interests. Large-scale migration to the US and New Zealand reflects the country's lack of jobs and the attractions of a Western lifestyle.

THE ECONOMY

Agricultural products include taro, coconut cream, cocoa, and copra. Growth of the service sector since 1989 launch of offshore banking. Dependent on aid and expatriate remittances. Rain forests are increasingly exploited for timber.

◆ INSIGHT: *Samoa was named for the sacred (sa) chickens (moa) of Lu, son of Tagaloa, the god of creation*

FACTFILE

OFFICIAL NAME: Independent State of Samoa

DATE OF FORMATION: 1962

CAPITAL: Apia

POPULATION: 180,000

TOTAL AREA: 1093 sq miles (2830 sq km)

DENSITY: 165 people per sq mile

LANGUAGES: Samoan*, English*

RELIGIONS: Christian 99%, other 1%

ETHNIC MIX: Polynesian 90%, Euronesian 9%, other 1%

GOVERNMENT: Parliamentary democracy

CURRENCY: Tala = 100 sene

San Marino

Perched on the slopes of Monte Titano in the Italian Appennino, San Marino has maintained its independence since the 4th century AD. Italy effectively controls most of its affairs.

GEOGRAPHY
Distinctive limestone outcrop of Monte Titano dominates wooded hills and pastures near Italy's Adriatic coast.

CLIMATE
High altitude and sea breezes moderate a Mediterranean climate. Hot summers and cool, wet winters.

PEOPLE & SOCIETY
Territory is divided into nine "castles," or districts. Tightly knit society, with 16 centuries of tradition. Strict immigration rules require 30-year residence before applying for citizenship. Catholic Church remains a more powerful influence than in neighboring Italy. Living standards are similar to those in northern Italy.

◆ **INSIGHT:** *Sales of postage stamps contribute 10% of the national income*

THE ECONOMY
Tourism provides 60% of total government income. Light industries – led by mechanical engineering and high-quality clothing – generate export revenue. Italian infrastructure is a boon.

FACTFILE

OFFICIAL NAME: Republic of San Marino
DATE OF FORMATION: 301
CAPITAL: San Marino
POPULATION: 26,937
TOTAL AREA: 24 sq miles (61 sq km)
DENSITY: 1122 people per sq mile

LANGUAGES: Italian*, other
RELIGIONS: Roman Catholic 93%, other and nonreligious 7%
ETHNIC MIX: Sammarinese 80%, Italian 19%, other 1%
GOVERNMENT: Parliamentary democracy
CURRENCY: Euro = 100 cents

São Tomé & Príncipe

A former Portuguese colony situated off the west coast of Africa, comprising two main islands and the surrounding islets. Elections in 1991 ended 15 years of Marxism.

 GEOGRAPHY
Islands are scattered across the Equator. São Tomé and Príncipe are heavily forested and mountainous.

 CLIMATE
Hot and humid, but cooled by the Benguela Current. Plentiful rainfall.

 PEOPLE & SOCIETY
Population is mostly black, although Portuguese culture pre-dominates. Blacks run the political parties. Society is well integrated and free of racial prejudice. Wealth disparities are not great, though there is a growing business class. Extended family offers main form of social security. Príncipe assumed autonomous status in April 1995.

◆ **INSIGHT:** *The population is entirely of immigrant descent: the islands were uninhabited when colonized in 1470*

THE ECONOMY
Cocoa provides 90% of export earnings. Palm oil, pepper and coffee are farmed. One of Africa's highest aid-to-population ratios.

 FACTFILE

OFFICIAL NAME: Democratic Republic of São Tomé and Príncipe
DATE OF FORMATION: 1975
CAPITAL: São Tomé
POPULATION: 159,883
TOTAL AREA: 370 sq miles (960 sq km)

DENSITY: 432 people per sq mile
LANGUAGES: Portuguese*, Portuguese Creole, other
RELIGIONS: Catholic 84%, other 16%
ETHNIC MIX: Black 90%, Portuguese and Creole 10%
GOVERNMENT: Multiparty republic
CURRENCY: Dobra = 100 centimos

Saudi Arabia

Occupying most of the Arabian peninsula, Saudi Arabia covers an area the size of Western Europe. It has the world's largest oil and gas reserves and a major petrochemicals industry.

GEOGRAPHY
Mostly desert or semidesert plateau. Mountain ranges in the west run parallel to the Red Sea and drop steeply to a coastal plain.

CLIMATE
In summer, temperatures often soar above 118°F (48°C), but in winter they may fall below freezing. Rainfall is rare.

PEOPLE & SOCIETY
Most Saudis are Sunni Muslims who follow the strictly orthodox *wahabi* interpretation of Islam and embrace *sharia* (Islamic law) in their daily lives. Women are obliged to wear the veil, cannot hold driving licenses, and have no role in public life. The Al-Saud family have been absolutist rulers since 1932. With the support of the religious establishment, they control all political life.

THE ECONOMY
Vast oil and gas reserves. Other minerals include coal, iron, and gold. Most food is imported.

INSIGHT: *Over two million Muslims a year make the haj – the pilgrimage to the holy city of Mecca*

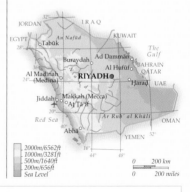

2000m/6562ft
1000m/3281ft
500m/1640ft
200m/656ft
Sea Level

0   200 km
0   200 miles

FACTFILE

OFFICIAL NAME: Kingdom of Saudi Arabia
DATE OF FORMATION: 1932
CAPITAL: Riyadh
POPULATION: 21.6 million
TOTAL AREA: 816,480 sq miles (2,114,690 sq km)

DENSITY: 26 people per sq mile
LANGUAGES: Arabic*, other
RELIGIONS: Sunni Muslim 85%, Shi'a Muslim 15%
ETHNIC MIX: Arab 90%, Afro-Asian 10%
GOVERNMENT: Monarchy
CURRENCY: Riyal = 100 malalah

Senegal

Senegal's capital, Dakar, stands on the westernmost cape of Africa. After independence from France, Senegal remained a single-party state until the first multiparty elections in 1981.

GEOGRAPHY
Arid semidesert in the north. The south is mainly savannah bushland. Plains in the southeast.

CLIMATE
Tropical, with humid rainy conditions June–October, and a drier season December–May. The coast is cooled by northern trade winds.

PEOPLE & SOCIETY
There is very little ethnic tension, due to the considerable amount of interethnic marriage. Groups can be identified regionally. Dakar is a Wolof area, the Senegal River is dominated by the Toucouleur, and the Malinke mostly live in the east. The Diola in Casamance have felt politically excluded and this has led to unrest. A French-influenced class system is still prevalent and has become more apparent in recent years.

THE ECONOMY
70% of people are farmers – peanuts are main export crop. Phosphate is mined. More industry than most West African countries.

INSIGHT: *Senegal's name derives from the Zenega Berbers who invaded in the 1300s, bringing Islam with them*

FACTFILE
OFFICIAL NAME: Republic of Senegal
DATE OF FORMATION: 1960
CAPITAL: Dakar
POPULATION: 9.5 million
TOTAL AREA: 74,336 sq miles (192,530 sq km)
DENSITY: 128 people per sq mile

LANGUAGES: French*, Wolof, Fulani, Serer, Diola, Malinke, Soninke
RELIGIONS: Sunni Muslim 90%, traditional beliefs 5%, Christian 5%
ETHNIC MIX: Wolof 44%, Serer 15% Fula 12%, Diola 5%, other 24%
GOVERNMENT: Presidential democracy
CURRENCY: CFA franc = 100 centimes

Seychelles

The Seychelles comprise 115 islands in the Indian Ocean. They support unique flora and fauna, including the giant tortoise and the world's largest seed, the *coco-de-mer*.

GEOGRAPHY

Mostly low-lying coral atolls, but 40 islands, including the largest, Mahé, are mountainous and are the only granitic islands in the world.

CLIMATE

Tropical oceanic climate. Hot and humid. Rainy season December–May.

PEOPLE & SOCIETY

The islands were uninhabited when French settlers arrived in the 18th century. Today, the population is homogeneous – a result of inter-marriage between ethnic groups. Almost 90% of people live on Malé. Living standards are among Africa's highest. Poverty is rare and the welfare system caters for all.

◆ **INSIGHT:** *Praised for their efforts in conservation, the islands helped to promote the idea of whale sanctuaries*

THE ECONOMY

Tourism is the main source of income, based on the appeal of beaches and exotic plants and animals. Tuna is fished and canned for export. There are virtually no mineral resources. All domestic requirements are imported.

FACTFILE

OFFICIAL NAME: Republic of the Seychelles
DATE OF FORMATION: 1976
CAPITAL: Victoria
POPULATION: 79,326
TOTAL AREA: 104 sq miles (270 sq km)

DENSITY: 763 people per sq mile
LANGUAGES: Creole*, French, English
RELIGIONS: Catholic 90%, Anglican 8%, other (inc. Muslim) 2%
ETHNIC MIX: Creole 89%, Indian 5%, Chinese 2%, other 4%
GOVERNMENT: Multiparty republic
CURRENCY: Rupee = 100 cents

Sierra Leone

The West African state of Sierra Leone achieved independence from the British in 1961. Today, it is still recovering from a devastating civil war, and is one of the world's poorest nations.

GEOGRAPHY

Flat plain, running the length of the coast, stretches inland for 83 miles (133 km). Beyond, forests rise to highlands near neighboring Guinea in the northeast.

CLIMATE

Hot tropical weather, with very high rainfall and humidity. The dusty, northeastern *harmattan* wind blows November–April.

PEOPLE & SOCIETY

Mende and Temne are major ethnic groups. Freetown's citizens are largely descended from slaves freed from Britain and the US, resulting in a strongly anglicized Creole culture. A military coup in 1992 halted plans to turn the government into a multi-party democracy. Rebel forces fought the government until 1999, when a peace agreement was signed.

THE ECONOMY

Vast majority of people are subsistance farmers. Cash crops include palm kernels, cocoa beans, and kola. Main export is diamonds.

INSIGHT: *The British philanthropist Granville Sharp set up a settlement for freed slaves in Sierra Leone in 1787*

FACTFILE

OFFICIAL NAME: Republic of Sierra Leone

DATE OF FORMATION: 1961

CAPITAL: Freetown

POPULATION: 4.9 million

TOTAL AREA: 27,652 sq miles (71,620 sq km)

DENSITY: 177 people per sq mile

LANGUAGES: English*, Krio (Creole)

RELIGIONS: Traditional beliefs 30%, Muslim 30%, Christian 30%, other 10%

ETHNIC MIX: Mende 35%, Temne 32%, Limba 8%, Kuranko 4%, other 21%

GOVERNMENT: Military republic

CURRENCY: Leone = 100 cents

Singapore

Linked to the southernmost tip of the Malay Peninsula by a causeway, Singapore was established as a trading settlement in 1819. It is still one of Asia's most important commercial centers.

GEOGRAPHY
Little remains of the original vegetation on Singapore island. The other 54 much smaller islands are little more than swampy jungle.

CLIMATE
Equatorial. Hot and humid, with heavy rainfall all year round.

PEOPLE & SOCIETY
Dominated by the Chinese, who make up three-quarters of the community. The old English-speaking Straits Chinese and newer Mandarin-speakers are now well integrated. Malays are generally the poorest group. There is a significant foreign workforce. Society is highly regulated and government campaigns to improve public behaviour are frequent. Crime is limited and punishment can be severe.

THE ECONOMY
Highly successful financial, banking, and manufacturing sectors. Produces 50% of the world's computer disk drives. All food and energy has to be imported.

INSIGHT: *Singapore has full employment, and the world's highest rate of home ownership and national savings*

Urban areas
Open areas
Nature reserves

Causeway

MALAYSIA

Pulau Ubin

Lim Chu Kang
Choa Chu Kang
Bukit Panjang
Bukit Timah
Houngang New Town
Pulau Tekong
Changi International Airport

Jurong Industrial Estate
Queenstown
Bedok New Town

Telok Blangah
City

Sedat Pandan
Sentosa
Pulau Brani

South China Sea

1°20'

103°40'   103°50'

Strait of Singapore

0   5 km
0   5 miles

FACTFILE

OFFICIAL NAME: Republic of Singapore
DATE OF FORMATION: 1965
CAPITAL: Singapore
POPULATION: 3.6 million
TOTAL AREA: 236 sq miles
(610 sq km)
DENSITY: 15,254 people per sq mile

LANGUAGES: Malay*, Chinese*, other
RELIGIONS: Buddhist 55%, Taoism 22%, Muslim 16%, other 7%
ETHNIC MIX: Chinese 78%, Malay 14%, Indian 6%, other 2%
GOVERNMENT: Parliamentary democracy
CURRENCY: Singapore $ = 100 cents

Slovakia

Landlocked in Central Europe, Slovakia became an independent state in 1993. It is the less-developed half of the former Czechoslovakia, with high levels of international debt.

GEOGRAPHY

The Carpathian Mountains stretch along the northern border with Poland. Southern lowlands include the fertile Danube plain.

CLIMATE

Continental. Moderately warm summers and steady rainfall. Cold winters with heavy snowfalls.

PEOPLE & SOCIETY

Slovaks are the largest and most dominant group. Tension between them and the Hungarian minority has increased, particularly over a directive that Hungarians should adopt Slovak name endings. Romanies have no official representation. Before partition, many skilled Slovaks took jobs in Prague, but few have returned to help structure the new Slovakia. The Catholic Church remains influential.

THE ECONOMY

Narrow emphasis on heavy industry, with a patchy record of innovation and capital investment. High inflation and unemployment. Growing tourism sector.

◆ **INSIGHT:** *Separation from the Czech Republic gave Slovakia full independence for the first time in over 1000 years*

2000m/6562ft	
1000m/3281ft	
500m/1640ft	
200m/656ft	
Sea Level	

0   50 km
0   50 miles

FACTFILE

OFFICIAL NAME: Slovak Republic
DATE OF FORMATION: 1993
CAPITAL: Bratislava
POPULATION: 5.4 million
TOTAL AREA: 18,933 sq miles (49,036 sq km)
DENSITY: 285 people per sq mile

LANGUAGES: Slovak*, Hungarian (Magyar), Romany, Czech, other
RELIGIONS: Catholic 60%, Atheist 8%, Protestant 8%, other 24%
ETHNIC MIX: Slovak 85%, Magyar 9%, Romany 1%, Czech 1%, other 2%
GOVERNMENT: Parliamentary democracy
CURRENCY: Koruna = 100 halura

Slovenia

The northernmost of the former Yugoslav republics, Slovenia has close links with Western Europe. Transition to independence in 1991 avoided the violence of the breakup of Yugoslavia.

GEOGRAPHY
Alpine terrain with hills and mountains. Forests cover almost half the country's area. There is a short coastline along the Adriatic Sea.

CLIMATE
Mediterranean climate on the small coastal strip. The alpine interior has continental extremes.

PEOPLE & SOCIETY
Ethnically homogeneous population accounts for the relatively peaceful transition to independence. A separate Slovene language and traditional links with Austria and Italy, each with Slovene populations, account for the "Alpine" rather than "Balkan" outlook. Unemployment is rising, though wages are the highest in Central Europe. Institutional change is proceeding slowly.

THE ECONOMY
Competitive manufacturing industry. There are prospects for growth in the electronics industry. Well-developed tourist sector.

INSIGHT: *Slovenia is a major producer of mercury, used in thermometers, and batteries*

FACTFILE

OFFICIAL NAME: Republic of Slovenia
DATE OF FORMATION: 1991
CAPITAL: Ljubljana
POPULATION: 2 million
TOTAL AREA: 7820 sq miles (20,250 sq km)
DENSITY: 256 people per sq mile

LANGUAGES: Slovene*, Serbo-Croatian
RELIGIONS: Roman Catholic 96%, Muslim 1%, other 3%
ETHNIC MIX: Slovene 88%, Croat 3%, Serb 2%, Muslim 1%, other 6%
GOVERNMENT: Parliamentary democracy
CURRENCY: Tolar = 100 stotins

Solomon Islands

The Solomons archipelago comprises several hundred coral reef islands scattered in the southwestern Pacific. Most of the population live on the six largest islands.

GEOGRAPHY
The six largest islands are volcanic, mountainous, and thickly forested. Flat coastal plains provide the only cultivable land.

CLIMATE
Northern islands are hot and humid all year round; further south a cool season develops. November–April wet season brings cyclones.

PEOPLE & SOCIETY
Most Solomon Islanders are of Melanesian descent. Around 87 native languages are spoken, but Pidgin English is used as a contact language between tribes. Most people live on shifting, subsistence agriculture in small rural villages. Villagers work collectively on community projects and there is much sharing among the various clans. Animist beliefs are maintained alongside Christianity.

THE ECONOMY
Main products are palm oil, copra, cocoa, fish, and timber. Bauxite deposits have been found on Rennell Island, but islanders persuaded the government that exploiting them would destroy the island.

◆ **INSIGHT:** *The Solomons have no television service; the islanders oppose TV as it might dilute their culture*

FACTFILE
OFFICIAL NAME: Solomon Islands
DATE OF FORMATION: 1978
CAPITAL: Honiara
POPULATION: 444,000
TOTAL AREA: 10,806 sq miles (27,990 sq km)
DENSITY: 41 people per sq mile

LANGUAGES: English*, Pidgin English, 87 (est.) native languages
RELIGIONS: Anglican 34%, Catholic 19%, other Christian 38%, other 9%
ETHNIC MIX: Melanesian 94%, Polynesian 4%, other 2
GOVERNMENT: Parliamentary democracy
CURRENCY: Solomon Is. $ = 100 cents

Somalia

Somalia is a semiarid state occupying the horn of Africa.
The colonies of Italian Somaliland and British Somaliland
were united in 1960 to form an independent Somalia.

GEOGRAPHY
Highlands in the north, flatter
scrub-covered land to the south.
Coastal areas are more fertile.

CLIMATE
Very dry, except for the north
coast, which is hot and humid.
The interior has among the world's
highest average annual temperatures.

PEOPLE & SOCIETY
The clan system forms the basis
of all commercial, political, and social
activities. The entire population is
ethnic Somali and national identity
remains strong. Most people are
herders (*Samaal*) while the rest are
farmers (*Sab*). Years of clan-based civil
war have resulted in the collapse of
central government. A US-led UN
peacekeeping force was deployed,
but it was withdrawn in 1994 due
to widespread Somali opposition.

THE ECONOMY
Somalia is heavily reliant on
foreign aid, since all commodities,
except arms, are in short supply.
Formal economy has collapsed
due to civil war and drought.

INSIGHT: *Somalia was known to
the Egyptians, Phoenicians and
Greeks as "the land of incense"*

FACTFILE
OFFICIAL NAME: Somali
Democratic Republic
DATE OF FORMATION: 1960
CAPITAL: Mogadishu
POPULATION: 10.1 million
TOTAL AREA: 242,215 sq miles
(627,340 sq km)

DENSITY: 42 people per sq mile
LANGUAGES: Somali*, Arabic*,
other
RELIGIONS: Sunni Muslim 98%,
other (inc. Christian) 2%
ETHNIC MIX: Somali 85%, other 15%
GOVERNMENT: Transitional regime
CURRENCY: Shilling = 100 cents

South Africa

South Africa is the southernmost nation on the African continent. After 80 years of white minority rule, the country's first multiracial, multiparty elections were held in 1994.

GEOGRAPHY

Much of the interior of South Africa is grassland plateau, or *veld*, drained in the west by the Orange River system and in the east by the Limpopo and its tributaries. Part of the Namib Desert lies along the west coast and the southern tip of the Kalahari Desert pushes into the north. Mountain ridges stretch across the east, south, and west. The highest form the Drakensberg range, a semicircular escarpment overshadowing a narrow, low-lying coastal strip to the east. The Great Karroo, a coastal mountain range, runs along the southern coast.

CLIMATE

South Africa is warm, temperate, and dry. The interior of the country gets most of the rain in summer. The coastal strip around Cape Town has a Mediterranean climate, with winter rains. Semiarid in the west.

PEOPLE & SOCIETY

Since the dismantling of apartheid in the early 1990s, racial segregation has ended, but tensions remain. Expected ethnic conflicts failed to materialize, though Zulus have made demands for independent homelands. While blacks now dominate politics, English-speaking whites continue to control the economy. The extended family has been undermined by regulations forcing men to migrate for work, leaving their wives and children in the rural areas. A small black middle class has developed, but most black South Africans are underemployed. Many women are now prominent in public life. The new constitution guarantees equality of the sexes.

◆ **INSIGHT:** *South Africa dominates the world market in diamonds and gold. Over the past century, it has produced almost half of the world's gold*

FACTFILE

OFFICIAL NAME: Republic of South Africa
DATE OF FORMATION: 1994
CAPITAL: Pretoria
POPULATION: 40.4 million
TOTAL AREA: 471,443 sq miles (1,221,040 sq km)

DENSITY: 86 people per sq mile
LANGUAGES: Afrikaans*, English, 11 African languages
RELIGIONS: Black independent 17%, Dutch reformed 11%, other 72%
ETHNIC MIX: Zulu 23% other 77%
GOVERNMENT: Parliamentary democracy
CURRENCY: Rand = 100 cents

South Africa

THE ECONOMY

Africa's largest and most developed economy; highly diversified, with modern infrastructure. Strong financial sector, though political fears deter foreign investment. Growing manufacturing sector. Diamonds, gold, platinum, coal, silver, uranium, copper, and asbestos mined. Varied agriculture. Falling gold price undermines many sectors. Growth too low to overcome deprivation among black majority.

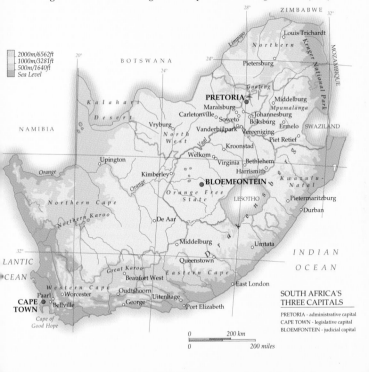

2000m/6562ft
1000m/3281ft
500m/1640ft
Sea Level

ZIMBABWE

Louis Trichardt

Limpopo
Northern

BOTSWANA

Pietersburg

NAMIBIA

Kalahari

Desert

Gauteng

PRETORIA

Maralsburg   Middelburg

Carletonville   Johannesburg   *Mpumalanga*

Vryburg   Soweto   Boksburg   Ermelo

North   Vanderbijlpark   Vereeniging   Piet Retief

West   SWAZILAND

Upington   Kroonstad

Vaal   Welkom

Orange   Virginia   Bethlehem

Kimberley   Harrismith

Orange Free   *Kwazulu-*

State   *Natal*

BLOEMFONTEIN

LESOTHO   Pietermaritzburg

Northern Cape   Durban

De Aar

Northern Karoo   *Drakensberg*

Middelburg

ATLANTIC   Umtata   INDIAN

OCEAN   Queenstown   OCEAN

Great Karoo   *Eastern Cape*

Beaufort West   East London

Western Cape   Oudtshoorn

Paarl   Worcester   George   Uitenhage

CAPE Bellville   Port Elizabeth

TOWN

Cape of
Good Hope

SOUTH AFRICA'S THREE CAPITALS

PRETORIA - administrative capital
CAPE TOWN - legislative capital
BLOEMFONTEIN - judicial capital

0   200 km

0   200 miles

Spain

Lodged between Europe and Africa, the Atlantic and the Mediterranean, Spain has occupied a pivotal global position since unification under Ferdinand and Isabella in 1492.

GEOGRAPHY
Mountain ranges in the north, center, and south, with a huge central plateau. Verdant valleys in the north-west. Mediterranean lowlands.

CLIMATE
Maritime in north. Hotter and drier in south. The central plateau has an extreme climate.

PEOPLE & SOCIETY
A vigorous ethnic regionalism, long suppressed under Franco's regime, now flourishes. There are now 17 autonomous regions. People remain churchgoing, though Catholic teachings on social issues are often flouted. Spanish women are increasingly emancipated, with strong political representation.

◆ **INSIGHT:** *Over 3000 festivals and feasts take place each year in Spain*

THE ECONOMY
Outdated labor practices and low investment hinder growth. Heavy industry, textiles, and food-processing lead exports. Tourism and agriculture are important.

FACTFILE
OFFICIAL NAME: Kingdom of Spain
DATE OF FORMATION: 1492
CAPITAL: Madrid
POPULATION: 39.6 million
TOTAL AREA: 192,834 sq miles (499,440 sq km)
DENSITY: 205 people per sq mile

LANGUAGES: Castilian Spanish*, Catalan*, Galician*, Basque*, other
RELIGIONS: Roman Catholic 96%, other 4%
ETHNIC MIX: Castilian Spanish 72%, Catalan 17%, Galician 6%, Basque 5%
GOVERNMENT: Parliamentary democracy
CURRENCY: Euro = 100 cents

Sri Lanka

Separated from India by the narrow Palk Strait, the state of Sri Lanka comprises one large island and several coral islets to the northwest known as Adam's Bridge.

GEOGRAPHY

The main island is dominated by rugged central highlands. Fertile northern plains are dissected by rivers. Much of the land is tropical jungle.

CLIMATE

Tropical, with breezes on the coast and cooler air in highlands. Northeast is driest and hottest.

PEOPLE & SOCIETY

The majority Sinhalese are mostly Buddhist, while minority Tamils are mostly Muslim or Hindu. Tamils were the minority group favored by the British colonists. Since independence from Britain in 1948, Tamils have felt sidelined, and support for secession has grown. Long-standing tensions between the groups erupted into civil war in 1983. Tamils demand an independent state in the north and east.

THE ECONOMY

World's largest tea exporter. Manufacturing now accounts for 60% of export earnings. Civil war is a drain on government funds and deters investors and tourists.

INSIGHT: *Sri Lanka elected the world's first woman prime minister in 1960*

Palk Strait
Jaffna
Bay of Bengal
Gulf of Mannar
0   50 km
0   50 miles
10°
Trincomalee
Anuradhapura
8°
Batticaloa
Negombo
Kandy
COLOMBO
Sri Jayawardanapura
Moratuwa
Ratnapura
INDIAN OCEAN
2000m/6562ft
1000m/3281ft
500m/1640ft
200m/656ft
Sea Level
Galle
6°
Matara
80°

FACTFILE

OFFICIAL NAME: Democratic Socialist Republic of Sri Lanka
DATE OF FORMATION: 1948
CAPITAL: Colombo
POPULATION: 18.8 million
TOTAL AREA: 24,996 sq miles (64,740 sq km)

DENSITY: 752 people per sq mile
LANGUAGES: Sinhala*, Tamil, English
RELIGIONS: Buddhist 69%, Hindu 15%, Christian 8%, Muslim 8%
ETHNIC MIX: Sinhalese 74%, Tamil 18%, Moor 7%, other 1%
GOVERNMENT: Presidential democracy
CURRENCY: Rupee = 100 cents

Sudan

The largest country in Africa, Sudan borders the Red Sea. Tensions between the Arab north and African south have led to two civil wars since independence from Britain and Egypt.

GEOGRAPHY
Lies within the upper Nile basin. Mostly arid plains, with marshes in the south. Highlands border the Red Sea in the northeast.

CLIMATE
North is hot, arid desert with constant dry winds. Rainy season ranging from two months in the center, to eight in the south.

PEOPLE & SOCIETY
Large number of ethnic and linguistic groups. Two million people are nomads, moving over ancient tribal areas in the south. Major social division is between Arabized Muslims in north, and mostly African, largely Christian or animist peoples in south. Attempts to impose Arab and Islamic values throughout Sudan have been the root cause of the civil war that has ravaged the south since 1983.

THE ECONOMY
Sudan is affected by drought and food shortages. Sesame seeds, cotton, gum arabic are cash crops.

◆ **INSIGHT:** *Sudan's Sudd plain contains the world's largest swamp*

FACTFILE
OFFICIAL NAME: Republic of Sudan
DATE OF FORMATION: 1956
CAPITAL: Khartoum
POPULATION: 29.5 million
TOTAL AREA: 917,373 sq miles (2,376,000 sq km)
DENSITY: 32 people per sq mile

LANGUAGES: Arabic*, other
RELIGIONS: Sunni Muslim 70%, traditional beliefs 20%, Christian 9%, other 1%
ETHNIC MIX: Arab 40%, Tribal 30%, Dinka and Beja 7%, other 23%
GOVERNMENT: Presidential regime
CURRENCY: Pound = 100 piastres

Suriname

Suriname is a former Dutch colony on the north coast of South America. Democracy was restored in 1991, after almost 11 years of military rule. The Netherlands is still the main supplier of aid.

GEOGRAPHY
Mostly covered by tropical rain forest. Coastal plain, central plateaus and the Guiana Highlands.

CLIMATE
Tropical. Hot and humid, but cooled by trade winds. High rainfall, especially in the interior.

PEOPLE & SOCIETY
About 200,000 people have emigrated to the Netherlands since independence. Of those left, 90% live near the coast, the rest live in scattered rain forest communities. Around 7000 are indigenous Indians. *Bosnegers* – descendants of runaway African slaves – fought the Creole-dominated government in the 1980s. Many South Asians and Javanese work in farming. Since return to civilian rule, each group has a political party representing its interests.

THE ECONOMY
Aluminum and bauxite are the leading exports. Rice and fruit are main cash crops. Oil reserves.

INSIGHT: *Suriname was ceded to Holland by the British, in exchange for New Amsterdam (New York), in 1667*

FACTFILE

OFFICIAL NAME: Republic of Suriname
DATE OF FORMATION: 1975
CAPITAL: Paramaribo
POPULATION: 417,000
TOTAL AREA: 62,343 sq miles (161,470 sq km)
DENSITY: 7 people per sq mile

LANGUAGES: Dutch*, Pidgin English (Taki-Taki), Hindi, Javanese, Carib
RELIGIONS: Hindu 27%, Protestant 25%, Catholic 23%, Muslim 20%, other 5%
ETHNIC MIX: South Asian 34%, Creole 34%, Javanese 18%, other 14%
GOVERNMENT: Parliamentary democracy
CURRENCY: Guilder = 100 cents

Swaziland

The tiny southern African kingdom of Swaziland is economically dependent on South Africa. The strong hereditary monarchy is being challenged by demands for a multiparty government.

GEOGRAPHY

Mainly high plateaus and mountains. Rolling grasslands and low scrub plains to the east. Pine forests on western border.

CLIMATE

Temperatures rise and rainfall declines as the land descends eastward, from high to low veld.

PEOPLE & SOCIETY

One of the most conservative states in Africa, though it is now coming under pressure from urban-based modernizers. The political system promotes Swazi tradition and is dominated by a powerful monarchy. Society is patriarchal and focused around clans and chiefs.

◆ **INSIGHT:** *Polygamy is practised in Swaziland – when King Sobhuza died in 1982, he left 100 wives*

THE ECONOMY

Sugarcane is the main cash crop. Others are pineapples, cotton, rice, and tobacco. Asbestos, coal, and wood pulp are also exported.

FACTFILE

OFFICIAL NAME: Kingdom of Swaziland

DATE OF FORMATION: 1968

CAPITAL: Mbabane

POPULATION: 1,008,000

TOTAL AREA: 6641 sq miles (17,200 sq km)

DENSITY: 152 people per sq mile

LANGUAGES: Siswati*, English*, Zulu

RELIGIONS: Christian 60%, traditional beliefs 40%

ETHNIC MIX: Swazi 97%, other 3%

GOVERNMENT: Monarchy

CURRENCY: Lilangeni = 100 cents

Sweden

The largest Scandinavian country in both population and area, Sweden has one of the world's most extensive welfare systems, and is among the leading proponents of equal rights for women.

GEOGRAPHY

Heavily forested, with many lakes. Northern plateau extends beyond the Arctic Circle. Southern lowlands are widely cultivated.

CLIMATE

Southern coasts warmed by Gulf Stream. Northern areas have more extreme continental climate.

PEOPLE & SOCIETY

As in all of Scandinavia, the nuclear family forms the basis of society. Traditions of hard work and economic success are balanced by permissiveness and egalitarianism. High taxes pay for extensive child-care provision, medical protection, and state education. Most industries and the bulk of the population are based in and around the southern cities. A 15,000-strong minority of Sami (Lapps) live in the north.

THE ECONOMY

Companies of global importance, including Volvo, Saab, SFK, Ericsson. Highly developed infra-structure. Up-to-date technology. Skilled labor force.

INSIGHT:

Sweden has maintained a position of armed neutrality since 1815

1000m/3281ft
500m/1640ft
200m/656ft
Sea Level

0   100 km
0   100 miles

FACTFILE

OFFICIAL NAME: Kingdom of Sweden
DATE OF FORMATION: 1905
CAPITAL: Stockholm
POPULATION: 8.9 million
TOTAL AREA: 158,926 sq miles (411,620 sq km)
DENSITY: 56 people per sq mile

LANGUAGES: Swedish*, Finnish, Lappish, other
RELIGIONS: Evangelical Lutheran 89%, Catholic 2%, other 9%
ETHNIC MIX: Swedish 91%, Finnish and Sami 3%, other European 6%
GOVERNMENT: Parliamentary democracy
CURRENCY: Krona = 100 öre

Switzerland

One of the world's most prosperous countries, Switzerland lies at the center of Western Europe. It has managed to retain its neutral status through every major European conflict since 1815.

GEOGRAPHY
Mostly mountainous, with river valleys. The Alps cover 60% of its area; the Jura in the west cover 10%. Lowlands lie along the east-west axis.

CLIMATE
Most rain falls in the warm summer months. Winters are snowy, but milder and foggy away from the mountains. Avalanches are a problem.

PEOPLE & SOCIETY
Switzerland is composed of distinct Swiss-German, Swiss-French, and Swiss-Italian linguistic groups, though national identity is strong. The country is divided into 26 autonomous cantons (states), each with control over housing and economic policy. There are tensions over membership of the EU, drug abuse, and the role of guest workers in the economy. The young see society as regimented and conformist.

THE ECONOMY
Diversified economy relies on services – with strong tourism and banking sectors – and specialized industries (engineering, watches).

◆ INSIGHT: *Though Switzerland itself is not a member, Genève is the headquarters of many UN agencies*

3000m/9843ft	
2000m/6562ft	
1000m/3281ft	
500m/1640ft	
200m/656ft	

0   50 km
0   50 miles

🗺 FACTFILE
OFFICIAL NAME: Swiss Confederation
DATE OF FORMATION: 1815
CAPITAL: Berne (Bern)
POPULATION: 7.4 million
TOTAL AREA: 15,355 sq miles (39,770 sq km)
DENSITY: 482 people per sq mile

LANGUAGES: German*, French*, Italian*, Romansch*, other
RELIGIONS: Catholic 46%, Protestant 40%, Muslim 2%, other 12%
ETHNIC MIX: German 65%, French 18%, Italian 10%, Romansch 1%, other 6%
GOVERNMENT: Parliamentary democracy
CURRENCY: Franc = 100 centimes

Syria

Stretching from the eastern Mediterranean to the River Tigris, Syria's borders are regarded as an artificial creation of French colonial rule by many Syrians. Foreign affairs are turbulent.

GEOGRAPHY
A northern coastal plain is backed by a low range of hills. The River Euphrates cuts through a vast interior desert plateau.

CLIMATE
Mediterranean coastal climate. Inland areas are arid. In winter, snow is common on the mountains.

PEOPLE & SOCIETY
Most Syrians live within 60 miles (100 km) the coast, where the largest cities are sited. 90% are Muslim, including the politically dominant Alawis. In the north and west are groups of Kurds, Armenians, and Turkish-speaking peoples. Some 300,000 Palestinian refugees have also settled in Syria. They, together with the urban unemployed, make up the poorest groups in a growing gulf between rich and poor.

THE ECONOMY
High defense spending is a major drain on economy. Exporter of crude oil. Agriculture is thriving: crops include cotton, wheat, olives.

◆ **INSIGHT:** *Aramaic, the language of the Bible, is still spoken by the people of two villages in Syria*

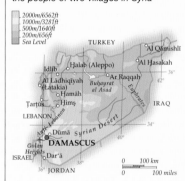

FACTFILE
OFFICIAL NAME: Syrian Arab Republic
DATE OF FORMATION: 1946
CAPITAL: Damascus
POPULATION: 16.1 million
TOTAL AREA: 71,065 sq miles (184,060 sq km)
DENSITY: 227 people per sq mile

LANGUAGES: Arabic*, French, Kurdish, Armenian, Circassian, Aramaic
RELIGIONS: Sunni Muslim 74%, other Muslim 16%, Christian 10%
ETHNIC MIX: Arab 89%, Kurdish 6%, other 5%
GOVERNMENT: One-party state
CURRENCY: Pound = 100 piastres

Taiwan

The island republic of Taiwan (formerly Formosa) lies 80 miles (130 km) off the southeast coast of mainland China. China still considers it to be a renegade province.

GEOGRAPHY
Mountain region covers two-thirds of the island. Highly fertile lowlands and coastal plains.

CLIMATE
Tropical monsoon. Hot and humid. Typhoons July–September. Snow falls in mountains in winter.

PEOPLE & SOCIETY
Most Taiwanese are Han Chinese, descendants of the 1644 migration of the Ming dynasty from the mainland. Taiwan came into existence in 1949, when the government was expelled from Beijing (then Peking) by the communists under Mao. 100,000 Nationalists established themselves as ruling class and monopolized the most prestigious jobs in the civil service. Countries wanting good relations with China cannot have formal links with Taiwan.

THE ECONOMY
Successful economy based on small, adaptable manufacturing companies. Goods include footwear, televisions and calculators.

◆ **INSIGHT:** *Taiwan has the second largest foreign currency reserves in the world*

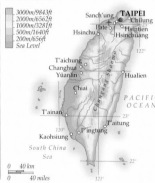

3000m/9843ft
2000m/6562ft
1000m/3281ft
500m/1640ft
200m/656ft
Sea Level

Sanch'ung · **TAIPEI**
· Chilung
Pate · · Hsintien
Hsinchu · · Hsinchuang
122°
T'aichung
Changhua · · Hualien
Yüanlin
Chiai
PACIFIC
OCEAN
T'ainan · 23°
120° · T'aitung
· P'ingtung
Kaohsiung
South China
Sea
Chungyang Shanmo
22°
0   40 km
0   40 miles
121°

FACTFILE
OFFICIAL NAME: Republic of China (Taiwan)
DATE OF FORMATION: 1949
CAPITAL: Taipei
POPULATION: 22.2 million
TOTAL AREA: 12,456 sq miles (32,260 sq km)

DENSITY: 1782 people per sq mile
LANGUAGES: Mandarin*, other
RELIGIONS: Buddhist, Confucian and Taoist 93%, Christian 5%, other 2%
ETHNIC MIX: Indigenous Chinese 84%, mainland Chinese 14%, other 2%
GOVERNMENT: Multiparty republic
CURRENCY: Taiwan $ = 100 cents

Tajikistan

Tajikistan lies landlocked on the western slopes of the Pamirs in Central Asia. The Tajiks' language and traditions are similar to those of Iran rather than those of Turkic Uzbekistan.

GEOGRAPHY
Mainly mountainous: the bare slopes of the Pamir ranges cover most of the country. Small but fertile Fergana Valley in northwest.

CLIMATE
Continental extremes in the valleys. Bitterly cold winters in the mountains. Rainfall is low.

PEOPLE & SOCIETY
The conflict between Tajiks, a Persian people, and minority Uzbeks (of Turkic origin), is coupled with civil war between supporters of the government and Tajik Islamic rebels. Despite a ceasefire in late 1994, clashes continued in 1995. Already low living standards have been worsened by the conflict. Many Russians have left, to escape discrimination.

THE ECONOMY
Formal economy is crippled by conflict. All sectors are in decline, and a barter economy is widespread. Uranium potential and hydroelectric schemes depend on peace.

◆ **INSIGHT:** *Carpetmaking, an ancient tradition learned from Persia, was a major source of revenue before the war*

4000m/13124ft
3000m/9843ft
2000m/6562ft
1000m/3281ft
500m/1640ft
200m/656ft

UZBEKISTAN
Fergana Valley
70°
Khŭjand   Isfara
68°   72°
Ŭroteppa   40°   KYRGYZSTAN
74°
Panjakent   CHINA
● **DUSHANBE**
Norak   *P a m i r s*   38°
Qŭrghonteppa   Kŭlob
Khorugh
Farkhor
Amu Darya
AFGHANISTAN   PAKISTAN

0   100 km
0   100 miles

FACTFILE

OFFICIAL NAME: Republic of Tajikistan
DATE OF FORMATION: 1991
CAPITAL: Dushanbe
POPULATION: 6.2 million
TOTAL AREA: 55,251 sq miles
(143,100 sq km)
DENSITY: 112 people per sq mile

LANGUAGES: Tajik*, Uzbek, Russian
RELIGIONS: Sunni Muslim 80%,
Shi'a Muslim 5%, other 15%
ETHNIC MIX: Tajik 62%, Uzbek 24%,
Russian 8%, Tatar 1%, Kyrgyz 1%,
other 4%
GOVERNMENT: Presidential regime
CURRENCY: Tajik rouble = 100 kopeks

Tanzania

The East African state of Tanzania was formed in 1964 by the union of Tanganyika, Zanzibar, and other islands. A third of its area is game reserve or national park.

GEOGRAPHY
The mainland is mostly a high plateau lying to the east of the Great Rift Valley. Forested coastal plain. Highlands in the north and south.

CLIMATE
Tropical on the coast and Zanzibar. Semiarid on central plateau, semitemperate in the highlands. March–May rains.

PEOPLE & SOCIETY
99% of people belong to one of 120 small ethnic Bantu groups. Arabs, Asians, and Europeans make up the remaining population. Use of Swahili as the *lingua franca* has eliminated ethnic rivalries. Politically, Tanzania is moving towards democracy.

◆ **INSIGHT:** *At 5895 m (19,340 ft), Kilimanjaro in northeast Tanzania is Africa's highest mountain*

THE ECONOMY
Heavily reliant on agriculture, including forestry and livestock. Cotton, coffee, tea, and cloves are cash crops. Diamonds are mined.

0   200 km
0   200 miles

3000m/9843ft
2000m/6562ft
1000m/3281ft
500m/1640ft
200m/656ft
Sea Level

FACTFILE
OFFICIAL NAME: United Republic of Tanzania
DATE OF FORMATION: 1964
CAPITAL: Dodoma
POPULATION: 33.5 million
TOTAL AREA: 342,100 sq miles (886,040 sq km)

DENSITY: 98 people per sq mile
LANGUAGES: English*, Swahili*
RELIGIONS: Muslim 33%, Christian 33%, traditional beliefs 30%, other 4%
ETHNIC MIX: Native African 99%, European and Asian 1%
GOVERNMENT: Presidential democracy
CURRENCY: Shilling = 100 cents

Thailand

Thailand lies at the heart of mainland Southeast Asia. Continuing rapid industrialization has resulted in massive congestion in the capital and a serious depletion of natural resources.

GEOGRAPHY
One third of the country is occupied by a low plateau, drained by tributaries of the Mekong River. Central plain is the most fertile area.

CLIMATE
Tropical. Hot, humid March–May, monsoon rains May–October, cooler season November–March.

PEOPLE & SOCIETY
Criticism of the king is not tolerated. Buddhism is a national binding force. The north and northeast are home to about 600,000 hill tribes-people, with their own languages and culture. Sex tourism is a problem. Women from the poor northeast enter prostitution in Bangkok and Pattaya.

INSIGHT: *Thailand, meaning "land of the free," is the only SE Asian nation never to have been colonized*

THE ECONOMY
Rapid economic growth. Rise in manufacturing. Chief world exporter of rice and rubber. Gas reserves. Successful tourist industry.

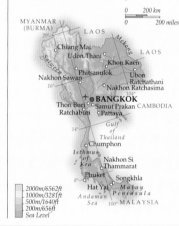

2000m/6562ft	
1000m/3281ft	
500m/1640ft	
200m/656ft	
Sea Level	

FACTFILE
OFFICIAL NAME: Kingdom of Thailand
DATE OF FORMATION: 1882
CAPITAL: Bangkok
POPULATION: 61.4 million
TOTAL AREA: 197,255 sq miles (510,890 sq km)
DENSITY: 311 people per sq mile

LANGUAGES: Thai*, Chinese, Malay, Khmer, Mon, Karen, Miao, English
RELIGIONS: Buddhist 95%, Muslim 4%, other (inc. Hindu, Christian) 1%
ETHNIC MIX: Thai 80%, Chinese 12%, Malay 4%, Khmer and other 4%
GOVERNMENT: Parliamentary democracy
CURRENCY: Baht = 100 stangs

Togo

Togo lies sandwiched between Ghana and Benin in West Africa. The president, General Eyadéma, has been in power since 1967. The port of Lomé is an important entrepôt for West African trade.

GEOGRAPHY

Central forested region bounded by savannah lands to the north and south. Mountain range stretches southwest to northeast.

CLIMATE

Coast hot and humid; drier inland. Rainy season March–July, with heaviest falls in the west.

PEOPLE & SOCIETY

Harsh resentment between Ewe in the south and Kabye in the north. Kabye control military, but are far less developed than people of the south. Extended family is important. Tribalism and nepotism are key factors in every-day life. Some ethnic groups, such as the Mina, have matriarchal societies.

◆ **INSIGHT:** *The "Nana Benz," the market-women of Lomé market, control Togo's retail trade*

THE ECONOMY

Most people are farmers. Self-sufficient in basic foodstuffs. Main export crops are coffee, cocoa, and cotton. Half of all export revenues come from phosphate deposits with the world's highest mineral content.

BURKINA

Dapaong

BENIN

Sansanné-Mango

Kara

Tchamba

GHANA

0   50 km
0   50 miles

Atakpamé

Mono

Kpalimé

Tsévié

Aného

LOMÉ

500m/1640ft
200m/656ft
Sea Level

ATLANTIC OCEAN

FACTFILE

OFFICIAL NAME: Togolese Republic
DATE OF FORMATION: 1960
CAPITAL: Lomé
POPULATION: 4.6 million
TOTAL AREA: 21,000 sq miles
(54,390 sq km)
DENSITY: 219 people per sq mile

LANGUAGES: French*, Ewe, Kabye, Gurma, other
RELIGIONS: Traditional beliefs 50%, Christian 35%, Muslim 15%
ETHNIC MIX: Ewe 46%, European 1%, other African 53%
GOVERNMENT: Presidential regime
CURRENCY: CFA franc = 100 centimes

Tonga

Tonga is an archipelago of 170 islands in the South Pacific. Only 45 of these islands are inhabited. The economy is based on agriculture, and politics is effectively controlled by the king.

GEOGRAPHY

Easterly islands are generally low and fertile. Those in the west are higher and volcanic in origin.

CLIMATE

Tropical oceanic. Temperatures range between 68°F (20°C) and 86°F (30°C) all year round. Heavy rainfall, especially February–March.

PEOPLE & SOCIETY

The last remaining Polynesian monarchy, and the only Pacific state never brought under foreign rule. All land is property of the crown, but is administered by nobles who allot it to the common people. Respect for traditional values remains high, although younger, Westernized Tongans are starting to question some attitudes.

INSIGHT: *Tonga has the world's lowest annual death rate: 1 in 2790*

THE ECONOMY

Most people are subsistence farmers. Commercial production of coconuts, cassava, and passion fruit. Tourism is increasing slowly.

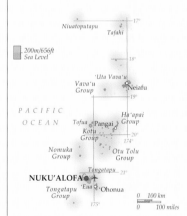

Niuatoputapu ° 17°
Tafahi

200m/656ft
Sea Level 18°

'Uta Vava'u

Vava'u Neiafu
Group 19°

PACIFIC

OCEAN Ha'apai
Tofua Group
Pangai 174°
Kotu 20°
Group

Nomuka Otu Tolu
Group Group

Tongatapu 21°

NUKU'ALOFA

'Eua ° Ohonua
Tongatapu
Group 175° 0   100 km
0   100 miles

FACTFILE

OFFICIAL NAME: Kingdom of Tonga
DATE OF FORMATION: 1970
CAPITAL: Nuku'alofa
POPULATION: 102,231
TOTAL AREA: 278 sq miles (720 sq km)

DENSITY: 368 people per sq mile
LANGUAGES: Tongan*, English
RELIGIONS: Free Weslyan 64%, Roman Catholic 15%, other 21%
ETHNIC MIX: Polynesian 99%, other 1%
GOVERNMENT: Monarchy
CURRENCY: Pa'anga = 100 seniti

Trinidad & Tobago

The two islands of the former British colony of Trinidad and Tobago are the most southerly of the Caribbean Windward Islands, lying just 9 miles (15 km) off the coast of Venezuela.

GEOGRAPHY
Both islands are hilly and wooded. Trinidad has a rugged mountain range in the north, and swamps on its east and west coasts.

CLIMATE
Tropical, with July–December wet season. Escapes the region's hurricanes, which pass to the north.

PEOPLE & SOCIETY
Blacks and South Asians are the biggest groups. Minorities of Chinese and Europeans. Politics has recently become fragmented, and dominated by the race issue. An attempted coup by a Muslim sect in 1990 strengthened black opposition to the possibility of a South Asian prime minister.

◆ **INSIGHT:** *Trinidad and Tobago is the birthplace of steel bands and Calypso music*

THE ECONOMY
Oil accounts for 70% of export earnings. Gas is increasingly being exploited to support new industries. Tourism, particularly on Tobago, is under development.

FACTFILE
OFFICIAL NAME: Republic of Trinidad and Tobago
DATE OF FORMATION: 1962
CAPITAL: Port-of-Spain
POPULATION: 1.3 million
TOTAL AREA: 1981 sq miles (5130 sq km)

DENSITY: 656 people per sq mile
LANGUAGES: English*, other
RELIGIONS: Catholic 32%, Hindu 24%, Anglican and Protestant 28%, other 16%
ETHNIC MIX: Asian 40%, Black 40%, mixed 19%, other 1%
GOVERNMENT: Parliamentary democracy
CURRENCY: Trin. & Tob. $ = 100 cents

Tunisia

Tunisia has traditionally been one of the more liberal Arab states, moving toward a multiparty democracy, but its government is now facing a challenge from Islamic fundamentalists.

GEOGRAPHY

Mountains in the north are surrounded by plains. Vast, low-lying salt pans in the center. To the south lies the Sahara.

CLIMATE

Summer temperatures are high. The north is often wet and windy in winter. Far south is arid.

PEOPLE & SOCIETY

The population is almost entirely of Arab-Berber descent, with Jewish and Christian minorities. Many still live in extended family groups, in which three or four generations are represented. Women have better rights than in any other Arab country and make up 25% of the total workforce. Politics, however, remains a male preserve. Low birth rate is a result of a long-standing family planning policy.

THE ECONOMY

Well-diversified, despite limited resources. Oil and gas exports. Expanding manufacturing. Tourism. European investment.

◆ **INSIGHT:** *Matmata – a Berber village – appeared in the film "Star Wars"*

FACTFILE

OFFICIAL NAME: Republic of Tunisia
DATE OF FORMATION: 1956
CAPITAL: Tunis
POPULATION: 9.6 million
TOTAL AREA: 59,984 sq miles (155,360 sq km)
DENSITY: 160 people per sq mile

LANGUAGES: Arabic*, French
RELIGIONS: Muslim (mainly Sunni) 98%, Christian 1%, Jewish 1%
ETHNIC MIX: Arab and Berber 98%, European 1%, other 1%
GOVERNMENT: Presidential democracy
CURRENCY: Dinar = 1000 millimes

Tuvalu

One of the world's smallest, most isolated states, Tuvalu lies in the central Pacific. The nine islands were linked to the Gilbert Islands as a British colony until independence.

GEOGRAPHY

A series of coral atolls, none more than 4.6 metres (15 feet) above sea level. Poor soils restrict vegetation to bush, coconut palms, and breadfruit trees.

CLIMATE

Hot all year round. Heavy annual rainfall. Hurricane season brings many violent storms.

PEOPLE & SOCIETY

People are mostly Polynesian. Almost half the population live on Funafuti, where government jobs are centred. Life is communal and traditional. Most people live by subsistence farming, digging pits out of the coral to grow crops. Fresh water is precious due to frequent droughts.

◆ **INSIGHT:** *Tuvaluans have a reputation as excellent sailors. Many work overseas as merchant seamen*

THE ECONOMY

World's smallest economy. Fish stocks exploited mainly by foreign boats in return for licensing fees. Exports are few: copra, stamps, and garments. Aid is crucial.

FACTFILE

OFFICIAL NAME: Tuvalu
DATE OF FORMATION: 1978
CAPITAL: Fongafale on Funafuti Atoll
POPULATION: 10,838
TOTAL AREA: 10 sq miles
(26 sq km)
DENSITY: 1084 people per sq mile

LANGUAGES: Tuvaluan, Kiribati, other
(no official language)
RELIGIONS: Church of Tuvalu 97%,
Seventh-day Adventist 1%, Baha'I 1%,
other 1%
ETHNIC MIX: Polynesian 96%, other 4%
GOVERNMENT: Non-party democracy
CURRENCY: Australian $ = 100 cents

Uganda

Landlocked in East Africa, Uganda has a history of ethnic strife. Under President Museveni, peace has been restored and steps taken to rebuild the economy and democracy.

GEOGRAPHY

Predominantly a large plateau with the Ruwenzori mountain range and the Great Rift Valley in the west. Lake Victoria lies to the southeast. Vegetation is of savannah type.

CLIMATE

Altitude and the influence of the lakes modify the equatorial climate. Rain falls throughout the year; spring is the wettest period.

PEOPLE & SOCIETY

The predominantly rural population comprises some 13 main ethnic groups. Since 1986, President Museveni has worked hard to break down traditional ethnic animosities. In 1993, he allowed the restoration of Uganda's four historical monarchies, whose borders form the basis of a federal system. Uganda now has one of the best human rights records in Africa.

THE ECONOMY

Coffee earns 93% of export income. Hydroelectric power is to be developed to replace 50% of oil imports. Reopening of mines should improve the economy.

INSIGHT: *Lake Victoria is the world's third largest lake*

3000m/9843ft
2000m/6562ft
1000m/3281ft
500m/1640ft

FACTFILE

OFFICIAL NAME: Republic of Uganda
DATE OF FORMATION: 1962
CAPITAL: Kampala
POPULATION: 21.8 million
TOTAL AREA: 77,046 sq miles (199,550 sq km)
DENSITY: 283 people per sq mile

LANGUAGES: English*, Luganda, Nkole, Chiga, Lango, Acholi, Teso
RELIGIONS: Roman Catholic 38%, Protestant 33%, traditional/other 29%
ETHNIC MIX: Bantu tribes 50%, Sudanese 5%, other 45%
GOVERNMENT: Non-party democracy
CURRENCY: Shilling = 100 cents

Ukraine

The former "breadbasket of the Soviet Union," Ukraine lies on the northern coast of the Black Sea. It balances assertive nationalism with concerns over its relations with Russia.

GEOGRAPHY
Mainly fertile steppes and forests. Carpathian Mountains in southwest, Crimean chain in south. Pripet Marshes in northwest.

CLIMATE
Mainly continental climate, with distinct seasons. Southern Crimea has Mediterranean climate.

PEOPLE & SOCIETY
Over 90% of the population in western Ukraine is Ukrainian. However, in several cities in the east and south, Russians form a majority. In the Crimea, the Tartars comprise around 10% of the population. At independence in 1991, most Russians accepted Ukrainian sovereignty. However, tensions are now rising as both groups adopt more extremist nationalist policies.

THE ECONOMY
Hyperinflation, corruption, and hostility from the economic elite stifle any reforms. Heavy industries and agriculture remain largely unchanged since independence.

◆ INSIGHT: *Ukraine means "frontier," a reference to the country's position along the Russian border*

FACTFILE

OFFICIAL NAME: Ukraine
DATE OF FORMATION: 1991
CAPITAL: Kiev
POPULATION: 50.5 million
TOTAL AREA: 233,089 sq miles (603,700 sq km)
DENSITY: 217 people per sq mile

LANGUAGES: Ukrainian*, Russian, Tartar
RELIGIONS: Ukrainian Orthodox 95%, Jewish 1%, other 4%
ETHNIC MIX: Ukranian 73%, Russian 22%, Jewish 1%, other 4%
GOVERNMENT: Presidential democracy
CURRENCY: Hyrvna

United Arab Emirates

Bordering the Gulf on the northern coast of the Arabian peninsula, the seven states of the United Arab Emirates are the Arab world's only working federation.

GEOGRAPHY

Mostly flat, semiarid desert with sand dunes, salt pans, and occasional oases. Cities are watered by extensive irrigation systems.

CLIMATE

Summers are humid, despite minimal rainfall. Sand-laden *shamal* winds blow in winter and spring.

PEOPLE & SOCIETY

People are mostly Sunni Muslims of Bedouin descent, and largely city-dwellers. In theory, women enjoy equal rights with men. Poverty is rare. Emirians make up only one-fifth of the population. They are outnumbered by immigrants who arrived during 1970s oil boom. Western expatriates are permitted a virtually unrestricted lifestyle. Islamic fundamentalism, however, is a growing force among the young.

THE ECONOMY

Major exporter of oil and natural gas. Fish and shellfish are caught in the Gulf, as well as oysters for their pearls. Most food and raw materials are imported.

◆ **INSIGHT:** *At present levels of production the country's crude oil reserves should last for over 100 years*

The Gulf

OMAN

RAS AL KHAIMAH

UMM AL QAYWAYN

SHARJAH

DUBAI · AJMAN

FUJAIRAH

QATAR

ABU DHABI

Ghuwayfāt · Al Maqṭa'

Ṭārif · Al 'Ayn

Ḥabshān

OMAN

SAUDI ARABIA

500m/1640ft
200m/656ft
Sea Level

0   50 km
0   50 miles

DUBAI *Emirate capital*

FACTFILE

OFFICIAL NAME: United Arab Emirates

DATE OF FORMATION: 1971

CAPITAL: Abu Dhabi

POPULATION: 2.4 million

TOTAL AREA: 32,278 sq miles (83,600 sq km)

DENSITY: 74 people per sq mile

LANGUAGES: Arabic*, Farsi (Persian), Urdu, Hindi, English

RELIGIONS: Muslim (mainly Sunni) 96%, Christian, Hindu and other 4%

ETHNIC MIX: Asian 50%, Emirian 19%, other Arab 23%, other 8%

GOVERNMENT: Monarchy

CURRENCY: Dirham = 100 fils

United Kingdom

Separated from continental Europe by the North Sea and the English Channel, the United Kingdom includes the countries of England, Wales, Scotland, and Northern Ireland.

GEOGRAPHY

Rugged uplands dominate the landscape of Scotland, Wales and northern England. All of the peaks in the United Kingdom over 1219 m (4000 ft) lie in highland Scotland. The Pennines, a mountain range known as the "backbone of England" run the length of northern England. Lowland England rises into several ranges of rolling hills, and there are no large-scale river systems. Over 600 islands, mostly uninhabited, lie west and north of the Scottish mainland.

CLIMATE

Generally mild, temperate, and highly changeable. Rain (synonymous with British weather) is fairly well distributed throughout the year. The west is generally wetter than the east, and the south warmer than the north. Winter snow is common in mountainous areas.

PEOPLE & SOCIETY

Although of mixed stock themselves, the British have an insular and ambivalent attitude towards Europe. The Welsh and Scottish are ethnically, culturally, and now politically distinct with the establishment of the Scottish Parliament and Welsh Assembly. Ethnic minorities account for less than 5% of the population, and over 50% were born in the UK. There are Asian and West Indian minorities in most cities. In key areas such as policing, multiethnic recruitment has made little progress and prejudices persist. Marriage is in decline; legalisation in 1996 has made divorce easier. A third of all births occur outside marriage, but most of them to cohabiting couples. Single-parent households account for one-fifth of all families with children under the age of 18.

FACTFILE

OFFICIAL NAME: United Kingdom of Great Britain and Northern Ireland
DATE OF FORMATION: 1707 (1922)
CAPITAL: London
POPULATION: 58.8 million
TOTAL AREA: 93,281 sq miles (241,600 sq km)

DENSITY: 630 people per sq mile
LANGUAGES: English*, other
RELIGIONS: Protestant 52%, Catholic 9%, Muslim 3%, other 36%
ETHNIC MIX: English 80%, Scottish 10%, Northern Irish 4%, Welsh 2%, other 4%
GOVERNMENT: Parliamentary democracy
CURRENCY: Pound sterling = 100 pence

United Kingdom

THE ECONOMY

World leader in financial services, pharmaceuticals, and defense industries. Strong multinationals. Precision engineering and high-tech industries, including biotechnology and telecommunications. Energy sector based on North Sea oil and gas production. Innovative in computer software development. Flexible working practices. Recent success in controlling inflationary tendencies. Decline of manufacturing sector, particularly heavy industries and car manufacture, matched by rise in financial and other services. High levels of government and consumer debt. Nonparticipation in euro threatens former status as EU's largest recipient of inward investment, and has prompted some major investors to close UK factories. Collapse of the Internet "dot.com" boom in 1999–2001 brought back fears of a possible recession.

INSIGHT: The UK has no formal written constitution, nevertheless Parliament has existed in its present form since the middle of the 14th century

Orkney Is.

Outer
Hebrides

Stornoway

58°

Scotland

Inverness

Aberdeen

Inner
Hebrides

Oban

Dundee

56°

Glasgow

Edinburgh

Londonderry

Newcastle
upon Tyne

*Northern
Ireland*

Carlisle

*North
Sea*

Belfast

Isle of
Man

54°

Blackpool

Leeds

REPUBLIC
OF
IRELAND

Liverpool

Blackburn

Sheffield

Manchester

England

Norwich

Birmingham

Derby

Leicester

Cambridge

52°

Wales

Swansea

Oxford

*Celtic
Sea*

Cardiff

Thames

LONDON

Bristol

Reading

ATLANTIC
OCEAN

Exeter

Southampton

Dover

Plymouth

0°

50°

English Channel

6°   4°   2°

1000m/3281ft
500m/1640ft
200m/656ft
Sea Level

0   100 km
0   100 miles

Shetlands
Is.
Lerwick

60°

2°

United States of America

Stretching across the most temperate part of North America, and with many natural resources, the US is the world's leading economic power and fourth largest country.

GEOGRAPHY
Central plain, mountains in west, hills and low mountains in east. Forested north and east, southwestern deserts. Volcanic islands in Hawaii. Forest and tundra in Alaska.

CLIMATE
Wide variety. Continental in north, hot summers and mild winters in southeast, desert climate in southwest. Arctic climate in Alaska; Florida and Hawaii are tropical.

PEOPLE & SOCIETY
A multiracial population, established through successive waves of immigration, initially from Europe and Africa, with more recent influxes from Latin America and Asia. Strong sense of nationhood, despite cultural diversity. Conservative, usually Christian consensus, is increasingly challenged by liberal, secular values.

FACTFILE
OFFICIAL NAME: United States of America
DATE OF FORMATION: 1776 (1959)
CAPITAL: Washington D.C.
POPULATION: 278.4 million
TOTAL AREA: 3,539,224 sq miles (9,166,600 sq km)

DENSITY: 79 people per sq mile
LANGUAGES: English*, Spanish, other
RELIGIONS: Protestant 61%, Catholic 25%, Jewish 2%, other 12%
ETHNIC MIX: White (inc. Hispanic) 84%, Black 12%, Native Indian 1%, other 3%
GOVERNMENT: Presidential democracy
CURRENCY: US $ = 100 cents

United States of America

$ **THE ECONOMY**
Traditions of innovation, skilled labor, and venture capital help high-tech industries replace outdated manufacturing. Global dominance of US culture boosts services, manufactures. Vast agriculture, mining sectors.

ARCTIC OCEAN

Bering Strait

Brooks Range

Alaska Range

Anchorage

ALASKA

CANADA

PACIFIC OCEAN

0   500 km
0   500 miles

CANADA

NORTH DAKOTA

MINNESOTA

Lake Superior

MICHIGAN

Lake Huron

St Lawrence

VERMONT

MAINE

NEW HAMPSHIRE

MASSACHUSETTS

RHODE I.

CONNECTICUT

SOUTH DAKOTA

Minneapolis

St Paul

WISCONSIN

Lake Michigan

Lake Ontario

NEW YORK

Boston

Milwaukee

Detroit

Buffalo

NEBRASKA

Chicago

Cleveland

Lake Erie

PENNSYLVANIA

NEW JERSEY

New York

Omaha

IOWA

Des Moines

Fort Wayne

INDIANA

OHIO

Pittsburgh

Philadelphia

Baltimore

DELAWARE

Denver

Springfield

Indianapolis

Columbus

WASHINGTON DC

COLORADO

KANSAS

Kansas City

St Louis

Cincinnati

WEST VIRGINIA

Richmond

MARYLAND

Newport News

MISSOURI

KENTUCKY

Louisville

VIRGINIA

NORTH CAROLINA

Albuquerque

Tulsa

Nashville

TENNESSEE

Charlotte

NEW MEXICO

OKLAHOMA

Oklahoma City

ARKANSAS

Little Rock

Memphis

SOUTH CAROLINA

ATLANTIC OCEAN

Lubbock

El Paso

Fort Worth

Dallas

MISSISSIPPI

ALABAMA

Birmingham

Atlanta

GEORGIA

Savannah

Edwards Plateau

Shreveport

Jackson

TEXAS

LOUISIANA

Mobile

Jacksonville

San Antonio

Baton Rouge

New Orleans

Tallahassee

FLORIDA

Houston

Corpus Christi

Gulf of Mexico

The Everglades

Tampa

Orlando

Miami

Mississippi

Missouri

Colorado

Rio Grande

3000m/9843ft
2000m/6562ft
1000m/3281ft
500m/1640ft
200m/656ft
Sea Level

◆ INSIGHT: *The United States of America has the world's oldest constitution. Devised in 1787, it has operated continuously ever since*

0   400 km
0   400 miles

Uruguay

Situated in southeastern South America, Uruguay returned to civilian government in 1985, after 12 years of military rule. Offshore banking brings in substantial foreign earnings.

GEOGRAPHY

Low, rolling grasslands cover 80% of the country. Narrow coastal plain. Alluvial flood plain in south-west. Five rivers flow westward and drain into the River Uruguay.

CLIMATE

Temperate throughout the country. Warm summers, mild winters, and moderate rainfall.

PEOPLE & SOCIETY

Uruguayans are largely second or third generation Italians or Spaniards. Wealth derived from cattle ranching enabled the country to become the first welfare state in South America. Economic decline since 1960s, but a large, if less prosperous, middle class remains. Although a Roman Catholic country, Uruguay is liberal in its attitude to religion and all forms are tolerated.

THE ECONOMY

Most land given over to crops and livestock. Wool, meat, and hides are exported. Buoyant tourism.

◆ **INSIGHT:** *Uruguay's literacy rates and life expectancy are the highest in South America*

200m/656ft
Sea Level

0   100 km
0   100 miles

FACTFILE

OFFICIAL NAME: Eastern Republic of Uruguay

DATE OF FORMATION: 1828

CAPITAL: Montevideo

POPULATION: 3.3 million

TOTAL AREA: 67,490 sq miles (174,810 sq km)

DENSITY: 49 people per sq mile

LANGUAGES: Spanish*, other

RELIGIONS: Roman Catholic 66%, Protestant 2%, Jewish 2%, other 30%

ETHNIC MIX: White 90%, Mestizo 6%, Black 4%

GOVERNMENT: Presidential democracy

CURRENCY: Peso = 100 centesimos

Uzbekistan

Sharing the Aral Sea coastline with its northern neighbor, Kazakhstan, Uzbekistan lies on the ancient Silk Road between Asia and Europe. It is the most populous Central Asian republic.

GEOGRAPHY

Arid and semiarid plains in much of the west. Fertile, irrigated farmland in the east lies below the peaks of the western Pamirs.

CLIMATE

Harsh continental climate. Summers can be extremely hot and dry, winters are cold.

PEOPLE & SOCIETY

Complex ethnic makeup, with potential for racial and regional conflict. Ex-communists are in firm control, but traditional social patterns based on family, religion, clan, and region have re-emerged. The population is concentrated in the fertile east. Birth rates are high, and the status of women continues to be low. Constitutional measures aim to control the influence of Islam.

THE ECONOMY

Strong agricultural sector, led by cotton production. Large unexploited deposits of oil, natural gas, gold, and uranium. Limited economic reform.

INSIGHT: *The Aral Sea has shrunk to half of the area it covered in 1960, due to diversion of rivers for irrigation*

FACTFILE

OFFICIAL NAME: Republic of Uzbekistan
DATE OF FORMATION: 1991
CAPITAL: Tashkent
POPULATION: 24.3 million
TOTAL AREA: 127,741 sq miles (447,400 sq km)
DENSITY: 190 people per sq mile

LANGUAGES: Uzbek*, Russian, other
RELIGIONS: Sunni Muslim 88%, Eastern Orthodox 9%, other 3%
ETHNIC MIX: Uzbek 71%, Russian 8%, Tajik 5%, Kazakh 4%, other 12%
GOVERNMENT: Presidential democracy
CURRENCY: Sum = 100 teen

Vanuatu

An archipelago of 82 islands and islets in the South Pacific, Vanuatu was ruled jointly by Britain and France from 1906 until independence. Politics are democratic but volatile.

GEOGRAPHY
Mountainous and volcanic, with coral beaches and dense rain forest. Cultivated land along the coasts.

CLIMATE
Tropical. Temperatures and rainfall decline from north to south.

PEOPLE & SOCIETY
Indigenous Melanesians form a majority. 80% of the population live on 16 main islands. People are among the most traditional in the Pacific: local social and religious customs are strong, despite centuries of missionary influence. Subsistence farming and fishing are the main activities. Women have lower social status than men and payment of bride-price is common.

INSIGHT: *With 105 indigenous languages, Vanuatu has the world's highest per capita density of languages*

THE ECONOMY
Copra and cocoa are the largest exports. Recent upsurge in tourist industry. Offshore financial services are also important.

FACTFILE
OFFICIAL NAME: Republic of Vanuatu
DATE OF FORMATION: 1980
CAPITAL: Port-Vila
POPULATION: 200,000
TOTAL AREA: 4706 sq miles (12,190 sq km)
DENSITY: 42 people per sq mile

LANGUAGES: Bislama (Melanesian pidgin)*, English*, French*, other
RELIGIONS: Protestant 77%, Catholic 15%, indigenous beliefs 8%
ETHNIC MIX: Melanesian 94%, Polynesian 3%, other 3%
GOVERNMENT: Parliamentary democracy
CURRENCY: Vatu = 100 centimes

Vatican City

The Vatican City, or Holy See, the seat of the Roman Catholic Church, is a walled enclave in the city of Rome. It is the world's smallest fully independent state.

GEOGRAPHY

The Vatican's territory includes ten other buildings in Rome, plus the papal residence. The Vatican Gardens cover half the City's area.

CLIMATE

Mild winters with regular rainfall. Hot, dry summers with occasional thunderstorms.

PEOPLE & SOCIETY

The Vatican has about 1000 permanent inhabitants, including several hundred lay persons, and employs a further 3400 lay staff. Citizenship can be acquired through stable residence and holding an office or job within the City. The reigning Pope has supreme legislative and judicial powers, and holds office for life. The state maintains a neutral stance in world affairs and has observer status in many international organizations.

THE ECONOMY

Investments and voluntary contributions made by Catholics worldwide (known as Peter's Pence), are backed up by tourist revenue and the issue of Vatican stamps and coins.

◆ **INSIGHT:** *The Vatican City is the only state to have Latin as an official language*

FACTFILE

OFFICIAL NAME: State of the Vatican City
DATE OF FORMATION: 1929
CAPITAL: Vatican City
POPULATION: 1000
TOTAL AREA: 0.17 sq miles (0.44 sq km)

DENSITY: 5,882 people per sq mile
LANGUAGES: Italian*, Latin*, other
RELIGIONS: Roman Catholic 100%
ETHNIC MIX: Italian 90%, Swiss 10% (including the Swiss Guard, which is responsible for papal security)
GOVERNMENT: Papal state
CURRENCY: Euro = 100 cents

Yemen

Located in southern Arabia, Yemen was formerly two countries: the People's Democratic Republic of Yemen in the south, and the Yemen Arab Republic in the north, were united in 1990.

GEOGRAPHY

Mountainous north with a fertile strip along the Red Sea. Arid desert and mountains in south and east.

CLIMATE

Desert climate, modified by altitude, which affects temperatures by as much as 54°F (12°C).

PEOPLE & SOCIETY

Yemenis are almost entirely of Arab and Bedouin descent. The majority are Sunni Muslims, of the Shafi sect. In rural areas and in the north, Islamic orthodoxy is strong and most women wear the veil. Tension continues to exist between the south, led by the cosmopolitan city of 'Adan, and the more conservative north. Clashes between their former armies escalated into a brief civil war in 1994.

THE ECONOMY

Poor economic development due to political instability. Large oil and gas reserves discovered in 1984. Agriculture is the largest employer.

INSIGHT: *Al Mukha (Mokha) on the Red Sea gave its name to the first coffee beans to be exported to Europe in the 17th and 18th centuries*

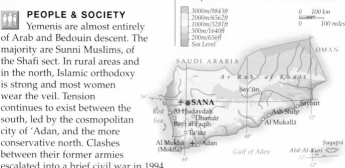

FACTFILE

OFFICIAL NAME: Republic of Yemen
DATE OF FORMATION: 1990
CAPITAL: Sana'a
POPULATION: 18.1 million
TOTAL AREA: 217,362 sq miles (562,970 sq km)
DENSITY: 83 people per sq mile

LANGUAGES: Arabic*, other
RELIGIONS: Sunni Muslim 55%, Shi'a Muslim 42%, Christian, Hindu and Jewish 3%
ETHNIC MIX: Arab 95%, Afro-Arab 3%, Indian, Somali, European 2%
GOVERNMENT: Multiparty republic
CURRENCY: Rial (North), Dinar (South)

Yugoslavia

The Federal Republic of Yugoslavia consists of Serbia and Montenegro – elements of former Yugoslavia. It is regarded as chiefly responsible for the 1990s conflict in the region.

GEOGRAPHY
Fertile Danube plain in the north, rolling uplands in center. Mountains in south, and behind narrow Adriatic coastal plain.

CLIMATE
Mediterranean along coast, continental inland. Hot summers and cold winters, with heavy snow.

PEOPLE & SOCIETY
Social order has disintegrated since dissolution of the former Yugoslavia. Serbia was vilified for its role in the conflict in the region, and invited international condemnation for its treatment of ethnic Albanians in Kosovo, which led to the launch of NATO air strikes against Serbs in 1999.

◇ **INSIGHT:** *Belgrade means "White City." There has been a settlement on this site for over 7000 years*

THE ECONOMY
Bosnian war, UN trade sanctions, and conflict in Kosovo have crippled the economy. Fuel and food shortages.

FACTFILE
OFFICIAL NAME: Federal Republic of Yugoslavia
DATE OF FORMATION: 1992
CAPITAL: Belgrade
POPULATION: 10.6 million
TOTAL AREA: 39,449 sq miles (102,173 sq km)

DENSITY: 268 people per sq mile
LANGUAGES: Serbo-Croatian*, other
RELIGIONS: Eastern Orthodox 65%, Muslim 19%, Catholic 4%, other 12%
ETHNIC MIX: Serb 62%, Albanian 17%, Montenegrin 5%, other 16%
GOVERNMENT: Multiparty republic
CURRENCY: Dinar = 100 para

Zambia

Bordered to the south by the Zambezi River, Zambia lies at the heart of southern Africa. In 1991, it made a peaceful transition from single-party rule to multiparty democracy.

GEOGRAPHY

A high savannah plateau, broken by mountains in northeast. Vegetation mainly trees and scrub.

CLIMATE

Tropical, with three seasons: cool and dry, hot and dry, and wet. Southwest is prone to drought.

PEOPLE & SOCIETY

One of the continent's most urbanized countries. There are more than 70 different ethnic groups, but there are fewer ethnic tensions than in many African states. The largest group is the Bemba in the northeast. Other major groups are the Tonga in the south, and the Lozi in the west. Urban life has done little to change the traditionally subordinate role of women in the family and politics. More than half the population live by subsistence farming.

THE ECONOMY

Copper mining is the main industry – exports bring in 80% of foreign income. However, domestic reserves are declining rapidly.

INSIGHT: *Zambia's Victoria Falls is known to Africans as Musi-o-Tunyi (The Smoke That Thunders)*

1000m/3281ft
500m/1640ft
200m/656ft

L. Tanganyika
TANZANIA
L. Mweru
DEM. REP.
CONGO
(ZAIRE)
Kasama
Mansa
Mufulira
Chingola
Kitwe
Ndola
Luanshya
Chipata
ANGOLA
Kabwe
Mongu
LUSAKA
Kafue
Zambezi
Monze
Choma
Lake
Kariba
ZIMBABWE
NAMIBIA
Livingstone
BOTSWANA
Victoria
Falls
MOZAMBIQUE
MALAWI

0   200 km
0   200 miles

FACTFILE

OFFICIAL NAME: Republic of Zambia
DATE OF FORMATION: 1964
CAPITAL: Lusaka
POPULATION: 9.2 million
TOTAL AREA: 285,992 sq miles (740,720 sq km)
DENSITY: 32 people per sq mile

LANGUAGES: English*, Bemba, Tonga, Nyanja, Lozi, Lunda
RELIGIONS: Christian 63%, indigenous beliefs 36%, other 1%
ETHNIC MIX: Bemba 34%, other African 65%, European 1%
GOVERNMENT: Presidential democracy
CURRENCY: Kwacha = 100 ngwee

Zimbabwe

Situated in southern Africa, the former British colony of
Southern Rhodesia became fully independent as Zimbabwe
in 1980, after 15 years of troubled white minority rule.

GEOGRAPHY

High plateaus in center
bordered by Zambezi River in the
north and Limpopo in the south.
Rivers crisscross central area.

CLIMATE

Tropical, though moderated
by the high altitude. Wet season
November–March. Drought is
common in the eastern highlands.

PEOPLE & SOCIETY

There are two main ethnic
groups, Shona in the north and east,
and Ndebele in the south. Shona
outnumber Ndebele by four to one.
Because of past colonial rule, whites
(numbering just 1% of the population)
are generally far more affluent than
blacks. This imbalance has been
somewhat redressed by government
policies to increase black education
and white-collar employment.

THE ECONOMY

Most broadly based African
economy after South Africa. Virtually
self-sufficient in food and energy.
Tobacco is the main cash crop.

◆ **INSIGHT:** *The city of Great
Zimbabwe, after which the country
is named, was built in the 8th century.
Its ruins are found near Masvingo*

FACTFILE

OFFICIAL NAME: Republic of Zimbabwe
DATE OF FORMATION: 1980
CAPITAL: Harare
POPULATION: 11.7 million
TOTAL AREA: 149,293 sq miles
(386,670 sq km)
DENSITY: 78 people per sq mile

LANGUAGES: English*, Shona, Ndebele
RELIGIONS: Syncretic (Christian and
traditional beliefs) 50%, Christian 25%,
traditional beliefs 24%, other 1%
ETHNIC MIX: Shona 71%, Ndebele 16%,
other African 11%, White 1%, Asian 1%
GOVERNMENT: Presidential regime
CURRENCY: Zimbabwe $ = 100 cents

Overseas territories

Despite the rapid process of global decolonization since World War II, around 10 million people in more than 50 territories around the world continue to live under the protection of France, Australia, Denmark, the Netherlands, Norway, New Zealand, the UK, or the USA. These remnants of former colonial empires may have persisted for economic, strategic, or political reasons and are administered by the protecting country in a variety of ways.

AUSTRALIA

Australia's overseas territories have not been an issue since Papua New Guinea became independent in 1975. Consequently there is no overriding policy toward them.
Norfolk Island is inhabited by descendants of the HMS Bounty mutineers and more recent Australian migrants. Phosphate is mined on Christmas Island.

ASHMORE & CARTIER IS. *Ref: 124 A3*

STATUS: External territory
CLAIMED: 1978
CAPITAL: Not applicable
POPULATION: None
AREA: 2 sq miles (5.2 sq km)

CHRISTMAS ISLAND *Ref: 123 E5*

STATUS: External territory
CLAIMED: 1958
CAPITAL: Flying Fish Cove
POPULATION: 1,275
AREA: 52 sq miles (135 sq km)

COCOS ISLANDS *Ref: 123 D5*

STATUS: External territory
CLAIMED: 1955
CAPITAL: Not applicable
POPULATION: 670
AREA: 5.5 sq miles (14 sq km)

CORAL SEA ISLANDS *Ref: 126 B4*

STATUS: External territory
CLAIMED: 1969
CAPITAL: Not applicable
POPULATION: 8 (Meteorologists)
AREA: 1.2 sq miles (3 sq km)

HEARD & MCDONALD IS. *Ref: 123 C7*

STATUS: External territory
CLAIMED: 1947
CAPITAL: Not applicable
POPULATION: None
AREA: 161 sq miles (417 sq km)

NORFOLK ISLAND *Ref: 124 D4*

STATUS: External territory
CLAIMED: 1774
CAPITAL: Kingston
POPULATION: 2181
AREA: 13 sq miles (34 sq km)

DENMARK

The Faeroe Islands have been under Danish administration since Queen Margreth I of Denmark inherited Norway in 1380. The Home Rule Act of 1948 gave the Faeroese control over all their internal affairs. Greenland first came under Danish rule in 1380. Denmark remains responsible for the island's foreign affairs.

Overseas territories

FAEROE ISLANDS *Ref: 65 F5*

STATUS: External territory
CLAIMED: 1380
CAPITAL: Tórshavn
POPULATION: 43,382
AREA: 540 sq miles (1399 sq km)

GREENLAND *Ref: 64 D3*

STATUS: External territory
CLAIMED: 1380
CAPITAL: Nuuk
POPULATION: 56,076
AREA: 840,000 sq miles (2,175,500 sq km)

FRANCE

France has developed economic
ties with its *Territoires d'Outre–Mer,*
thereby stressing interdependence
over independence. Overseas
départements, officially part of
France, have their own governments.
Territorial *collectivités* and overseas
territoires have varying degrees
of autonomy.

CLIPPERTON ISLAND *Ref: 135 F3*

STATUS: Dependency of
French Polynesia
CLAIMED: 1930
CAPITAL: Not applicable
POPULATION: None
AREA: 2.7 sq miles (7 sq km)

FRENCH GUIANA *Ref: 41 H3*

STATUS: Overseas department
CLAIMED: 1817
CAPITAL: Cayenne
POPULATION: 152,300
AREA: 35,135 sq miles
(91,000 sq km)

FRENCH POLYNESIA *Ref: 127 H4*

STATUS: Overseas territory
CLAIMED: 1843
CAPITAL: Papeete
POPULATION: 219,521
AREA: 1608 sq miles (4165 sq km)

GUADELOUPE *Ref: 37 G4*

STATUS: Overseas department
CLAIMED: 1635
CAPITAL: Basse-Terre
POPULATION: 419,500
AREA: 687 sq miles (1780 sq km)

MARTINIQUE *Ref: 37 G4*

STATUS: Overseas department
CLAIMED: 1635
CAPITAL: Fort-de-France
POPULATION: 381,200
AREA: 425 sq miles (1100 sq km)

MAYOTTE *Ref: 61 G2*

STATUS: Territorial collectivity
CLAIMED: 1843
CAPITAL: Mamoudzou
POPULATION: 131,320
AREA: 144 sq miles (374 sq km)

NEW CALEDONIA *Ref: 126 D5*

STATUS: Overseas territory
CLAIMED: 1853
CAPITAL: Nouméa
POPULATION: 196,836
AREA: 7347 sq miles (19,100 sq km)

RÉUNION *Ref: 61 H4*

STATUS: Overseas department
CLAIMED: 1638
CAPITAL: Saint-Denis
POPULATION: 632,000
AREA: 970 sq miles (2500 sq km)

Overseas territories

ST PIERRE & MIQUELON
Ref: 21 G4

STATUS: Territorial collectivity
CLAIMED: 1604
CAPITAL: Saint-Pierre
POPULATION: 6600
AREA: 93 sq miles (242 sq km)

WALLIS & FUTUNA
Ref: 127 E4

STATUS: Overseas territory
CLAIMED: 1842
CAPITAL: Matā'Utu
POPULATION: 15,000
AREA: 106 sq miles (274 sq km)

NETHERLANDS

The country's two remaining
territories were formerly part
of the Dutch West Indies. Both
are now self-governing, but the
Netherlands remains responsible
for their defense.

ARUBA *Ref: 37 E5*

STATUS: Autonomous part
of the Netherlands
CLAIMED: 1643
CAPITAL: Oranjestad
POPULATION: 88,000
AREA: 75 sq miles (194 sq km)

NETHERLANDS ANTILLES *Ref: 37 E5*

STATUS: Autonomous part
of the Netherlands
CLAIMED: 1816
CAPITAL: Willemstad
POPULATION: 207,175
AREA: 308 sq miles (800 sq km)

NEW ZEALAND

New Zealand's government has
no desire to retain any overseas
territories. However, the economic
weakness of Tokelau, Niue, and
the Cook Islands has forced it
to remain responsible for their
foreign policy and defense.

COOK ISLANDS *Ref: 127 G4*

STATUS: Associated
territory
CLAIMED: 1901
CAPITAL: Avarua
POPULATION: 20,200
AREA: 113 sq miles (293 sq km)

NIUE *Ref: 127 F5*

STATUS: Associated
territory
CLAIMED: 1901
CAPITAL: Alofi
POPULATION: 2080
AREA: 102 sq miles (264 sq km)

TOKELAU *Ref: 127 F3*

STATUS: Dependent territory
CLAIMED: 1926
CAPITAL: Not applicable
POPULATION: 1577
AREA: 4 sq miles (10 sq km)

NORWAY

In 1920, 41 nations signed the
Spits-bergen treaty recognizing
Norwegian sovereignty over
Svalbard. There is a Nato base
on Jan Mayen. Bouvet Island
is a nature reserve.

Overseas territories

BOUVET ISLAND *Ref: 49 D7*
STATUS: Dependency
CLAIMED: 1928
CAPITAL: Not applicable
POPULATION: None
AREA: 22 sq miles (58 sq km)

JAN MAYEN *Ref: 65 F3*
STATUS: Dependency
CLAIMED: 1929
CAPITAL: Not applicable
POPULATION: None
AREA: 147 sq miles (381 sq km)

PETER I. ISLAND *Ref: 136 A3*
STATUS: Dependency
CLAIMED: 1931
CAPITAL: Not applicable
POPULATION: None
AREA: 69 sq miles (180 sq km)

SVALBARD *Ref: 65 F2*
STATUS: Dependency CLAIMED: 1920
CAPITAL: Longyearbyen
POPULATION: 3231
AREA: 24,289 sq miles (62,906 sq km)

UNITED KINGDOM

The UK has the largest number
of overseas territories. These are
locally governed by a mixture of
elected representatives and
appointed officials.

ANGUILLA *Ref: 37 G3*

STATUS: Dependent territory
CLAIMED: 1650
CAPITAL: The Valley
POPULATION: 10,300
AREA: 37 sq miles (96 sq km)

ASCENSION ISLAND *Ref: 49 C5*
STATUS: Dependency of St Helena
CLAIMED: 1673
CAPITAL: Georgetown
POPULATION: 1099
AREA: 34 sq miles (88 sq km)

BERMUDA *Ref: 17 E6*

STATUS: Crown colony
CLAIMED: 1612
CAPITAL: Hamilton
POPULATION: 60,144
AREA: 20 sq miles (53 sq km)

**BRITISH INDIAN OCEAN
TERRITORY** *Ref: 122 C4*

STATUS: Dependent territory
CLAIMED: 1814
CAPITAL: Diego Garcia
POPULATION: 930
AREA: 23 sq miles (60 sq km)

BRITISH VIRGIN IS. *Ref: 37 F3*

STATUS: Dependent territory
CLAIMED: 1672
CAPITAL: Road Town
POPULATION: 17,896
AREA: 59 sq miles (153 sq km)

CAYMAN ISLANDS *Ref: 36 B3*

STATUS: Dependent territory
CLAIMED: 1670
CAPITAL: George Town
POPULATION: 35,000
AREA: 100 sq miles (259 sq km)

FALKLAND ISLANDS *Ref: 47 D7*

STATUS: Dependent territory
CLAIMED: 1832
CAPITAL: Stanley
POPULATION: 2564
AREA: 4699 sq miles (12,173 sq km)

Overseas territories

GIBRALTAR *Ref: 74 D5*

STATUS: Crown colony
CLAIMED: 1713
CAPITAL: Gibraltar
POPULATION: 27,086
AREA: 2.5 sq miles (6.5 sq km)

GUERNSEY *Ref: 71 D8*

STATUS: Crown dependency
CLAIMED: 1066
CAPITAL: St. Peter Port
POPULATION: 56,681
AREA: 25 sq miles (65 sq km)

ISLE OF MAN *Ref: 71 C5*

STATUS: Crown dependency
CLAIMED: 1765
CAPITAL: Douglas
POPULATION: 71,714
AREA: 221 sq miles (572 sq km)

JERSEY *Ref: 71 D8*

STATUS: Crown dependency
CLAIMED: 1066
CAPITAL: St. Helier
POPULATION: 85,150
AREA: 45 sq miles (116 sq km)

MONTSERRAT *Ref: 37 G4*

STATUS: Dependent
territory
CLAIMED: 1632
CAPITAL: Plymouth (uninhabitable)
POPULATION: 2850
AREA: 40 sq miles (102 sq km)

PITCAIRN ISLANDS *Ref: 125 G4*

STATUS: Dependent
territory
CLAIMED: 1887
CAPITAL: Adamstown POPULATION: 55
AREA: 1.4 sq miles (3.5 sq km)

ST HELENA *Ref: 49 D5*

STATUS: Dependent territory
CLAIMED: 1673
CAPITAL: Jamestown
POPULATION: 6472
AREA: 47 sq miles (122 sq km)

SOUTH GEORGIA & THE SANDWICH ISLANDS *Ref: 49 C7*

STATUS: Dependent territory
CLAIMED: 1775 CAPITAL: Not applicable
POPULATION: None
AREA: 1387 sq miles (3592 sq km)

TRISTAN DA CUNHA *Ref: 49 D6*

STATUS: Dependency of St. Helena
CLAIMED: 1612 CAPITAL: Edinburgh
POPULATION: 297
AREA: 38 sq miles (98 sq km)

TURKS & CAICOS ISLANDS *Ref: 37 E2*

STATUS: Dependent territory
CLAIMED: 1766
CAPITAL: Cockburn Town
POPULATION: 13,800
AREA: 166 sq miles (430 sq km)

UNITED STATES

US Commonwealth territories
are self-governing incorporated
territories that are an integral part
of the US. Unincorporated territories
have varying degrees of autonomy.

AMERICAN SAMOA *Ref: 127 F4*

STATUS: Unincorporated
territory
CLAIMED: 1900
CAPITAL: Pago Pago
POPULATION: 60,000
AREA: 75 sq miles (195 sq km)

Overseas territories

BAKER & HOWLAND ISLANDS
Ref: 127 E2
STATUS: Unincorporated territory
CAPITAL: Not applicable
CLAIMED: 1856 POPULATION: None
AREA: 0.5 sq miles (1.4 sq km)

GUAM *Ref: 126 B1*

STATUS: Unincorporated territory
CLAIMED: 1898
CAPITAL: Hågatña
POPULATION: 149,249
AREA: 212 sq miles (549 sq km)

JARVIS ISLAND *Ref: 127 G2*
STATUS: Unincorporated territory
CLAIMED: 1856
CAPITAL: Not applicable
POPULATION: None
AREA: 1.7 sq miles (4.5 sq km)

JOHNSTON ATOLL *Ref: 125 E1*
STATUS: Unincorporated territory
CLAIMED: 1858
CAPITAL: Not applicable
POPULATION: 327
AREA: 1 sq miles (2.8 sq km)

KINGMAN REEF *Ref: 127 F2*
STATUS: Administered territory
CLAIMED: 1856
CAPITAL: Not applicable
POPULATION: None
AREA: 0.4 sq miles (1 sq km)

MIDWAY ISLANDS *Ref: 134 D2*
STATUS: Administered territory
CLAIMED: 1867
CAPITAL: Not applicable
POPULATION: 453
AREA: 2 sq miles (5.2 sq km)

NAVASSA ISLAND *Ref: 36 D3*
STATUS: Unincorporated territory
CLAIMED: 1856 CAPITAL: Not applicable
POPULATION: None
AREA: 2 sq miles (5.2 sq km)

NORTHERN MARIANA ISLANDS
Ref: 124 C1

STATUS: Commonwealth territory
CLAIMED: 1947
CAPITAL: Saipan POPULATION: 58,846
AREA: 177 sq miles (457 sq km)

PALMYRA ATOLL *Ref: 127 G2*
STATUS: Unincorporated territory
CLAIMED: 1898 CAPITAL: Not applicable
POPULATION: None
AREA: 5 sq miles (12 sq km)

PUERTO RICO *Ref: 37 F3*

STATUS: Commonwealth territory
CLAIMED: 1898
CAPITAL: San Juan
POPULATION: 3.8 million
AREA: 3458 sq miles (8959 sq km)

VIRGIN ISLANDS *Ref: 37 F3*
STATUS: Unincorporated territory
CLAIMED: 1917
CAPITAL: Charlotte Amalie
POPULATION: 101,809
AREA: 137 sq miles (355 sq km)

WAKE ISLAND *Ref: 124 D1*
STATUS: Unincorporated territory
CLAIMED: 1898
CAPITAL: Not applicable
POPULATION: 302
AREA: 2.5 sq miles (6.5 sq km)

International organizations

This listing provides acronym definitions for the main international organizations concerned with worldwide economics, trade and defense, plus an indication of membership.

ASEAN

Association of Southeast Asian Nations
ESTABLISHED: 1967
MEMBERS: Brunei, Thailand, Laos, Malaysia, Singapore, Ind., Philippines, Vietnam, Myanmar

CIS

Commonwealth of Independent States
ESTABLISHED: 1991
MEMBERS: Armenia, Az., Belarus, Kazakhstan, Kyrgyzstan, Moldova, Russia, Tajikistan, Turkmenistan, Ukraine, Uzbekistan, Georgia

COMM

The Commonwealth
ESTABLISHED: 1931; evolved out of the British Empire. Formerly known as the British Commonwealth of Nations.
MEMBERS: 53

EU

European Union
ESTABLISHED: 1965; formerly known as EEC (European Economic Community) and EC (Economic Community)
MEMBERS: Belgium, Denmark, France, Germany, Greece, Ireland, Italy, Luxembourg, Netherlands, Portugal, Spain, UK, Austria, Finland and Sweden

GATT

General Agreement on Tariffs and Trade
ESTABLISHED: 1947
MEMBERS: 104

G7

Group of 7
ESTABLISHED: 1975
MEMBERS: Canada, France, Germany, Italy, Japan, UK, US

IMF

International Monetary Fund
(UN agency)
ESTABLISHED: 1945 MEMBERS: 182

NAFTA

North American Free Trade Agreement
ESTABLISHED: 1994
MEMBERS: Canada, Mexico, US

NATO

North Atlantic Treaty Organization
ESTABLISHED: 1949 MEMBERS: Belgium, Canada, Czech Rep., Denmark, Fr., Ger., Greece, Hung., Iceland, Italy, Lux., Neth., Norway, Poland, Port., Spain, Turkey, UK, US

OPEC

Organization of Petroleum Exporting Countries
ESTABLISHED: 1960 MEMBERS: Algeria, Indonesia, Iran, Iraq, Kuwait, Libya, Nigeria, Qatar, Saudi Arabia, United Arab Emirates, Venezuela

UN

United Nations
ESTABLISHED: 1945 MEMBERS: 185; all nations are represented, except Kiribati, Nauru, Taiwan, Tonga and Tuvalu. Switzerland and Vatican City have "observer status" only.

Abbreviations

This glossary provides a comprehensive guide to the abbreviations used in this atlas.

abbrev. abbreviation
Afgh. Afghanistan
Amh. Amharic
anc. ancient
Ar. Arabic
Arm. Armenia/Armenian
Aus. Austria
Aust. Australia
Az. Azerbaijan

Bas Basque
Bel. Belorussian
Belg. Belgium/Belgian
Bos. & Herz. Bosnia & Herzegovina
Bul. Bulgarian
Bulg. Bulgaria
Bur. Burmese

C Central
C. Cape
Cam. Cambodian
Cast. Castilian
Chin. Chinese
Cord. Cordillera (Sp. mountain range)
Cz. Czech
Czech Rep. Czech Republic

D.C. District of Columbia
Dan. Danish
Dominican Rep. Dominican Republic

E East
Emb. Embalse
Eng. English
Est. Estonia/Estonian

Faer. Faeroese
Fin. Finnish
Flem. Flemish
Fr. France/French

Geo. Georgia
Geor. Georgian
Ger. German
Gk. Greek

Heb. Hebrew
Hung. Hungary/Hungarian

I. Island
Ind. Indonesian
Is. Islands
It. Italian

Kaz. Kazakh
Kep. Kepulauan (Ind. island group)
Kir. Kirghiz
Kor. Korean
Kurd. Kurdish
Kyrgy. Kyrgyzstan

L. Lake, Lago
Lat. Latvia
Latv. Latvian
Leb. Lebanon
Liech. Liechtenstein
Lith. Lithuania/Lithuanian
Lux. Luxembourg

m meters
Mac. Macedonia
Med. Sea Mediterranean Sea
Mold. Moldova
Mt. Mount/Mountain
Mts Mountains

N North
N. Korea North Korea
Neth. Netherlands
NW Northwest
NZ New Zealand

P. Pulau (Ind. island)
Peg. Pegunungan (Ind. mountain range)
Per. Persian
Pol. Poland/Polish
Port. Portuguese
prev. previously

R. River, Rio, Río
Res. Reservoir
Rom. Romania/Romanian
Rus. Russian
Russ. Fed. Russian Federation

S South
S. Korea South Korea
SA South Africa
SCr. Serbian and Croatian
Slvka. Slovakia
Slvna. Slovenia
Som. Somali
Sp. Spanish
St, St. Saint
Str. Strait
Swed. Swedish
Switz. Switzerland

Tajik. Tajikistan
Th. Thai
Turk. Turkish
Turkm. Turkmen
Turkmen. Turkmenistan

U.A.E. United Arab Emirates
UK United Kingdom
Ukr. Ukranian
US United States of America
Uzb. Uzbek
Uzbek. Uzbekistan

var. variant
Vdkhr. Vodokhranilishche (Rus. reservoir)
Vdskh. Vodoskhovyshche (Ukr. reservoir)
Ven. Venezuela

W West
W. Sahara Western Sahara
Wel. Welsh

Yugo. Yugoslavia

——— **A** ———

Aachen Germany 76 A4

Aalst Belgium 69 B5

Aba Nigeria 57 G5

Ābādān Iran 102 C4

Abashiri Japan 112 D2

Abéché Chad 58 D3

Åbenrå Denmark 67 A8

Aberdeen Scotland, UK 70 D3

Aberdeen South Dakota, USA 25 E2

Aberdeen Washington, USA 26 A2

Aberystwyth Wales, UK 71 C6

Abhā Saudi Arabia 103 B6

Abidjan Côte d'Ivoire 56 D5

Abilene Texas, USA 29 F3

Abomey Benin 57 F4

Abu Dhabi *capital of* United Arab Emirates *var.* Abū Z̧aby 103 D5

Abuja *capital of* Nigeria 57 G4

Abū Z̧aby *see* Abu Dhabi

Acapulco Mexico 33 E5

Acarai Mountains *mountain range* Brazil/Guyana 41 F3

Acarigua Venezuela 40 D1

Accra *capital of* Ghana 57 E5

Acklins Island *island* Bahamas 36 B2

Aconcagua, Cerro *peak* Argentina 46 B4

A Coruña Spain *Cast.* La Coruña 74 C1

ACT *see* Australian Capital Territory

Adalia *see* Antalya

Adalia, Gulf of *see* Antalya Körfezi

'Adan Yemen *Eng.* Aden 103 B7

Adana Turkey *var.* Seyhan 98 D4

Adapazarı Turkey *var.* Sakarya 98 B2

Ad Dahnā' *desert* Saudi Arabia 103 C5

Ad Dakhla Western Sahara 52 A4

Ad Dawḩah *see* Doha

Addis Ababa *capital of* Ethiopia *Amh.* Ādīs Ābeba 55 C5

Adelaide Australia 131 B6

Adélie, Terre d' *territory* Antarctica 136 C4

Aden *see* 'Adan

Aden, Gulf of *sea feature* Indian Ocean 122 A3

Adige *river* Italy 78 C2

Ādīs Ābeba *see* Addis Ababa

Adıyaman Turkey 99 E4

Adriatic Sea *Mediterranean Sea* 78 D4

Aegean Sea *Mediterranean Sea* *Gk.* Aigaío Pélagos, *Turk.* Ege Denizi 87 D5

Aeolian Islands *see* Isole Eolie

Afghanistan *country* C Asia 104-105

Africa 50-51

Africa, Horn of *physical region* Ethiopia/Somalia 122 A3

Afyon Turkey *prev.* Afyonkarahisar 98 B3

Afyonkarahisar *see* Afyon

Agadez Niger 57 G3

Agadir Morocco 52 B2

Agassiz Fracture Zone *tectonic feature* Pacific Ocean 135 E4

Agen France 73 B6

Āgra India 116 D3

Agrigento Italy 79 C7

Agrinio Greece 87 B5

Aguarico *river* Ecuador/Peru 40 B4

Aguascalientes Mexico 32 D4

Ahaggar *mountains* Algeria *var.* Hoggar 53 E4

Ahmadābād India 116 C4

Ahvāz Iran 102 C4

Ahvenanmaa *see* Åland

Aigaío Pélagos *see* Aegean Sea

Aintab *see* Gaziantep

Aïr, Massif de l' *region* Niger 57 G2

Aix-en-Provence France 73 D6

Ajaccio Corse, France 73 E7

Ajdābiyā Libya 53 G2

Ajmer India 116 D3

Akaba *see* Al 'Aqabah

Akchâr *desert* Mauritania 56 C2

Akimiski Island *island* Canada 20 C3

Akita Japan 112 D3

Akjoujt Mauritania 56 C2

Akmola *see* Astana

Akmolinsk *see* Astana

Akpatok Island *island* Canada 21 E1

Akra Kanestron *see* Palioúri, Akrotírio

Akron Ohio, USA 22 D3

Aksai Chin *disputed region* China/India 108 B4

Aktau Kazakhstan *prev.* Shevchenko 96 A4

Akureyri Iceland 65 E4

Akyab *see* Sittwe

Alabama *state* USA 30 D3

Alajuela Costa Rica 34 D4

Alamogordo New Mexico, USA 28 D3

Åland *island group* Finland *Fin.* Ahvenanmaa 67 D6

Al 'Aqabah Jordan *var.* Akaba 101 B7

Alaska *state* USA 18

Alaska, Gulf of *sea feature* Pacific Ocean 16 C3

Alaska Range *mountain range* Alaska, USA 18 C3

Albacete Spain 75 E3

Alba Iulia Romania 90 B4

Albania *country* SE Europe 83

Albany Australia 129 B7

Albany Georgia, USA 31 E3

Albany New York, USA 23 F3

Albany Oregon, USA 26 A3

Albany *river* Canada 20 B3

Al Başrah Iraq *var.* Basra 102 C4

Al Bayḑā' Libya 53 G2

Albert, Lake *lake* Uganda/Congo (Zaire) 59 E5

Alberta *province* Canada 19 E4

Albi France 73 C6

Ålborg Denmark 67 B7

Albuquerque New Mexico, USA 28 D2

Alcácer do Sal Portugal 74 C4

Aldabra Group *island group* Seychelles 61 G2

Aleg Mauritania 56 C3

Aleksandriya *see* Oleksandriya

Aleksandropol' *see* Gyumri

Aleksinac Yugoslavia 82 E4

Alençon France 72 B3

Alessandria Italy 78 B2

Ålesund Norway 67 A5

Aleutian Basin *undersea feature* Bering Sea 134 D1

Aleutian Islands *islands* Alaska, USA 18 A3

Aleutian Trench *undersea feature* Pacific Ocean 134 D1

Alexander Island *island* Antarctica 136 A3

Alexandra New Zealand 133 B7

Alexandretta *see* İskenderun

Alexandria Egypt 54 B1

Alexandria Louisiana, USA 30 B3

Alexandroúpoli Greece 86 D3

Al Fāshīr *see* El Fasher

Alföld *see* Great Hungarian Plain

Algarve *region* Portugal 74 C4

Algeciras Spain 74 D5

Algeria *country* N Africa 52-53

Alghero Italy 79 A5

Algiers *capital of* Algeria 52 D1

Al Ḥasakah Syria 100 D2

Al Ḥudaydah Yemen 103 B7

Al Ḥufūf Saudi Arabia 103 C5

Alicante Spain 75 F4

Alice Springs Australia 130 A4

Al Jawf Saudi Arabia 102 B4

Al Jazīrah *region* Iraq/Syria 100 E2

Al Jīzah *see* El Gîza

Al Karak Jordan 101 B6

Al Khalīl *see* Hebron

Al Khārijah *see* El Khârga

Al Khums Libya 53 F2

Al Khurṭūm *see* Khartoum

Alkmaar Netherlands 68 C2

Al Kufrah Libya 53 H4

Al Lādhiqīyah Syria *Eng.* Latakia 100 B3

Allahābād India 117 E4

Allenstein *see* Olsztyn

Allentown Pennsylvania, USA 23 F4

Alma-Ata *capital of* Kazakhstan *Rus./Kaz.* Almaty 96 C5

Al Madīnah Saudi Arabia *Eng.* Medina 102 A5

Al Mafraq Jordan 101 B5

Almalyk Uzbekistan *Uzb.* Olmaliq 105 F2

Al Manāmah *see* Manama

Al Marj Libya 53 G2

Almaty *see* Alma-Ata

Al Mawṣil Iraq *Eng.* Mosul 102 B3

Almelo Netherlands 68 E3

Almería Spain 75 E5

Al Mukallā Yemen 103 C7

Alofi *capital of* Niue 127 F5

Alor, Kepulauan *island group* Indonesia 121 E5

Alps *mountain range* C Europe 62 D4

Al Qāhirah *see* Cairo

Al Qāmishlī Syria *var.* Kamishli 100 E1

Al Qunayṭirah Syria 100 B4

Altai Mountains *mountain range* C Asia 108 C2

Altamura Italy 79 E5

Altar, Desierto de *Desert* Mexico/USA *var.* Sonoran Desert 32 A1

Altay China 108 C2

Altay Mongolia 108 D2

Altun Shan *mountain range* China 108 C3

Alturas California, USA 26 B4

Alytus Lithuania *Pol.* Olita 89 B5

Amadeus, Lake *seasonal lake* Australia 129 E5

Amakusa-nada *island group* Japan 113 A8

Amami-Ō-shima *island* Japan 113 A8

Amarillo Texas, USA 29 E2

Amazon *river* South America 38 C3

Amazon Basin *region* C South America 42 D2

Ambanja Madagascar 61 G2

Ambarchik Russian Federation 97 G2

Ambato Ecuador 40 A4

Amboasary Madagascar 61 F4

Ambon Indonesia 121 F4

Ambositra Madagascar 61 G3

Ambriz Angola 60 B1

Amdo China 108 C4

Ameland *island* Netherlands 68 D1

American Falls Reservoir *Reservoir* Idaho, USA 26 E4

American Samoa *external territory* USA, Pacific Ocean 127 F4

Amersfoort Netherlands 68 D3

Amga *river* Russian Federation 95 F2

Amiens France 72 C3

Amindivi Islands *island group* India 114 C2

Amirante Islands *island group* Seychelles 61 H1

Amman *capital of* Jordan 101 B5

Ammassalik Greenland *var.* Angmagssalik 64 D4

Ammochostos *see* Gazimağusa

Āmol Iran 102 C3

Amorgós *island* Greece 87 D6

Amritsar India 116 D2

Amsterdam *capital of* Netherlands 68 C3

Amsterdam Island *island* French Southern and Antarctic Territories 123 C6

Am Timan Chad 58 C3

Amu Darya *river* C Asia 104 D3

Amundsen Gulf *sea feature* Canada 19 E2

Amundsen Plain *undersea feature* Pacific Ocean 136 B4

Amundsen Sea Antarctica 97 G4

Amur *river* E Asia 97 G4 107 E1

Anabar *river* Russian Federation 95 E2

Anadolu Dağları *see* Doğu Karadeniz Dağları

Anadyr' Russian Federation 97 H1

Anápolis Brazil 43 F4

Anatolia *region* SE Europe 85 G3

Anchorage Alaska, USA 18 C3

Ancona Italy 78 C3

Andalucía *region* Spain 74 D4

Andaman Islands *island group* India 115 H2 119 A5

Andaman Sea Indian Ocean 122 B3

Andes *mountain range* South America 39 B6

Andijon Uzbekistan *Rus.* Andizhan 105 F2

Andizhan *see* Andijon

Andorra *country* SW Europe 73 B6

Andorra la Vella *capital of* Andorra 73 B6

Ándros *island* Greece 87 D5

Andros Island *island* Bahamas 36 C1

Angara *river* C Asia 95 D3

Ángel de la Guarda, Isla *island* Mexico 32 B2

Angel Falls *see* Salto Ángel

Angeles Philippines 121 E1

Ángel, Salto *waterfall* Venezuela 40 D2 *Eng.* Angel Falls 41 F2

Ångermanälven *river* Sweden 66 C4

Angers France 72 B4

Anglesey *island* Wales, UK 71 C5

Angmagssalik *see* Ammassalik

Angola *country* C Africa 60

Angola Basin *undersea feature* Atlantic Ocean 49 D6

Angora *see* Ankara

Angoulême France 73 B5

Angren Uzbekistan 105 E2

Anguilla *external territory* UK, West Indies 37

Anhui *province* China *var.* Anhwei, Wan 111 C5

Anhwei *see* Anhui

Anjouan *island* Comoros 61 F2

Ankara *capital of* Turkey *prev.* Angora 98 C3

Annaba Algeria 53 E1

An Nafūd *desert region* Saudi Arabia 102 B4

An Najaf Iraq *var.* Najaf 102 B4

Annapolis Maryland, USA 23 F4

Ann Arbor Michigan, USA 22 C3

Annecy France 73 D5

Anshan China 110 D4

Ansongo Mali 57 E3

Antakya Turkey *var.* Hatay 98 D4

Antalaha Madagascar 61 G2

Antalya Turkey *prev.* Adalia 98 B4

Antalya, Gulf of *see* Antalya Körfezi

Antalya Körfezi *sea feature* Mediterranean Sea *Eng.* Gulf of Antalya, *var.* Gulf of Adalia 98 B4

Antananarivo *capital of* Madagascar *prev.* Tananarive 61 G3

Antarctica 136

Antarctic Peninsula *peninsula* Antarctica 136 A2

Antequera Spain 74 D5

Anticosti, Île d' *island* Canada 21 E3

Antigua *island* Antigua & Barbuda 37 G3

Antigua & Barbuda *country* West Indies 37

Anti-Lebanon *mountains* Lebanon/Syria 100 B4

Antipodes Islands *island group* New Zealand 124 D5

Antofagasta Chile 46 B2

Antsiranana Madagascar 61 G2

Antsohihy Madagascar 61 G2

Antwerp *see* Antwerpen

Antwerpen Belgium *Eng.* Antwerp 69 C5

Anyang China 110 C4

Aoga-shima *island* Japan 113 D6

Aomori Japan 112 D3

Aorangi *see* Cook, Mount

Aosta Italy 78 A2

Aoukâr *plateau* Mauritania 56 D3

Apeldoorn Netherlands 68 D3

Apennines *see* Appennino

Apia *capital of* Samoa 127 F4

Appalachian Mountains *mountain range* E USA 17 D5

Appennino *mountain range* Italy *Eng.* Apennines 78 C4

Apure *river* Venezuela 40 D2

Aqaba *see* Al 'Aqabah

Aqaba, Gulf of *sea feature* Red Sea *Ar.* Khalīj al 'Aqabah 101 A8

'Aqaba, Khalīj al *see* Aqaba, Gulf of

Āqchah Afghanistan *var.* Āqcheh 104 D3

Āqcheh *see* Āqchah

Arabian Basin *undersea feature* Indian Ocean 122 B3

Arabian Peninsula *peninsula* Asia 85 H5 94 B5 103 C5

Arabian Sea Indian Ocean 122 B3

Aracaju Brazil 43 H3

Arad Romania 90 A4

Arafura Sea Asia/Australasia 126 A4

Araguaia *river* Brazil 43 F3

Arāk Iran 102 C3

Araks *see* Aras

Arak's *see* Aras

Aral Sea *inland sea* Kazakhstan/Uzbekistan 104 C

Araouane Mali 57 E2

Ararat, Mount peak Turkey var. Great Ararat, Turk. Büyükağrı Dağı 94 F3

Aras river SW Asia Arm. Arak's, Per. Rūd-e Aras, Rus. Araks, Turk. Aras Nehri 99 G3

Aras Nehri see Aras

Arauca Colombia 40 C2

Arauca river Colombia/Venezuela 40 C2

Arbīl Iraq Kurd. Hawlēr 102 B3

Arctic Ocean 18-19 137

Arda river Bulgaria/Greece 86 C3

Ardabīl Iran 102 C3

Ardennes region W Europe 69 D7

Arendal Norway 67 A6

Arensburg see Kuressaare

Arequipa Peru 42 B4

Arezzo Italy 78 C3

Argentina country S South America 46-47

Argentine Basin undersea feature Atlantic Ocean 49 B7

Argun river China/Russian Federation 95 E3

Århus Denmark 67 A7

Arica Chile 46 B1

Arizona state USA 28 B2

Arkansas state USA 30 B1

Arkansas river C USA 17 C5

Arkhangel'sk Russian Federation 92 C3 96 C2

Arles France 73 D6

Arlington Texas, USA 29 G3

Arlington Virginia, USA 23 E4

Arlon Belgium 69 D8

Armenia country SW Asia 99 G2

Armenia Colombia 40 B3

Armidale Australia 131 D5

Arnhem Netherlands 68 D4

Arnhem Land region Australia 128 E2

Arno river Italy 78 B3

Arran island Scotland, UK 70 C4

Ar Raqqah Syria 100 C2

Arras France 72 C3

Ar Riyāḍ see Riyadh

Ar Rub 'al Khālī desert Asia Eng. Empty Quarter, Great Sandy Desert 103 C6

Ar Rustāq Oman var. Rostak 103 D5

Artesia New Mexico, USA 28 D3

Artigas Uruguay 44 B4

Aru, Kepulauan island group Indonesia 121 G5

Arua Uganda 55 B6

Aruba external territory Netherlands, West Indies 37 E5

Arusha Tanzania 55 C7

Asad, Buḥayrat al Lake Syria Eng. Lake Assad 100 C2

Asadābād Afghanistan 105 E4

Asahikawa Japan 112 D2

Asamankese Ghana 57 E5

Ascension island Atlantic Ocean 49 C5

Ascoli Piceno Italy 78 C4

Aseb Eritrea var. Assab 54 D4

Ashburton New Zealand 133 C6

Asheville North Carolina, USA 31 E1

Ashgabat capital of Turkmenistan prev. Ashkhabad, Poltoratsk 104 C3

Ashkhabad see Ashgabat

Ashmore and Cartier Islands Australian external territory Indian Ocean 124 A3

Ash Shāriqah see Sharjah

Asia 94-95 106-107

Asmara capital of Eritrea Amh. Asmera 54 C4

Asmera see Asmara

Assab see Aseb

As Salţ Jordan var. Salt 101 B5

Assamakka Niger 57 F2

Assen Netherlands 68 E2

Assad, Lake see Asad, Buḥayrat al

As Sulayyil Saudi Arabia 103 B6

As Suwaydā' Syria 101 B5

Astana country capital Kazakhstan prev. Akmola, Akmolinsk, Tselinograd, Kaz. Aqmola. 96 C4

Astoria Oregon, USA 26 A2

Astrakhan' Russian Federation 93 B7

Astypálaia island Greece 87 D6

Asunción capital of Paraguay 44 B3

Aswân Egypt 54 B2

Asyût Egypt 54 B2

Atacama Desert desert Chile 46 B2

Aţâr Mauritania 56 C2

Atbara Sudan 54 C3

Athabasca, Lake lake Canada 19 F4

Athens capital of Greece Gk. Athína, prev. Athínai 87 C5

Athens Georgia, USA 31 E1

Athína see Athens

Athínai see Athens

Athlone Ireland 71 B5

Ati Chad 58 C3

Atlanta Georgia, USA 30 D2

Atlantic City New Jersey, USA 23 F4

Atlantic Ocean 48-49

Atlantic-Indian Basin undersea feature Indian Ocean 136 B1

Atlantic-Indian Ridge undersea feature Atlantic Ocean 49 D7

Atlas Mountains mountain range Morocco 52 C2

Aţ Ţafīlah Jordan 101 B6

Aţ Ţā'if Saudi Arabia 102 B6

Attapu Laos 119 E5

Attawapiskat Canada 20 C3

Attawapiskat river Canada 20 B3

Attu Island island Alaska, USA 18 A2

Auch France 73 B6

Auckland New Zealand 132 D3

Auckland Islands *island group*
New Zealand124 D5

Audijon Kyrgyzstan 105 F2

Augsburg Germany 77 C6

Augusta Australia 129 B7

Augusta Georgia, USA 31 E2

Augusta Maine, USA 23 G2

Aurillac France 73 C5

Aurora Colorado, USA 24 D4

Aurora Illinois, USA 22 B3

Aussig *see* Ústí nad Labem

Austin Texas, USA 29 G4

Australasia 124-125

Australes, Îles *island group*
French Polynesia 125 F4

Austral Fracture Zone
tectonic feature Pacific Ocean
125 H4

Australia *country* Pacific Ocean
124

Australian Alps Australia
131 D7

Australian Capital Territory
territory Australia *abbrev.*
A.C.T. *131* D6

Austria *country* C Europe 77

Auxerre France 72 C4

Avarua *capital of* Cook Islands
127 G5

Aveiro Portugal 74 C2

Avignon France 73 D6

Ávila Spain 74 D2

Avilés Spain 74 D1

Awbārī Libya 53 F3

Axel Heiberg Island *island*
Canada 19 F1

Axios *see* Vardar

Ayacucho Peru 42 B4

Aydarkul', Ozero *lake*
Uzbekistan 104 D2

Aydın Turkey 98 A3

Ayer's Rock *see* Uluru

Ayr Scotland, UK 70 C4

Ayutthaya Thailand 119 C5

Ayvalık Turkey 98 A3

Azaouâd *desert* Mali 57 E2

A'zāz Syria 100 B2

Azerbaijan *country* SW Asia
99 G2

Azores *islands* Portugal,
Atlantic Ocean 48 C3

Azov, Sea of Black Sea *Ukr.*
Azovs'ke More, *Rus.*
Azovskoye More 93 A6 91 G4

Azovs'ke More *see* Azov, Sea of

Azovskoye More *see*
Azov, Sea of

Azul Argentina 46 D4

Azur, Côte d' *coastal region*
France 73 E6

Az Zarqā' Jordan 101 B5

Az Zāwiyah Libya 53 F2

B

Baalbek Lebanon *var.*
Ba'labakk 100 B4

Babeldaob *island* Palau 124 B2

Babruysk Belarus *Rus.*
Bobruysk 89 D6

Babuyan Channel *channel*
Philippines 121 E1

Bacan, Pulau *island* Indonesia
121 F4

Bačka Topola Yugoslavia 82 D3

Bacău Romania 90 C4

Badajoz Spain 74 C4

Baden Switzerland 77 E6

Bādiyat ash Shām *see* Syrian
Desert

Baffin Bay *sea feature* Atlantic
Ocean 48 B1

Baffin Island *island* Canada
19 G2

Bafing *river* Africa 56 C3

Bafoussam Cameroon 58 B4

Bagdad *see* Baghdad

Bagé Brazil 44 C4

Baghdad *capital of* Iraq *var.*
Bagdad, *Ar.* Baghdād 102 B3

Baghdād *see* Baghdad

Baghlān Afghanistan 105 E3

Bagoé *river* Côte d'Ivoire/Mali
56 D4

Baguio Philippines 121 E1

Bahamas *country* West Indies,
Atlantic Ocean 36

Baharden *see* Bakherden

Bahāwalpur Pakistan 116 C3

Bäherden *see* Bakherden

Bahía Blanca Argentina 47 C5

Bahía, Islas de la *islands*
Honduras 34 D2

Bahir Dar Ethiopia 54 C4

Bahrain *country* SW Asia
103 C5

Baia Mare Romania 90 B3

Baikal, Lake *see* Baykal, Ozero

Bairiki *capital of* Kiribati
127 E2

Baja Hungary 81 C7

Baja California *peninsula*
Mexico *Eng.* Lower California
32 B2

Bajo Nuevo *island* Colombia
35 F2

Baker Oregon, USA 26 C3

Baker & Howland Islands
external territory USA, Pacific
Ocean 125 E2

Bakersfield California, USA
27 C7

Bakharden *see* Bakherden

Bakherden Turkmenistan *prev.*
Bakharden, *var.* Baharden,
Turkm. Bäherden 104 B3

Bākhtarān Iran *prev.*
Kermānshāh 102 C3

Bakı *see* Baku

Baku *capital of* Azerbaijan
Az. Bakı, *var.* Baky 99 H2

Baky *see* Baku

Balabac Strait *sea feature*
South China Sea/Sulu Sea
120 D2

Ba'labakk *see* Baalbek

Balakovo Russian Federation
93 C6

Bālā Morghāb Afghanistan
104 D4

Balaton *lake* Hungary *var.* Lake
Balaton, *Ger.* Plattensee
81 C7

Balaton, Lake *see* Balaton

Balbina, Represa *Reservoir*
Brazil 42 D2

Baleares, Islas *island group* Spain *Eng.* Balearic Islands 75 H3

Balearic Islands *see* Baleares, Islas

Bali *island* Indonesia 120 D5

Balikesir Turkey 98 A3

Balikpapan Indonesia 120 D4

Balkan Mountains *mountain range* Bulgaria *Bul.* Stara Planina 86 C2

Balkhash Kazakhstan 96 C5

Balkhash, Lake *see* Balkhash, Ozero

Balkhash, Ozero *lake* Kazakhstan *Eng.* Lake Balkhash 94 C3

Ballarat Australia 131 C7

Balsas *river* Mexico 33 E5

Bălţi Moldova 90 D3

Baltic Port *see* Paldiski

Baltic Sea Atlantic Ocean 67 C7

Baltimore Maryland, USA 23 F4

Baltischport *see* Paldiski

Baltiski *see* Paldiski

Bamako *capital of* Mali 56 D3

Bambari Central African Republic 58 D4

Bamenda Cameroon 58 B4

Banaba *island* Kiribati *prev.* Ocean Island 127 E2

Bandaaceh Indonesia 120 A3

Banda, Laut *see* Banda Sea

Banda Sea *sea feature* Pacific Ocean *Ind.* Laut Banda 121 F4

Bandar-e 'Abbās Iran 102 D4

Bandar-e Būshehr Iran 102 C4

Bandarlampung Indonesia *prev.* Tanjungkarang 120 C4

Bandarlampung Indonesia 120 C4

Bandar Seri Begawan *capital of* Brunei 120 D3

Bandon Oregon, USA 26 A3

Bandundu Congo (Zaire) 59 C6

Bandung Indonesia 120 C5

Bangalore India 114 D2

Banggai, Kepulauan *island group* Indonesia 121 E4

Banghāzī Libya *Eng.* Benghazi 53 G2

Bangka, Palau *island* Indonesia 120 C4

Bangkok *capital of* Thailand *Th.* Krung Thep 119 C5

Bangladesh *country* S Asia 117

Bangor Northern Ireland, UK 71 B5

Bangor Maine, USA 23 G2

Bangui *capital of* Central African Republic 59 C5

Bani *river* Mali 56 D3

Banī Suwayf *see* Beni Suef

Banja Luka Bosnia & Herzegovina 82 B3

Banjarmasin Indonesia 120 D4

Banjul *capital of* Gambia 56 B3

Banks Island *island* Canada 19 E2

Banks Islands *island group* Vanuatu, Pacific Ocean 126 D4

Banks Peninsula *peninsula* New Zealand 133 C6

Banks Strait *sea feature* Tasman Sea 131 C7

Banská Bystrica Slovakia *Ger.* Neusohl, *Hung.* Besztercebánya 81 C6

Bantry Bay *sea feature* Ireland 71 A6

Banyo Cameroon 58 B4

Banzare Seamounts *undersea feature* Indian Ocean 123 C7

Baotou China 109 F3

Baranavichy Belarus *Rus.* Baranovichi, *Pol.* Baranowicze 89 C6

Baranovichi *see* Baranavichy

Baranowicze *see* Baranavichy

Barbados *country* West Indies 37 H4

Barbuda *island* Antigua & Barbuda 37 G3

Barcaldine Australia 130 C4

Barcelona Spain 75 G2

Barcelona Venezuela 41 E1

Barcolod City Philippines 121 E2

Bareilly India 117 E3

Barentsburg Svalbard 65 F2

Barentsøya *island* Svalbard 65 G2

Barents Sea Arctic Ocean 137 H5

Bari Italy 79 E5

Barinas Venezuela 40 D2

Barisan, Pegunungan *mountains* Indonesia 120 B4

Barkly Tableland *plateau* Australia 130 B3

Barlavento, Ilhas de *island group* Cape Verde *var.* Windward Islands 56 A2

Bar-le-Duc France 72 D3

Barlee, Lake *lake* Australia 129 B 5

Barlee Range *mountain range* Australia 128 B4

Barnaul Russian Federation 96 D4

Barnstaple England, UK 71 C7

Barquisimeto Venezuela 40 D1

Barra *island* Scotland, UK 70 B3

Barranquilla Colombia 40 B1

Barrier Range *mountain range* Australia 131 C5

Barrow *river* Ireland 71 B6

Barstow California, USA 27 C7

Bartang *river* Tajikistan 105 F3

Bartica Guyana 41 G2

Baruun-Urt Mongolia 109 F2

Barwon River *river* Australia 131 D5

Barysaw Belarus *Rus.* Borisov 89 D5

Basarabeasca Moldova 90 D4

Basel Switzerland 77 B6

Basra *see* Al Başrah

Bassein Myanmar 118 A4

Basse-Terre *capital of* Guadeloupe 37 G4

Basseterre *capital of* St Kitts & Nevis 37 G3

Bass Strait *sea feature* Australia 131 C7

Bastia Corse, France 73 E7

Bastogne Belgium 69 D7

Bata Equatorial Guinea 58 A5

Batangas Philippines 121 E2

Bătdâmbâng Cambodia 119 D5

Bath England, UK 71 D6

Bathurst Canada 21 F4

Bathurst Island *island* Australia 128 D2

Bathurst Island *island* Canada 19 F2

Bāțin, Wādī al *dry watercourse* Asia 102 C4

Batman Turkey *var.* İluh 99 E4

Batna Algeria 53 E1

Baton Rouge Louisiana, USA 30 B3

Batticaloa Sri Lanka 115 E3

Bat'umi Georgia 99 F2

Bauru Brazil 44 D2

Bavarian Alps *mountains* Austria/Germany 77 C6

Bayamo Cuba 36 C2

Bayan Har Shan *mountain range* China 108 D4

Bayanhongor Mongolia 108 D2

Bay City Michigan, USA 22 C3

Baydhabo Somalia 55 D6

Baykal, Ozero *lake* Russian Federation *Eng.* Lake Baikal 95 E3

Bayonne France 73 A6

Bayramaly Turkmenistan 104 C3

Bayrūt *see* Beirut

Beaufort Sea Arctic Ocean 137 F2

Beaufort West South Africa 60 D5

Beaumont Texas, USA 29 H4

Beauvais France 72 C3

Béchar Algeria 52 C2

Be'ér Sheva' Israel 101 A6

Beijing *capital of* China *var.* Peking 110 C4

Beira Mozambique 61 E3

Beirut *capital of* Lebanon *var.* Beyrouth, Bayrūt 100 B4

Beja Portugal 74 C4

Béjaïa Algeria 53 E1

Bek-Budi *see* Karshi

Békéscsaba Hungary 81 D7

Belarus *country* E Europe *var.* Belorusia 89

Belau *see* Palau

Belcher Islands *islands* Canada 20 C2

Beledweyne Somalia 55 D5

Belém Brazil 43 F2

Belfast Northern Ireland, UK 71 B5

Belfort France 72 E4

Belgaum India 114 C1

Belgium *country* W Europe 69

Belgorod Russian Federation 93 A5

Belgrade *capital of* Yugoslavia *SCr.* Beograd 82 D3

Belitung, Pulau *island* Indonesia 120 C4

Belize *country* Central America 34

Belize City Belize 34 C1

Belle Île *island* France 72 A4

Belle Isle, Strait of *sea feature* Canada 21 G3

Bellevue Washington, USA 26 B3

Bellingham Washington, USA 26 B1

Bellingshausen Sea Antarctica 136 A3

Bello Colombia 40 B2

Bellville South Africa 60 C5

Belmopan *capital of* Belize 34 C1

Belo Horizonte Brazil 45 F1

Belorussia *see* Belarus

Belostok *see* Białystok

Beloye More Arctic Ocean *Eng.* White Sea 63 F1

Belyy, Ostrov *island* Russian Federation 137 H4

Bend Oregon, USA 26 B3

Bendery *see* Tighina

Bendigo Australia 131 C7

Benevento Italy 79 D5

Bengal, Bay of *sea feature* Indian Ocean 122 D3

Bengbu China 111 D5

Benghazi *see* Banghāzī

Bengkulu Indonesia 120 B4

Benguela Angola 60 B2

Beni *river* Bolivia 42 C4

Benidorm Spain 75 F4

Beni Mellal Morocco 52 C2

Benin *country* N Africa *prev.* Dahomey 57

Benin, Bight of *sea feature* W Africa 57 F5

Benin City Nigeria 57 F5

Beni Suef Egypt *var.* Banī Suwayf 54 B1

Ben Nevis *mountain* Scotland, UK 70 C4

Benue *river* Cameroon/Nigeria 57 G4

Beograd *see* Belgrade

Berat Albania 83 D6

Berbera Somalia 54 D4

Berbérati Central African Republic 58 C5

Berdyans'k Ukraine 91 G4

Berezina *see* Byerazino

Bergamo Italy 78 B2

Bergen Norway 67 A5

Bergse Maas *river* Netherlands 68 D4

Bering Sea Pacific Ocean 134 D1

Bering Strait *sea feature* Bering Sea/Chukchi Sea 134 D1

Berkeley California, USA 27 B6

Berlin *capital of* Germany 76 D3

Bermejo *river* Argentina 46 D2

Bermuda *external territory* UK Atlantic Ocean 48 B3

Bern *capital of* Switzerland *Fr.* Berne 77 B7

Berne *see* Bern

Berner Alpen *mountain range* Switzerland 77 B7

Bertoua Cameroon 59 B5

Besançon France 72 D4

Besztercebánya *see* Banská
Bystrica
Bethlehem West Bank 101 A5
Beyrouth *see* Beirut
Béziers France 73 C6
Bezmein *see* Byuzmeyin
Bhamo Myanmar 118 B2
Bhāvnagar India 116 C4
Bhōpal India 116 D4
Bhutan *country* S Asia 117
Biak, Pulau *island* Indonesia
121 G4
Białystok Poland *Rus.* Belostok
80 E3
Biel Switzerland 77 B7
Bielefeld Germany 76 B4
Bielitz-Biala *see* Bielsko-Biała
Bielsko-Biała Poland *Ger.*
Bielitz-Biala 81 C5
Bighorn Mountains *mountains*
C USA 24 C2
Bignona Senegal 56 B3
Big Spring Texas, USA 29 E3
Bihać Bosnia & Herzegovina
82 B3
Bihār *state* India 117 F3
Bijelo Polje Yugoslavia 82 D4
Bikāner India 116 C3
Bila Tserkva Ukraine 91 E2
Bilbao Spain 75 E1
Billings Montana, USA 24 C2
Bilma, Grand Erg de *desert*
Niger 57 G3
Biloela Australia 130 D4
Biloxi Mississippi, USA 30 C3
Biltine Chad 58 D3
Binghamton New York, USA
23 F3
Birāk Libya 53 F3
Biratnagar Nepal 117 F3
Birmingham England, UK
71 D6
Birmingham Alabama, USA
30 D2
Bîr Mogreïn Mauritania 56 C1
Birsen *see* Biržai
Biržai Lithuania *Ger.* Birsen
88 C4
Biscay, Bay of *sea feature*

Atlantic Ocean 62 C4
Bishkek *capital of* Kyrgyzstan
prev. Frunze, Pishpek 105 F2
Bishop California, USA 27 C6
Biskra Algeria 53 E2
Bismarck North Dakota, USA
25 E2
Bismarck Archipelago *island
group* Papua New Guinea
126 B3
Bismarck Sea *sea* Pacific Ocean
124 B3
Bissau *capital of* Guinea-Bissau
56 B4
Bitola Macedonia 83 E6
Bitterroot Range *mountains*
NW USA 26 D2
Biwa-ko *lake* Japan 113 C5
Bizerte Tunisia 53 E1
Bjelovar Croatia 82 B2
Bjørnøya *Island* N Norway *Eng.*
Bear Island 65 G3
Black Drin *river*
Albania/Macedonia 83 D5
Black Forest *see* Schwarzwald
Black Hills *mountains* C USA
24 D3
Blackpool England, UK 71 D5
Black River *river* China/Vietnam
118 D3
Black Sea Asia/Europe 63 F4
Black Volta *river* Ghana/Côte
d'Ivoire 57 E4
Blackwater *river* Ireland 71 A6
Blagoevgrad Bulgaria 86 C3
Blagoveshchensk Russian
Federation 97 G4
Blanca, Bahía *sea feature*
Argentina 39 D5
Blanche, Lake *lake* Australia
131 B5
Blantyre Malawi 61 E2
Blenheim New Zealand 133 D5
Blida Algeria 52 D1
Bloemfontein South Africa
60 D4
Blois France 72 C4
Bloomington Indiana, USA
22 C4
Bluefields Nicaragua 35 E3

Blue Mountains *mountains* W
USA 26 C2
Blue Nile *river* Ethiopia/Sudan
54 C4
Blumenau Brazil 44 D3
Bo Sierra Leone 56 C4
Boa Vista Brazil 42 D1
Boa Vista *island* Cape Verde
56 A3
Bobo-Dioulasso Burkina 56 D4
Bobruysk *see* Babruysk
Boca de la Serpiente *see*
Serpent's Mouth, The
Bochum Germany 76 B4
Bodø Norway 66 C3
Bodrum Turkey 98 A4
Bogor Indonesia 120 C5
Bogotá *capital of* Colombia
40 B3
Bo Hai *sea feature* Yellow Sea
110 D4
Bohemian Forest *region*
Germany 77 D5
Bohol Sea Philippines
121 E2
Boise Idaho, USA 26 D3
Boké Guinea 56 C4
Bokhara *see* Bukhoro
Bol Chad 58 B3
Bolivia *country* C South
America 42-43
Bologna Italy 78 C3
Bolton England, UK 71 D5
Bolzano Italy *Ger.* Bozen 78 C2
Boma Congo (Zaire) 59 B7
Bombay *see* Mumbai
Bomu *river* Central African
Republic/Congo (Zaire) 59 D5
Bongo, Massif des *upland*
Central African Republic
58 D4
Bongor Chad 58 C3
Bonn Germany 76 B4
Boosaaso Somalia 54 E4
Borås Sweden 67 B7
Bordeaux France 73 B5
Borger Texas, USA 29 E2
Borisov *see* Barysaw
Borlänge Sweden 67 C6

Borneo *island* SE Asia 120-121
Bornholm *island* Denmark 67 C8
Bosanski Šamac Bosnia & Herzegovina 82 C3
Bosna *river* Bosnia & Herzegovina 82 C3
Bosna I Hercegovina, Federacija Admin. region *republic* Bosnia and Herzegovina 82 C4
Bosnia & Herzegovina *country* SE Europe 82-83
Bosporus *sea feature* Turkey *Turk.* İstanbul Boğazi 98 B2
Bossangoa Central African Republic 58 C4
Bosten Hu *Lake* China 108 C3
Boston Massachusetts, USA 23 G3
Bothnia, Gulf of *sea feature* Baltic Sea 67 C5
Botoşani Romania 90 C3
Botswana *country* southern Africa 60
Bouar Central African Republic 58 C4
Bougainville Island *island* Papua New Guinea 126 C3
Bougouni Mali 56 D4
Boulder Colorado, USA 24 C4
Boulogne-sur-Mer France 72 C2
Bourges France 72 C4
Bourgogne *region* France *Eng.* Burgundy 72 D4
Bourke Australia 131 C5
Bournemouth England, UK 71 D7
Bouvet Island *external territory* Norway, Atlantic Ocean 49 D7
Bowen Australia 130 D3
Bowling Green Kentucky, USA 22 C5
Bozeman Montana, USA 24 B2
Bozen *see* Bolzano
Brač *island* Croatia 82 B4
Bradford England, UK 71 D5
Braga Portugal 74 C2
Bragança Portugal 74 C2
Brahmaputra *river* Asia 117 G3

Brăila Romania 90 D4
Brainerd Minnesota, USA 25 F2
Brandon Canada 19 F5
Brasília *capital of* Brazil 43 F4
Braşov Romania 90 C4
Bratislava *capital of* Slovakia *Ger.* Pressburg, *Hung.* Pozsony 81 C6
Bratsk Russian Federation 97 E4
Braunau am Inn Austria 77 D6
Braunschweig Germany *Eng.* Brunswick 76 C4
Brazil *country* South America 42-43
Brazil Basin *undersea feature* Atlantic Ocean 49 C5
Brazilian Highlands *upland* Brazil 43 G4
Brazos *river* SW USA 29 G3
Brazzaville *capital of* Congo 59 B6
Brecon Beacons *hills* Wales, UK 71 C6
Breda Netherlands 68 C4
Bregenz Austria 77 B7
Bremen Germany 76 B3
Bremerhaven Germany 76 B3
Brescia Italy 78 B2
Breslau *see* Wrocław
Brest Belarus *Pol.* Brześć nad Bugiem, *prev.* Brześć Litewski, *Rus.* Brest-Litovsk 89 B6
Brest France 72 A3
Brest-Litovsk *see* Brest
Bretagne *region* France *Eng.* Brittany 72 A3
Brezhnev *see* Naberezhnyye Chelny
Bria Central African Republic 58 D4
Bridgetown *capital of* Barbados 37 H4
Brig Switzerland 77 B5
Brighton England, UK 71 E7
Brindisi Italy 79 E5
Brisbane Australia 131 E5
Bristol England, UK 71 D6

British Columbia *province* Canada 18-19
British Indian Ocean Territory *external territory* UK, Indian Ocean 122 C4
British Isles *islands* W Europe 70-71
British Virgin Islands *external territory* UK, West Indies 37
Brittany *see* Bretagne
Brno Czech Republic *Ger.* Brünn 81 B5
Broken Arrow Oklahoma, USA 29 G1
Broken Hill Australia 131 B6
Broken Ridge *undersea feature* Indian Ocean 123 D6
Bromberg *see* Bydgoszcz
Brooks Range *mountains* Alaska, USA 18 D2
Brookton Australia 129 B6
Broome Australia 128 C3
Brownfield Texas, USA 29 E2
Brownsville Texas, USA 29 G5
Bruges *see* Brugge
Brugge Belgium *Fr.* Bruges 69 A5
Brunei *country* E Asia 120 D3
Brünn *see* Brno
Brunswick Georgia, USA 31 E3
Brunswick *see* Braunschweig
Brusa *see* Bursa
Brussel *see* Brussels
Brussels *capital of* Belgium *Fr.* Bruxelles, *Flem.* Brussel 69 C6
Brüx *see* Most
Bruxelles *see* Brussels
Bryan Texas, USA 29 G3
Bryansk Russian Federation 93 A5 96 A2
Brześć Litewski *see* Brest
Brześć nad Bugiem *see* Brest
Bucaramanga Colombia 40 C2
Buchanan Liberia 56 C5
Bucharest *capital of* Romania 90 C5
Budapest *capital of* Hungary 81 C6
Budweis *see* České Budějovice

Buenaventura Colombia 40 B3

Buenos Aires *capital of* Argentina 46 D4

Buenos Aires, Lago *lake* Argentina/Chile 47 B6

Buffalo New York, USA 23 E3

Bug *river* E Europe 90 C1

Bujumbura *capital of* Burundi *prev.* Usumbura 55 B7

Bukavu Congo (Zaire) 59 E6

Bukhara *see* Bukhoro

Bukhoro Uzbekistan *var.* Bokhara, *Rus.* Bukhara 104 D2

Bulawayo Zimbabwe 60 D3

Bulgan Mongolia 109 E2

Bulgaria *country* E Europe 86

Bumba Congo (Zaire) 59 D5

Bunbury Australia 129 B6

Bundaberg Australia 130 E4

Bunia Congo (Zaire) 59 E5

Buraydah Saudi Arabia 103 B5

Burē Ethiopia 54 C4

Burgas Bulgaria 86 E2

Burgos Spain 75 E2

Burgundy *see* Bourgogne

Burketown Australia 130 B3

Burkina *country* W Africa 57

Burlington Iowa, USA 25 G4

Burlington Vermont, USA 23 F2

Burma *see* Myanmar

Burnie Tasmania 131 C8

Burns Oregon, USA 26 C3

Bursa Turkey *prev.* Brusa 98 B3

Burtnieku Ezers *lake* Latvia 88 C3

Buru, Pulau *island* Indonesia 121 E4

Burundi *country* C Africa 55

Busselton Australia 129 B7

Butembo Congo (Zaire) 59 E5

Buton, Pulau *Island* Indonesia 121 E4

Butte Montana, USA 24 B2

Butuan Philippines 121 F2

Büyükağrı Dağı *see* Ararat, Mount

Buzău Romania 90 C4

Bydgoszcz Poland *Ger.* Bromberg 80 C3

Byerazino *river* Belarus *Rus.* Berezina 89 D6

Byuzmeyin Turkmenistan *prev.* Bezmein 104 B3

Byzantium *see* İstanbul

C

Caazapá Paraguay 44 C3

Cabanatuan Philippines 121 E1

Cabimas Venezuela 40 C1

Cabinda *exclave* Angola 60 B1

Cabot Strait *sea feature* Atlantic Ocean 21 G4

Čačak Yugoslavia 82 D4

Cáceres Spain 74 D3

Cachoeiro de Itapemirim Brazil 45 F1

Cadiz Philippines 121 E2

Cádiz Spain 74 D5

Caen France 72 B3

Cagayan de Oro Philippines 121 F2

Cagliari Italy 79 A5

Cahors France 73 B5

Cairns Australia 130 D3

Cairo *capital of* Egypt *Ar.* Al Qāhirah, *var.* El Qâhira 54 B1

Čakovec Croatia 82 B2

Calabar Nigeria 57 G5

Calabria *region* Italy 79 D6

Calafate *see* El Calafate

Calais France 72 C2

Calais Maine, USA 23 H1

Calama Chile 46 B2

Calbayog Philippines 121 F2

Calcutta India *var.* Kolkata 117 F4

Caldas da Rainha Portugal 74 B3

Caldwell Idaho, USA 27 C3

Caleta Olivia Argentina 47 C6

Calgary Canada 19 E5

Cali Colombia 40 A3

Calicut India *var.* Kozhikode 114 D2

California *state* USA 26-27

California, Golfo de *sea feature* Pacific Ocean *Eng.* California, Gulf of 32 C2 123 F2

Callabonna, Lake *lake* Australia131 B5

Callao Peru 42 A3

Caltanissetta Italy 79 C7

Camagüey Cuba 36 C2

Cambodia *country* SE Asia *Cam.* Kampuchea 119

Cambridge England, UK 71 E6

Cambridge New Zealand 132 D2

Cameroon *country* W Africa 58-59

Campbell Plateau *undersea feature* Pacific Ocean 134 C5

Campeche Mexico 33 G4

Campeche, Bahía de *sea feature* Mexico *Eng.* Gulf of Campeche 33 G4

Campina Grande Brazil 43 H3

Campinas Brazil 45 E2

Campo Grande Brazil 44 C1

Campos Brazil 45 F2

Canada *country* North America 16-17

Canada Basin *undersea feature* Arctic Ocean *var.* Laurentian Basin 137 F2

Canadian River *river* SW USA 29 E2

Çanakkale Turkey 98 A3

Çanakkale Boğazı *see* Dardanelles

Canarias, Islas *islands* Spain *Eng.* Canary Islands 50 A2

Canary Basin *undersea feature* Atlantic Ocean 48 C4

Canary Islands *see* Canarias, Islas

Canaveral, Cape *coastal feature* Florida, USA 31 F4

Canberra *capital of* Australia 131 D6

Cancún Mexico 33 H3

Caniapiscau *river* Canada 21 E2

Caniapiscau, Réservoir
Reservoir Canada 21 E3

Canik Dağları *mountains*
Turkey 98 D2

Çankırı Turkey 98 C2

Cannes France 73 D6

Canoas Brazil 44 D4

Canterbury England, UK 71 E6

Canterbury Bight *sea feature*
Pacific Ocean 133 C6

Canterbury Plains *plain* New
Zealand 133 B6

Cân Thơ Vietnam 119 D6

Canton Ohio, USA 22 D4

Canton *see* Guangzhou

Cape Basin *undersea feature*
Atlantic Ocean 49 C6

Cape Town South Africa 60 C5

Cape Verde *country* Atlantic
Ocean 52 A2

Cape Verde Basin *undersea
feature* Atlantic Ocean 48 C4

Cape York Peninsula *peninsula*
Australia 124 B3

Cap-Haïtien Haiti 36 D3

Capri, Isola di *island* Italy
79 D5

Caquetá *river* Colombia 40 C4

CAR *see* Central African
Republic

Caracas *capital of* Venezuela
40 D1

Carazinho Brazil 44 C3

Carbondale Illinois, USA 22 B5

Carcassonne France 73 C6

Cardiff Wales, UK 71 C6

Cardigan Bay *sea feature*
Wales, UK 71 C6

Carey, Lake *lake* Australia
129 C5

Caribbean Sea Atlantic Ocean
36-37

Carlisle England, UK 70 D4

Carlsbad New Mexico, USA
28 D3

Carlsberg Ridge *undersea
feature* Indian Ocean 122 B4

Carnavon Australia 128 A5

Carnegie, Lake *lake* Australia
129 C5

Carolina Brazil 43 F3

Caroline Island *see* Millennium
Island

Caroline Islands *island group*
Micronesia 126 B1

Caroni *river* Venezuela 41 F2

Carpathian Mountains
mountain range E Europe
var. Carpathians 63 E4

Carpathians *see* Carpathian
Mountains

Carpaţii Meridionali *mountain
range* Romania *Eng.* South
Carpathians, Transylvanian
Alps 90 B4

Carpentaria, Gulf of *sea feature*
Australia 130 B2

Carson City Nevada, USA 27 B5

Cartagena Colombia 40 B1

Cartagena Spain 75 F4

Cartago Costa Rica 35 E4

Cartwright Canada 21 G2

Carúpano Venezuela 41 E1

Casablanca Morocco 52 C2

Casa Grande Arizona, USA
28 B3

Cascade Range *mountain range*
Canada/USA 26 B2

Cascais Portugal 74 B3

Casper Wyoming, USA 24 C3

Caspian Sea *inland sea*
Asia/Europe 94 B4

Castelló de la Plana Spain
75 F3

Castelo Branco Portugal 74 C3

Castries *capital of* St Lucia 37
G4

Castro Chile 47 B6

Cat Island *island* Bahamas
36 D1

Catania Italy 79 D7

Catanzaro Italy 79 D6

Cauca *river* Colombia 40 B2

Caucasus *mountains*
Asia/Europe 93 A7

Caura *river* Venezuela 41 E2

Caviana, Ilha *island* Brazil
43 F1

Cawnpore *see* Kānpur

Caxias do Sul Brazil 44 D4

Cayenne *capital of* French
Guiana 41 H3

Cayman Islands *external
territory* UK, West Indies 36

Cebu Philippines 121 E2

Cedar Rapids Iowa, USA 25 G3

Cedros, Isla *island* Mexico
32 A2

Ceduna Australia 131 A6

Cefalù Italy 79 C6

Celebes *see* Sulawesi

Celebes Sea Pacific Ocean *Ind.*
Laut Sulawesi 134 B3

Celje Slovenia 77 E7

Central African Republic
country C Africa
abbrev. CAR 58-59

Central, Cordillera *mountain
range* Philippines 121 E1

Central Makrān Range
mountains Pakistan 116 A3

Central Pacific Basin *undersea
feature* Pacific Ocean 125 E1

Central Russian Upland *upland*
Russian Federation 94 B3

Central Siberian Plateau *see*
Srednesibirskoye Ploskogor'ye

Central Siberian Uplands *see*
Srednesibirskoye Ploskogor'ye

Central, Sistema *mountain
range* Spain 74 D3

Cephalonia *see* Kefallinía

Ceram Sea *see* Indonesia 121 F4

Cernăuţi *see* Chernivtsi

Cēsis Latvia *Ger.* Wenden
88 C3

České Budějovice Czech
Republic *Ger.* Budweis 81 B5

Ceuta *external territory* Spain,
N Africa 52 C1

Cévennes *mountains* France
73 C6

Ceylon *see* Sri Lanka

Ceylon Plain *undersea feature*
Indian Ocean 122 C4

Chad *country* C Africa 58

Chad, Lake *lake* C Africa 58 B3

Chāgai Hills *mountains* Pakistan 116 A2

Chagos-Laccadive Plateau *undersea feature* Indian Ocean 122 C4

Chagos Trench *undersea feature* Indian Ocean 122 C4

Chalkida Greece 87 C5

Challenger Deep *undersea feature* Pacific Ocean 134 B3

Châlons-en-Champagne France 72 D3

Chambéry France 73 D5

Champaign Illinois, USA 22 B4

Chañaral Chile 46 B2

Chandīgarh India 116 D2

Chang, Ko *island* Thailand 119 C5

Changchun China 110 D3

Chang Jiang *river* China *var.* Yangtze 111 B6

Changsha China 111 C6

Chaniá Greece 87 C7

Channel Islands *island group* California, USA 27 B8

Channel Islands *islands* UK 71 D8

Channel-Port-aux-Basques Canada 21 G4

Channel Tunnel France/UK 71 E7

Chapala, Lago de *lake* Mexico 32 D4

Chardzhev Turkmenistan *prev.* Chardzhou, *prev.* Leninsk, *Turkm.* Chärjew 104 D3

Chardzhou *see* Chardzhev

Chari *river* C Africa 58 C3

Chārīkār Afghanistan 105 E4

Chärjew *see* Chardzhev

Charleroi Belgium 69 C6

Charleston South Carolina, USA 31 F2

Charleston West Virginia, USA 22 D5

Charleville Australia 130 C4

Charlotte North Carolina, USA 31 F1

Charlotte Amalie *capital of* Virgin Islands 37 F3

Charlottesville Virginia, USA 23 E5

Charlottetown Canada 21 G4

Charters Towers Australia 130 D3

Chartres France 72 C3

Charus Nuur *lake* Mongolia 108 C2

Châteauroux France 72 C4

Chatham Islands *islands* New Zealand 134 D4

Chattanooga Tennessee, USA 30 D1

Chauk Myanmar 118 A3

Chaves Portugal 74 C2

Cheboksary Russian Federation 93 C5

Cheboygan Michigan, USA 22 C2

Chech, Erg *desert* Algeria/Mali 56 D1

Che-chiang *see* Zhejiang

Cheju-do *island* South Korea 111 E5

Cheju Strait *sea feature* South Korea 111 E5

Chekiang *see* Zhejiang

Cheleken Turkmenistan 104 A2

Chelyabinsk Russian Federation 96 C3

Chemnitz Germany *prev.* Karl-Marx-Stadt 76 D4

Chenāb *river* Pakistan 116 C2

Chengdu China 111 B5

Chennai India *prev.* Madras 115 E2

Cherbourg France 72 B3

Cherepovets Russian Federation 92 B4

Cherkasy Ukraine 91 E2

Cherkessk Russian Federation 93 A7

Chernigov *see* Chernihiv

Chernihiv Ukraine *Rus.* Chernigov 91 E1

Chernivtsi Ukraine *Rus.* Chernovtsy, *Rom.* Cernăuţi 90 C3

Chernobyl' *see* Chornobyl'

Chernovtsy *see* Chernivtsi

Chernyakhovsk Kaliningrad, Russian Federation 88 B4

Chesapeake Bay *sea feature* USA 23 F5

Chester England, UK 71 D5

Cheyenne Wyoming, USA 24 D4

Chiang-hsi *see* Jiangxi

Chiang Mai Thailand 118 B4

Chiang-su *see* Jiangsu

Chiba Japan 113 D5

Chicago Illinois, USA 22 B3

Chiclayo Peru 42 A3

Chico California, USA 27 B5

Chicoutimi Canada 21 E4

Chifeng China 109 F2

Chihli *see* Hebei

Chihuahua Mexico 32 C2

Chile *country* S South America 46-47

Chile Basin *undersea feature* Pacific Ocean 135 G4

Chile Chico Chile 47 B6

Chile Rise *undersea feature* Pacific Ocean 135 G4

Chi-lin *see* Jilin

Chillán Chile 46 B4

Chiloé, Isla de *island* Chile 47 B6

Chimborazo *peak* Ecuador 38 A3

Chimbote Peru 42 A3

Chimkent *see* Shymkent

Chimoio Mozambique 61 E3

China *country* E Asia 108-109

Chinandega Nicaragua 34 C3

Chindwin *river* Myanmar 118 A2

Chinghai *see* Qinghai

Chingola Zambia 60 D2

Chinook Trough *undersea feature* Pacific Ocean 134 D1

Chíos Greece 87 D5

Chíos *island* Greece *prev.* Khíos 87 D5

Chirchik Uzbekistan *Uzb.* Chirchiq 105 E2

Chirchiq *see* Chirchik

Chiriquí, Golfo de *sea feature* Panama 35 E5

Chişinău *capital of* Moldova, *var.* Kishinev 90 D3

Chita Russian Federation 97 F4

Chitré Panama 35 F5

Chittagong Bangladesh 117 G4

Chitungwiza Zimbabwe 60 D3

Choluteca Honduras 34 C3

Choma Zambia 60 D3

Chona *river* Russian Federation 95 E2

Chon Buri Thailand 119 C5

Ch'ŏngjin North Korea 110 E3

Chongqing *province* China *var.* Chungking 111 B5

Chonos, Archipiélago de los *island group* Chile 47 B6

Chornobyl' Ukraine *Rus.* Chernobyl 91 E1

Choûm Mauritania 56 C2

Choybalsan Mongolia 109 F2

Christchurch New Zealand 133 C6

Christmas Island *external territory* Australia, Indian Ocean 122 D5

Christmas Island *see* Kiritimati

Christmas Ridge *undersea feature* Pacific Ocean 125 F1

Chuan *see* Sichuan

Chubut *river* Argentina 47 B6

Chudskoye Ozero *see* Peipus, Lake

Chuí *see* Chuy

Chukchi Plain *undersea feature* Arctic Ocean 137 G2

Chukchi Sea Arctic Ocean *Rus.* Chukotskoye More 137 F1

Chukotskoye More *see* Chukchi Sea

Chula Vista California, USA 27 C8

Chulym *river* Russian Federation 94 D3

Chumphon Thailand 119 C6

Chungking *see* Chongqing

Chuquicamata Chile 46 B2

Chur Switzerland 77 B7

Churchill Canada 19 G4

Chuuk Islands *island group* Micronesia 126 B1

Chuy Brazil *var.* Chuí 44 C5

Cienfuegos Cuba 36 B2

Cieza Spain 75 F4

Cilacap Indonesia 120 C5

Cincinnati Ohio, USA 22 C4

Cirebon Indonesia 120 C5

Ciudad Bolívar Venezuela 41 E2

Ciudad del Este Paraguay 44 C3

Ciudad de México *see* Mexico City

Ciudad Guayana Venezuela 41 E2

Ciudad Juárez Mexico 32 C1

Ciudad Obregón Mexico 32 B2

Ciudad Ojeda Venezuela 40 C1

Ciudad Real Spain 75 E3

Ciudad Valles Mexico 33 E3

Ciudad Victoria Mexico 33 E3

Clarence *river* New Zealand 133 C5

Clarion Fracture Zone *tectonic feature* Pacific Ocean 125 G1

Clarksville Tennessee, USA 30 D1

Clearwater Florida, USA 31 E4

Clermont Australia 130 D4

Clermont-Ferrand France 73 C5

Cleveland Ohio, USA 22 D3

Clipperton Fracture Zone *tectonic feature* Pacific Ocean 125 G2

Clipperton Island *external territory* France, Pacific Ocean 135 F3

Cloncurry Australia 130 C3

Clovis New Mexico, USA 29 E2

Cluj-Napoca Romania 90 B3

Clutha *river* New Zealand 133 B7

Coast Ranges *mountain range* W USA 26 A5

Coats Island *island* Canada 20 C1

Coats Land *physical region* Antarctica 136 B2

Coatzacoalcos Mexico 33 G4

Cobán Guatemala 34 B2

Cochabamba Bolivia 42 C4

Cochin India 114 D3

Cochrane Canada 20 C4

Cochrane Chile 47 B6

Coco *river* Honduras/Nicaragua 34 D2

Cocos Basin *undersea feature* Indian Ocean 122 D4

Cocos Islands *external territory* Australia, Indian Ocean 122 D5

Cod, Cape *coastal feature* NE USA 23 G3

Coeur d'Alene Idaho, USA 26 C2

Coffs Harbour Australia 131 E6

Coihaique Chile 47 B6

Coimbatore India 114 D3

Coimbra Portugal 74 C3

Colchester England, UK 71 E6

Colmar France 72 E4

Cologne *see* Köln

Colombia *country* N South America 40-41

Colombo *capital of* Sri Lanka 115 E4

Colón Panama 35 F4

Colón, Archipiélago de *see* Galapagos Islands

Colorado *state* USA 24 C4

Colorado *river* USA 16 B5

Colorado *river* Argentina 47 C5

Colorado Plateau *upland region* S USA 28 B1

Colorado Springs Colorado, USA 24 D4

Columbia South Carolina, USA 31 F2

Columbia *river* NW USA 26 C1

Columbus Georgia, USA 30 D3

Columbus Mississippi, USA 30 C2

Columbus Nebraska, USA 25 E4

Columbus Ohio, USA 22 D4

Comayagua Honduras 34 C2

Comilla Bangladesh 117 G4

Communism Peak *peak* Tajikistan *Rus.* Pik Kommunizma, *prev.* Stalin Peak, Garmo Peak 105 F3

Czech Republic *country* C
Europe 80-81

Częstochowa Poland *Ger.*
Tschenstochau 80 C4

Człuchów Poland 80 C3

D

Dacca *see* Dhaka

Dagden *see* Hiiumaa

Dagö *see* Hiiumaa

Dagupan Philippines 121 E1

Da Hinggan Ling *mountain
range* China *Eng.* Great
Khingan Range 109 G1

Dahomey *see* Benin

Dakar *capital of* Senegal 56 B3

Đakovo Croatia 82 C3

Dalaman Turkey 98 B4

Dalandzadgad Mongolia 109 E3

Đa Lat Vietnam 119 E5

Dalby Australia 131 D5

Dalian China 110 D4

Dallas Texas, USA 129 G3

Dalmacija *region* Croatia 82 B4

Daly Waters Australia 128 E3

Damān India 116 C5

Damas *see* Damascus

Damascus Syria *var.* Esh Sham,
Fr. Damas, *Ar.* Dimashq
100 B4

Dampier Australia 128 B4

Damxung China 108 C5

Đa Nâng Vietnam 119 E4

Dandong China 110 D4

Daneborg Greenland 65 E3

Dangara Tajikistan 105 E3

Danmarksstraedet *see*
Denmark Strait

Danube *river* C Europe 63 E4

Danville Virginia, USA 23 E5

Danzig *see* Gdańsk

Danzig, Gulf of *76 C2 Gulf*
Poland 80 C2

Darã Syria 101 B5

Dardanelles *sea feature* Turkey
Turk. Çanakkale Boğazı
98 A2

Dar es Salaam Tanzania 55 C7

Darfur *Cultural region* Sudan
54 A4

Darhan Mongolia 109 E2

Darien, Gulf of *sea feature*
Caribbean Sea 35 G5

Darling *river* Australia 131 C6

Darmstadt Germany 77 B5

Darnah Libya 53 H2

Dartmoor *region* England, UK
71 C7

Dartmouth Canada 21 F4

Darwin Australia 128 D2

Dashhowuz *see* Dashkhovuz

Dashkhovuz Turkmenistan
prev. Tashauz, *Trkm.*
Dashhowuz 104 C2

Datong China 110 C4

Daugava *see* Western Dvina

Daugavpils Latvia *Ger.*
Dünaburg, *Rus.* Dvinsk 88 D4

Dāvangere India 114 D2

Davao Philippines 121 F3

Davao Gulf *gulf* Philippines
121 F3

Davenport Iowa, USA 25 G3

David Panama 35 E5

Davie Ridge *undersea feature*
Indian Ocean 123 A5

Davis Sea Indian Ocean 136 D3

Davis Strait *sea feature*
Atlantic Ocean 64 C3

Dayr az Zawr Syria 100 D3

Dayton Ohio, USA 22 C4

Daytona Beach Florida, USA
31 F4

Dead Sea *salt lake* SW Asia *Ar.*
Al Bahr al Mayyit, Bahrat Lūt,
Heb. Yam HaMelah 101 B5

Debrecen Hungary *prev.*
Debreczen, *Ger.* Debreczin
81 D6

Debreczen *see* Debrecen

Debreczin *see* Debrecen

Decatur Illinois, USA 22 B4

Deccan *plateau* India 106 B3
115 D1

Děčín Czech Republic *Ger.*
Tetschen 80 B4

Dej Romania 90 B3

Delaware *state* USA 23 F4

Delémont Switzerland 77 A7

Delft Netherlands 68 C4

Delfzijl Netherlands 68 E1

Delhi India 116 D3

Del Rio Texas, USA 29 F4

Demchok *disputed region*
China/India *var.* Dêmqog
108 B4

Demopolis Alabama, USA *30 C2*

Dêmqog *see* Demchok

Denali *see* Mount McKinley

Denham Australia 129 A5

Den Helder Netherlands 68 C2

Denizli Turkey 98 B4

Denmark *country* NW Europe
67

Denmark Strait *sea feature*
Greenland/Iceland *var.*
Danmarksstraedet 65 C4

Denpasar Indonesia 120 D5

Denton Texas, USA 29 G2

Denver Colorado, USA 24 D4

Dera Ghāzi Khān Pakistan
116 C2

Derby England, UK 71 D6

Derg, Lough *lake* Ireland 71 B6

Desē Ethiopia 54 C4

Deseado *river* Argentina 47 C6

Des Moines Iowa, USA 25 F3

Despoto Planina *see* Rhodope
Mountains

Dessau Germany 76 D4

Detroit Michigan, USA 22 D3

Deutschendorf *see* Poprad

Deva Romania 90 B4

Deventer Netherlands 68 D3

Devolli, Lumi i *river* Albania
83 D6

Devon Island *island* Canada
19 F2

Devonport Tasmania, Australia
131 C8

Dezfūl Iran 102 C3

Dhaka *capital of* Bangladesh
var. Dacca 117 G4

Dhanbād India 117 F4

Dhrepanon, Ákra *see* Drépano, Akrotírio

Diamantina Fracture Zone *tectonic feature* Indian Ocean 123 E6

Dickinson North Dakota, USA 24 D2

Diekirch Luxembourg 69 D7

Dieppe France 72 C3

Digul *River* Indonesia 121 H5

Dijon France 72 D4

Dikson Taymyrskiy (Dolgano-Nenetskiy) Russian Federation 137 H4

Dili *capital of* East Timor 121 F5

Dilling Sudan 54 B4

Dilolo Congo (Zaire) 59 D8

Dimashq *see* Damascus

Dimitrovo *see* Pernik

Dinant Belgium 69 C7

Dinaric Alps *mountains* Bosnia & Herzegovina/Croatia 82 B4

Diourbel Senegal 56 B3

Dirê Dawa Ethiopia 55 D5

Dirk Hartog Island *island* Australia 129 A5

Disappointment, Lake *salt lake* Australia 128 C4

Dispur India 117 G3

Divinópolis Brazil 45 F1

Diyarbakır Turkey 99 E4

Dkaraganda *see* Zhezkazgan

Djambala Congo 59 B6

Djibouti *country* E Africa 54

Djibouti *capital of* Djibouti *var.* Jibuti 54 D4

Dnieper *river* E Europe 63 F4

Dniester *river* Moldova/Ukraine 90 D3

Dnipropetrovs'k Ukraine 91 F3

Dobele Latvia *Ger.* Doblen 88 C3

Doberai, Jazirah *Peninsula* Indonesia 121 G4

Doblen *see* Dobele

Doboj Bosnia & Herzegovina 82 C3

Dobrich Bulgaria 86 E1

Dodecanese *see* Dodekánisos

Dodekánisos *islands* Greece *Eng.* Dodecanese 87 E6

Dodge City Kansas, USA 25 E5

Dodoma *capital of* Tanzania 55 C7

Doğu Karadeniz Dağlarıi *mountains* Turkey *var.* Anadolu Dağları 99 E2

Doha *capital of* Qatar *Ar.* Ad Dawhah 103 C5

Dolisie Congo 59 B6

Dolomites *see* Dolomitiche, Alpi

Dolomitiche, Alpi *mountains* Italy *Eng.* Dolomites 78 C2

Dolores Argentina 46 D4

Dolores Hidalgo Mexico 33 E4

Dominica *country* West Indies 37

Dominican Republic *country* West Indies 37

Don *river* Russian Federation 93 B6 96 A3

Donegal Bay *sea feature* Ireland 71 A5

Donets *river* Russian Federation/Ukraine 93 A6

Donets'k Ukraine 91 G3

Dongguan China 111 C6

Dongola Sudan 54 B3

Donostia *see* San Sebastián

Dordogne *river* France 73 B5

Dordrecht Netherlands 68 C4

Dorpat *see* Tartu

Dortmund Germany 76 B4

Dothan Alabama, USA 30 D3

Douai France 72 D3

Douala Cameroon 59 A5

Douglas UK 71 C5

Douglas Arizona, USA 28 C3

Dourados Brazil 44 C2

Douro *river* Portugal/Spain *Sp.* Duero 74 C2

Dover England, UK 71 E7

Dover Delaware, USA 23 F4

Drakensberg *mountain range* Lesotho/South Africa 60 D5

Drake Passage *sea feature* Atlantic Ocean/Pacific Ocean 39 C8

Dráma Greece 86 C3

Drammen Norway 67 B6

Drau *river* C Europe *var.* Drava 77 D7 82 C3

Drava *river* C Europe *var.* Drau 81 C7

Drépano, Akrotírio *coastal feature* Greece *var.* Dhrepanon Ákra 86 C4

Dresden Germany 76 D4

Drina *river* Bosnia & Herzegovina/Yugoslavia 82 D4

Drobeta-Turnu Severin Romania *prev.* Turnu Severin 90 B4

Dronning Maud Land *region* Antarctica 137 B1

Druskieniki *see* Druskininkai

Druskininkai Lithuania *Pol.* Druskieniki 89 B5

Dubayy United Arab Emirates 103 D5

Dubăsari Moldova 90 D3

Dubawnt *river* Canada 19 F4

Dubbo Australia 131 D6

Dublin *capital of* Ireland 71 B5

Dubrovnik Croatia 83 C5

Dubuque Iowa, USA 25 G3

Duero *river* Portugal/Spain *Port.* Douro 74 D2

Dugi Otok *island* Croatia 82 A4

Duisburg Germany 76 A4

Dulan China 108 D4

Duluth Minnesota, USA 25 F2

Dumfries Scotland, UK 70 C4

Düna *see* Western Dvina

Dünaburg *see* Daugavpils

Dundalk Ireland 71 B5

Dundee Scotland, UK 70 D3

Dunedin New Zealand 133 B7

Dunkerque France *Eng.* Dunkirk 72 C2

Dunkirk *see* Dunkerque

Duqm Oman 103 E6

Durango Mexico 32 D3

Durango Colorado, USA 24 C5
Durazno Uruguay 44 C5
Durban South Africa 60 E4
Durham North Carolina, USA 31 F1
Durrës Albania 83 C5
Dushanbe *capital of* Tajikistan *var.* Dyushambe, *prev.* Stalinabad 105 E3
Düsseldorf Germany 76 A4
Dutch Harbor Alaska, USA 18 B3
Dutch West Indies *see* Netherland Antilles
Dvinsk *see* Daugavpils
Dyushambe *see* Dushanbe
Dzaudzhikau *see* Vladikavkaz
Dzhalal-Abad Kyrgyzstan *Kir.* Jalal-Abad 105 F2
Dzhambul *see* Taraz
Dzhezkazgan *see* Zhezkazgan
Dzvina *see* Western Dvina

E

Eagle Pass Texas, USA 29 F4
East Cape *coastal feature* New Zealand 132 E2
East China Sea Pacific Ocean 111 E5
Easter Fracture Zone *tectonic feature* Pacific Ocean 135 G4
Easter Island *island* Pacific Ocean 135 F4
Eastern Ghats *mountain range* India 117 B5
Eastern Sierra Madre *see* Sierra Madre Oriental
East Falkland *island* Falkland Islands 47 D7
East Indiaman Ridge *undersea feature* Indian Ocean 123 D5
East Indies *island group* Asia 122 E4
East London South Africa 60 D5
Eastmain *river* Canada 20 D3

East Pacific Rise *undersea feature* Pacific Ocean 135 F4
East Siberian Sea *see* Vostochno-Sibirskoye More
East St Louis Illinois, USA 22 B4
East Novaya Zemlya Trench *var.* Novaya Zemlya Trench. *Undersea feature* Kara Sea 137 H4
Eau Claire Wisconsin, USA 22 A2
Ebolowa Cameroon 59 B5
Ebro *river* Spain 75 F2
Ecuador *country* NW South America 40
Ede Netherlands 68 D3
Ede Nigeria 57 F4
Edgeøya *island* Svalbard 65 G2
Edinburgh Scotland, UK 70 C4
Edirne Turkey 98 A2
Edmonton Canada 19 E5
Edward, Lake *lake* Uganda/Congo (Zaire) 59 E6
Edwards Plateau *upland* S USA 29 F4
Efate *Island* Vanuatu *prev.* Sandwich Island 124 D4
Effingham Illinois, USA 22 B4
Eforie-Sud Romania 90 D5
Egadi, Isole *island group* Italy 79 B6
Ege Denizi *see* Aegean Sea
Eger *see* Ohře
Egypt *country* NE Africa 54
Eighty Mile Beach *beach* Australia 128 C3
Eindhoven Netherlands 69 D5
Eisenstadt Austria 77 E6
Eivissa *island* Spain *Cast.* Ibiza 75 G4
Ejin Qi China 108 D3
Elat Israel 101 B7
Elâzığ Turkey 99 E3
Elba, Isola d' *island* Italy 78 B4
Elbasan Albania 83 D6
Elbe *river* Czech Republic/Germany 81 B5
Elbing *see* Elbląg
Elbląg Poland *Ger.* Elbing 80 D2

El'brus *peak* Russian Federation 93 A7
El Calafate Argentina *var.* Calafate 47 B7
Elche Spain 75 F4
Elda Spain 75 F4
Eldoret Kenya 55 C6
Eleuthera *island* Bahamas 36 C1
El Fasher Sudan *var.* Al Fāshir 54 A4
El Geneina Sudan 54 A4
Elgin Scotland, UK 70 C3
El Gîza Egypt *var.* Al Jīzah 54 B1
El Ḥank *cliff* Mauritania 56 D1
Elista Russian Federation 93 B6
El Khalīl *see* Hebron
El Khārga Egypt *var.* Al Khārijah 54 B2
Elko Nevada, USA 27 D5
Ellensburg Washington, USA 26 B2
Ellesmere Island *island* Canada 19 F1
Ellsworth Land *region* Antarctica 136 A3
El Minya Egypt 54 B2
Elmira New York, USA 23 E3
El Mreyyé *desert* Mauritania 56 D2
El Obeid Sudan 54 B4
El Paso Texas, USA 28 D3
El Puerto de Santa María Spain 74 D5
El Qâhira *see* Cairo
El Salvador *country* Central America 34
Eltanin Fracture Zone *tectonic feature* Pacific Ocean 135 E5
El Tigre Venezuela 41 E2
Ely Nevada USA 27 D5
Emden Germany 76 B3
Emerald Australia 130 D4
Emmen Netherlands 68 E2
Empty Quarter *see* Ar Rub' al Khali
Ems *river* Germany/Netherlands 76 B3

Fayetteville North Carolina, USA 31 F1

Fdérik Mauritania 56 C1

Fear, Cape coastal feature North Carolina, USA 31 G2

Fehmarn island Germany 76 C2

Fehmarn Belt sea feature Germany 76 C2

Feira de Santana Brazil 43 G3

Fellin see Viljandi

Fénérive see Fenoarivo

Fengtien see Liaoning

Fenoarivo Madagascar prev. Fénérive 61 G3

Fens, The wetland England, UK 71 E6

Fergana Uzbekistan prev. Novyy Margilan, Uzb. Farghona 105 F2

Ferrara Italy 78 C3

Ferrol Spain 74 C1

Fès Morocco Eng. Fez 52 C2

Feyzābād Afghanistan var. Faizabad 105 E3

Fez see Fès

Fianarantsoa Madagascar 61 G3

Fier Albania 83 D6

Figueira da Foz Portugal 74 C3

Figueres Spain 75 G2

Figuig Morocco 52 D2

Fiji country Pacific Ocean 127

Finland country N Europe 66-67

Finland, Gulf of sea feature Baltic Sea 67 E6

Fiordland physical region New Zealand 133 A7

Firenze Italy Eng. Florence 78 C3

Fishguard Wales, UK 71 C6

Fitzroy river Australia 128 C3

Fitzroy Crossing Australia 128 D3

Fiume see Rijeka

Flagstaff Arizona, USA 28 B2

Flanders region Belgium 69 A5

Flensburg Germany 76 B2

Flinders Island island Australia 131 C7

Flinders Ranges mountain range Australia 131 B6

Flinders River river Australia 130 C3

Flin Flon Canada 19 F5

Flint Michigan, USA 22 C3

Flint Island island Kiribati 127 H4

Florence Alabama, USA 30 C2

Florence South Carolina, USA 31 F2

Florence see Firenze

Florencia Colombia 40 B3

Flores Guatemala 34 B1

Flores island Indonesia 121 E5

Flores, Laut see Flores Sea

Flores Sea Pacific Ocean Ind. Laut Flores 121 E5

Florianópolis Brazil 44 D3

Florida state USA 31 E4

Florida, Straits of sea feature Bahamas/USA 31 F5 36 B1

Florida Keys island chain Florida, USA 31 F5

Flórina Greece 86 B3

Flushing see Vlissingen

Foča Bosnia & Herzegovina 82 C4

Focşani Romania 90 C4

Foggia Italy 79 D5

Fogo island Cape Verde 56 A3

Foligno Italy 78 C4

Fongafale capital of Tuvalu 127 E3

Fonseca, Gulf of sea feature El Salvador/Honduras 34 C3

Forlì Italy 78 C3

Formentera island Spain 75 G4

Former Yugoslav Republic of Macedonia see Macedonia

Formosa Argentina 46 D2

Formosa see Taiwan

Formosa Strait see Taiwan Strait

Fóroyar see Faeroe Islands

Fortaleza Brazil 43 H2

Fortescue River river Australia 128 B4

Fort Collins Colorado, USA 24 D4

Fort-de-France capital of Martinique 37 G4

Forth river Scotland, UK 70 C4

Forth, Firth of inlet Scotland, UK 70 D4

Fort Lauderdale Florida, USA 31 F5

Fort McMurray Canada 19 F4

Fort Myers Florida, USA 31 E4

Fort Peck Lake lake Montana, USA 24 C1

Fort Saint John Canada 19 E4

Fort Smith Canada 19 E4

Fort Smith Arkansas, USA 30 A1

Fort Wayne Indiana, USA 22 C4

Fort William Scotland, UK 70 C3

Fort Worth Texas, USA 29 G3

Foveaux Strait sea feature New Zealand 133 A7

Fox Glacier New Zealand 133 B6

Franca Brazil 45 E1

France country W Europe 72-73

Francistown Botswana 60 D3

Frankfort Kentucky, USA 22 C5

Frankfurt see Frankfurt am Main

Frankfurt am Main Germany Eng. Frankfurt 77 B5

Frankfurt an der Oder Germany 76 D5

Fränkische Alb mountains Germany 77 C6

Frantsa-Iosifa, Zemlya islands Russian Federation Eng. Franz Josef Land 137 G4

Franz Josef Land see Frantsa-Iosifa, Zemlya

Fraser Island island Australia 130 E4

Frauenburg see Saldus

Fray Bentos Uruguay 44 B5

Fredericksburg Virginia, USA 23 E4

Fredericton Canada 21 F4

Frederikshavn Denmark 67 B7

Fredrikstad Norway 67 B6

Freeport Bahamas 36 C1

Freeport Texas, USA 29 G4

Freetown *capital of* Sierra Leone 56 C4

Freiburg im Breisgau Germany 77 B6

Fremantle Australia 129 B6

French Guiana *external territory* France, N South America 41

French Polynesia *external territory* France, Pacific Ocean 135 E3

French Southern and Antarctic Territories *French overseas territory* Indian Ocean *Fr.* Terres Australes et Antarctiques Françaises 123 C7

Fresnillo Mexico 32 D1

Fresno California, USA 27 B6

Frome, Lake *salt lake* Australia 131 B5

Frunze *see* Bishkek

Fu-chien *see* Fujian

Fuerte Olimpo Paraguay 44 B1

Fuerteventura *island* Spain 52 A3

Fuhkien *see* Fujian

Fujian *province* China *var.* Fu-chien, Fuhkien, Fukien, Min 111 D6

Fukien *see* Fujian

Fukui Japan 113 C5

Fukuoka Japan 113 A6

Fukushima Japan 112 D4

Fulda Germany 77 C5

Fünfkirchen *see* Pécs

Fushun China 110 D3

Furnas, Represa de *Reservoir* Brazil 45 E1

Fuxin China 110 D3

Fuzhou China 111 D6

FYR Macedonia *see* Macedonia

G

Gaalkacyo Somalia 55 E5

Gabès Tunisia 53 E2

Gabon *country* W Africa 59

Gaborone *capital of* Botswana 60 D4

Gabrovo Bulgaria 86 D2

Gadsden Alabama, USA 30 D2

Gaeta, Golfo di *sea feature* Italy 79 C5

Gafsa Tunisia 53 E2

Gagnoa Côte d'Ivoire 56 D5

Gagra Georgia 99 E1

Gairdner, Lake *lake* Australia 131 B6

Galapagos Fracture Zone *tectonic feature* Pacific Ocean 135 F3

Galapagos Islands *islands* Ecuador, Pacific Ocean *var.* Tortoise Islands, *Sp.* Archipiélago de Colón 135 G3

Galapagos Rise *undersea feature* Pacific Ocean 135 G3

Galați Romania 90 D4

Galesburg Illinois, USA 22 B4

Galicia *region* Spain 74 C1

Galilee, Sea of *see* Tiberias, Lake

Galle Sri Lanka 115 E4

Gallego Rise *undersea feature* Pacific Ocean 135 F3

Gallipoli Italy 79 E5

Gällivare Sweden 66 D3

Gallup New Mexico, USA 28 C2

Galveston Texas, USA 29 G4

Galway Ireland 71 A5

Gambia *country* W Africa 56

Gambia *River* Africa 56 C3

Gambier, Îles *island group* French Polynesia 135 E4

Gan *see* Gansu

Gan *see* Jiangxi

Gand *see* Gent

Gander Canada 21 H3

Gandia Spain 75 F3

Ganges *river* S Asia 116 F4

Ganges Fan *Undersea feature* Bay of Bengal 122 D3

Ganges, Mouths of the *wetlands* Bangladesh/India 117 G4

Gangtok India 117 G3

Gansu *province* China *var.* Gan, Kansu 111 B5

Gao Mali 57 E3

Gaoual Guinea 56 C4

Gar China 108 A4

Garagum *see* Karakumy

Garagum Kanaly *see* Karakumskiy Kanal

Garagumy *desert* Turkmenistan *var.* Kara Kum, Karakumy 104 C2

Garda, Lago di *lake* Italy 78 B2

Gardēz Afghanistan 105 E4

Garissa Kenya 55 C6

Garmo Peak *see* Communism Peak

Garonne *river* France 73 B5

Garoowe Somalia 55 E5

Garoua Cameroon 58 B4

Gary Indiana, USA 22 B3

Gaspé Canada 21 F4

Gastonia North Carolina, USA 31 E1

Gävle Sweden 67 C5

Gaya India 117 F4

Gaza Gaza Strip 101 A6

Gazandzhik Turkmenistan *var.* Kazandzhik, *Turkm.* Gazanjyk 104 B2

Gazanjyk *see* Gazandzhik

Gaza Strip *disputed territory* SW Asia 101 A6

Gaziantep Turkey *prev.* Aintab 98 D4

Gazimağusa Cyprus *var.* Famagusta *Gk.* Ammochostos 98 C5

Gdańsk Poland *Ger.* Danzig 80 C2

Gdingen *see* Gdynia

Gdynia Poland *Ger.* Gdingen 80 C2

Gedaref Sudan 54 C4

Geelong Australia 131 C7

Gëkdepe Turkmenistan *prev.* Geok-Tepe, *Turkm.* Gökdepe 104 B3

Gemena Congo (Zaire) 59 C5
General Eugenio A. Garay Paraguay 44 A1
General Santos Philippines 121 F3
Geneva see Genève
Geneva, Lake lake France/Switzerland Fr. Lac Léman, var. Le Léman, Ger. Genfer See 77 A7
Genève Switzerland Eng. Geneva 77 A7
Genfer See see Geneva, Lake
Genk Belgium 69 D5
Genoa see Genova
Genova Italy Eng. Genoa 78 B3
Genova, Golfo di sea feature Italy 78 B3
Gent Belgium Fr. Gand, Eng. Ghent 69 B5
Geok-Tepe see Gëkdepe
George South Africa 60 D5
George V Land physical region Antarctica 134 C4
Georgenburg see Jurbarkas
George Town capital of Cayman Islands 36 B3
Georgetown capital of Guyana 41 G2
George Town Malaysia 120 B3
Georgia country SW Asia 99 F2
Georgia state USA 31 E3
Gera Germany 76 C4
Geraldton Australia 129 A5
Gereshk Afghanistan 104 D5
Germany country W Europe 76-77
Getafe Spain 75 E3
Gettysburg Pennsylvania, USA 23 E4
Gevgelija Macedonia 83 E6
Ghana country W Africa 57
Ghanzi Botswana 60 C3
Ghardaïa Algeria 52 D2
Gharyān Libya 53 F2
Ghaznī Afghanistan 105 E4
Ghent see Gent
Gibraltar external territory UK, SW Europe 74 D5

Gibson Desert desert region Australia 128 C4
Gijón Spain 74 D1
Gilbert Islands see Tungaru
Gilbert River river Australia 130 C3
Gillette Wyoming, USA 24 C3
Gingin Australia 129 B6
Girin see Jilin
Girne Cyprus var. Kyrenia 98 C5
Girona Spain 75 G2
Gisborne New Zealand 132 E3
Giurgiu Romania 90 C5
Gjirokastër Albania 83 D6
Gjøvik Norway 67 B5
Glasgow Scotland, UK 70 C4
Gleiwitz see Gliwice
Glendale Arizona, USA 28 B2
Glendive Montana, USA 24 D2
Gliwice Poland Ger. Gleiwitz 81 C5
Gloucester England, UK 71 D6
Glubokoye see Hlybokaye
Gobi desert China/Mongolia 108 D3
Godāveri river India 106 B3 115 E1
Godoy Cruz Argentina 46 B4
Godthåb see Nuuk
Godwin Austin, Mount see K2
Goiânia Brazil 43 F4
Gökdepe see Gëkdepe
Golan Heights disputed territory SW Asia 100 B4
Gold Coast coastal region Australia 131 E5
Goldingen see Kuldiga
Golmud China 108 D4
Goma Congo (Zaire) 59 E6
Gomel' see Homyel'
Gómez Palacio Mexico 32 D2
Gonaïves Haiti 36 D3
Gonder Ethiopia 54 C4
Gongola river Nigeria 57 G4
Good Hope, Cape of coastal feature South Africa 60 C5
Goondiwindi Australia 131 D5
Goose Lake lake W USA 26 B4

Goré Chad 58 C4
Gorē Ethiopia 55 C5
Gore New Zealand 133 B7
Gorgān Iran 102 D3
Gorki see Horki
Gor'kiy see Nizhniy Novgorod
Gorlovka see Horlivka
Gorontalo Indonesia 121 E4
Gorzów Wielkopolski Poland Ger. Landsberg 80 B3
Gospić Croatia 82 B3
Gosford Australia 131 D6
Gostivar Macedonia 83 D5
Göteborg Sweden 67 B7
Gotel Mountains mountain range Nigeria 57 G4
Gotland island Sweden 67 C7
Gotō-rettō island group Japan 113 A6
Göttingen Germany 76 C4
Gouda Netherlands 68 C4
Gough Island external territory UK, Atlantic Ocean 49 D7
Gouin, Réservoir Reservoir Canada 20 D4
Gouré Niger 57 G3
Governador Valadares Brazil 43 G4 45 F1
Govĭ Altayn Nuruu mountain range Mongolia 109 E3
Gozo island Malta 79 C7
Grafton Australia 131 E5
Grampian Mountains mountains Scotland, UK 70 C3
Granada Nicaragua 34 D3
Granada Spain 75 E4
Gran Canaria island Spain 52 A3
Gran Chaco region C South America 38 C4 44 A2 46 D2
Grand Bahama island Bahamas 36 C1
Grand Banks undersea feature Atlantic Ocean 48 B3
Grand Canyon valley SW USA 28 B1
Grande, Rio river Brazil 45 E1

Grande, Rio *River* Mexico/USA 17 B6

Grande Comore *island* Comoros 61 F2

Grande Prairie Canada 19 E4

Grand Erg Occidental *desert region* Algeria 52 D2

Grand Erg Oriental *desert region* Algeria/Tunisia 53 E3

Grand Falls Canada 21 G3

Grand Forks North Dakota, USA 25 E1

Grand Junction Colorado, USA 24 C4

Grand Rapids Michigan, USA 22 C3

Graudenz *see* Grudziądz

Graz Austria 77 E7

Great Abaco *island* Bahamas 36 C1

Great Ararat *see* Ararat, Mount

Great Australian Bight *sea feature* Australia 129 D6

Great Barrier Island *island* N NZ 132 D2

Great Barrier Reef *coral reef* Coral Sea 130 C4

Great Basin *region* USA 26 D4

Great Bear Lake *lake* Canada 19 E3

Great Dividing Range *mountain range* Australia 130-131

Great Exhibition Bay *inlet* New Zealand 132 C1

Great Wall of China *ancient monument* China 110 C4

Greater Antarctica *region* Antarctica 136 C3

Greater Antilles *island group* West Indies 36 C3

Great Exuma Island *island* Bahamas 36 C2

Great Falls Montana, USA 24 B1

Great Hungarian Plain *plain* SE Europe *Hung.* Alföld 81 D7

Great Inagua *island* Bahamas 36 D2

Great Khingan Range *see* Da Hinggan Ling

Great Lakes, The *lakes* N America *see* Erie, Huron, Michigan, Ontario, Superior 17 C5

Great Nicobar *island* India 115 H3

Great Plain of China *region* China 106 E2

Great Plains *region* N America 16-17 C5

Great Rift Valley *valley* E Africa/SW Asia 55 C6

Great Salt Desert *see* Kavir, Dasht-e

Great Salt Lake *salt lake* Utah, USA 24 B3

Great Sand Sea *desert region* Egypt/Libya 53 H3

Great Sandy Desert *desert* Australia 129 C5

Great Sandy Desert *see* Ar Rub' al Khali

Great Slave Lake *lake* Canada 19 E4

Great Victoria Desert *desert* Australia 129 C5

Greece *country* SE Europe 86-87

Green Bay Wisconsin, USA 22 B2

Greenland *external territory* Denmark, Atlantic Ocean *var.* Grønland 64

Greenland Sea Atlantic Ocean 65 F2

Greenock Scotland, UK 70 C4

Greensboro North Carolina, USA 31 F1

Greenville South Carolina, USA 31 E2

Greifswald Germany 76 D2

Gregory Range *mountain range* Australia 130 C3

Grenada *country* West Indies 37 H5

Grenoble France 73 D5

Greymouth New Zealand 133 B5

Grey Range *mountain range* Australia 124 B4

Grimsby England, UK 71 E5

Groningen Netherlands 68 E1

Grønland *see* Greenland

Groote Eylandt *island* Australia 130 B2

Grootfontein Namibia 60 C3

Grosseto Italy 78 B4

Grosskanizsa *see* Nagykanizsa

Groznyy Russian Federation 93 B7 96 A4

Grudziądz Poland *Ger.* Graudenz 80 C3

Grünberg in Schlesien *see* Zielona Góra

Guadalajara Mexico 32 D4

Guadalcanal *island* Solomon Islands 124 C3

Guadalquivir *river* Spain 74 D4

Guadeloupe *external territory* France, West Indies 37 G4

Guadiana *river* Portugal/Spain 74 C4

Gualeguaychú Argentina 46 D4

Guam *external territory* USA, Pacific Ocean 126 B1

Guanare Venezuela 40 D1

Guanare *river* Venezuela 40 D2

Guangdong *province* China *var.* Kuang-tung, Kwangtung, Yue 111 C6

Guangxi *autonomous region* China *var.* Kwangsi 111 B6

Guangzhou China *Eng.* Canton 111 C6

Guantánamo Cuba 36 D3

Guaporé *River* Bolivia/Brazil 32 D3

Guarapuava Brazil 44 D3

Guatemala *country* Central America 34

Guatemala Basin *undersea feature* Pacific Ocean 135 G3

Guatemala City *capital of* Guatemala 34 B2

Guaviare *river* Colombia 40 D3

Guayaquil Ecuador 40 A4

Guayaquil, Golfo do *sea feature* Ecuador/Peru 40 A5

Guernsey *island* Channel Islands 71 D8

Guiana Highlands *upland* N South America 38 C2

Guider Cameroon 58 B4

Guimarães Portugal 74 C2

Guinea *country* W Africa 56

Guinea, Gulf of *sea feature* Atlantic Ocean 49 D5

Guinea-Bissau *country* W Africa 56

Guiyang China 111 B6

Guizhou *province* China *var.* Kuei-chou, Kweichow, Qian 111 B6

Gujarāt *state* India 116 C4

Gujrānwāla Pakistan 116 C2

Gujrāt Pakistan 116 C2

Gulf, The *sea feature* Arabian Sea *var.* Persian Gulf 122 B2

Gulfport Mississippi, USA 30 C3

Gulu Uganda 55 B6

Gumbinnen *see* Gusev

Gunnbjørn Fjeld *mountain* Greenland 64 D4

Gurbantünggüt Shamo *desert* China 108 C2

Guri, Embalse de *Reservoir* Venezuela 41 E2

Gusau Nigeria 57 F3

Gusev Kaliningrad, Russian Federation *prev.* Gumbinnen 88 B3

Gushgy Turkmenistan *prev.* Kushka 104 C4

Guwāhāti India 117 G3

Guyana *country* NE South America 41

Gwalior India 116 D3

Gyandzha *see* Gäncä

Gyangzê China 108 C5

Győr Hungary *Ger.* Raab 81 C6

Gyumri Armenia *Rus.* Kumayri, *prev.* Leninakan, Aleksandropol'** 99 F2

Gyzylarbat Turkmenistan *prev.* Kizyl-Arvat 104 B2

H

Ha'apai Group *islands* Tonga 127 F5

Haapsalu Estonia *Ger.* Hapsal 88 C2

Haarlem Netherlands 68 C3

Haast New Zealand 133 B6

Hachijō-jima *island* Japan 113 D5

Hachinohe Japan 112 D3

Hadejia river Nigeria 57 G3

Ḥaḍramawt *Mountain range* Yemen 103 C7

Hagåtña Guam 126 B1

Hague, The *see* 's-Gravenhage

Haicheng China 110 D4

Haifa Israel *Heb.* Ḥefa 85 G4

Ḥā'il Saudi Arabia 102 B4

Hailar China 109 F1

Hainan *island* China *var.* Hainan Dao 106 D3 111 C8

Hainan *province* China *var.* Qiong 111 C7

Hainan Dao *see* Hainan Dao

Hai Phong Vietnam 118 D3

Haiti *country* West Indies 36

Hajdarken *see* Khaydarkan

Hakodate Japan 112 D3

Ḥalab Syria 100 B2

Ḥalāniyāt, Juzur al *Island group* Oman 103 D6

Halden Norway 67 B6

Halfmoon Bay New Zealand 133 A7

Halifax Canada 21 F4

Halle Germany 76 C4

Hallein Austria 77 D7

Halls Creek Australia 128 D3

Halmahera, Pulau *island* Indonesia 121 F3

Halmahera Sea *Sea* Indonesia 121 F4

Halmstad Sweden 67 B7

Hamada Japan 113 B5

Hamadān Iran 102 C3

Ḥamāh Syria 100 B3

Hamamatsu Japan 113 C5

Hamar Norway 67 B5

Hamburg Germany 76 C3

Hämeenlinna Finland 67 D5

HaMelah, Yam *see* Dead Sea

Hamersley Range *mountain range* Australia 128 B4

Hamhŭng North Korea 110 E4

Hami China 108 C3

Hamilton Canada 20 D5

Hamilton New Zealand 132 D3

Hamm Germany 76 B4

Hammerfest Norway 66 D2

Handan China 110 C4

HaNegev *desert region* Israel *Eng.* Negev 101 A6

Hangayn Nuruu *mountain range* Mongolia 108 D2

Hangzhou China 111 D5

Hannover Germany *Eng.* Hanover 76 B4

Hanoi *capital of* Vietnam 118 D3

Hanover *see* Hannover

Hanzhong China 111 B5

Hapsal *see* Haapsalu

Ḥaraḍ Yemen 103 C5

Harare *capital of* Zimbabwe 61 E3

Harbin China 110 E3

Hargeysa Somalia 55 D5

Hari *river* Indonesia 120 B4

Harīrūd *river* C Asia 104 D4

Harper Liberia 56 D5

Harrisburg Pennsylvania, USA 23 E4

Harstad Norway 66 C2

Hartford Connecticut, USA 23 G3

Hasselt Belgium 69 D5

Hastings New Zealand 132 E4

Hastings Nebraska, USA 24 E4

Hatay *see* Antakya

Hatteras, Cape *coastal feature* North Carolina, USA 31 G1

Hattiesburg Mississippi, USA 30 C3

Hat Yai Thailand 119 C7

Haugesund Norway 67 A6

Hauraki Gulf *gulf* New Zealand 132 D2

Havana *capital of* Cuba *Sp.* La Habana 36 B2

Havelock North Carolina, USA 31 G1

Havre Montana, USA 24 C1

Havre-Saint-Pierre Canada 21 F3

Hawaii *state* USA 135 E2

Hawaiian Islands *islands* USA 125 F1

Hawaiian Ridge *undersea feature* Pacific Ocean 134 D2

Hawera New Zealand 132 D4

Hawke Bay *bay* New Zealand 132 E4

Hawlêr *see* Arbīl

Hawthorne Nevada, USA 27 C6

Hay River Canada 19 E4

Hays Kansas, USA 25 E4

Heard & McDonald Islands *islands* Indian Ocean 123 C7

Hebei *province* China *var.* Hopeh, Hopei, Ji; *prev.* Chihli 110 C4

Hebron West Bank *var.* Al Khalīl, El Khalil, *Heb.* Hevron 101 D7

Heerenveen Netherlands 68 D2

Heerlen Netherlands 69 D6

Hefa Israel *prev.* Haifa 101 A5

Hefei China 111 D5

Hei *see* Heilongjiang

Heidelberg Germany 77 B5

Heilbronn Germany 77 B5

Heilongjiang *province* China *var.* Hei, Hei-lung-chiang 110 E3

Hei-lung-chiang *see* Heilongjiang

Helena Montana, USA 24 B2

Hells Canyon *valley* Idaho/Oregon USA 26 C3

Helmand *river* Afghanistan 104 C5

Helmond Netherlands 69 D5

Helsingborg Sweden 67 B7

Helsinki *capital of* Finland 67 D6

Henan *province* China *var.* Honan, Yu 111 C5

Hengduan Shan *mountain range* China 111 A6

Hengelo Netherlands 68 E3

Hengyang China 111 C6

Henzada Myanmar 118 A4

Herāt Afghanistan 104 C4

Hermansverk Norway 67 A5

Hermosillo Mexico 32 B2

Herning Denmark 67 A7

Heywood Islands *island group* Australia 128 C3

Hiiumaa *island* Estonia *Ger.* Dagden, *Swed.* Dagö 88 C2

Hildesheim Germany 76 C4

Hilversum Netherlands 68 C3

Himalayas *mountain range* S Asia 106 D2

Himora Ethiopia 54 C4

Ḥimṣ Syria 100 B3

Hinchinbrook Island *island* Australia 130 D3

Hindu Kush *mountain range* C Asia 105 C4

Hiroshima Japan 113 B5

Hitachi Japan 112 D4

Hjørring Denmark 67 A7

Hlybokaye Belarus *Rus.* Glubokoye 89 D5

Hobart Tasmania 131 C8

Hobbs New Mexico, USA 29 E3

Hồ Chí Minh Vietnam *var.* Ho Chi Minh City, *prev.* Saigon 119 E6

Ho Chi Minh City *see* Hồ Chí Minh

Hodeida *see* Al Ḥudaydah

Hoek van Holland Netherlands 68 B4

Hoggar *see* Ahaggar

Hohe Tauern *mountain range* Austria 77 C7

Hohhot China 109 F3

Hokitika New Zealand 133 B5

Hokkaidō *island* Japan 112 D2

Holguín Cuba 36 C2

Holland *see* Netherlands

Hollabrunn Austria 77 E6

Holon Israel 101 A5

Holyhead Wales, UK 71 C5

Hombori Mopti, Mali 57 E3

Homyel' Belarus *Rus.* Gomel' 89 E7

Honan *see* Henan

Honduras *country* Central America 34-35

Honduras, Gulf of *sea feature* Caribbean Sea 34 C2

Hønefoss Norway 67 B6

Hông Gai Vietnam 118 D3

Hong Kong China *var.* Xianggang 111 C6

Honiara *capital of* Solomon Islands 126 C3

Honshū *island* Japan 112 D3

Hoorn Netherlands 68 C2

Hopa Turkey 99 E2

Hopedale Canada 21 F2

Hopeh *see* Hebei

Hopei *see* Hebei

Hopkinsville Kentucky, USA 22 B5

Horki Belarus *Rus.* Gorki 89 E5

Horlivka Ukraine *Rus.* Gorlovka 90 G3

Horn, Cape *see* Hornos, Cabo

Hornos, Cabo *Eng* Cape Horn *coastal feature* Chile 47 C8

Horsham Australia 131 C7

Hospitalet *see* L'Hospitalet de Llobregat

Hot Springs Arkansas, USA 30 B2

Houston Texas, USA 29 G4

Hovd Mongolia 108 C2

Hövsgöl Nuur *lake* Mongolia 108 D1

Hradec Králové Czech Republic *Ger.* Königgrätz 81 B5

Hrodna Belarus *Rus.* Grodno 89 B5

Huacho Peru 42 A3

Huainan China 111 D5

Huambo Angola 60 B2

Huancayo Peru 42 B4

Huang He *river* China *Eng.* Yellow River 110 C4

Huánuco Peru 42 B3

Huaraz Peru 42 B3

Hubei *province* China 111 C5

Hubli India 114 C2

Hudson *river* NE USA 23 F3

Hudson Bay *sea feature* Canada 16 C4

Hudson Strait *sea feature* Canada 19 H3

Huê Vietnam 118 E4

Huehuetenango Guatemala 34 B2

Huelva Spain 74 C4

Huesca Spain 75 F2

Hughenden Australia 130 C4

Hull *see* Kingston upon Hull

Hulun Nur *lake* China 109 F1

Humboldt *river* W USA 27 C5

Hunan *province* China *var.* Xiang 111 C6

Hungarian Plain *plain* C Europe 85 E2

Hungary *country* C Europe 81

Huntington Beach California, USA 27 C8

Huntington West Virginia, USA 22 D5

Huntsville Alabama, USA 30 D2

Hurghada Egypt 54 B2

Huron, Lake *lake* Canada/USA 22 D2

Hurunui *river* New Zealand 133 C5

Húsavík Iceland 65 E4

Huvadhu Atoll *island* Maldives 114 C5

Hvar *island* Croatia 82 B4

Hyargas Nuur *lake* Mongolia 108 D2

Hyderābād India 114 D1 116 B3

Hyères, Îles d' *islands* France 73 D6

I

Iaşi Romania 90 D3

Ibadan Nigeria 57 F4

Ibagué Colombia 40 B3

Ibarra Ecuador 40 A4

Iberian Peninsula *peninsula* SW Europe 84 B3

Ibérico, Sistema *Mountain range* Spain 75 F2

Ibiza *see* Eivissa

Ica Peru 42 B4

İçel *see* Mersin

Iceland *country* Atlantic Ocean 65 E4

Idaho *state* USA 26

Idaho Falls Idaho, USA 26 E3

Idfu Egypt 54 B2

Idlib Syria 100 B2

Ieper Belgium *Fr.* Ypres 69 A6

Ifôghas, Adrar des *upland* Mali *var.* Adrar des Iforas 57 F2

Iforas, Adrar des *see* Ifôghas, Adrar des

Iglau *see* Jihlava

Iglesias Italy 79 A5

Iguaçu *River* Argentina/Brazil 44 C3

Iguîdi, 'Erg *Desert* Algeria/Mauritania 56 D1

Ihosy Madagascar 61 G4

Iisalmi Finland 66 E4

IJssel *river* Netherlands 68 D3

IJsselmeer *lake* Netherlands *prev.* Zuider Zee 68 D2

Ikaria *island* Greece 87 D5

Iki *island* Japan 113 A6

Ilagan Philippines 121 E1

Ilebo Congo (Zaire) 59 C6

Ili River China/Kazakhstan 94 D3

Iligan Philippines 121 F2

Illapel Chile 46 B3

Illinois *state* USA 22 B4

Iloilo Philippines 121 E2

Ilorin Nigeria 57 F4

Iluh *see* Batman

Imatra Finland 67 E5

Imperatriz Brazil 43 F2

Impfondo Congo 59 C5

Imphāl India 117 H4

Independence Missouri, USA 25 F4

India *country* S Asia 114-115, 116-117

Indian Ocean 122-123

Indiana *state* USA 22 C4

Indianapolis Indiana, USA 22 C4

Indigirka *river* Russian Federation 95 F2

Indonesia *country* SE Asia 120-121

Indonesian Borneo *see* Kalimantan

Indore India 116 D4

Indus *river* S Asia 116 C1

Indus Cone *see.* Indus Fan

Indus Fan *var.* Indus Cone. *Undersea feature* Arabian Sea 122 B3

Indus, Mouths of the *wetlands* Pakistan 116 B4

Ingolstadt Germany 77 C6

Inguri *see* Enguri

Inhambane Mozambique 61 E4

Inn *river* C Europe 77 D6

Innaanganeq *headland* Greenland 64 C1

Inner Islands *islands* Seychelles 61 H1

Inner Mongolia *autonomous region* China 109 F3

Innsbruck Austria 77 C7

I-n-Sâkâne, Erg *Desert* Mali 57 E2

I-n-Salah Algeria 52 D3

Insein Myanmar 118 B4

Inukjuak Canada 20 D2

Inuvik Canada 19 E3

Invercargill New Zealand 133 A7

Inverness Scotland, UK 70 C3

Investigator Ridge *undersea feature* Indian Ocean 122 D4

Ioánnina Greece 86 A4

Ionian Islands *see* Iónioi Nísoi

Ionian Sea Mediterranean Sea 87 A6

Iónioi Nísoi *island group* Greece *Eng.* Ionian Islands 87 A5

Íos *island* Greece 87 D6

Iowa *state* USA 25 F3

Ipoh Malaysia 120 B3

Ipswich England, UK 71 E6

Iqaluit Canada 19 H3

Iquique Chile 46 B1

Iquitos Peru 42 B2

Irákleio Greece 87 D7

Iran *country* SW Asia 102-103

Iranian Plateau *upland* Iran 102 D4

Irapuato Mexico 33 E4

Iraq *country* SW Asia 102

Irbid Jordan 101 B5

Ireland *country* W Europe 70-71

Irian Jaya *province* Indonesia 121 H4

Iringa Tanzania 55 C7

Irish Sea British Isles 71 C5

Irkutsk Russian Federation 97 E4

Iron Mountain Michigan, USA 22 B2

Ironwood Michigan, USA 22 B1

Irrawaddy *river* Myanmar 118 B2

Irrawaddy, Mouths of the *wetlands* Myanmar 118 A4

Irtysh River Asia 94 C3

Ishim *River* Kazakhstan/Russian Federation 94 C3

Isiro Congo (Zaire) 59 E5

İskenderun Turkey *Eng.* Alexandretta 98 D4

Iskŭr *river* Bulgaria 86 C1

Iskŭr, Yazovir *Reservoir* Bulgaria 86 C2

Islay Scotland, UK 70 B4

Islāmābād *capital* of Pakistan 116 C1

Ismaila *see* Ismâ`ilîya

Ismâ`ilîya Egypt *Eng.* Ismaila 54 B1

Isna Egypt 54 B2

İsparta Turkey 98 B4

Israel *country* SW Asia 100-101

Issyk-Kul, Ozero *lake* Kyrgyzstan 105 G2

İstanbul Turkey *var.* Stambul, *prev.* Constantinople, Byzantium, *Bul.* Tsarigrad 98 B2

İstanbul Boğazı *see* Bosporus

Itabuna Brazil 43 G4

Itagüi Colombia 40 B2

Italy *country* S Europe 78-79

Ittoqqortoormiit Greenland 65 E3

Iturup *island* Japan/Russian Federation (disputed) 112 E1

Ivanhoe Australia 131 C6

Ivano-Frankivs'k Ukraine 90 C2

Ivanovo Russian Federation 92 B4

Ivittuut Greenland 64 B4

Ivory Coast *see* Côte d'Ivoire

Ivujivik Canada 20 D1

Iwaki Japan 112 D4

Izabal, Lago de *lake* Guatemala 34 C2

Izhevsk Russian Federation 93 C5 96 B3

İzmir Turkey *prev.* Smyrna 98 A3

İzmit Turkey *var.* Kocaeli 98 B2

Izu-shotō *island group* Japan 113 D6

J

Jabal ash Shifā *desert* Saudi Arabia 102 A4

Jabalpur India 116 E4

Jackson Mississippi, USA 30 C2

Jacksonville Florida, USA 31 E3

Jacksonville Texas, USA 29 G3

Jacmel Haiti 36 D3

Jaén Spain 75 E4

Jaffna Sri Lanka 115 E3

Jagdaqi China 109 G1

Jiangxi *province* China 111 C6

Jaipur India 116 D3

Jajce Bosnia & Herzegovina 82 C4

Jakarta *capital* of Indonesia 120 C5

Jakobstad Finland 66 D4

Jakobstadt *see* Jēkabpils

Jalālābād Afghanistan 105 E4

Jalal-Abad *see* Dzhalal-Abad

Jalandhar India 116 D2

Jalapa *see* Xalapa

Jamaame Somalia 55 D6

Jamaica *country* West Indies 36

Jamālpur Bangladesh 117 G4

Jambi Indonesia 120 B4

James Bay *sea feature* Canada 20 C4

Jammu & Kashmir *disputed region* India/Pakistan 116 D2

Jāmnagar India 116 B4

Jan Mayen *external territory* Norway, Arctic Ocean 65 F3

Japan *country* E Asia 112-113

Japan, Sea of Pacific Ocean 112 B3

Jarvis Island *external territory* USA, Pacific Ocean 125 F2

Java *see* Jawa

Java Sea Pacific Ocean *var.* Laut Jawa 122 D4

Java Trench *undersea feature* Indian Ocean 122 D4

Jawa *island* Indonesia *var.* Java 120 C5

Jawa, Laut *see* Java Sea

Jayapura Indonesia 121 H4

Jaz Mūriān, Hāmūn-e *lake* Iran 102 E4

Jedda *see* Jiddah

Jedda *see* Jiddah

Jefferson City Missouri, USA 25 G4

Jēkabpils Latvia *Ger.* Jakobstadt 88 C4

Jelgava Latvia *Ger.* Mitau 88 C3

Jember Indonesia 120 D5

Jena Germany 76 C4

Jenin *var.* Janin, Jinin; *anc.* Engannim. West Bank 101 D6

Jérémie Haiti 36 D3

Jerevan *see* Yerevan

Jericho West Bank 101 B5

Jerid, Chott el *salt lake* Africa 84 D4

Jersey *island* Channel Islands 71 D8

Jerusalem *capital* of Israel 101 B5

Jhelum Pakistan 116 C2

Ji *see* Hebei

Ji *see* Jilin

Jiangsu *province* China *var.* Chiang-su, Kiangsu, Su 111 D5

Jiangxi *province* China *var.* Chiang-hsi, Gan, Kiangsi 111 C6

Jiaxing Zhejiang, China 111 D5

Jibuti *see* Djibouti

Jiddah Saudi Arabia *Eng.* Jedda 103 A5

Jiftlik Post West Bank 101 D7

Jihlava Czech Republic *Ger.* Iglau 81 B5

Jilin *province* China *var.* Chi-lin, Girin, Ji, Kirin 110 E3

Jilin China 110 E3

Jīma Ethiopia 55 C5

Jin *see* Shanxi

Jinan China 111 C4

Jingdezhen China 111 D5

Jinhua China 111 D5

Jining China 109 F3

Jinotega Nicaragua 34 D3

Jinsha Jiang *river* China 108 D5

Jinzhou China 110 D4

Jīzān Saudi Arabia 103 B6

João Pessoa Brazil 43 H3

Jodhpur India 116 C3

Joensuu Finland 67 E5

Johannesburg South Africa 60 D4

Johnston Atoll *US unincorporated territory* Pacific Ocean 125 E1

Johor Bahru Malaysia 120 C3

Joinville Brazil 44 D3

Joliet Illinois, USA 22 B3

Jönköping Sweden 67 B7

Jonquière Canada 21 E4

Jordan *country* SW Asia 100-101

Jordan SW Asia 101 B5

Joseph Bonaparte Gulf *gulf* Australia 128 D2

Jos Plateau *upland* Nigeria 57 G4

Juan Fernandez, Islas *islands* Chile 46 A4

Juàzeiro Brazil 43 G3

Juàzeiro do Norte Brazil 43 G3

Juba Sudan 55 B5

Júcar *river* Spain 75 E3

Judenburg Austria 77 D7

Juigalpa Nicaragua 34 D3

Juiz de Fora Brazil 43 G5 45 F2

Juneau Alaska, USA 18 D4

Junín Argentina 46 D4

Jura *mountains* France/Switzerland 77 A7

Jura *island* Scotland, UK 70 B4

Jurbarkas Lithuania *Ger.* Jurburg, *var.* Georgenburg 88 B4

Jurburg *see* Jurbarkas

Juruá *river* Brazil/Peru 42 C2

Juticalpa Honduras 34 D2

Jutland *see* Jylland

Juventud, Isla de la *island* Cuba 36 B2

Jylland *peninsula* Denmark *Eng.* Jutland 67 A7

Jyväskylä Finland 67 D5

K

K2 *peak* China/Pakistan *Eng.* Mount Godwin Austen 116 D1

Kaachka *see* Kaka

Kaaka Turkmenistan *prev.* Kaahkka, *var.* Kaachka 104 C3

Kaahkka *see* Kaka

Kabale Uganda 55 B6

Kabinda Congo (Zaire) 59 D7

Kābol *see* Kābul

Kābul *capital of* Afghanistan *Per.* Kābol 105 E4

Kachch, Gulf of *sea feature* Arabian Sea 116 B4

Kachch, Rann of *wetland* India/Pakistan *var.* Rann of Kutch 116 B4

Kadugli Sudan 54 B4

Kaduna Nigeria 57 G4

Kaédi Mauritania 56 C3

Kâghet *Physical region* Mauritania 56 D1

Kagoshima Japan 113 A6

Kahramanmaraş Turkey *var.* Marash, Maraş 98 D4

Kai, Kepulauan *island group* Indonesia 121 G4

Kaifeng China 111 C5

Kaikohe New Zealand 132 C2

Kaikoura New Zealand 133 C5

Kainji Reservoir *Reservoir* Nigeria 57 F4

Kairouan Tunisia 53 E1

Kaiserslautern Germany 77 B5

Kaitaia New Zealand 132 C2

Kajaani Finland 66 E4

Kakhovka Ukraine 91 F4

Kakhovs'ka Vodoskhovyshche *Reservoir* Ukraine 91 F3

Kalahari Desert *desert* southern Africa 60 C4

Kalamariá Greece 86 C3

Kalámata Greece 87 B6

Kalāt Afghanistan 104 D5

Kalbarri Australia 129 A5

Kalemie Congo (Zaire) 59 E7

Kalgoorlie Australia 129 C6

Kalimantan *geopolitical region* Indonesia *Eng.* Indonesian Borneo 120 D4

Kaliningrad *external territory* Russian Federation 96 A2

Kaliningrad Kaliningrad, Russian Federation *prev.* Königsberg 88 A4

Kalinkavichy Belarus *Rus.* Kalinkovichi 89 D7

Kalinkovichi *see* Kalinkavichy

Kalisch *see* Kalisz

Kalispell Montana, USA 24 B1

Kalisz Poland *Ger.* Kalisch 80 C4

Kalmar Sweden 67 C7

Kalpeni Island *island* India 114 C3

Kama *river* Russian Federation 92 D4

Kamchatka *peninsula* Russian Federation 97 H3

Kamchiya *river* Bulgaria 86 E2

Kamina Congo (Zaire) 59 D7

Kamishli *see* Al Qāmishlī
Kamloops Canada 19 E5
Kampala *capital of* Uganda 55 B6
Kâmpóng Cham Cambodia 119 D6
Kâmpóng Chhnăng Cambodia 119 D5
Kâmpóng Saôm Cambodia 119 D6
Kâmpôt Cambodia 119 D6
Kampuchea *see* Cambodia
Kam"yanets'-Podil's'kyy Ukraine 90 C3
Kananga Congo (Zaire) 59 D7
Kanazawa Japan 112 C4
Kandahār Afghanistan *var.* Qandahār 104 D5
Kandi Benin 57 F4
Kanivs'ke Vodoskhovyshche *Reservoir* Ukraine 91 E2
Kandy Sri Lanka 115 E3
Kanestron, Ákra *see* Palioúri, Akrotírio
Kangaroo Island *island* Australia 131 B7
Kangertittivaq *region* Greenland 64 E3
Kangikajik *headland* Greenland 65 E4
Kanjiža Yugoslavia 82 D2
Kankan Guinea 56 D4
Kano Nigeria 57 G4
Kānpur India *prev.* Cawnpore 117 E3
Kansas *state* USA 24-25
Kansas City Kansas, USA 25 F4
Kansas City Missouri, USA 25 F4
Kansk Russian Federation 97 E4
Kansu *see* Gansu
Kaohsiung Taiwan 111 D7
Kaolack Senegal 56 B3
Kapfenberg Austria 77 E7
Kaposvár Hungary 81 C7
Kapsukas *see* Marijampolė
Kapuas *river* Indonesia 120 D4
Kara-Balta Kyrgyzstan 105 F2
Karabük Turkey 98 C2

Karáchi Pakistan 116 B4
Karaganda Kazakhstan 96 C4
Karakol Kyrgyzstan *prev.* Przheval'sk 105 G2
Kara Kum *see* Garagumy
Karakumskiy Kanal *canal* Turkmenistan Turkm. Garagum Kanaly 104 C3
Karakumy *see* Garagum
Karamay China 108 C2
Karamea Bight *gulf* New Zealand 133 C5
Karasburg Namibia 60 C4
Kara Sea *see* Karskoye More
Karditsa Greece 86 B4
Kariba, Lake *lake* Zambia/Zimbabwe 60 D3
Karimata, Selat *strait* Indonesia 120 C4
Karkinits'ka Zatoka *sea feature* Black Sea 91 E4
Karl-Marx-Stadt *see* Chemnitz
Karlovac Croatia 82 B3
Karlovy Vary Czech Republic *Ger.* Karlsbad 81 A5
Karlsbad *see* Karlovy Vary
Karlskrona Sweden 67 C7
Karlsruhe Germany 77 B5
Karlstad Sweden 67 B6
Karnātaka *state* India 114 D1
Kárpathos *island* Greece 87 E7
Kars Turkey 99 F2
Karshi Uzbekistan *prev.* Bek-Budi, *Uzb.* Qarshi 104 D3
Karskoye More Arctic Ocean *Eng.* Kara Sea 137 H3
Kasai *river* Congo (Zaire) 59 C6
Kasama Zambia 61 F4
Kaschau *see* Košice
Kāshān Iran 102 C3
Kashi China 108 A3
Kasongo Congo (Zaire) 59 E6
Kassa *see* Košice
Kassala Sudan 54 C4
Kassel Germany 76 B4
Kastamonu Turkey 98 C2
Katanning Australia 129 B6
Kateríni Greece 86 B4
Katha Myanmar 118 B2

Katherine Australia 128 E2
Kathmandu *capital of* Nepal 117 F3
Katsina Nigeria 57 G3
Katowice Poland 81 C5
Kauen *see* Kaunas
Kaunas Lithuania *Ger.* Kauen, *Pol.* Kowno, *Rus.* Kovno 88 B4
Kavadarci Macedonia 82 E5
Kavála Greece 86 C3
Kavaratti Island *island* India 114 C3
Kavir, Dasht-e *Salt pan* Iran 102 D3
Kawasaki Japan 113 D5
Kayan *river* Indonesia 120 D3
Kayes Mali 56 C3
Kayseri Turkey 98 D3
Kazakhstan *country* C Asia 96
Kazan' Russian Federation 96 B3
Kazandzhik *see* Gazandzhyk
Kazanlŭk Bulgaria 86 D2
Kéa *island* Greece 87 C5
Kecskemét Hungary 81 D7
Kediri Indonesia 120 D5
Keetmanshoop Namibia 60 C4
Kefallinía *island* Greece *Eng.* Cephalonia 87 A5
Kelang *see* Klang
Kelmė Lithuania 88 B4
Kelowna Canada 19 E5
Kemerovo Russian Federation 96 D4
Kemi Finland 66 D4
Kemi *river* Finland 66 D3
Kemijärvi Finland 66 D3
Kendari Indonesia 121 E4
Këneurgench Turkmenistan *prev.* Kunya-Urgench, *Turkm.* Köneürgench 104 C2
Kénitra Morocco 52 C2
Kennewick Washington, USA 26 C2
Kenora Canada 20 A3
Kentucky *state* USA 22 C5
Kenya *country* E Africa 55
Kerala *state* India 114 D3

Kerch Ukraine 91 G4

Kerguelen *island group* Indian Ocean 123 C7

Kerguelen Plateau *undersea feature* Indian Ocean 123 C7

Kerki Turkmenistan 104 D3

Kérkira *see* Kérkyra

Kérkyra Greece 86 A4

Kérkyra *island* Greece *prev.* Kérkira, *Eng.* Corfu 86 A4

Kermadec Islands *island group* Pacific Ocean 125 E4

Kermadec Trench *undersea feature* Pacific Ocean 125 E4

Kermān Iran *var.* Kirman 102 D4

Kermānshāh *see* Bākhtarān

Kerulen *river* China/Mongolia 109 E2

Ketchikan Alaska, USA 18 D4

Key West Florida, USA 31 E5

Khabarovsk Russian Federation 97 G4

Khanka, Lake *lake* China/Russian Federation 110 E3

Khankendy *see* Xankändi

Kharkiv Ukraine *Rus.* Khar'kov 91 G2

Khar'kov *see* Kharkiv

Khartoum *capital of* Sudan *var.* Al Khurţūm 54 B4

Khâsh Iran 102 E4

Khaskovo Bulgaria 86 D2

Khaydarkan Kyrgyzstan *var.* Khaydarken, Hajdarken 105 E2

Khaydarken *see* Khaydarkan

Kherson Ukraine 91 E4

Kheta *river* Russian Federation 94 D2

Khios *see* Chios

Khirbet el 'Aujā et Tahtā West Bank 101 D6

Khmel 'nyts'kyy Ukraine 90 D2

Khodzhent *see* Khŭjand

Khojend *see* Khŭjand

Khokand *see* Kokand

Kholm Afghanistan 105 E3

Khon Kaen Thailand 118 C4

Khorog *see* Khorugh

Khorugh Tajikistan *Rus.* Khorog 105 F3

Khouribga Morocco 52 C2

Khudzhand *see* Khŭjand

Khŭjand Tajikistan *var.* Khodzheut, Khojend, *Rus.* Khudzhand *prev.* Leninabad 105 E2

Khulna Bangladesh 117 G4

Khvoy Iran 102 B3

Kiangsi *see* Jiangxi

Kiangsu *see* Jiangsu

Kičevo Macedonia 83 D5

Kiel Germany 76 C2

Kielce Poland 80 D4

Kiev *capital of* Ukraine *Ukr.* Kyyiv 91 E2

Kiffa Mauritania 56 C3

Kigali *capital of* Rwanda 55 B6

Kigoma Tanzania 55 B7

Kikládhes *see* Kyklades

Kikwit Congo (Zaire) 59 C6

Kilimanjaro *peak* Tanzania 55 C7

Kilkis Greece 86 B3

Killarney Ireland 71 A6

Kimberley South Africa 60 D4

Kimberley Plateau *upland* Australia 128 D3

Kindia Guinea 56 C4

Kindu Congo (Zaire) 59 D6

King Island *island* Australia 131 C7

Kingissepp *see* Kuressaare

Kingman Reef *external territory* USA, Pacific Ocean 125 F2

King Sound *sound* Australia 128 C3

Kingsport Tennessee, USA 31 E1

Kingsville Texas, USA 27 G5

Kingston Canada 20 C5

Kingston *capital of* Jamaica 36 C3

Kingston upon Hull England, UK *var.* Hull 71 E5

Kingstown St Vincent & The Grenadines 36 G4

King William Island *island* Canada 19 F3

Kinneret, Yam *see* Tiberius, Lake

Kinshasa *capital of* Congo (Zaire) *prev.* Léopoldville 59 B6

Kirghizia *see* Kyrgyzstan

Kiribati *country* Pacific Ocean 127

Kirin *see* Jilin

Kiritimati *island* Kiribati *var.* Christmas Island 127 G2

Kirkenes Norway 66 E2

Kirklareli Turkey 98 A2

Kirksville Missouri, USA 25 F4

Kirkūk Iraq 102 B3

Kirkwall Scotland, UK 70 E1

Kirman *see* Kermān

Kirov Russian Federation 92 C4 96 B3

Kirovabad *see* Gäncä

Kirovakan *see* Vanadzor

Kirovohrad Ukraine 91 E3

Kiruna Sweden 66 C3

Kisangani Congo (Zaire) *prev.* Stanleyville 59 D5

Kishinev *see* Chişinău

Kismaayo Somalia 55 D6

Kisumu Kenya 55 C6

Kitakyūshū Japan 113 A5

Kitami Japan 112 D2

Kitchener Canada 20 C5

Kitwe Zambia 60 D2

Kivu, Lake *lake* Rwanda/Congo (Zaire) 55 B6 59 E6

Kızıl Irmak *river* Turkey 98 C2

Kizyl-Arvat *see* Gyzylarbat

Kladno Czech Republic 81 A5

Klagenfurt Austria 77 D7

Klaipėda Lithuania *Ger.* Memel 88 B4

Klamath Falls Oregon, USA 26 B4

Khang Malaysia *var.* Kelang 120 B2

Ključ Bosnia & Herzegovina 82 B3

Knin Croatia 82 B4

Knoxville Tennessee, USA 31 E1

Knud Rasmussen Land *region* Greenland 64 D1

Kōbe Japan 113 C5

Koblenz Germany 77 B5

Kobryn Belarus 89 B6

Kocaeli *see* İzmit

Kočani Macedonia 83 E5

Kōchi Japan 113 B6

Kodiak Alaska, USA 18 C3

Kodiak Island *island* Alaska, USA 18 C3

Koedoes *see* Kudus

Kohima India 117 H3

Kohtla-Järve Estonia 88 D2

Kokand Uzbekistan *var.* Khokand, *Uzb.* Qŭqon 105 E2

Kokchetav Kazakhstan 96 C4

Kokkola Finland 66 D4

Koko Nor *see* Qinghai

Koko Nor *see* Qinghai Hu

Kokshaal-Tau *mountain range* Kyrgyzstan 105 G2

Kola Peninsula *see* Kol'skiy Poluostrov

Kolguyev, Ostrov *island* Russian Federation 92 D2

Kolhumadulu Atoll *island* Maldives 114 C5

Kolka Latvia 88 C3

Kolkata *see* Calcutta

Köln Germany *Eng.* Cologne 76 B4

Kol'skiy Poluostrov *peninsula* Russian Federation *Eng.* Kola Peninsula 63 F1 92 C2

Kolwezi Congo (Zaire) 59 D8

Kolyma *river* Russian Federation 95 G2

Kommunizma, Pik *see* Communism Peak

Komoé *river* Côte d'Ivoire 57 E4

Komotiní Greece 86 D3

Komsomol'sk-na-Amure Russian Federation 97 G4

Kondoz *see* Kunduz

Kondūz *see* Kunduz

Köneürgench *see* Këneurgench

Kong Christian IX Land *region* Greenland 64 D4

Kong Christian X Land *region* Greenland 64 E3

Kong Frederik VI Kyst *region* Greenland 64 C4

Kong Frederik VIII Land *region* Greenland 64 E3

Kong Frederik IX Land *region* Greenland 64 C3

Kong Karls Land *island group* Svalbard 65 G2

Kong Oscar Fjord *fjord* Greenland 65 E3

Konia *see* Konya

Königgrätz *see* Hradec Králové

Königsberg *see* Kaliningrad

Konispol Albania 83 D7

Konjic Bosnia & Herzegovina 82 C4

Konya Turkey *prev.* Konia 98 C4

Kopaonik *mountains* Yugoslavia 83 D4

Koper Slovenia 77 D8

Koprivnica Croatia 82 B2

Korçë Albania 83 D6

Korčula *island* Croatia 82 B4

Korea Bay *bay* China/North Korea 110 D4

Korea Strait *sea feature* Japan/South Korea 110-111 E5

Korinthiakós Kólpos *sea feature* Greece *Eng.* Gulf of Corinth 87 B5

Kórinthos Greece *Eng.* Corinth 87 B5

Kōriyama Japan 113 D4

Korla China 108 C3

Koror *see* Oreor

Korosten' Ukraine 90 D1

Kortrijk Belgium 69 A6

Kos *island* Greece 87 E6

Kosciusko, Mount *peak* Australia 131 D7

Košice Slovakia *Ger.* Kaschau, *Hung.* Kassa 81 D6

Köslin *see* Koszalin

Kosovo *province* Yugoslavia 83 D5

Kosovska Mitrovica Yugoslavia 82 D4

Kosrae *island* Micronesia 126 C2

Kossou, Lac de *lake* Côte d'Ivoire 56 D4

Kostanay Kazakhstan *var.* Kustanay 96 C4

Kostyantynivka Ukraine 91 G3

Koszalin Poland *Ger.* Köslin 80 B2

Kota India 116 D4

Kota Bharu Malaysia 120 B3

Kota Kinabalu Malaysia 120 D3

Kotka Finland 67 E5

Kotlas NW Russia 92 D4

Kotuy *river* Russian Federation 95 E2

Koudougou Burkina 57 E4

Kourou French Guiana 41 H2

Kousséri Cameroon 58 B3

Kouvola Finland 67 E5

Kovel' Ukraine 90 C1

Kovno *see* Kaunas

Kowno *see* Kaunas

Kozáni Greece 86 B4

Kozhikode *see* Calicut

Kra, Isthmus of *coastal feature* Myanmar/Thailand 119 B6

Kragujevac Yugoslavia 82 D4

Krakau *see* Kraków

Kraków Poland *Eng.* Cracow, *Ger.* Krakau 81 D5

Kraljevo Yugoslavia 82 D4

Kranj Slovenia 77 D7

Krasnodar Russian Federation 93 A6

Krasnovodsk *see* Turkmenbashy

Krasnoyarsk Russian Federation 96 D4

Krasnyy Luch Ukraine 91 H3

Kremenchuk Ukraine 91 F2

Kremenchuts'ke Vodoskhovyshche *Reservoir* Ukraine 91 E2

Krems an der Donau Austria 77 E6

Kretinga Lithuania Ger. Krottingen 88 B3

Krichev see Krychaw

Krishna river India 114 C1

Kristiansand Norway 67 A6

Kristianstad Sweden 67 B7

Kriti island Greece Eng. Crete 87 F7

Kritikó Pélagos see Crete, Sea of

Krivoy Rog see Kryvyy Rih

Krk island Croatia 82 A3

Kroonstad South Africa 60 D4

Krottingen see Kretinga

Krung Thep see Bangkok

Kruševac Yugoslavia 83 E4

Krušné Hory see Erzgebirge

Krychaw Belarus Rus. Krichev 89 E6

Kryms'kyy Pivostriv peninsula Ukraine var. Crimea 90 F4

Kryvyy Rih Ukraine Rus. Krivoy Rog 91 E3

Kuala Lumpur capital of Malaysia 120 B3

Kuala Terengganu Malaysia 120 B3

Kuang-tung see Guangdong

Kuantan Malaysia 120 C3

Kuba see Quba

Kuching Malaysia 120 C3

Kuçovë Albania prev. Qyteti Stalin 83 D6

Kudus Indonesia prev. Koedoes 120 D5

Kuei-chou see China Guizhou

Kugluktuk Canada prev. Coppermine 19 E3

Kuito Angola 60 C2

Kuldiga Latvia Ger. Goldingen 88 B3

Kullorsuaq Greenland 64 C2

Külob Tajikistan Rus. Kulyab 105 E3

Kulyab see Külob

Kum see Qom

Kuma river Russian Federation 93 B7

Kumamoto Japan 113 B6

Kumanovo Macedonia 83 E5

Kumasi Ghana 57 E5

Kumayri see Gyumri

Kumo Nigeria 57 G4

Kumon Range mountain range Myanmar 118 B1

Kunashir island Japan/Russian Federation (disputed) 112 E1

Kunduz Afghanistan var. Kondūz, Qondūz, Kondoz 105 E3

Kunja-Urgenç see Këneurgench

Kunlun Mountains see Kunlun Shan

Kunlun Shan mountain range China Eng. Kunlun Mountains 106 B4

Kunming China 111 B6

Kununurra Australia 128 D3

Kupang Indonesia 120 E5

Kür see Kura

Kura river Azerbaijan/Georgia Az. Kür 99 G2

Kurashiki Japan 113 B5

Küre Dağları mountains Turkey 98 C2

Kuressaare Estonia prev. Kingissepp, Ger. Arensburg 88 C2

Kurgan–Tyube see Qürghonteppa

Kurile Islands islands Pacific Ocean 112 E1

Kurile Trench undersea feature Pacific Ocean 134 C2

Kurnool India 114 D2

Kushiro Japan 112 E2

Kushka see Gushgy

Kustanay see Kostanay

Kütahya Turkey prev. Kutaiah 98 B3

Kutaiah see Kütahya

K'ut'aisi Georgia 99 F2

Kutch, Rann of see Kachch, Rann of

Kuujjuaq Canada 21 E2

Kuujjuarapik Canada 20 D2

Kuusamo Finland 66 E3

Kuwait country SW Asia 102 C4

Kuwait City capital of Kuwait 102 C4

Kuytun China 108 C2

Kvitøya island Svalbard 65 G1

Kwangju South Korea 111 E4

Kwango river Congo (Zaire) 59 C7

Kwangtung see Guangdong

Kweichow see Guizhou

Kykládes island group Greece prev. Kikládhes, Eng. Cyclades 87 D6

Kyrenia see Girne

Kyrgyzstan country C Asia var. Kirghizia 105

Kýthira island Greece 87 B6

Kyushu-Palau Ridge undersea feature Pacific Ocean 124 B1

Kyyiv see Kiev

Kyyiv's'ke Vodoskhovyshche Reservoir Ukraine 91 E1

Kyōto Japan 113 C5

Kyūshū island Japan 113 B6

Kyzylorda Kazakhstan 96 C3

L

Laâyoune Western Sahara 52 B3

Labé Guinea 56 C4

Laborca see Laborec

Laborec river Slovakia Hung. Laborca 81 E5

Labrador region Canada 21 F2

Labrador Sea Atlantic Ocean 64 B5

Laccadive Islands see Lakshadweep

La Ceiba Honduras 34 D2

Lachlan River river Australia 131 C6

La Coruña see A Coruña

La Crosse Wisconsin, USA 22 A2

Ladoga, Lake see Ladozhskoye Ozero

Ladozhskoye Ozero *lake*
Russian Federation *Eng.* Lake
Ladoga 92 B3
Ladysmith Wisconsin, USA
22 A2
Lae Papua New Guinea 126 B3
La Esperanza Honduras 34 C2
Lafayette Louisiana, USA 30 B3
Laghouat Algeria 52 D2
Lagos Nigeria 57 F5
Lagos Portugal 74 C4
Lagouira Western Sahara 52 A4
La Grande Oregon, USA 26 C3
La Habana *see* Havana
Lahore Pakistan 116 C2
Laï Chad 58 C4
Laila *see* Laylá
Lajes Brazil 44 D3
Lake Charles Louisiana, USA 30
B3
Lake District *region* England,
UK 71 C5
Lakewood Colorado, USA
24 D4
Lakshadweep *island group*
India *Eng.* Laccadive Islands
114 B2
La Ligua Chile 46 B4
La Louvière Belgium 69 B6
Lambaré Paraguay 44 B3
Lambaréné Gabon 59 B6
Lamia Greece 86 B4
Lancaster England, UK 71 D5
Lancaster California, USA 27 C7
Lancaster Sound *sea feature*
Canada 19 F2
Landsberg *see* Gorzów
Wielkopolski
Land's End *coastal feature*
England, UK 71 C7
Landshut Germany 77 D6
Lang Son Vietnam 118 D3
Länkäran Azerbaijan *Rus.*
Lenkoran' 99 H3
Lansing Michigan, USA 22 C3
Lanzarote *island* Spain 52 B3
Lanzhou China 110 B4
Laon France 72 D3
La Oroya Peru 42 B3

Laos *country* SE Asia 118
La Palma *island* Spain 52 A3
La Paz *capital of* Bolivia 42 C4
La Paz Mexico 32 B3
La Pérouse Strait *sea feature*
Japan 112 D1
Lapland *region* N Europe
66 C3
La Plata Argentina 46 D4
Lappeenranta Finland 67 E5
Laptev Sea *see*
Laptevykh, More
Laptevykh, More Arctic Ocean
Eng. Laptev Sea 97 F2
L'Aquila Italy 78 C4
Laramie Wyoming, USA 24 C4
Laredo Texas, USA 29 F5
La Rioja Argentina 46 C3
Lárisa Greece 86 B4
Lārkāna Pakistan 116 B3
Larnaca Cyprus *var.* Larnaka,
Larnax 98 C5
Larnaka *see* Larnaca
Larnax *see* Larnaca
La Rochelle France 72 B4
La Roche-sur-Yon France 72 B4
La Romana Dominican Republic
36 E3
Las Cruces New Mexico, USA
28 D3
Las Piedras Uruguay 44 C5
La Serena Chile 46 B3
La Spezia Italy 78 B3
Las Tablas Panama 35 F5
Las Vegas Nevada, USA 27 D7
Latakia *see* Al Lādhiqīyah
Latvia *country* NE Europe 88
Launceston Tasmania 131 C8
Laurentian Basin *see* Canada
Basin
Laurentian Mountains *upland*
Canada 16 D4
Lausanne Switzerland 77 A7
Laut, Pulau *prev.* Laoet. *Island*
Indonesia 120 D4
Laval France 72 B4
Lawton Oklahoma, USA 29 F2
Laylá Saudi Arabia 103 C5

Lazarev Sea *sea* Antarctica
136 B2
Lebanon *country* SW Asia
100-101
Lebu Chile 47 B5
Lecce Italy 79 E5
Leduc Canada 19 E5
Leeds England, UK 71 D5
Leeuwarden Netherlands 68 D1
Leeward Islands *see* Sotavento,
Ilhas de
Lefkáda *island* Greece *prev.*
Levkás 87 A5
Lefkoşa *see* Nicosia
Lefkosia *see* Nicosia
Legaspi Philippines 120 E2
Legnica Poland *Ger.* Liegnitz
80 B4
Le Havre France 72 B3
Leicester England, UK 71 D6
Leiden Netherlands 68 C3
Leipzig Germany 76 D4
Lek *river* Netherlands 68 C4
Le Léman *see* Geneva, Lake
Lelystad Netherlands 68 D3
Léman, Lac *see* Geneva, Lake
Le Mans France 72 B4
Lemesos *see* Limassol
Lemnos *see* Limnos
Lena *river* Russian Federation
97 F3
Leninabad *see* Khŭjand
Leninakan *see* Gyumri
Leningrad *see* St Petersburg
Leninsk *see* Chardzhev
Lenkoran' *see* Länkäran
León Mexico 33 E4
León Nicaragua 34 C3
León Spain 74 D1
Léopoldville *see* Kinshasa
Lepel' *see* Lyepyel'
Le Puy France 73 C5
Lérida *see* Lleida
Lerwick Scotland, UK 70 D1
Lesbos *see* Lésvos
Leshan China 111 B5
Leskovac Yugoslavia 82 E4

Lesotho *country* southern Africa 60

Lesser Antarctica *region* Antarctica 134 B3

Lesser Antilles *island group* West Indies 37 G4

Lésvos *island* Greece *Eng.* Lesbos 86 D4

Lethbridge Canada 19 E5

Leti, Kepulauan *island group* Indonesia 121 F5

Leuven Belgium 69 C6

Leverkusen Germany 76 A4

Levin New Zealand 132 D4

Levkás *see* Lefkáda

Lewis *island* Scotland, UK 70 B2

Lewiston Idaho, USA 26 C2

Lewiston Maine, USA 23 G2

Lexington Kentucky, USA 22 C5

Lezhë Albania 83 D5

Lhasa China 108 C5

Lhazê China 108 C4

L'Hospitalet de Llobregat *var.* Hospitalet. Spain 75 G2

Liao *see* Liaoning

Liaoning *province* China *var.* Liao, Shengking; *hist.* Fengtien, Shenking. Admin. region 110 D3

Libau *see* Liepāja

Liberec Czech Republic *Ger.* Reichenberg 80 B4

Liberia *country* W Africa 56

Liberia Costa Rica 34 D4

Libreville *capital* of Gabon 59 A5

Libya *country* N Africa 53

Libyan Desert *desert* N Africa 50 C3

Lichuan China 111 B5

Liechtenstein *country* C Europe 77 B7

Liège Belgium 69 D6

Liegnitz *see* Legnica

Lienz Austria 77 D7

Linz Austria 77 D7

Liepāja Latvia *Ger.* Libau 88 B3

Liffey *river* Ireland 71 B5

Ligurian Sea Mediterranean Sea 78 A3

Likasi Congo (Zaire) 59 E8

Lille France 72 D2

Lillehammer Norway 67 B5

Lilongwe *capital* of Malawi 61 D2

Lima *capital* of Peru 42 B4

Limassol Cyprus *var.* Lemesos 98 C5

Limerick Ireland 71 A6

Limnos *island* Greece *var.* Lemnos 86 D4

Limoges France 72 C5

Limón Costa Rica 35 E4

Limpopo *river* southern Africa 60 D3

Linares Chile 46 B4

Linares Spain 75 E4

Linchuan China 111 D6

Lincoln England, UK 71 D5

Lincoln Nebraska, USA 25 F4

Lincoln Sea Arctic Ocean 64 E1

Linden Guyana 41 G2

Lindi Tanzania 55 C8

Line Islands *island group* Kiribati 127 G2

Linköping Sweden 67 C6

Linz Austria 77 D6

Lion, Golfe du *sea feature* Mediterranean Sea 73 D6

Lipari, Isola *island* Italy 79 D6

Lipari Islands *see* Isole Eolie

Lira Uganda 55 B6

Lisbon *capital* of Portugal *Port.* Lisboa 74 B3

Litani *river* SW Asia 91 B4

Lithuania *country* E Europe 88-89

Little Andaman *island* India 115 G2

Little Minch *sea feature* Scotland, UK 70 B3

Little Rock Arkansas, USA 30 B2

Liuzhou China 111 C6

Liverpool England, UK 71 D5

Livingstone Zambia 60 D3

Livno Bosnia & Herzegovina 82 B4

Livorno Italy 78 B3

Ljubljana *capital* of Slovenia 77 D7

Ljusnan *river* Sweden 67 B5

Llanos *region* Colombia/Venezuela 41 E2

Lleida Spain *Cast.* Lérida 75 F2

Lobatse Botswana 60 D4

Lobito Angola 60 B2

Locarno Switzerland 77 B7

Lodja Congo (Zaire) 59 D6

Łódź Poland *Rus.* Lodz 80 D4

Lofoten *island group* Norway 66 B3

Logroño Spain 75 E2

Loire *river* France 72 B4

Loja Ecuador 40 A5

Lokitaung Kenya 55 C5

Loksa Estonia *Ger.* Loxa 88 D2

Lombok, Pulau *island* Indonesia 120 D5

Lomé *capital* of Togo 57 E5

Lomond, Loch *lake* Scotland, UK 70 C4

London Canada 20 C5

London *capital* of UK 71 E6

Londonderry Northern Ireland, UK 70 A4

Londonderry, Cape *coastal feature* Australia 128 D2

Londrina Brazil 44 D2

Long Beach California, USA 27 C8

Long Island *island* Bahamas 34 D2

Long Island *island* NE USA 23 G3

Longreach Australia 130 C4

Long Strait *Strait* Russian Federation 95 H2

Longview Texas, USA 29 G3

Longview Washington, USA 26 B2

Longyearbyen Svalbard 65 F2

Lop Nur *lake* China 108 C3

Lorca Spain 75 E4

Lord Howe Island *island* Australia 124 C4

Lord Howe Rise *undersea feature* Pacific Ocean 124 D4

Lorient France 72 A4

Los Alamos New Mexico, USA 28 D1

Los Angeles California, USA 27 C7

Loslau *see* Wodzisław Śląski

Los Mochis Mexico 32 C3

Losonc *see* Lučenec

Losontz *see* Lučenec

Lot *river* France 73 B5

Louangphrabang Laos 118 C3

Loubomo Congo 59 B6

Louisiana *state* USA 30 B3

Louisville Kentucky, USA 22 C5

Louisville Ridge *undersea feature* Pacific Ocean 125 E4

Lovech Bulgaria 86 C2

Lower California *see* Baja California

Lower Hutt New Zealand

Loxa *see* Loksa

Loyauté, Îles *island group* New Caledonia 126 D5

Loznica Yugoslavia 82 C3

Lu *see* Shandong

Luanda *capital of* Angola 60 B1

Luanshya Zambia 60 D2

Lubango Angola 60 B2

Lubbock Texas, USA 29 E2

Lübeck Germany 76 C3

Lublin Poland *Rus.* Lyublin 80 E4

Lubny Ukraine 91 F2

Lubumbashi Congo (Zaire) 59 E8

Lucapa Angola 60 C1

Lucena Philippines 120 E2

Lučenec Slovakia *Hung.* Losonc, *Ger.* Losontz 81 D6

Lucerne *see* Luzern

Lucknow India 117 E3

Lüderitz Namibia 60 C4

Ludhiāna India 116 D2

Lugano Switzerland 77 B7

Lugo Spain 74 C1

Luhans'k Ukraine 91 H3

Luleå Sweden 66 D4

Lumsden New Zealand 133 A7

Lüneburg Germany 76 C3

Luninyets Belarus 89 C6

Luoyang *var.* Honan, Lo-yang. China 110 C4

Lusaka *capital of* Zambia 60 D2

Lushnjë Albania 83 D6

Lūt, Baḥrat *see* Dead Sea

Luts'k Ukraine 90 C1

Luxembourg *country* W Europe 69 D8

Luxembourg *capital of* Luxembourg 69 D8

Luxor Egypt 54 B2

Luzern Switzerland *Fr.* Lucerne 77 B7

Luzon *island* Philippines 121 E1

Luzon Strait *sea feature* Philippines/Taiwan 107 E3

L'viv Ukraine *Rus.* L'vov 90 C2

L'vov *see* L'viv

Lyepyel' Belarus *Rus.* Lepel' 89 D5

Lyon France 73 D5

Lyublin *see* Lublin

M

Ma'ān Jordan 101 B6

Maas *see* Meuse

Maastricht Netherlands 69 D6

Macao *external territory* Portugal, E Asia *var.* Macau 111 C7

Macapá Brazil 43 F1

Macau *see* Macao

Macdonnell Ranges *mountains* Australia 130 A4

Macedonia *country* SE Europe officially Former Yugoslav Republic of Macedonia, *abbrev.* FYR Macedonia 83

Maceió Brazil 43 H3

Machala Ecuador 40 A5

Mackay Australia 130 D4

Mackay, Lake *lake* Australia 128 D4

Mackenzie *river* Canada 19 E4

Mackenzie Bay *sea feature* Atlantic Ocean 136 D3

Macleod, Lake *lake* Australia 128 A4

Mâcon France 72 D5

Macon Georgia, USA 31 E2

Madagascar *country* Indian Ocean 61

Madagascar Basin *undersea feature* Indian Ocean 123 B5

Madagascar Plateau *undersea feature* Indian Ocean 123 A6

Madang Papua New Guinea 126 B3

Madeira *river* Bolivia/Brazil 42 D2

Madeira *island group* Portugal 52 A2

Madhya Pradesh *state* India 117 E4

Madison Wisconsin, USA 22 B3

Madiun *prev.* Madioen. Indonesia 120 D5

Madona Latvia *Ger.* Modohn 88 D3

Madras *see* Chennai

Madre de Dios *river* Bolivia/Peru 42 C3

Madrid *capital of* Spain 75 E3

Madurai India 114 D3

Magadan Russian Federation 97 G3

Magallanes *see* Punta Arenas

Magallanes, Estrecho de *see* Magellan, Strait of

Magdalena *river* Colombia 40 B2

Magdeburg Germany 76 C4

Magelang Indonesia 120 C5

Magellan, Strait of *sea feature* S South America *Sp.* Estrecho de Magallanes 47 B8

Maggiore, Lake *lake* Italy/Switzerland 78 B2

Mahajanga Madagascar 61 G3

Mahalapye Botswana 60 D4

Mahanādi *river* India 117 F5

Mahārāshtra *state* India 116 D5

Mahé *island* Seychelles 61 H1

Mahilyow Belarus *Rus.* Mogilëv 89 E6

Mährisch-Ostrau *see* Ostrava

Maicao Colombia 40 C1

Maiduguri Nigeria 57 H4

Maimana *see* Meymaneh

Maine *state* USA 23 G1

Maine, Gulf of *gulf* USA 23 G2

Mainz Germany 77 B5

Maio *island* Cape Verde 56 A3

Maíz, Islas del *islands* Nicaragua 35 E3

Majorca *see* Mallorca

Majuro *island* Marshall Islands 126 D1

Makarska Croatia 82 B4

Makarov Basin *undersea feature* Arctic Ocean 137 G3

Makassar Strait *strait* Indonesia 120 D4

Makeyevka *see* Makiyivka

Makhachkala Russian Federation 93 B7 96 A4

Makiyivka Ukraine *Rus.* Makeyevka 91 G5

Makkah Saudi Arabia *Eng.* Mecca 103 A5

Makkovik Canada 21 F2

Malabo *capital of* Equatorial Guinea 59 A5

Malacca, Strait of *sea feature* Indonesia/ Malaysia 106 C4 119 C8 120 B3

Maladzyechna Belarus *Rus.* Molodechno, *Pol.* Molodeczno 89 C5

Málaga Spain 74 D5

Malakal Sudan 55 B5

Malang Indonesia 120 D5

Malanje Angola 60 C2

Malatya Turkey 99 E3

Malawi *country* southern Africa 61

Malay Peninsula *peninsula* Malaysia/Thailand 119 D8

Malaysia *country* Asia 120

Malden Island *atoll* Kiribati 125 F2

Maldives *country* Indian Ocean 114 C4

Male' *capital of* Maldives 114 C4

Malekula *island* Vanuatu 124 D3

Mali *country* W Africa 57

Malindi Kenya 55 C7

Mallorca *island* Spain *Eng.* Majorca 75 H3

Malmö Sweden 67 B7

Malta *country* Mediterranean Sea 79 C8

Malta Montana, USA 24 C1

Malta Channel *sea feature* Mediterranean Sea 79 C7

Maluku *island group* Indonesia *var.* Moluccas 107 E4 121 F4

Maluku, Laut *Pacific Ocean Eng.* Molucca Sea 121 F4

Mamberamo *river* Indonesia 121 H4

Mamoudzou *capital of* Mayotte 61 G2

Man, Isle of *island* UK 71 C5

Manado Indonesia 121 F3

Managua *capital of* Nicaragua 34 D3

Manama *capital of* Bahrain *Ar.* Al Manāmah 103 C5

Mananjary Madagascar 61 G3

Manaus Brazil 42 D2

Manchester England, UK 71 D5

Manchester New Hampshire, USA 23 G2

Manchurian Plain *plain* E Asia 107 E1

Mandalay Myanmar 118 B3

Mangalia Romania 90 D5

Mangalore India 114 C2

Manicouagan, Réservoir *Reservoir* Canada 21 E3

Manihiki *atoll* Cook Islands 125 F3

Maniitsoq Greenland 64 C3

Manila *capital of* Philippines 121 E1

Manisa Turkey *prev.* Saruhan 98 A3

Manitoba *province* Canada 19 G4

Manizales Colombia 40 B3

Manjimup Australia 129 B7

Mannar Sri Lanka 115 E3

Mannar, Gulf of *sea feature* Indian Ocean 114 D3

Mannheim Germany 77 B5

Manono Congo (Zaire) 59 E7

Mansel Island *island* Canada 20 C1

Mansfield Ohio, USA 22 D4

Manta Ecuador 40 A4

Mantes-la-Jolie France 72 C3

Mantova Italy *Eng.* Mantua 78 B2

Mantua *see* Mantova

Manurewa New Zealand 132 D3

Manzhouli China 109 F1

Mao Chad 58 B3

Maoke, Pegunungan *mountains* Indonesia 121 H4

Maputo *capital of* Mozambique 61 E4

Mar, Serra do *mountains* Brazil 38 D4

Maracaibo Venezuela 40 C1

Maracaibo, Lago de *inlet* Venezuela 40 C1

Maracay Venezuela 40 D1

Maradi Niger 57 F3

Marāgheh Iran 102 C3

Marajó, Ilha de *island* Brazil 43 F2

Marañón *river* Peru 42 B2

Maraş *see* Kahramanmaraş

Marash *see* Kahramanmaraş

Marbella Spain 74 D5

Marble Bar Australia 128 B4

Mar Chiquita, Laguna *salt lake* Argentina 46 C3

Mardān Pakistan 116 C1

Mar del Plata Argentina 47 D5

Mardin Turkey 99 E4

Margarita, Isla de *island* Venezuela 41 E1

Mārgow, Dasht-e- *desert* Afghanistan 104 C5

Mariana Trench *undersea feature* Pacific Ocean 124 B1 126 B1

Marías, Islas *islands* Mexico 32 C4

Maribor Slovenia 77 E7

Marie Byrd Land *region* Antarctica 136 B4

Mariehamn Finland 67 D6

Marijampolė Lithuania *prev.* Kapsukas 88 B4

Marília Brazil 44 D2

Maringá Brazil 44 D2

Marion, Lake *lake* South Carolina, USA 31 F2

Mariscal Estigarribia Paraguay 44 B2

Maritsa *river* SE Europe 86 D3

Mariupol' Ukraine *prev.* Shdanov 91 G3

Marka Somalia 55 D6

Marmara, Sea of *see* Marmara Denizi

Marmara Denizi Turkey *Eng.* Sea of Marmara 98 B2

Marne *river* France 72 D3

Marotiri *Island group* French Polynesia 125 F4

Maroua Cameroon 58 B3

Marowijne *river* French Guiana/Suriname 41 H3

Marquesas Fracture Zone *tectonic feature* Pacific Ocean 125 G3

Marquesas Islands *island group* French Polynesia *Fr.* Îles Marquises 125 G3

Marquette Michigan, USA 22 B1

Marquisas, Îles *see* Marquesas Islands

Marrakech Morocco *Eng.* Marrakesh 52 C2

Marrawah Australia 131 C8

Marree Australia 131 B5

Marsala Italy 79 C6

Marseille France 73 D6

Marshall Islands *country* Pacific Ocean 126-127

Martin Slovakia *prev.* Turčiansky Svätý Martin, *Ger.* Sankt Martin, *Hung.* Turócszentmárton 81 C5

Martinique *external territory* France, West Indies 37

Mary Turkmenistan *prev.* Merv 104 C3

Maryborough Australia 131 E5

Maryland *state* USA 23 F4

Masai Steppe *grassland* Tanzania 55 C7

Mascarene Basin *undersea feature* Indian Ocean 123 B5

Mascarene Islands *island group* Indian Ocean 61 H4

Mascarene Plain *undersea feature* Indian Ocean 123 B5

Mascarene Plateau *undersea feature* Indian Ocean 123 B5

Maseru *capital of* Lesotho 60 D4

Mas-ha Bank 101 D6

Mashhad Iran *var.* Meshed 100 E3

Masindi Uganda 55 B6

Maṣīra, Jazīrat *Island* Oman 103 E6

Maṣīrah, Khalīj *bay* Oman 103 E6

Mason City Iowa, USA 25 F3

Masqaṭ *see* Muscat

Massachusetts *state* USA 23 G3

Massawa Eritrea 54 C4

Massif Central *upland* France 73 C5

Massoukou Gabon 59 B6

Masterton New Zealand 133 D5

Matadi Congo (Zaire) 59 B7

Matagalpa Nicaragua 34 D3

Matamoros Mexico 33 E2

Matanzas Cuba 36 B2

Matara Sri Lanka 115 E4

Mataram Indonesia 120 D5

Mataró Spain 75 G2

Mato Grosso *upland* Brazil 43 E3

Matosinhos Portugal 74 C2

Matsue Japan 113 B5

Matsuyama Japan 113 B5

Maturín Venezuela 41 E1

Maun Botswana 60 D3

Mauritania *country* W Africa 56

Mauritius *country* Indian Ocean 61 H4 123 B5

Mayaguana *island* Bahamas 36 D2

Mayfield New Zealand 133 C6

Mayotte *external territory* France, Indian Ocean 61 G2

Mayyit, Al Baḥr *see* Dead Sea

Mazār-e Sharīf Afghanistan 104 D3

Mazatlán Mexico 32 C3

Mažeikiai Lithuania 88 B3

Mazury *region* Poland 80 D3

Mazyr Belarus *Rus.* Mozyr' 89 D7

Mbabane *capital of* Swaziland 61 E4

Mbaké Senegal 56 B3

Mbala Zambia 61 E1

Mbale Uganda 55 C6

Mbandaka Congo (Zaire) 59 C5

Mbeya Tanzania 55 B8

Mbuji-Mayi Congo (Zaire) 59 D7

McKinley, Mount *peak* Alaska, USA *var.* Denali 18 C3

Mead, Lake *lake* SW USA 28 A1

Mecca *see* Makkah

Mechelen Belgium 69 C5

Mecklenburger Bucht *bay* Germany 76 C2

Medan Indonesia 120 B3

Medellín Colombia 40 B2

Médenine Tunisia 53 F2

Medford Oregon, USA 26 A4

Medina *see* Al Madīnah

Mediterranean Sea Atlantic Ocean 84-85

Meekatharra Australia 129 B5

Meerut India 116 D3

Minneapolis Minnesota, USA 23 F2

Minnesota *state* USA 25 F2

Miño *river* Portugal/Spain *Port.* Minho 74 C1

Minorca *see* Menorca

Minot North Dakota, USA 24 D1

Minā' Qābūs Oman 122 B3

Minsk *capital of* Belarus 89 C5

Minto, Lake *lake* Canada 20 D2

Miranda de Ebro Spain 75 E1

Mirim, Lake *see* Mirim Lagoon

Mirim Lagoon *lagoon* Brazil/Uruguay *var.* Mirim, Lake 44 C5

Mírtóo Pelagos *sea feature* Mediterranean Sea 87 C6

Miskitos Cayos *islands* Nicaragua 35 E2

Miskolc Hungary 81 D6

Mişrātah Libya 53 F2

Mississippi *state* USA 30 C2

Mississippi *river* USA 16 C5

Mississippi Delta *wetlands* USA 30 C4

Missoula Montana, USA 24 B2

Missouri *state* USA 25 G4

Missouri *river* USA 17 C5

Mistassini, Lake *lake* Canada 20 D3

Mitau *see* Jelgava

Mitchell South Dakota, USA 25 E3

Mitchell River *river* Australia 130 C3

Mitilíni Greece 86 D4

Mito Japan 112 D4

Mitumba, Monts *Mountain range* Dem. Rep. Congo (Zaire) 59 E7

Miyazaki Japan 113 B6

Mjøsa *lake* Norway 67 B5

Mljet *island* Croatia 83 C5

Mmabatho South Africa 60 D4

Mo Norway 66 C3

Mobile Alabama, USA 30 C3

Moçambique Mozambique 61 F2

Mocímboa da Praia Mozambique 61 F2

Mocoa Colombia 40 B4

Mocuba Mozambique 61 E3

Modena Italy 78 B3

Modesto California, USA 27 B6

Modohn *see* Madona

Modriča Bosnia & Herzegovina 82 C3

Mogadiscio *see* Mogadishu

Mogadishu *capital of* Somalia *Som.* Muqdisho, *It.* Mogadiscio 55 D6

Mogilëv *see* Mahilyow

Mohéli *island* Comoros 61 G2

Mo i Rana Norway 66 C3

Mojave California, USA 27 C7

Mojave Desert *desert* W USA 27 C7

Moldavia *see* Moldova

Molde Norway 67 A5

Moldova *country* E Europe *var.* Moldavia 90

Molodechno *see* Maladzyechna

Molodeczno *see* Maladzyechna

Molotov *see* Perm'

Moluccas *see* Maluku

Molucca Sea *see* Maluku, Laut

Mombasa Kenya 55 C7

Monaco *country* W Europe 73 E6

Monclova Mexico 33 E2

Moncton Canada 21 F4

Mongo Chad 58 C3

Mongolia *country* NE Asia 108-109

Monroe Louisiana, USA 30 B2

Monrovia *capital of* Liberia 56 C5

Mons Belgium 69 B6

Montague Seamount *undersea feature* Atlantic Ocean 45 H1

Montana *state* USA 24 C2

Montauban France 73 C6

Mont Blanc *peak* France/Italy 62 D4

Mont-de-Marsan France 72 B6

Monte Cristi Dominican Republic 37 E3

Montego Bay Jamaica 36 C3

Montenegro *Republic* Yugoslavia 83 D5

Monterey California, USA 27 B6

Montería Colombia 40 B2

Montero Bolivia 42 D4

Monterrey Mexico 33 E2

Montes Claros Brazil 43 G4

Montevideo *capital of* Uruguay 44 C5

Montgomery Alabama, USA 30 D2

Monthey Switzerland 77 A7

Montpelier Vermont, USA 23 F2

Montpellier France 73 C6

Montréal Canada 21 E4

Montserrat *external territory* UK, West Indies 37

Monywa Myanmar 118 A3

Monza Italy 78 B2

Moora Australia 129 B6

Moore, Lake *lake* Australia 129 B6

Moorhead Minnesota, USA 25 E2

Moosonee Canada 20 C3

Mopti Mali 57 E3

Morava *river* C Europe 82 E4

Moravská Ostrava *see* Ostrava

Moray Firth *inlet* Scotland, UK 70 C3

Moree Australia 131 D5

Morelia Mexico 33 E4

Morena, Sierra *mountain range* Spain 74 D4

Morghāb *river* Afghanistan/Turkmenistan 104 D3

Morioka Japan 112 D3

Mornington Abyssal Plain *undersea feature* Pacific Ocean 135 C6

Morocco *country* N Africa 52

Morogoro Tanzania 55 C7

Mörön Mongolia 108 D2

Morondava Madagascar 61 F3

Moroni *capital of* Comoros 61 F2

Morotai, Pulau *island* Indonesia 121 F3

Morova *river* Poland 80 C6

Morris Jesup, Kap *headland* Greenland 65 E1

Moscow *capital of* Russian Federation *Rus.* Moskva 92 B4 96 B2

Mosel *river* W Europe *Fr.* Moselle 77 A5

Moselle *river* W Europe *Ger.* Mosel 72 E4

Mosgiel New Zealand 133 B7

Moshi Tanzania 55 C7

Moskva *see* Moscow

Mosquito Coast *coastal region* Nicaragua 35 E3

Moss Norway 67 B6

Mossendjo Congo 59 B6

Mossoró Brazil 43 H2

Most Czech Republic *Ger.* Brüx 80 A4

Mostaganem Algeria 52 D1

Mostar Bosnia & Herzegovina 82 C4

Mosul *see* Al Mawşil

Motril Spain 75 E5

Motueka New Zealand 133 C5

Moulins France 72 C4

Moulmein Myanmar 118 B4

Moundou Chad 58 C4

Mount Gambier Australia 131 B7

Mount Isa Australia 130 B4

Mount Magnet Australia 129 B5

Mount Vernon Illinois, USA 22 B5

Mouscron Belgium 69 A6

Moyobamba Peru 42 B2

Moyu China 108 B2

Mozambique *country* SE Africa 61

Mozambique Channel *sea feature* Indian Ocean 61 F3

Mozyr' *see* Mazyr

Mpika Zambia 61 E2

Mtwara Tanzania 55 C8

Muang Không Laos 119 D5

Muang Xaignabouri *see* Xaignabouri

Mudanjiang China 110 B3

Mufulira Zambia 60 D2

Mugla Turkey 98 A4

Mulhouse France 72 E4

Mull *island* Scotland, UK 70 B3

Muller, Pegunungan *mountains* Indonesia 120 C3

Multán Pakistan 116 C2

Mumbai India *var.* Bombay 117 C5

München Germany *Eng.* Munich 77 C6

Muncie Indiana, USA 22 C4

Munich *see* München

Münster Germany 76 B4

Muqdisho *see* Mogadishu

Mur *river* C Europe 77 E7

Murchison River *river* Australia 129 B5

Murcia Spain 75 F4

Mures *river* Hungary/Romania 81 D7

Murfreesboro Tennessee, USA 30 D1

Murgab Tajikistan 105 F3

Murgab *river* Turkmenistan *var.* Murghab 104 C3

Murghab *see* Murgab

Müritz *lake* Germany 76 D3

Murmansk Russian Federation 92 C2 96 C1

Murray *river* Australia 131 B6

Murray Fracture Zone *tectonic feature* Pacific Ocean 135 E2

Murray Ridge *Undersea feature* Arabian Sea 122 B3

Murwillumbah Australia 131 E5

Murzuq Libya 53 F3

Muş Turkey 99 F3

Muscat *capital of* Oman *Ar.* Masqaţ 103 E5

Musgrave Ranges *mountain range* Australia 129 D5

Musters, Lago *lake* Argentina 46 C6

Mu Us Shamo *Desert* China 109 E4

Mvonioälv *river* Finland/Sweden 66 D3

Mwanza Tanzania 55 B6

Mwene-Ditu Congo (Zaire) 59 D7

Mweru, Lake *lake* Congo (Zaire)/Zambia 59 D7

Myanmar *country* SE Asia *var.* Myanmar 118-119

Mykolayiv Ukraine *Rus.* Nikolayev 91 E4

Mykonos *island* Greece 87 D5

Mysore India 114 D2

Mzuzu Malawi 61 E2

N

Naberezhnyye Chelny Russian Federation *prev.* Brezhnev 93 C5

Nablus West Bank *var.* Nābulus, *Heb.* Shekhem 101 D6

Nābulus *see* Nablus

Nacala Mozambique 61 F2

Naga Philippines 120 E2

Nagano Japan 112 C4

Nagasaki Japan 113 A6

Nāgercoil India 114 D3

Nagorno-Karabakh *region* Azerbaijan 99 G2

Nagoya Japan 113 C5

Nāgpur India 116 D4

Nagqu China 108 C5

Nagykanizsa Hungary *Ger.* Grosskanizsa 81 C7

Nagyszombat *see* Trnava

Naha Japan 113 A8

Nain Canada 21 F2

Nairobi *capital of* Kenya 55 C6

Najaf *see* An Najaf

Najrān Saudi Arabia 103 B6

Nakamura Japan 113 B6

Nakhichevan' *see* Naxçivan

Nakhon Ratchasima Thailand 119 C5

Nakhon Sawan Thailand 119 C5

Nakhon Si Thammarat Thailand 119 C6

Nakuru Kenya 55 C6

Nal'chik Russian Federation 96 A4

Namangan Uzbekistan 105 E2

Nam Co *lake* China 108 C4

Nam Dinh Vietnam 118 D3

Namib Desert *desert* Namibia 60 B3

Namibe Angola 60 B2

Namibia *country* southern Africa 60

Nampa Idaho, USA 26 C3

Namp'o North Korea 110 E4

Nampula Mozambique 61 F2

Namur Belgium 69 C6

Nanchang China 111 C5

Nancy France 72 D3

Nânded India 116 D5 114 D1

Nanjing China 111 D5

Nanning China 111 B6

Nanortalik Greenland 64 C5

Nansen Basin *undersea feature* Arctic Ocean 137 G4

Nantes France 72 B4

Napier New Zealand 132 E4

Naples *see* Napoli

Napo *river* Ecuador/Peru 42 B2

Napoli Italy *Eng.* Naples 79 D5

Narbonne France 73 C6

Nares Strait *sea feature* Canada/Greenland 64 C1

Narew *river* Poland 80 E3

Narmada *river* India 116 D4

Narva Estonia 88 E2

Narva *river* Estonia/Russian Federation 88 E2

Narva Bay *sea feature* Gulf of Finland *Est.* Narva Laht, *Rus.* Narvskiy Zaliv 88 E2

Narva Laht *see* Narva Bay

Narvik Norway 66 C3

Narvskiy Zaliv *see* Narva Bay

Naryn Kyrgyzstan 105 G2

Näshik India 116 C5

Nashville Tennessee, USA 30 D1

Nâsir, Buheiret *see* Nasser, Lake

Nassau *capital of* Bahamas 36 C1

Nasser, Lake *reservoir* Egypt *var.* Nâsir, Buheiret 54 B2

Natal Brazil 43 H3

Natal Basin *Undersea feature* Indian Ocean 123 A5

Natitingou Benin 57 E4

Naturaliste Plateau *undersea feature* Indian Ocean 123 E6

Nauru *country* Pacific Ocean 126 D3

Navapolatsk Belarus *Rus.* Novopolotsk 89 D5

Navassa Island *external territory* USA, West Indies 36 D3

Nawâbshâh Pakistan 116 B3

Nawoiy Uzbekistan *Uzb.* Nawoly 104 D2

Nawoly *see* Navoi

Naxçivan Azerbaijan *Rus.* Nakhichevan' 99 G3

Náxos *island* Greece 87 D6

Nazareth *see* Nazerat

Nazca Peru 42 B4

Nazerat Israel *Eng.* Nazareth 101 A5

Nazrêt Ethiopia 55 C5

Nazwá Oman 103 E5

N'Dalatando Angola 60 B2

Ndélé Central African Republic 58 C4

N'Djamena *capital of* Chad 58 B3

Ndola Zambia 60 D2

Nebitdag Turkmenistan 104 B2

Nebraska *state* USA 24-25 E3

Neches *river* S USA 29 H3

Neckar *river* Germany 77 B5

Necochea Argentina 47 D5

Neftezavodsk *see* Seydi

Negêlê Ethiopia 55 C5

Negev *see* HaNegev

Negro, Rio *river* Argentina 47 C5

Negro, Rio *river* Brazil/Uruguay 44 C4

Negro, Rio *river* N South America 40 C1

Neiva Colombia 40 B3

Nellore India 115 E2

Neman *river* NE Europe *Bel.* Nyoman, *Lith.* Nemunas, *Ger.* Memel, *Pol.* Niemen 88 B4

Nemunas *see* Neman

Nemuro Japan 112 E2

Nepal *country* S Asia 117

Neris *river* Belarus/Lithuania *Bel.* Viliya, *Pol.* Wilja 88 C4

Ness, Loch *lake* Scotland, UK 70 C3

Netherlands *country* W Europe *var.* Holland 68-69

Netherlands Antilles *external territory* Netherlands, West Indies *prev.* Dutch West Indies 37 E5

Netze *see* Noteć

Neubrandenburg Germany 76 D3

Neuchâtel, Lac de *lake* Switzerland 77 A7

Neumünster Germany 76 C2

Neuquén Argentina 47 C5

Neusiedler See *lake* Austria/Hungary 77 E6

Neusohl *see* Banská Bystrica

Neutra *see* Nitra

Nevada *state* USA 26-27

Nevers France 72 C4

Nevşehir Turkey 98 C3

New Amsterdam Guyana 41 G2

Newark New Jersey, USA 23 F3

New Britain *island* Papua New Guinea 126 B3

New Brunswick *province* Canada 21 F4

New Caledonia *external territory* France, Pacific Ocean 126 C5

New Caledonia *island* Pacific Ocean 124 D3

New Caledonia Basin *undersea feature* Pacific Ocean 124 D4

Newcastle Australia 131 D6

Newcastle upon Tyne England, UK 70 D4

New Delhi *capital of* India
116 D3

Newfoundland *province*
Canada 21 F2

Newfoundland *island* Canada
21 G3

Newfoundland Basin *undersea
feature* Atlantic Ocean 48 B3

New Georgia Islands *island
group* Solomon Is 126 C3

New Guinea *island* Pacific
Ocean 126 B3

New Hampshire *state* USA
23 G2

New Haven Connecticut, USA
23 G3

New Ireland *island* Papua New
Guinea 126 C3

New Jersey *state* USA 23 F4

Newman Australia 128 B4

New Mexico *state* USA
28-29

New Orleans Louisiana, USA
30 C3

New Plymouth New Zealand
132 D3

Newport Oregon, USA 26 A3

Newport News Virginia, USA
23 F5

New Providence *island*
Bahamas 36 C1

Newry Northern Ireland, UK
71 B5

New Siberian Islands *see*
Novosibirskiye Ostrova

New South Wales *state*
Australia 131 C6

New York *state* USA 23 F3

New York New York, USA 23 F3

New Zealand *country* Pacific
Ocean 132-133

Neyshābūr Iran 102 D3

Ngaoundéré Cameroon 58 B4

N'Giva Angola 60 C3

N'Guigmi Niger 57 H3

Nha Trang Vietnam 119 E5

Niagara Falls *waterfall*
Canada/USA 23 E3

Niamey *capital of* Niger 57 F3

Niangay, Lac *lake* Mali 56 E3

Nias, Pulau *island* Indonesia
120 B3

Nicaragua *country* Central
America 34-35

Nicaragua, Lago de *lake*
Nicaragua 34 D3

Nice France 73 E6

Nicobar Islands *island group*
India 115 H3

Nicosia *capital of* Cyprus *var.*
Lefkosia, *Turk.* Lefkoşa 98 C5

Nicoya, Peninsula de *peninsula*
Costa Rica 34 D4

Niemen *see* Neman

Nieuw Amsterdam Suriname
41 H2

Niğde Turkey 98 D4

Niger *country* W Africa 57

Niger *river* W Africa 56-57 D3

Niger, Mouths of the *delta*
Nigeria 57 F5

Nigeria *country* W Africa 57

Niigata Japan 112 C4

Nijmegen Netherlands 68 D4

Nikolayev *see* Mykolayiv

Nikopol' Ukraine 91 F3

Nile *river* N Africa 54 B3

Nile Delta *wetlands* Egypt
54 B1

Nîmes France 73 D6

Ninetyeast Ridge *undersea
feature* Indian Ocean 123 C5

Ningbo China 111 D5

Ningxia *autonomous region*
China 110-111 B4

Nioro Mali 56 D3

Nipigon, Lake *lake* Canada
20 B4

Niš Yugoslavia 82 E4

Nitra Slovakia *Ger.* Neutra,
Hung. Nyitra 81 C6

Nitra *river* Slovakia *Ger.*
Neutra, *Hung.* Nyitra 81 C6

Niue *external territory* New
Zealand, Pacific Ocean 127 F4

Nizāmābād India 114 D1

Nizhnevartovsk Russian
Federation 96 D3

Nizhniy Novgorod Russian
Federation *prev.* Gor'kiy 93
C5 96 B3

Nkongsamba Cameroon 58 B4

Norak Tajikistan 105 E3

Nord Greenland 65 E2

Nordaustlandet *island* Svalbard
65 G1

Norfolk Virginia, USA 23 F5

Norfolk Island *external territory*
Australia, Pacific Ocean
124 D4

Norfolk Ridge *undersea feature*
Pacific Ocean 124 D4

Norman Oklahoma, USA 28 F2

Normandie *region* France *Eng.*
Normandy 72 B3

Normandy *see* Normandie

Normanton Australia 130 C3

Norrköping Sweden 67 C6

Norseman Australia 129 C6

North Albanian Alps *mountains*
Albania/Yugoslavia 83 D5

North America 16-17

North Andaman *island* India
115 G2

North Atlantic Ocean 64-65

North Australian Basin
undersea feature Indian
Ocean 124 A2 128 A2

North Bay Canada 20 D4

North Cape *coastal feature*
New Zealand 132 C1

North Cape *coastal feature*
Norway 66 D2

North Carolina *state* USA 31 F1

North Dakota *state* USA 24-25
D2

North Fiji Basin *undersea
feature* Coral Sea 124 D3

Northern Cook Islands *islands*
Cook Islands 127 G4

**Northern Cyprus, Turkish
Republic of** *disputed region*
Cyprus 98 C5

Northern Dvina *river* Russian
Federation *see* Severnaya
Dvina 63 G2

Northern Ireland *province* UK 70-71

Northern Mariana Islands *external territory* USA, Pacific Ocean 124 C1

Northern Sporades *see* Voreíoi Sporades

Northern Territory *territory* Australia 130 A3

North European Plain *region* N Europe 62 E3

North Frisian Islands *islands* Denmark/Germany 76 B2

North Island *island* New Zealand 132 G2

North Korea *country* E Asia 110

North Little Rock Arkansas, USA 30 B1

North Platte Nebraska, USA 25 E4

North Platte *river* C USA 24 D3

North Pole *ice feature* Arctic Ocean 137 G3

North Sea Atlantic Ocean 70 E2

North Siberian Lowland *lowlands* Russian Federation 94-95

North Taranaki Bight *gulf* New Zealand 132 D3

North Uist *island* Scotland, UK 70 B3

Northwest Territories *territory* Canada 19 E3

Norway *country* N Europe 66-67

Norwegian Sea Arctic Ocean 137 G5

Norwich England, UK 71 E6

Noteć *river* Poland *Ger.* Netze 80 C3

Nottingham England, UK 71 D6

Nottingham Island *island* Hudson Strait 20 D1

Nouâdhibou Mauritania 56 B2

Nouakchott *capital of* Mauritania 56 B2

Nouméa *capital of* New Caledonia 126 D5

Nova Gradiška Croatia 82 C3

Nova Iguaçu Brazil 43 F5 45 F2

Novara Italy 78 B2

Nova Scotia *province* Canada 21 F4

Novaya Zemlya *islands* Russian Federation 137 H4

Novaya Zemlya Trench *see* East Novaya Zemlya Trench

Novgorod Russian Federation 92 B4 96 B2

Novi Sad Yugoslavia 82 D3

Novokuznetsk Russian Federation *prev.* Stalinsk 96 D4

Novopolotsk *see* Navapolatsk

Novosibirsk Russian Federation 96 D4

Novosibirskiye Ostrova *islands* Russian Federation *Eng.* New Siberian Islands 95 F1

Novo Urgench *see* Urgench

Novyy Margilan *see* Fergana

Nsanje Malawi 61 E3

Nsawam Ghana 57 E5

Nubian Desert *desert* Sudan 54 B3

Nu'eima West Bank 101 D7

Nuevo Laredo Mexico 33 E2

Nuku'alofa *capital of* Tonga 127 F5

Nukus Uzbekistan 104 C2

Nullarbor Plain *region* Australia 129 D6

Nunap Isua Island *coastal region* Greenland *var.* Uummannaruaq *Dan.* Kap Farvel 64 C5

Nunavut *Territory* Canada 19 F3

Nunivak Island *island* Alaska, USA 18 B2

Nuoro Italy 79 A5

Nuremberg *see* Nürnberg

Nürnberg Germany *Eng.* Nuremberg 77 C5

Nusa Tenggara *islands* East Timor / Indonesia 120 E5

Nuuk Greenland *var.* Godthåb 64 C4

Nyaingêntanglha Shan *mountain range* China 108 D5

Nyala Sudan 54 A4

Nyasa, Lake *lake* E Africa 51 D5

Nyeri Kenya 55 C6

Nyima China 108 C4

Nyíregyháza Hungary 81 E6

Nyitra *see* Nitra

Nykøbing Denmark 67 B8

Nyköping Sweden 67 C6

Nyngan Australia 131 D6

Nyoman *see* Neman

O

Oakland California, USA 27 B6

Oakley Kansas, USA 25 E4

Oamaru New Zealand 133 B7

Oaxaca Mexico 33 F5

Ob' *river* Russian Federation 96 D4

Oban Scotland, UK 70 C4

Obihiro Japan 112 D2

Obo Central African Republic 58 D4

Oceania 124-125

Ocean Island *see* Banaba

Oceanside California, USA 27 C8

Ochamchira *see* Och'amch'ire

Och'amch'ire Georgia *Rus.* Ochamchira 99 E1

Ödenburg *see* Sopron

Odense Denmark 67 B7

Oder *river* C Europe 80 C4

Odesa Ukraine *Rus.* Odessa 91 E4

Odessa *see* Odesa

Odessa Texas, USA 29 E3

Odienné Côte d'Ivoire 56 D4

Oesel *see* Saaremaa

Ofanto *river* Italy 79 D5

Offenbach Germany 77 B5

Ogadēn *plateau* Ethiopia 55 D5

Ogallala Nebraska, USA 24 D4

Ogbomosho Nigeria 57 F4

Ogden Utah, USA 24 B3

Ottawa *river* Canada 20 D4
Ou *river* Laos 118 C3
Ouachita *river* SE USA 30 B2
Ouagadougou *capital of* Burkina 57 E3
Ouarâne *desert* Mauritania 56 D2
Ouargla Algeria 53 E2
Ouessant, Île d' *island* France 72 A3
Ouésso Congo 59 C5
Oujda Morocco 52 D2
Oulu Finland 66 D4
Oulu *river* Finland 66 D4
Oulujärvi *lake* Finland 66 E4
Ounasjoki *river* Finland 66 D3
Our *river* W Europe 69 E7
Ourense Spain *Cast.* Orense 74 C2
Ourinhos Brazil 44 D2
Ourthe *river* Belgium 69 D6
Outer Hebrides *island group* UK *var.* Western Isles 70 B3
Outer Islands *island group* Seychelles 61 H2
Ouyen Australia 131 C6
Oviedo Spain 74 D1
Owando Congo 59 C6
Owen Fracture Zone *tectonic feature* Arabian Sea 122 B3
Owensboro Kentucky, USA 22 B5
Oxford England, UK 71 D6
Oxnard California, USA 29 C7
Oyem Gabon 59 B5
Oyo Nigeria 57 F4
Ozark Plateau *plain* Arkansas/Missouri, USA 25 G5
Ózd Hungary 81 D6

P

Paamiut Greenland 64 B4
Pachuca Mexico 33 E4
Pacific-Antarctic Ridge *undersea feature* Pacific Ocean 136 B5
Pacific Ocean 134-135

Padang Indonesia 120 B4
Paderborn Germany 76 B4
Padova Italy *Eng.* Padua 78 C2
Padre Island *island* Texas, USA 29 G5
Padua *see* Padova
Paducah Kentucky, USA 22 B5
Paeroa Waikato, New Zealand 132 D3
Pafos *see* Paphos
Pag *island* Croatia 82 A3
Pago Pago *capital of* American Samoa 127 F4
Paide Estonia *Ger.* Weissenstein 88 D2
Paihia New Zealand 132 D2
Painted Desert *desert* SW USA 28 C1
País Valenciano *cultural region* Spain 75 F3
Pakistan *country* S Asia 116
Pakokku Myanmar 118 A3
Palagruža *island* Croatia 83 B5
Palau *country* Pacific Ocean *var.* Belau 124 B2 126
Palawan *island* Philippines 121 E2
Palawan Passage *passage* Philippines 121 E2
Paldiski Estonia *prev.* Baltiski, *Eng.* Baltic Port, *Ger.* Baltischport 88 C2
Palembang Indonesia 120 C4
Palencia Spain 74 D2
Palermo Italy 79 C6
Palikir *capital of* Micronesia 126 C2
Palioúri, Akrotírio *coastal feature* Greece *var.* Akra Kanestron 86 C4
Palk Strait *sea feature* India/Sri Lanka 115 E3
Palliser, Cape *headland* New Zealand 133 D5
Palm Springs California, USA 27 D8
Palma Spain 75 G3
Palmer Land *physical region* Antarctica 136 A3

Palmerston North New Zealand 132 D4
Palmyra *see* Tudmur
Palmyra Atoll *external territory* USA, Pacific Ocean 125 F2
Palu Indonesia 121 E4
Pamir *river* Afghanistan/Tajikistan 105 F3
Pamirs *mountains* Tajikistan 105 F3
Pampa Texas, USA 29 E2
Pampas *region* South America 46 C4
Pamplona Spain 75 F1
Pānāji India 114 C2
Panama *country* Central America 35
Panamá, Golfo de *sea feature* Panama 35 F5
Panama Canal *canal* Panama 35 F4
Panama City *capital of* Panama 35 F5
Panama City Florida, USA 30 D3
Pančevo Yugoslavia 82 D3
Panevėžys Lithuania 88 C4
Pantanal *region* Brazil 38 C4
Pantelleria *island* Italy 79 B7
Papeete *capital of* French Polynesia 127 H4
Paphos Cyprus *var.* Pafos 98 C5
Papua New Guinea *country* Pacific Ocean 126
Paracel Islands *disputed territory* Asia 120 D1
Paragua *river* Venezuela 41 E3
Paraguay *country* South America 44
Paraguay *river* C South America 38 C4 44 B2
Parakou Benin 57 F4
Paramaribo *capital of* Suriname 41 G2
Paraná Argentina 46 D4
Paraná *river* C South America 46 D3
Paranaíba Brazil 43 G2
Paraparaumu New Zealand 132 D4

Pardubice Czech Republic *Ger.*
  Pardubitz 81 B5
Pardubitz *see* Pardubice
Parepare Indonesia 121 E4
Paris *capital of* France 72 C3
Paris Texas, USA 29 G2
Parma Italy 78 B3
Pärnu Estonia *Rus.* Pyarnu,
  prev. Pernov, *Ger.* Pernau
  88 C2
Páros *island* Greece 87 D6
Pasadena California, USA 27 C7
Pasadena Texas, USA 29 G4
Passo Fundo Brazil 44 D3
Pasto Colombia 40 B4
Patagonia *region* S South
  America 47 C6
Patna India 117 F3
Patos, Lagoa dos *lagoon* Brazil
  44 D4
Pátra Greece 87 B5
Pattani Thailand 119 C7
Pattaya Thailand 119 C5
Patuca *river* Honduras 34 D2
Pau France 73 B6
Pavlodar Kazakhstan 96 C4
Pavlograd *see* **Pavlohrad**
Pavlohrad Ukraine *Rus.*
  Pavlograd 91 G3
Paysandú Uruguay 44 B4
Pazardzhik Bulgaria *prev.* Tatar
  Pazardzhik 86 C2
Pearl *river* SE USA 30 C3
Peć Yugoslavia 83 D5
Pechora *river* Russian
  Federation 92 D3
Pecos Texas, USA 29 E3
Pecos *river* SW USA 28 D2
Pécs Hungary *Ger.* Fünfkirchen
  81 C7
Pegasus Bay *bay* New Zealand
  133 C5
Pegu Myanmar 118 B4
Peipsi Järv *see* Peipus, Lake
Peipus, Lake *lake*
  Estonia/Russian Federation
  Est. Peipsi Järv, *Rus.*
  Chudskoye Ozero 88 D2

Peiraías Greece *var.* Piraiévs,
  Eng. Piraeus 87 C5
Pekalongan Jawa, Indonesia
  120 C4
Pekanbaru Indonesia 120 B3
Peking *see* Beijing
Pelagie, Isola *island* Italy 79 B8
Peloponnese *see* Pelopónnisos
Pelopónnisos *peninsula* Greece
  Eng. Peloponnese 87 B5
Pelotas Brazil 44 C4
Pelotas *river* Brazil 44 C3
Pematangsiantar Indonesia
  120 B3
Pemba *island* Tanzania 51 E5
Pendleton Oregon, USA 26 C2
Pennines *hills* England, UK
  70 D4
Pennsylvania *state* USA 23 E3
Penong Australia 131 A6
Penonomé Panama 35 F5
Penrhyn *atoll* Cook Islands
  125 F3
Penrhyn Basin *undersea feature*
  Pacific Ocean 135 E2
Pensacola Florida, USA 30 D3
Penza Russian Federation
  93 B5
Penzance England, UK 71 C7
Peoria Illinois, USA 22 B4
Percival Lakes *lakes* Australia
  128 C4
Pereira Colombia 40 B3
Périgueux France 73 B5
Perm' Russian Federation *prev.*
  Molotov 93 D5 96 B3
Pernau *see* Pärnu
Pernik Bulgaria *prev.* Dimitrovo
  86 C2
Pernov *see* Pärnu
Perpignan France 73 C6
Persian Gulf *see* The Gulf
Perth Australia 129 B6
Perth Scotland, UK 70 C3
Perth Basin *undersea feature*
  Indian Ocean 123 E6
Peru C South America 42
Peru-Chile Trench *undersea
  feature* Pacific Ocean 135 G3

Perugia Italy 78 C4
Pescara Italy 78 D4
Peshāwar Pakistan 116 C1
Petah Tiqwa Israel 101 A5
Peterborough England, UK
  71 E6
Peterborough Canada 20 D5
Peter the First Island *island*
  Antarctica 154 C1
Petra *see* Wādī Mūsā
Petrich Bulgaria 86 C3
Petroaleksandrovsk *see* Turtkul'
Petrograd *see* St Petersburg
Petropavlovsk Russian
  Federation 96 C4
Petropavlovsk-Kamchatskiy
  Russian Federation 97 H3
Petrozavodsk Russian
  Federation 92 B3
Pevek Russian Federation
  97 G1
Pforzheim Germany 77 B6
Phangan, Ko *island* Thailand
  119 C6
Philadelphia Pennsylvania, USA
  23 F4
Philippine Basin *undersea
  feature* Pacific Ocean 124 B1
Philippine Trench *undersea
  feature* Philippine Sea 124 A2
Philippines *country* Asia 121
Philippine Sea Pacific Ocean
  121 F1 124 A1
Philippopolis *see* Plovdiv
Phnom Penh *capital of*
  Cambodia 119 D6
Phoenix Arizona, USA 28 B2
Phoenix Islands *island group*
  Kiribati 127 F3
Phôngsali Laos 118 C3
Phuket Thailand 119 B7
Phuket, Ko *island* Thailand
  119 B7
Phumĭ Sâmraông Cambodia
  119 D5
Piacenza Italy 78 B2
Piatra-Neamţ Romania 90 C3
Piave *river* Italy 78 C2
Picton New Zealand 133 C5

Pielinen *lake* Finland 66 E4

Pierre South Dakota, USA 25 E3

Piešťany Slovakia *Ger.* Pistyan, *Hung.* Pöstyén 81 C6

Pietermaritzburg South Africa 60 D4

Pihkva Järv *see* Pskov, Lake

Piła Poland *Ger.* Schneidemühl 80 C3

Pilar Paraguay 44 B3

Pilchilemu Chile 46 B4

Pilcomayo *river* C South America 44 B2 46 D2

Pilsen *see* Plzeň

Pinar del Río Cuba 36 A2

Pindos *mountain range* Greece *Eng.* Pindus Mountains 86 A4

Pindus Mountains *see* Pindos

Pine Bluff Arkansas, USA 30 B2

Pine Creek Australia 128 E2

Pinega *river* Russian Federation 92 C3

Pineiós *river* Greece 86 B4

Ping, Mae Nam *river* Thailand 118 C4

Pinnes, Ákra *coastal feature* Greece 86 C4

Pinsk Belarus *Pol.* Pińsk 89 B4

Piraeus *see* Peiraiás

Piraiévs *see* Peiraiás

Pisa Italy 78 B3

Pisco Peru 42 B4

Pishpek *see* Bishkek

Pistyan *see* Piešťany

Pitcairn Islands *external territory* UK, Pacific Ocean 125 G4

Piteå Sweden 66 D4

Pitești Romania 90 C4

Pittsburgh Pennsylvania, USA 23 E4

Piura Peru 42 A2

Pivdennyy Bug *river* Ukraine 91 E3

Plasencia Spain 74 D3

Plata, Río de la *river* Argentina/Uruguay *var.* River Plate 44 B5 46 D4

Plate, River *see* Plata, Río de la

Platte *river* C USA 25 E4

Plattensee *see* Balaton

Plenty, Bay of *bay* New Zealand 132 E3

Pleven Bulgaria 86 C1

Płock Poland 80 D3

Ploiești Romania 90 C4

Plovdiv Bulgaria *Gk.* Philippopolis 86 C2

Plungė Lithuania 88 B4

Plymouth *capital of* Montserrat 37 G3

Plymouth England, UK 71 C7

Plzeň Czech Republic *Ger.* Pilsen 81 A5

Po *river* Italy 78 B2

Pocatello Idaho, USA 26 E4

Po Delta *wetland* Italy 78 C3

Podgorica Yugoslavia 83 C5

Pohnpei Island *island* Micronesia 126 C2

Pointe-Noire Congo 59 B6

Poitiers France 72 B4

Poland *country* E Europe 80-81

Polatsk Belarus 89 D5

Pol-e Khomrī Afghanistan 105 E4

Poltava Ukraine 91 F2

Poltoratsk *see* Ashgabat

Polynesia *region* Pacific Ocean 127

Pomeranian Bay *bay* Germany/Poland 80 B2

Pompano Beach Florida, USA 31 F5

Ponca City Oklahoma, USA 29 G1

Pondicherry India 115 E2

Ponta Grossa Brazil 44 D2

Pontevedra Spain 74 C1

Pontianak Indonesia 120 C4

Poona *see* Pune

Poopó, Lake *lake* Bolivia 42 C5

Popayán Colombia 40 B3

Poprad Slovakia *Ger.* Deutschendorf 81 D5

Porbandar India 116 B4

Pori Finland 67 D5

Porsgrunn Norway 67 B6

Portalegre Portugal 74 C3

Port Angeles Washington, USA 26 A1

Port Arthur Texas, USA 29 H4

Port Augusta Australia 131 B6

Port-au-Prince *capital of* Haiti 36 D3

Port Blair India 115 G2

Port Douglas Australia 130 D3

Port Elizabeth South Africa 60 D5

Port-Gentil Gabon 59 A6

Port Harcourt Nigeria 57 F5

Port Hardy Canada 18 D5

Port Hedland Australia 128 B4

Portland Australia 131 B7

Portland Maine, USA 23 G2

Portland Oregon, USA 26 B2

Port Lincoln Australia 131 A6

Port Louis *capital of* Mauritius 61 H4

Port Macquarie Australia 131 E6

Port Moresby *capital of* Papua New Guinea 126 B3

Porto Portugal *Eng.* Oporto 74 C2

Porto Alegre Sao Tome and Principe 44 D4

Port-of-Spain *capital of* Trinidad & Tobago 37 G5

Porto-Novo *capital of* Benin 57 F5

Porto Velho Brazil 42 C3

Portoviejo Ecuador 40 A4

Port Said Egypt 54 B1

Portsmouth England, UK 71 D7

Port Sudan Sudan 54 C3

Portugal *country* SW Europe 74

Port-Vila *capital of* Vanuatu 126 D5

Porvenir Chile 47 B7

Posadas Argentina 46 E3

Posen *see* Poznań

Pöstyén *see* Piešťany

Potenza S Italy 79 D5

P'ot'i Georgia 99 E2

Potosí Bolivia 42 C5

Potsdam Germany 76 D4

Póvoa de Varzim Portugal 74 C2

Powder *river* N USA 24 C2

Powell, Lake *lake* SW USA 24 B5

Poza Rica Mexico 33 F4

Poznań Poland *Ger.* Posen 80 C3

Pozo Colorado Paraguay 44 B2

Pozsony *see* Bratislava

Prag *see* Prague

Prague *capital of* Czech Republic *Cz.* Praha, *Ger.* Prag 81 B5

Praha *see* Prague

Praia *capital of* Cape Verde 56 A3

Prato Italy 78 B3

Pratt Kansas, USA 25 E5

Preschau *see* Prešov

Prescott Arizona, USA 28 B2

Presidente Prudente Brazil 44 D2

Prešov Slovakia *Ger.* Eperies, *var.* Preschau, *Hung.* Eperjes 81 D5

Prespa, Lake *lake* SE Europe 83 D6 86 A3

Presque Isle Maine, USA 23 G1

Pressburg *see* Bratislava

Preston England, UK 71 D5

Pretoria *capital of* South Africa 60 D4

Préveza Greece 86 A4

Prijedor Bosnia & Herzegovina 82 B3

Prilep Macedonia 83 E5

Prince Albert Canada 19 F5

Prince Edward Island *province* Canada 21 F4

Prince Edward Islands *island group* South Africa 123 A7

Prince George Canada 19 E5

Prince of Wales Island *island* Canada 19 F2

Prince Rupert Canada 18 D4

Princess Charlotte Bay *bay* Australia 130 C2

Princess Elizabeth Land *region* Antarctica 136 C3

Principe *island* Sao Tome & Principe 59 A5

Pripet *river* Belarus/Ukraine 90 C1

Pripet Marshes *wetlands* Belarus/Ukraine 90 C1

Priština Yugoslavia 83 D5

Prizren Yugoslavia 83 D5

Prome Myanmar 118 A4

Prossnitz *see* Prostějov

Prostějov Czech Republic *Ger.* Prossnitz 81 C5

Provence *region* France 73 D6

Providence Rhode Island, USA 23 G3

Providencia, Isla de *island* Colombia 35 E3

Provo Utah, USA 24 B4

Prudhoe Bay Alaska, USA 18 D2

Przheval'sk *see* Karakol

Pskov Russian Federation 92 A4

Pskov, Lake *lake* Estonia/Russian Federation *Est.* Pihkva Järv, *Rus.* Pskovskoye Ozero 88 D3

Pskovskoye Ozero *see* Pskov, Lake

Ptich' *see* Ptsich

Ptsich *river* Belarus *Rus.* Ptich' 89 D6

Pucallpa Peru 42 B3

Puebla Mexico 33 F4

Pueblo Colorado, USA 22 D4

Puerto Aisén Chile 47 B6

Puerto Barrios Guatemala 34 C2

Puerto Carreño Colombia 40 D2

Puerto Cortés Honduras 34 C2

Puerto Deseado Argentina 47 C6

Puerto Maldonado Peru 42 C4

Puerto Montt Chile 47 B5

Puerto Natales Chile 47 B7

Puerto Plata Dominican Republic 37 E3

Puerto Princesa Philippines 120 E2

Puerto Rico *external territory* USA, West Indies 37 F3

Puerto San Julián Argentina 47 C7

Puerto Suárez Bolivia 42 D4

Puerto Vallarta Mexico 32 D4

Pula Croatia 82 A3

Pune India *prev.* Poona 114 C1

Puno Peru 42 C4

Punta Arenas Chile *prev.* Magallanes 47 B7

Puntarenas Costa Rica 34 D4

Purmerend Netherlands 68 C3

Purus *river* Brazil/Peru 42 C3

Pusan South Korea 110 E4

Putumayo *river* NW South America 38 B3

Pyapon Myanmar 118 B4

Pyarnu *see* Pärnu

Pyinmana Myanmar 118 B3

Pyongyang *capital of* North Korea 110 E4

Pyramid Lake *lake* Nevada, USA 27 C5

Pyrenees *mountain range* SW Europe 62 C4

Q

Qaanaaq Greenland *var.* Thule 64 D1

Qābatiya West Bank 101 D7

Qaidam Pendi *basin* China 108 D4

Qalqilya West Bank 101 D7

Qamdo China 108 D5

Qandahār *see* Kandahār

Qaqortoq Greenland 64 C4

Qara Qum *see* Karakumy

Qarshi *see* Karshi

Qasigiannguit Greenland 64 C3

Qatar *country* SW Asia 103 D5

Qattara Depression *see* Qaṭṭâra, Monkhafad el

Qaṭṭâra, Monkhafad el *desert basin* Egypt *Eng.* Qattara Depression 54 A1

Qena Egypt 54 B2

Qeqertarsuaq Greenland 64 B3

Qeqertarsuaq *island* Greenland 64 B3

Qian *see* Guizhou

Qilian Shan *mountain range* China 108 A4

Qimusseriarsuaq *bay* Greenland 64 C2

Qingdao China 110 D4

Qinghai *province* China *var.* Chinghai, Koko Nor, Qing, Tsinghai 108 B4

Qinghai Hu *lake* China *var.* Koko Nor 108 D4

Qingzang Gaoyuan *plateau* China *Eng.* Plateau of Tibet 110 A4

Qiong *see* Hainan

Qiqihar China 110 D3

Qira China 108 B4

Qitai China 108 C3

Qom Iran *var.* Kum 102 C3

Qonduz *river* Afghanistan 105 E4

Qonduz *see* Kunduz

Quba Azerbaijan *Rus.* Kuba 99 H2

Québec Canada 21 E4

Quebec *province* Canada 20 D3

Queen Charlotte Islands *islands* Canada 18 D4

Queen Charlotte Sound *sea feature* Canada 18 D5

Queen Elizabeth Islands *islands* Canada 19 F1

Queensland *state* Australia 130 C4

Queenstown New Zealand 133 B6

Quelimane Mozambique 61 E3

Querétaro Mexico 33 E4

Quetta Pakistan 116 B2

Quezaltenango Guatemala 34 B2

Quibdó Colombia 40 B2

Quimper France 72 A3

Qui Nhon Vietnam 119 E5

Qing *see* Qinghai

Quito *capital of* Ecuador 40 A4

Qüqon *see* Kokand

Qürghonteppa Tajikistan *Rus.* Kurgan–Tynbe 105 E3

Qyteti Stalin *see* Kuçovë

R

Raab *see* Győr

Raab *see* Rába

Rába *river* Austria/Hungary *Ger.* Raab 81 C7

Rabat *capital of* Morocco 52 C2

Race, Cape *coastal feature* Canada 21 H4

Rach Gia Vietnam 119 D6

Radom Poland 80 D4

Radviliškis Lithuania 88 C4

Ragusa Italy 79 D7

Rahīmyār Khān Pakistan 116 C3

Raipur India 117 E5

Rājahmundry India 115 E1

Rājasthān *state* India 116 C3

Rājkot India 116 C4

Rājshāhi Bangladesh 117 G4

Rakaia *river* New Zealand 133 C6

Rakvere Estonia *Ger.* Wesenberg 84 D2

Raleigh North Carolina, USA 31 F1

Ralik Chain *islands* Marshall Islands 126 D1

Râmnicu Vâlcea Romania *prev.* Rîmnicu Vîlcea 90 B4

Ramallah West Bank 101 D7

Ramree Island *island* Myanmar 118 A3

Rancagua Chile 46 B4

Rānchi India 117 F4

Randers Denmark 67 A7

Rangiora New Zealand 133 C6

Rangitikei *river* New Zealand 132 D4

Rangoon *capital of* Myanmar *Bur.* Yangon 118 B4

Rankin Inlet Canada 19 G3

Rapid City South Dakota, USA 24 D3

Rarotonga *island* Cook Islands 127 G5

Rasht Iran 102 C3

Ratak Chain *islands* Marshall Islands 126 D1

Ratchaburi Thailand 119 C5

Rat Islands *island group* Alaska, USA 18 A2

Raukumara Range *mountain range* New Zealand 132 E3

Rauma Finland 67 D5

Ravenna Italy 78 C3

Rāwalpindi Pakistan 116 C1

Rawson Argentina 47 C6

Razgrad Bulgaria 86 D1

Reading England, UK 71 D7

Rebecca, Lake *lake* Australia 129 C6

Rebun-tō *island* Japan 112 D1

Rechytsa Belarus 89 D7

Recife Brazil 43 H3

Recklinghausen Germany 76 G4

Red Deer Canada 19 E5

Redding California, USA 27 B5

Red River *river* S USA 30 B3

Red River *river* China/ Vietnam 118

Red Sea Indian Ocean 122 A3

Reefton New Zealand 133 C5

Regensburg Germany 77 C5

Reggane Algeria 52 D3

Reggio di Calabria Italy 79 D6

Reggio nell' Emilia Italy 78 B3

Regina Canada 19 F5

Rehoboth Namibia 60 C4

Reichenberg *see* Liberec

Reid Australia 129 D6

Reims France *Eng.* Rheims 72 D3

Reindeer Lake *lake* Canada 17 C4

Reni Ukraine 90 D4

Rennes France 72 B3

Reno Nevada, USA 27 B5

Resistencia Argentina 46 D3

Reşiţa Romania 90 B4

Resolute Canada 19 F2

Réunion *external territory* France, Indian Ocean 123 B5

Reus Spain 75 G2

Reutlingen Germany 77 B6

Reval *see* Tallinn

Revel *see* Tallinn

Revillagigedo, Islas *island* Mexico 32 B4

Rey, Isla del *island* Panama 35 F5

Reykjavík *capital of* Iceland 65 E5

Reynosa Mexico 33 E2

Rēzekne Latvia *Ger.* Rositten, *Rus.* Rezhitsa 88 D4

Rezhitsa *see* Rēzekne

Rheims *see* Reims

Rhine *river* W Europe 62 D3

Rhode Island *state* USA 23 G3

Rhodes *see* Ródos

Rhodope Mountains *mountain range* Bulgaria/Greece *Gk.* Orosirá Rodópis, *Bul.* Despoto Planina 86 C3

Rhône *river* France/Switzerland 62 C4

Ribeirão Preto Brazil 45 E1

Riberalta Bolivia 42 C3

Ribniţa Moldova 90 D3

Richfield Utah, USA 24 B4

Richland Washington, USA 24 C2

Richmond Kentucky, USA 22 C5

Richmond New Zealand 133 C5

Richmond Virginia, USA 23 E5

Richmond Range *mountain range* New Zealand 133 C5

Ricobayo, Embalse de *reservoir* Spain 74 D2

Riga *capital of* Latvia *Latv.* Rīga 88 C3

Riga, Gulf of *sea feature* Baltic Sea 88 C3

Riihimäki Finland 67 D5

Rijeka Croatia *It.* Fiume 82 A3

Rimah, Wādī ar *dry watercourse* Saudi Arabia 103 B5

Rimini Italy 78 C3

Râmnicu Vâlcea *see* Râmnicu Vâlcea

Riobamba Ecuador 40 A4

Rio Branco Brazil 42 C3

Rio Cuarto Argentina 46 C4

Rio de Janeiro Brazil 45 F2

Rio Gallegos Argentina 47 C7

Rio Grande Brazil 44 D4

Rio Grande *river* N America 16 B6

Rio Grande Rise *undersea feature* Atlantic Ocean 49 C6

Rio Verde Mexico 33 E3

Rishiri-tō *island* Japan 112 D1

Rivas Nicaragua 34 D3

Rivera Uruguay 44 C4

Riverside California, USA 27 C8

Riverton New Zealand 133 A7

Rivne Ukraine *Rus.* Rovno 90 C2

Riyadh *capital of* Saudi Arabia *Ar.* Ar Riyāḍ 103 C5

Rize Turkey 99 E2

Rkîz Mauritania 56 C2

Road Town *capital of* British Virgin Islands 37 F3

Roanne France 73 D5

Roanoke Virginia, USA 23 E5

Roanoke *river* SE USA 31 G1

Robinson Range *mountain range* Australia 129 B5

Rochester Minnesota, USA 25 F3

Rochester New York, USA 23 E3

Rockford Illinois, USA 22 B3

Rockhampton Australia 130 D4

Rock Island Illinois, USA 22 B3

Rock Springs Wyoming, USA 24 C3

Rockstone Guyana 41 G2

Rocky Mountains *mountain range* Canada/USA 18-19 D4

Rodez France 73 C6

Ródhos *see* Ródos

Ródos *island* Greece *var.* Ródhos, *Eng.* Rhodes 87 E6

Ródos Greece *Eng.* Rhodes 87 E6

Rodosto *see* Tekirdağ

Roeselare Belgium 69 A5

Roma Australia 131 D5

Roma *see* Rome

Romania *country* SE Europe 90

Rome *capital of* Italy *It.* Roma 78 C4

Rome Georgia, USA 30 D2

Ronne Denmark 67 B8

Ronne Ice Shelf *ice feature* Antarctica 136 B3

Roosendaal Netherlands 68 C4

Rosario Argentina 46 D4

Roseau *capital of* Dominica 37 G4

Rosenau *see* Rožňava

Rositten *see* Rēzekne

Ross Ice Shelf *ice feature* Antarctica 136 B4

Ross Sea Antarctica 136 B4

Rostak *see* Ar Rustāq

Rostock Germany 76 C2

Rostov-na-Donu Russian Federation 96 A3

Roswell New Mexico, USA 28 D2

Rotorua New Zealand 132 D3

Rotorua, Lake *lake* New Zealand 132 D3

Rotterdam Netherlands 68 C4

Rouen France 72 C3

Rovaniemi Finland 66 D3

Rovno *see* Rivne

Rovuma *river* Mozambique/ Tanzania 61 F2

Roxas City Philippines 121 E2

Rožňava Slovakia *Ger.* Rosenau, *Hung.* Rozsnyó 81 D6

Rozsnyó *see* Rožňava

Ruatoria New Zealand 132 E3

Ruawai New Zealand 132 D2

Rudnyy Kazakhstan 96 C4

Rudolf, Lake *see* Lake Turkana

Rügen *headland* Germany 76 D2

Rukwa, Lake *lake* Tanzania 55 B7

Rumbek Sudan 55 B5

Rundu Namibia 60 C3

Ruoqiang China 108 C3

Ruse Bulgaria 86 D1

Russian Federation *country* Europe/Asia 92-93 96-97

Rust'avi Georgia 99 F2

Rutland Vermont, USA 23 F2

Rutog China 108 B4

Rwanda *country* C Africa 55

Ryazan' Russian Federation 93 B5 96 B3

Rybinskoye Vodokhranilishche *Reservoir* Russian Federation *Eng.* Rybinsk Reservoir 92 B4

Rybnik Poland 81 C5

Ryūkyū-rettō *island group* Japan 113 A8

Ryukyu Trench *Undersea feature* East China Sea 134 B2

Rzeszów Poland 81 E5**Saale** *river* Germany 76 C4

S

Saarbrücken Germany 77 A5

Saare *see* Saaremaa

Saaremaa *island* Estonia *var.* Saare, Sarema, *Ger.* Ösel, *var.* Oesel 88 C2

Šabac Serbia, Yugoslavia 82 C3

Sabadell Spain 75 G2

Sabah *cultural region* Borneo 120 D3

Sab'atayn, Ramlat as *desert* Yemen 103 C7

Sabhā Libya 53 F3

Sabzevār Iran 102 D3

Sacramento California, USA 27 B6

Şa'dah Yemen 103 B6

Sado *island* Japan 112 C4

Safi Morocco 52 B2

Saginaw Michigan, USA 22 C3

Sahara *desert* N Africa 50 B3

Sahel *region* W Africa 50 B3

Saïda Lebanon *anc.* Sidon 100 B4

Saidpur Bangladesh 117 G3

Saigon *see* Hồ Chi Minh

Saimaa *lake* Finland 67 E5

Saint-Brieuc France 72 A3

Saint Catherines Canada 20 D5

Saint-Chamond France 73 D5

St Christopher & Nevis *see* St Kitts & Nevis

St Cloud Minnesota, USA 25 F2

St-Denis *capital of* Réunion 61 H4

Saintes France 72 B5

Saint-Étienne France 73 D5

Saint George Australia 131 D5

St. George's *capital of* Grenada 37 G5

St Helena *external territory* UK, Atlantic Ocean 49 D5

St Helier *capital* Jersey 71 D8

Saint-Jean, Lake *lake* Canada 21 E4

Saint John Canada 21 F4

St John's *country capital* Antigua and Barbuda 37 G3

Saint John's Canada 21 H3

St Joseph Missouri, USA 25 F4

St Kitts & Nevis *country* West Indies *var.* St Christopher & Nevis 37

St.-Laurent-du-Maroni French Guiana 41 H2

Saint Lawrence *river* Canada 21 E4

Saint Lawrence, Gulf of *sea feature* Canada 21 F3

St. Lawrence Island *island* Alaska, USA 18 C2

Saint-Lô France 73 B3

Saint Louis Senegal 56 B3

St Louis Missouri, USA 25 G4

St Lucia *country* West Indies 37

Saint-Malo France 72 B3

Saint-Nazaire France 72 B4

Saint Paul Minnesota, USA 25 F2

St-Paul, Île *island* French Southern and Antarctic Territories 123 C6

St Peter Port *capital of* Guernsey 71 D8

St Petersburg Russian Federation *Rus.* Sankt-Peterburg, *prev.* Leningrad, Petrograd 92 B3 96 B2

St Petersburg Florida, USA 31 E4

Saint Pierre & Miquelon *external territory* France, Atlantic Ocean 21 G4

St Vincent, Cape *see* São Vicente, Cabo de

St Vincent & The Grenadines *country* West Indies 37

Saipan *island country capital* Northern Mariana Islands 124 B1

Sakākah Saudi Arabia 102 B4

Sakakawea, Lake *lake* North Dakota, USA 24 D2

Sakarya *see* Adapazari

Sakhalin *island* Russian Federation 97 H4

Sal *island* Cape Verde 56 A2

Salado *river* Argentina 46 C3

Şalālah Oman 103 D6

Salamanca Spain 74 D2

Sala y Gómez *island* Chile, Pacific Ocean 135 F4

Saldus Latvia *Ger.* Frauenburg 88 B3

Salekhard Russian Federation 96 D3

Salem India 114 D2

Salem Oregon, USA 26 A3

Salerno Italy 79 D5

Salerno, Golfo di *sea feature* Italy 79 D5

Salihorsk Belarus *Rus.* Soligorsk 89 C6

Salima Malawi 61 E2

Salinas California, USA 27 B6

Salisbury England, UK 71 D7

Salisbury Island *island* Canada 20 D1

Salonica *see* Thessaloníki

Salso *river* Italy 79 C7
Salt *see* As Salt
Salta Argentina 46 C2
Saltillo Mexico 33 E2
Salt Lake City Utah, USA 24 B4
Salto Uruguay 44 B4
Salton Sea *lake* California, USA 27 D8
Salvador Brazil 43 G4
Salween *river* SE Asia 111 A6
Salzburg Austria 77 D6
Salzgitter Germany 76 C4
Samara Russian Federation 93 C6 96 B3
Samarinda Indonesia 121 E4
Samarkand Uzbekistan 104 D2
Sambre *river* Belgium 69 B7
Samoa *country* Pacific Ocean 127 F4
Samobor Croatia 82 B3
Sámos *island* Greece 87 D5
Samothrace *see* Samothráki
Samothráki *island* Greece *Eng.* Samothrace 86 D3
Samsun Turkey 98 D2
Samui, Ko *island group* Thailand 119 C6
San *river* Poland 81 E5
Saña Peru 42 A3
Sana *capital of* Yemen *var.* Şan'ā' 103 B7
Sanandaj Sinneh. Iran 102 C3
San Andrés, Isla de *island* Colombia 35 E3
San Angelo Texas, USA 29 F3
San Antonio Chile 46 B4
San Antonio Texas, USA 29 F4
San Antonio *river* S USA 29 G4
San Antonio Oeste Argentina 47 C5
Sanāw Yemen 103 C6
San Bernardino California, USA 27 C7
San Carlos Uruguay 44 C5
San Carlos de Bariloche Argentina 47 B5
San Clemente Island *island* W USA 27 C8
San Cristóbal Venezuela 40 C2

San Diego California, USA 27 C8
Sandwich Island *see* Efate
San Fernando Trinidad & Tobago 37 G5
San Fernando Venezuela 40 D2
San Fernando de Noronha *island* Brazil 43 H2
San Francisco California, USA 27 B6
Sangir, Kepulauan *island group* Indonesia 121 F3
San Ignacio Belize 34 C1
San Joaquin Valley *valley* W USA 27 B6
San José *capital of* Costa Rica 34 D4
San Jose California, USA 27 B6
San José del Guaviare Colombia 40 C3
San Juan Argentina 46 B3
San Juan *river* Costa Rica/Nicaragua 34 D4
San Juan *capital of* Puerto Rico 37 F3
San Juan Bautista Paraguay 44 B3
San Juan de los Morros Venezuela 40 D1
Sankt Martin *see* Martin
Sankt-Peterburg *see* St Petersburg
Sankt Pölten Austria 77 E6
Şanlıurfa Turkey *prev.* Urfa 98 E4
San Lorenzo Honduras 34 C3
San Luis Potosí Mexico 33 E3
San Marino *country* S Europe 78 C3
San Matías, Golfo *sea feature* Argentina 39 C6
San Miguel El Salvador 34 C3
San Miguel de Tucumán Argentina 46 C3
San Nicolas Island *island* W USA 27 B8
San Pedro Sula Honduras 34 C2
San Remo Italy 78 A3
San Salvador *capital of* El Salvador 34 C3

San Salvador de Jujuy Argentina 46 C2
San Sebastián Spain *Bas.* Donostia 75 E1
Santa Ana El Salvador 34 B2
Santa Ana California, USA 27 C8
Santa Barbara California, USA 27 B7
Santa Catalina Island *island* W USA 27 C8
Santa Clara Cuba 36 B2
Santa Cruz Bolivia 42 D4
Santa Cruz California, USA 27 B6
Santa Cruz Islands *island group* Solomon Islands 126 C4
Santa Fe Argentina 46 D3
Santa Fe New Mexico, USA 28 D2
Santa Maria Brazil 44 C4
Santa Marta Colombia 40 C1
Santander Spain 75 E1
Santanilla, Islas *islands* Honduras 35 E1
Santarém Brazil 43 E2
Santarém Portugal 74 C3
Santaren Channel *Channel* Bahamas 36 C2
Santa Rosa Argentina 47 C4
Santa Rosa California, USA 27 A6
Santa Rosa de Copán Honduras 34 C2
Santa Rosa Island *island* W USA 27 B8
Santiago *island* Cape Verde 56 A3
Santiago *capital of* Chile 46 B4
Santiago Dominican Republic 37 E3
Santiago Panama 35 F5
Santiago Spain 74 C1
Santiago de Cuba Cuba 36 C3
Santiago del Estero Argentina 46 C3
Santo Antão *island* Cape Verde 56 A2
Santo Domingo *capital of* Dominican Republic 37 E3

Severnaya Dvina *river* Russian Federation *Eng.* Northern Dvina 92 D3

Severnaya Zemlya *island group* Russian Federation 137 H3

Sevilla Spain *Eng.* Seville 74 D4

Seville *see* Sevilla

Seychelles *country* Indian Ocean 61 122 B4

Seydhisfjördhur Iceland 65 E4

Seydi Turkmenistan *prev.* Neftezavodsk 104 D2

Seyhan *see* Adana

Sfax Tunisia 53 F2

's-Gravenhage *capital of* Netherlands *Eng.* The Hague 68 B3

Shaan *see* Shaanxi

Shaanxi *province* China *var.* Shaan, Shan-hsi, Shenshi, Shensi 111 C5

Shache China 108 A3

Shackleton Ice Shelf *ice feature* Antarctica 136 D3

Shandong *province* China *var.* Lu, Shantung 110 D4

Shanghai China 111 D5

Shangrao China 111 D6

Shan-hsi *see* Shaanxi

Shan-hsi *see* Shanxi

Shannon *river* Ireland 71 B5

Shan Plateau *upland* Myanmar 118 B3

Shantou China 111 D6

Shanxi Sheng *see* Shanxi

Shantung *see* Shandong

Sharjah United Arab Emirates *Ar.* Ash Shāriqah 103 D5

Shawnee Oklahoma, USA 29 G2

Shdanov *see* Mariupol'

Shebeli *river* Ethiopia/Somalia 55 D5

Sheberghän Afghanistan 104 D3

Sheffield England, UK 71 D5

Shengking *see* Liaoning

Shenking *see* Liaoning

Shenshi *see* Shaanxi

Shensi *see* Shaanxi

Shenyang China 110 D3

Sherbrooke Canada 21 E4

Sheridan Wyoming, USA 22 C2

's-Hertogenbosch Netherlands 68 C4

Shetland *islands* Scotland, UK 70 D1

Shevchenko *see* Aktau

Shihezi China 108 C2

Shijiazhuang China 110 C4

Shikoku *island* Japan 113 B6

Shikoku Basin *undersea feature* Philippine Sea 134 B2

Shikotan *island* Japan/Russian Federation (disputed) 112 E2

Shikārpur Pakistan 116 B3

Shimonoseki Japan 113 A5

Shinano-gawa *river* Japan 112 C4

Shingū Japan 113 C6

Shinyanga Tanzania 55 B7

Shīrāz Iran 102 D4

Shkodër Albania 83 D5

Shostka Ukraine 91 E1

Shreveport Louisiana, USA 30 A2

Shrewsbury England, UK 71 D6

Shumen Bulgaria 86 D2

Shymkent Kazakhstan *prev.* Chimkent 96 B5

Šiauliai Lithuania *Ger.* Schaulen 88 B4

Šibenik Croatia 82 B4

Siberia *region* Russian Federation 97 E3

Siberut, Pulau *island* Indonesia 120 B4

Sibiu Romania 90 B4

Sibolga Indonesia 120 B3

Sibu Malaysia 120 C3

Sibut Central African Republic 58 C4

Sibuyan Sea *sea* Philippines 121 E2

Sichuan *province* China *var.* Chuan, Ssu-ch'uan, Szechwan 111 B5

Sichuan Pendi *depression* China 111 B5

Sicilia *island* Italy *Eng.* Sicily 79 C7

Sicily, Strait of *sea feature* Mediterranean Sea 79 B7

Sicily *see* Sicilia

Sidi Bel Abbès Algeria 52 D1

Sidon *see* Saïda

Siednesibirskoye Ploskogor'ye *plateau* Russian Federation *Eng.* Central Siberian Plateau 97 E3

Siegen Germany 76 B4

Siena Italy 78 B3

Sierra Leone *country* W Africa 56

Sierra Madre del Sur *mountain range* Mexico 33 E5

Sierra Madre Occidental *mountain range* Mexico *var.* Western Sierra Madre 17 B6

Sierra Madre Oriental *mountain range* Mexico *var.* Eastern Sierra Madre 32 D2

Sierra Nevada *mountain range* Spain 75 E4

Sierra Nevada *mountain range* W USA 27 B5

Sighişoara Romania 90 C4

Siglufjördhur Iceland 65 E4

Siguiri Guinea 56 D4

Siirt Turkey 99 F3

Siling Co *lake* China 108 C5

Silkeborg Denmark 67 A7

Sillein *see* Žilina

Šilutė Lithuania 88 B4

Simeulue, Pulau *island* Indonesia 120 A3

Simferopol' Ukraine 91 F5

Simpson Desert *desert* Australia 130 C4

Sinai *desert* Egypt 54 B1

Sincelejo Colombia 40 B1

Sines Portugal 74 B4

Singapore *country* SE Asia 120

Singapore *capital of* Singapore 120 C3

Sinkiang *see* Xinjiang Uygur Zizhiqu

Sinnamary French Guiana 41 H2

Sinop Turkey 98 D2

Sint-Niklaas Belgium 69 B5

Sülüktü *see* Sulyukta
Sulu Sea Pacific Ocean 121 E2
Sulyukta Kyrgyzstan *Kir.*
  Sülüktü 105 E2
Sumatra *island* Indonesia
  120 B4
Sumba, Selat *island* Indonesia
  121 E5
Sumbawanga Tanzania 55 B7
Sumbe Angola 60 B2
Sumgait *see* Sumqayıt
Sumqayıt Azerbaijan *Rus.*
  Sumgait 99 H2
Sumy Ukraine 91 F1
Sunda, Selat *strait* Indonesia
  120 D5
Sunderland England, UK 70 D4
Sundsvall Sweden 67 C5
Suntar Russian Federation
  97 F3
Sunyani Ghana 57 E4
Superior Wisconsin, USA 22 A1
Superior, Lake *lake*
  Canada/USA 16 C5
Suqutrá *island* Yemen *var.*
  Socotra 103 D7 122 B3
Şūr Oman 103 E5
Surabaya Indonesia 120 D5
Surakarta Indonesia 120 D5
Sūrat India 116 C5
Surat Thani Thailand 119 C6
Sûre *river* W Europe 69 D7
Surfers Paradise Australia
  131 E5
Surinam *see* Suriname
Suriname *country* NE South
  America *var.* Surinam 41
Surkhob *river* Tajikistan 105 E3
Surt Libya *var.* Sidra 53 G2
Surt, Khalīj *sea feature*
  Mediterranean Sea *Eng.* Gulf
  of Sirte, Gulf of Sidra 85 E4
Surtsey *island* S Iceland 65 E5
Susanville California, USA
  27 B5
Suways, Qanāt as *see* Suez
  Canal
Suva *capital* of Fiji 127 E4
Svalbard *external territory*
  Norway, Arctic Ocean 65 G2

Svay Riĕng Cambodia 119 D6
Sverdlovsk *see* Yekaterinburg
Svetlogorsk *see* Svyatlahorsk
Svyataya Anna Trough
  undersea feature Kara Sea
  137 H4
Svyetlahorsk Belarus *Rus.*
  Svetlogorsk 89 D6
Swakopmund Namibia 60 B3
Swansea Wales, UK 71 C6
Swaziland *country* southern
  Africa 61
Sweden *country* N Europe
  66-67
Sweetwater Texas, USA 29 F3
Swindon England, UK 71 D6
Switzerland *country* C Europe
  77
Sydney Australia 131 D6
Sydney Canada 21 G4
Syeverodonets'k Ukraine 91 G1
Syktyvkar Russian Federation
  92 D4 96 C3
Sylhet Bangladesh 117 G4
Syracuse *see* Siracusa
Syracuse New York, USA 23 E3
Syr Darya *river* C Asia 104 D1
Syria *country* SW Asia 100-101
Syrian Desert *desert* SW Asia
  Ar. Bādiyat ash Shām 101 C5
Szczecin Poland *Ger.* Stettin
  80 B3
Szczeciński, Zalew *bay*
  Germany/Poland 80 A2
Szechwan *see* Sichuan
Szeged Hungary *Ger.* Szegedin
  81 D7
Szegedin *see* Szeged
Székesfehérvár Hungary *Ger.*
  Stuhlweissenburg 81 C6
Szekszárd Hungary 81 C7
Szolnok Hungary 81 D6
Szombathely Hungary *Ger.*
  Steinamanger 81 B6

T

Tabariya, Bahrat *see*
  Tiberius, Lake

Tábor Czech Republic 81 B5
Tabora Tanzania 55 B7
Tabrīz Iran 102 C2
Tabuaeran *island* Kiribati
  127 G2
Tabūk Saudi Arabia 102 A4
Tacloban Philippines 120 F2
Tacna Peru 42 C4
Tacoma Washington, USA
  26 B2
Tacuarembó Uruguay 44 C4
Tadmur *see* Tudmur
Taegu South Korea 110 E4
Taejŏn South Korea 110 E4
Tafassâsset, Ténéré du *desert*
  Niger 57 G2
Taguatinga Brazil 43 F3
Tagus *river* Portugal/Spain
  Port. Tejo, *Sp.* Tajo 74 C3
Tahiti *island* French Polynesia
  127 H5
Tahoe, Lake *lake* W USA 27 B5
Tahoua Niger 57 F3
T'aichung Taiwan 111 D6
Taieri *129* New Zealand 133 B7
Taihape New Zealand 132 D4
T'ainan Taiwan 111 D6
Taipei *capital* of Taiwan 111 D6
Taiping Malaysia 120 B3
Taiwan *country* E Asia *prev.*
  Formosa 111
Taiwan Strait *sea feature* East
  China Sea/South China Sea
  var. Formosa Strait 111 D7
Taiyuan China 110 C4
Ta‘izz Yemen 103 B7
Tajikistan *country* C Asia 105
Tajo *see* Tagus
Takamaka New Zealand 132 D2
Takla Makan *see* Taklimakan
  Shamo
Taklimakan Shamo *desert*
  region China *var.* Takla
  Makan 108 B3
Talamanca, Cordillera de
  mountains Costa Rica 35 E4
Talas Kyrgyzstan 105 F2
Talaud, Kepulauan *island group*
  Indonesia 121 F3

Tennant Creek Australia 130 A3
Tennessee *state* USA 30 D1
Tennessee *river* USA 31 C1
Tepelenë Albania 83 D6
Tepic Mexico 32 D4
Teplice Czech Republic *Ger.* Teplitz, *prev.* Teplice-Šanov, *Ger.* Teplitz-Schönau 80 A4
Teplice-Šanov *see* Teplice
Teplitz *see* Teplice
Teplitz-Schönau *see* Teplice
Teraina *island* Kiribati 127 G2
Teresina Brazil 43 G2
Termez Uzbekistan 105 E3
Terneuzen Netherlands 69 B5
Terni Italy 78 C4
Ternopil' Ukraine *Rus.* Ternopol' 90 C2
Ternopol' *see* Ternopil'
Terrassa Spain 75 G2
Terre Haute Indiana, USA 22 B4
Terres Australes et Antarctiques Françaises *see* French Southern and Antarctic Territories
Terschelling *island* Netherlands 68 C1
Teruel Spain 75 F3
Teseney Eritrea 54 C4
Tessalit Mali 57 E2
Tete Mozambique 61 E3
Tétouan Morocco 52 C1
Tetovo Macedonia 83 D5
Tetschen *see* Děčín
Tevere *river* Italy 78 C4
Texas *state* USA 28-29 F3
Texarkana Arkansas, USA 30 A2
Texas City Texas, USA 29 G4
Texel *island* Netherlands 68 C2
Thailand *country* SE Asia 118-119
Thailand, Gulf of *sea feature* South China Sea 119 C6
Thames *river* England, UK 71 D6
Thar Desert *desert* India/Pakistan 116 C3
Tharthār, Buḩayrat ath *lake* Iraq 102 B3
Thásos *island* Greece 86 C3

Thaton Myanmar 118 B4
Theiss *see* Tisza
Thermaic Gulf *see* Thermaïkós Kólpos
Thermaïkós Kólpos *sea feature* Greece *Eng.* Thermaic Gulf 86 B4
Thessaloníki Greece *var.* Salonica 86 B3
The Valley *dependent territory capital* Anguilla 37 G5
Thimphu *capital of* Bhutan 117 G3
Thionville France 72 E3
Thíra *island* Greece 87 D6
Thompson Canada 19 F4
Thorn *see* Toruń
Thorshavn *see* Tórshavn
Thracian Sea Greece *Gk.* Thrakikó Pélagos 86 D3
Thrakikó Pélagos *see* Thracian Sea
Three Kings Islands *island group* New Zealand 132 C1
Thule *see* Qaanaaq
Thunder Bay Canada 20 B4
Thuner See *lake* Switzerland 77 B7
Thurso Scotland, UK 70 C2
Tianjin China *var.* Tientsin 110 D4
Tiberias, Lake *lake* Israel *var.* Sea of Galilee, *Heb.* Yam Kinneret, *Ar.* Bahrat Tabariya 101 B5
Tibesti *mountains* Chad/Libya 50 C3
Tibet *autonomous region* China *Chin.* Xizang 108 C5
Tibet, Plateau of *see* Qingzang Gaoyuan
Tienen Belgium 69 C6
Tien Shan *mountain range* C Asia 105 G2
Tientsin *see* Tianjin
Tierra del Fuego *island* Argentina/Chile 47 C8
Tiflis *see* Tbilisi
Tighina Moldova *prev.* Bendery 90 D4
Tigris *river* SW Asia 94 B4

Tijuana Mexico 32 A1
Tiki Basin *undersea feature* Pacific Ocean 135 E3
Tiksi Russian Federation 97 F2
Tilburg Netherlands 68 C4
Timaru New Zealand 133 B6
Timişoara Romania 90 A4
Timmins Canada 20 C4
Timor *island* Indonesia 121 F5
Timor Sea Indian Ocean 121 F5
Tindouf Algeria 52 B3
Tínos *island* Greece 87 D5
Tirana *capital of* Albania 83 D6
Tiraspol Moldova 90 D4
Tîrgovişte *see* Târgovişte
Tîrgu Mureş *see* Târgu Mureş
Tirol *region* Austria *var.* Tyrol 77 C7
Tiruchchiràppalli India 114 D3
Tisa *see* Tisza
Tisza *river* E Europe *Ger.* Theiss, *Cz./Rom./SCr.* Tisa 81 D6
Titicaca, Lake *lake* Bolivia/Peru 42 C4
Tlemcen Algeria 52 D2
Toamasina Madagascar 61 G3
Toba, Danau *lake* Indonesia 120 B3
Tobago *island* Trinidad and Tobago 37 G5
Toba Kākar Range *mountains* Pakistan 116 B2
Tobruk *see* Ṭubruq
Tocantins *river* Brazil 43 F3
Tocopilla Chile 46 B2
Togo *country* W Africa 57 E4
Tokat Turkey 98 D3
Tokelau *external territory* New Zealand, Pacific Ocean 127 F3
Tokmak Kyrgyzstan 105 F2
Tokuno-shima *island* Japan 113 A8
Tokushima Japan 113 B5
Tokyo *capital of* Japan 113 D5
Toledo Spain 75 E3
Toledo Ohio, USA 22 C3
Toledo Bend Reservoir *Reservoir* S USA 29 H3

Toliara Madagascar 61 E3

Tol'yatti prev. Stavropol'
Russian Federation 93 C5

Tomakomai Japan 112 D2

Tombouctou Mali 57 E3

Tombua Angola 60 B2

Tomini, Gul of sea feature
Indonesia 121 E4

Tomsk Russian Federation
96 D4

Tonga country Pacific Ocean
127

Tongatapu island Tonga 125 E3

Tongking, Gulf of sea feature
South China Sea var. Gulf of
Tonkin 111 B7

Tongliao China 109 G2

Tongtian He river China 108 C4

Tonkin, Gulf of see Tongking,
Gulf of

Tônle Kông river
Cambodia/Vietnam 118 E5

Tônlé Sap lake Cambodia
119 D5

Tonopah Nevada, USA 27 C6

Toowoomba Australia 131 D5

Topeka Kansas, USA 25 F4

Top Springs Roadhouse
Australia 130 A3

Torino Italy Eng. Turin 78 A2

Tornio Finland 66 D4

Tornionjoki river
Finland/Sweden 66 D3

Toronto Canada 20 D5

Toros Dağları mountain range
Turkey Eng. Taurus
Mountains 98 C4

Torre del Greco Italy 79 D5

Torrens, Lake lake Australia
131 B5

Torreón Mexico 32 D2

Torres Strait sea feature
Arafura Sea/Coral Sea 126 B4

Torrington Wyoming, USA 24
D3

Tórshavn capital of Faeroe
Islands Dan. Thorshavn 65 F5

Tortoise Islands see Galapagos
Islands

Tortosa Spain 75 F2

Toruń Poland Ger. Thorn 80 C3

Toscana region Italy Eng.
Tuscany 78 B3

Toscano, Archipelago island
group Italy 78 B4

Toshkent see Tashkent

Tottori Japan 113 B5

Touggourt Algeria 53 E2

Toulon France 73 D6

Toulouse France 73 B6

Toungoo Myanmar 118 B4

Tournai Belgium 69 B6

Tours France 72 C4

Townsville Australia 130 D3

Toyama Japan 112 C4

Tozeur Tunisia 53 E2

Trâblous see Tripoli, Lebanon

Trabzon Turkey Eng. Trebizond
99 F2

Tralee Ireland 71 A6

Trang Thailand 119 C7

Transantarctic Mountains
mountain range Antarctica
136 B3

Transylvania region Romania
90 B3

Transylvanian Alps see Carpaţii
Meridionali

Trapani Italy 79 C6

Traralgon Australia 131 C7

Trasimeno, Lago lake Italy
78 C4

Traverse City Michigan, USA
22 C2

Travis, Lake lake Texas, USA
29 F4

Trebinje Bosnia & Herzegovina
83 C5

Trebizond see Trabzon

Trelew Argentina 47 C6

Trenčín Slovakia Ger. Trentschin
Hung. Trencsén 81 C6

Trencsén see Trenčín

Trento Italy Ger. Trient 78 C2

Trenton New Jersey, USA 23 F4

Trentschin see Trenčín

Tres Arroyos Argentina 47 D5

Treviso Italy 78 C2

Trient see Trento

Trieste Italy 78 D2

Trikala Greece 86 B4

Trincomalee Sri Lanka 115 E3

Trindade external territory
Brazil, Atlantic Ocean 49 C6

Trinidad Bolivia 42 C4

Trinidad Uruguay 44 B5

Trinidad island Trinidad &
Tobago 38 C2

Trinidad & Tobago country
West Indies 37 G5

Tripoli Greece 87 B5

Tripoli Lebanon var. Trâblous,
Ţarābulus 100 B4

Tripoli capital of Libya Ar.
Ţarābulus al-Gharb 53 F2

Tristan da Cunha external
territory UK, Atlantic Ocean
49 D6

Trivandrum India 114 D3

Trnava Slovakia Ger. Tyrnau,
Hung. Nagyszombat 81 C6

Trois-Rivières Canada 21 E4

Trollhättan Sweden 67 B6

Tromsø Norway 66 C2

Trondheim Norway 66 B4

Trondheimsfjorden inlet
Norway 66 B4

Troyes France 72 D4

Trujillo Honduras 34 D2

Trujillo Peru 42 A3

Tsarigrad see İstanbul

Tschenstochau see
Częstochowa

Tselinograd see Astana

Tsetserleg Mongolia 108 D2

Tshikapa Congo (Zaire) 59 C7

Tsinghai see Qinghai

Tsumeb Namibia 60 C3

Tsushima island Japan 113 A5

Tuamotu Fracture Zone tectonic
feature Pacific Ocean 125 H3

Tuamotu Islands island group
French Polynesia 125 G3

Tubmanburg Liberia 56 C4

Ţubruq Libya Eng. Tobruk
53 H2

Tucson Arizona, USA 28 B3

Tucupita Venezuela 41 F1

Uruguay *country* SE South America 44

Uruguay *river* S South America 46 D3

Urumchi *see* Ürümqi

Ürümqi China *prev.* Urumchi 108 C3

Usa *river* Russian Federation 92 D3

Uşak Turkey *prev.* Ushak 98 B3

Ushak *see* Uşak

Ushuaia Argentina 47 C8

Ust'-Chaun Russian Federation 97 G1

Ustica, Isola de *island* Italy 79 C6

Ústí nad Labem Czech Republic *Ger.* Aussig 80 A4

Ust'-Kamchatsk Russian Federation 97 H2

Ust'-Kamenogorsk Kazakhstan 96 D5

Ustyurt Plateau *upland* Kazakhstan/Uzbekistan 104 B1

Usumacinta *river* Guatemala/Mexico 34 B1

Usumbura *see* Bujumbura

Utah *state* USA 24 B4

Utena Lithuania 88 C4

Utica New York, USA 23 F2

Utrecht Netherlands 68 C3

Uttar Pradesh *state* India 117 E3

Uummannarsuaq *see* Nunap Isua

Uvs Nuur *lake* Mongolia 108 C2

Uyo Nigeria 57 G5

Uyuni Bolivia 43 C5

Uzbekistan *country* C Asia 104–105

Uzhgorod *see* Uzhhorod

Uzhhorod Ukraine *Rus.* Uzhgorod 90 B2

V

Vaal *river* South Africa 60 D4

Vaasa Finland 67 D5

Vadodara India 116 C4

Vaduz *capital of* Liechtenstein 77 B7

Våg *see* Váh

Váh *river* Slovakia *Ger.* Waag, *Hung.* Vág 81 C6

Valdés, Península *peninsula* Argentina 47 C5

Valdez Alaska, USA 18 D3

Valdivia Chile 47 B5

Valdosta Georgia, USA 31 E3

Valence France 73 D5

Valencia Spain 75 F3

Valencia Venezuela 40 D1

Valencia *region* Spain 75 F3

Valera Venezuela 40 C1

Valga Estonia *Ger.* Walk 88 D3

Valladolid Spain 74 D2

Valledupar Colombia 40 C1

Vallenar Chile 46 B3

Valletta *capital of* Malta 79 C8

Valley, The *capital of* Anguilla 37 G3

Valmiera Latvia *Ger.* Wolmar 88 C3

Valparaíso Chile 46 B4

Van Turkey 99 F3

Van, Lake *see* Van Gölü

Vanadzor Armenia *prev.* Kirovakan 99 F2

Vancouver Canada 19 E5

Vancouver Washington, USA 26 B2

Vancouver Island *island* Canada 18 D5

Vänern *lake* Sweden 67 B6

Vangaindrano Madagascar 61 G4

Van Gölü *lake* Turkey *Eng.* Lake Van 99 F3

Vantaa Finland 67 D5

Vanua Levu *island* Fiji 127 E4

Vanuatu *country* Pacific Ocean 134

Vārānasi India 117 E3

Varaždin Croatia 82 B2

Vardar *river* Greece/Macedonia *prev.* Axios 83 E6

Vardø Norway 66 E2

Varkaus Finland 67 E5

Varna Bulgaria 86 E2

Västerås Sweden 67 C6

Vatican City *country* S Europe 78 C4

Vättern *lake* Sweden 67 B6

Vava'u Group *island group* Tonga 127 F4

Vawkavysk Belarus *Rus.* Volkovysk, *Pol.* Wołkowysk 89 B5

Växjö Sweden 67 C7

Vaygach, Ostrov *island* Russian Federation 92 E3

Veles Macedonia 83 E5

Velikaya *river* Russian Federation 95 G2

Velikiye Luki Russian Federation 92 A4

Velingrad Bulgaria 86 C2

Vellore India 114 D2

Venezia Italy *Eng.* Venice 78 C2

Venezuela *country* N South America 40–41

Venezuela, Gulf of *sea feature* Caribbean Sea 40 C1

Venice *see* Venezia

Venice, Gulf of *sea feature* Adriatic Sea 78 C2

Venlo Netherlands 69 D5

Venta *river* Latvia/Lithuania 88 B3

Ventspils Latvia *Ger.* Windau 88 B3

Vera Argentina 46 D3

Veracruz Mexico 33 F4

Verkhoyanskiy Khrebet *mountain range* Russian Federation *Eng.* Verkhoyansk Range 97 F3

Verkhoyansk Range *see* Verkhoyanskiy Khrebet

Vermont *state* USA 23 F2

Vernon Texas, USA 29 F2

Véroia Greece 86 B3

Verona Italy 78 C2

Versailles France 72 C3

Verviers Belgium 69 D6

Vesoul France 72 D4

Veszprém Hungary *Ger.*
Veszprim 81 C7

Veszprim *see* Veszprém

Viana do Castelo Portugal
74 C2

Viareggio Italy 78 B3

Vicenza Italy 78 C2

Vichy France 73 C5

Victoria *state* Australia 131 C7

Victoria Canada 18 D5

Victoria *capital of* Seychelles
61 H1

Victoria Texas, USA 29 G4

Victoria *river* Australia 128 D3

Victoria, Lake *lake* E Africa *var.*
Victoria Nyanza 55 B6

Victoria Falls *waterfall*
Zambia/Zimbabwe 51 C6

Victoria Island *island* Canada
19 F2

Victoria Land *region* Antarctica
137 C4

Victoria Nyanza *see*
Victoria, Lake

Vidin Bulgaria 86 B1

Viedma Argentina 47 C5

Vienna *capital of* Austria
Ger. Wien 77 E6

Vientiane *capital of* Laos
118 C4

Vietnam *country* SE Asia
118-119

Vigo Spain 74 C2

Vijayawāda India 115 E1

Vila Nova de Gaia Portugal
74 C2

Vila Real Portugal 74 C2

Viliya *see* Neris

Viljandi Estonia *Ger.* Fellin
88 D2

Villach Austria 77 D7

Villahermosa Mexico 33 G4

Villa Mercedes Argentina 46 C4

Villarrica *peak* Chile 39 B6

Villavicencio Colombia 40 C3

Villeurbanne France 73 D5

Vilna *see* Vilnius

Vilnius *capital of* Lithuania *Pol.*
Wilno, *Ger.* Wilna, *Rus.* Vilna
89 C5

Viña del Mar Chile 46 B4

Vinh Vietnam 118 D4

Vinnitsa *see* Vinnytsya

Vinnytsya Ukraine *Rus.*
Vinnitsa 90 D2

Virgin Islands *external territory*
USA, West Indies 37 F3

Virginia Minnesota, USA 25 F2

Virginia *state* USA 22-23

Virovitica Croatia 82 C3

Virtsu Estonia *Ger.* Werder
88 C2

Visākhapatnam India 117 E5

Visalia California, USA 27 C7

Visby Sweden 67 C7

Viscount Melville Sound *sea
feature* Arctic Ocean 19 F2

Viseu Portugal 74 C3

Vistula *see* Wisła

Vitebsk *see* Vitsyebsk

Viterbo Italy 78 C4

Viti Levu *island* Fiji 127 E4

Vitim *river* Russian Federation
95 E3

Vitória Brazil 43 G5 45 G1

Vitória da Conquista Brazil
43 G4

Vitoria-Gasteiz Spain 75 E1

Vitsyebsk Belarus *Rus.* Vitebsk
88 E5

Vjosës, Lumi i *river* Albania
83 D6

Vladikavkaz Russian Federation
prev. Ordzhonikidze,
Dzaudzhikau 93 B7

Vladimir Russian Federation
93 B5

Vladimirovka *see*
Yuzhno-Sakhalinsk

Vladivostok Russian Federation
97 G5

Vlieland *island* Netherlands
68 C1

Vlissingen Netherlands
Eng. Flushing 69 B5

Vlorë Albania 83 D6

Vojvodina *region* Yugoslavia
82 D3

Volga *river* Russian Federation
96 A3

Volgograd Russian Federation
prev. Stalingrad 93 B6 96 A3

Volkovysk *see* Vawkavysk

Vologda Russian Federation
96 B2

Vólos Greece 86 B4

Volta *river* Ghana 57 E4

Volta, Lake *lake* Ghana 57 E4

Volta Redonda Brazil 45 E2

Voreioi Sporades *island group*
Greece *Eng.* Northern
Sporades 86 C4

Vorkuta Russian Federation
92 E3 96 C2

Vormsi *island* Estonia *Ger.*
Worms, *Swed.* Ormsö 88 C2

Voronezh Russian Federation
93 B5

Võru Estonia *Ger.* Werro 88 D3

Vosges *mountain range* France
72 E4

Vostochno-Sibirskoye More
Arctic Ocean *Eng.* East
Siberian Sea 137 G2

Vostok Island *island* Kiribati
127 H4

Vrangel'ya, Ostrov *island*
Russian Federation *Eng.*
Wrangel Island 97 G1

Vratsa Bulgaria 86 C2

Vršac Yugoslavia 82 D3

Vukovar Croatia 82 C3

Vulcano, Isola *island* Italy
79 D6

Vyatka *river* Russian Federation
93 C5

W

Wa Ghana 57 E4

Waag *see* Váh

Waal *river* Netherlands 68 D4

Wabash *river* C USA 22 B4

Waco Texas, USA 29 G3

Waddeneilanden *island group*
Netherlands *Eng.* West
Frisian Islands 68 C1

Waddenzee *sea feature*
Netherlands 68 D1